The Book of Heaven

The Book *of* Heaven

An Anthology of Writings from Ancient to Modern Times

Edited by
CAROL ZALESKI *and* PHILIP ZALESKI

OXFORD
UNIVERSITY PRESS
2000

OXFORD
UNIVERSITY PRESS

Oxford New York
Athens Auckland Bangkok Bogotá Buenos Aires Calcutta
Cape Town Chennai Dar es Salaam Delhi Florence Hong Kong Istanbul
Karachi Kuala Lumpur Madrid Melbourne Mexico City Mumbai
Nairobi Paris São Paulo Singapore Taipei Tokyo Toronto Warsaw

and associated companies in
Berlin Ibadan

Published by Oxford University Press, Inc.
198 Madison Avenue, New York, New York 10016

Oxford is a registered trademark of Oxford University Press

Library of Congress Cataloging-in-Publication Data
The book of heaven : an anthology of writings from ancient
to modern times / edited by Carol Zaleski and Philip Zaleski.
p. cm.
Includes bibliographical references and index.
ISBN 0-19-511933-9
1. Heaven—literary collections.
I. Zaleski, Carol. II. Zaleski, Philip.
PN6071.H37 B66 2000
291.2'3—dc21 99-056045

9 8 7 6 5 4 3 2 1
Printed in the United States of America
on acid-free paper

Contents

Note: Scriptures and anonymous works are identified by title; other works by author, then title.

Acknowledgments		*xi*
Introduction		*3*

I. The Journey

Introduction		*11*
Dante Alighieri	*Paradiso,* Canto 1	*15*
St. Bede the Venerable	From "The Vision of Drythelm" in *Bede's Ecclesiastical History of the English People*	*21*
John Bunyan	From *The Pilgrim's Progress*	*27*
Henry Fielding	From *A Journey from This World to the Next*	*35*
Percy Bysshe Shelley	From *Adonais*	*42*
"How the Weaver Went to Heaven"		*47*
From The Tibetan Book of the Dead		*49*
"The Far-Off Journey"		*54*
C. G. Jung	From *Memories, Dreams, Reflections*	*60*
Poems, Prayers, and Spells:		
"The Mithras Liturgy"	From *The Greek Magical Papyri*	*67*
"Spell for Ascending through the Heavens"	From *The Second Book of Jeu*	*69*
"Commendation of the Soul"	From *The Book of the Craft of Dying*	*71*
Sir Walter Ralegh	"The Passionate Mans Pilgrimage"	*73*
Iroquois Mother's Lament	From *League of the Ho-dé-no-sau-nee*	*75*
"The Hobo's Last Lament"	From *Hobo News*	*76*

II. Lands of Bliss

Introduction		79
"Fysh"	"Where Is No More Sea"	83
Rupert Brooke	"Heaven"	85
	"Rangi and Papatua"	87
Louis Ginzberg	"The First Day" From *The Legends of the Jews*	89
Snorri Sturluson	"The Deluding of Gylfi" From *The Prose Edda*	93
From *The Sukhavativyuha Sutra*		102
Marcus Tullius Cicero	From "The Dream of Scipio" in *On the Republic*	106
Howard Schwartz	"The Celestial Orchestra"	111
The Passion of Saints Perpetua and Felicity		116
John G. Neihardt	From *Black Elk Speaks*	119
Robert Hare	From *Experimental Investigation of the Spirit Manifestations*	127
Elizabeth Stuart Phelps	From *The Gates Ajar*	135

III. The Vision of God

Introduction		149
St. Augustine	From *Confessions*	153
As-Suyuti	From *La'ālī al-maṣnū'a*	155
From *The Shi'ur Qomah*		158
From *The Kausitaki Upanishad*		161
From *The Sukhavativyuha Sutra*		166
Dante Alighieri	*Paradiso*, Canto 33	168
Jonathan Edwards	From Sermon VIII on Romans 2:10	174

Marie Corelli	From *A Romance of Two Worlds*	176
Songs of Adoration:		
Pygmy Hymn		182
Bible	Psalm 104: 1–4	183
	Ezekiel 1	184
	Isaiah 6:1–7	187
	Revelation 4, 5	188
From the *Hekhalot Rabbati*		191
Edmund Spenser	From "An Hymne of Heavenly Beautie"	193
John Henry Cardinal Newman	"God Is All in All"	197

IV. THE CELESTIAL COURT

Introduction		199
Homer	From *The Iliad*	203
Pseudo-Dionysius	From *The Celestial Hierarchy*	207
From *The Vision of Adamnan*		210
From the Bhagavata Purana		218
John Milton	From *Paradise Lost*	221
Robert Southey	From *A Vision of Judgment*	226
George Gordon, Lord Byron	From *The Vision of Judgment*	228
John Henry Cardinal Newman	From *On the Fitness of the Glories of Mary*	233
Pope Pius XII	Assumption Prayer	237
G. K. Chesterton	From *The Man Who Was Thursday*	239

V. HEAVENLY SOCIETY

Introduction		251
Mark Twain	From *Extract from Captain Stormfield's Visit to Heaven*	255
Emanuel Swedenborg	From *Heaven and Its Wonders and Hell*	266

Sir Arthur Conan Doyle	From *The Land of Mist*	273
Julian Barnes	From *A History of the World in 10½ Chapters*	286
Hildegard of Bingen	"Concerning the Heavenly Joys of Virgins," from *The Book of the Rewards of Life*	295
Tales of Heavenly Intercession:		
St. Thérèse of Lisieux	From *Story of a Soul*	298
Evelyn Underhill	"The Window of Paradise," from *The Miracles of Our Lady Saint Mary*	301
Louis Ginzberg	"Elijah"	304
Jalal ad-Din ar-Rumi	"The Spirit of the Saints"	311

VI. Heaven on Earth

Introduction		313
Plato	From *Phaedo*	317
	From *The Voyage of Bran*	320
Guillaume de Lorris and Jean de Meun	From *The Romance of the Rose*	330
John Milton	From *Paradise Lost*	341
From the Bhagavata Purana		347
Rinpung Ngawang Jigdag	From "The Knowledge-bearing Messenger"	349
Thomas Traherne	From *Centuries*	355
Hans Christian Andersen	"A Leaf from Heaven"	357
Charles Fourier	From the Preface to *Théorie de l'unité universelle*	360
William James	From "What Makes a Life Significant"	362
Songs and Poems:		
"An Invitation to Lubberland"		365
George Herbert	"Prayer"	368

Mikhail Lermontov	"The Angel"	369
Shaker songs	"Simple Gifts"	370
	"Heavenly Display"	371

VII. New Heaven, New Earth

Introduction		373
"Belief"	From *Legends of the Hasidim*	377
Shmuel Yosef Agnon	"On the Sea," from *In the Heart of the Seas*	378
Bible	Daniel 12:1–3	384
	Isaiah 65:17–25	385
	1 Corinthians 15:35–54	386
	Revelation 21:1–4	388
Qu'ran	Sura 55: 37–78	389
From the Bundahishn		391
George Sword	Report on the Ghost Dance, From James Mooney, *The Ghost-Dance Religion and the Sioux Outbreak of 1890*	396
St. Augustine	From *The City of God*	400
C. S. Lewis	From *The Last Battle*	405
Songs and Poems:		
Henry Vaughan	"Easter-day"	416
	"Easter Hymn"	417
John Donne	"At the round earths imagin'd corners, blow . . ."	418
Spirituals	"In That Great Getting-up Morning"	419
	"I'll Hear the Trumpet Sound"	422
Credits		425
Name Index		431

Acknowledgments

We would like to express our gratitude first of all to Cynthia Read of Oxford University Press, who suggested this project; Linda Halvorson, who launched it; Nancy Toff, who kept it in orbit; and Catherine Carter, who saw it through to completion. In addition, we are grateful for help from the Rev. Anselm Atkinson, O.S.B.; the Rev. Ian Boyd, C.S.B.; Eleanor Cartelli; Stratford and Léonie Caldecott; Shaye Cohen; the Rev. Giles Conacher, O.S.B.; Stephen D. Crites; Craig Davis; Paul Dietrich; Annie Dillard; Michelle Dilts; Karl Donfried; Lois Dubin; Peggy Ellsberg; Robert Ellsberg; Daniel Gardner; Jay Garfield; the Rt. Rev. Abbot Hugh Gilbert, O.S.B.; Jennifer Hengen; Jamie Hubbard; Dennis Hudson; William Johnston; Joel Kaminsky; the Rev. Bede Kierney, O.S.B.; Quinn Lai; Will McCormack; Richard Millington; Kimberley Patton; Claire Renkin; Robert Richardson; Bruce Sajdak; Howard Schwartz; Alan Segal; Alison Share; Vera Shevzov; Gretchen Sullivan; Jean Sulzberger; Taitetsu Unno; and the Very Rev. Mother Mary Clare Vincent, O.S.B. We thank Smith College for generous research grants, and the staff at Smith College's Neilson Library, especially in interlibrary loan and reference, for unfailing and cheerful assistance. Finally, thanks to Andy, John, and Kriston for giving us a glimpse of heaven on earth.

The Book of Heaven

INTRODUCTION

Heaven is everywhere: in the writings of poets, the prayers of the dying, the lyrics of popular song. In every culture, in every epoch, human beings have dreamed of heaven, thirsted for heaven, even killed for heaven. Heaven is safety, goodness, beauty, truth; it is the kingdom of God, abode of the elect, crown of the martyrs, comfort of the bereaved, fount of enlightenment, mirror of fantasy and hope. Heaven is also the sky—home of the four winds, storehouse of rain and snow, concourse of the moving planets, vault of the fixed stars.

Heaven is a timeless realm but it has a history, or perhaps it is truer to say that it has multiple histories, running concurrently, all in the present tense. Maps change but no picture of heaven has ever become completely obsolete. In every flourishing culture the image of heaven is perpetually renewed.

The Book of Heaven is a literary tour of heaven, moving thematically through its many mansions, and highlighting both the diversity and the universality of reflection on heaven. Sacred chants from the Tibetan Book of the Dead reverberate alongside John Donne's holy sonnets, Shaker gift songs alongside Gnostic hymns, in what must be an unprecedented combination. Selections span the millennia as well, for we wish, in G. K. Chesterton's words, to "have the dead at our councils." At the same time, in order to trace a particular lineage in depth, we emphasize the heaven literature of the West, where visions of the heavenly city reflect the cultural patterns, ideals, and longings of the earthly cities of Athens, Jerusalem, and Rome.

The history of heaven in the West begins with the Bible. The heavens of the ancient Hebrews, created out of primordial chaos, form a vast watery sky-dome, supported by massive pillars and covering the earth. Rain falls down from the open windows of the firmament; stars shine through it; God dwells enthroned within it, or perhaps beyond it (for how can God be contained by a visible scaffolding of his own creation?). The prophets of Israel visit heaven in visions, dreams, even bodily ascents. But the dead are nowhere to be seen—they have descended into a shadowy realm beneath the earth. Yet after the Babylonian exile, a new hope gradually emerges: that the righteous will be raised up from death and enter into a state of blessedness in the world to come. Heaven now belongs to astronomers and mystics. A hierarchy of seven or ten celestial spheres, it reveals its secrets to visionaries who, in the tradition of Ezekiel, contemplate the divine throne and the chariot on which it rests. Although God remains utterly transcendent, a few may be privileged to behold the radiance of his glory.

St. Paul, after being lowered from the window of a Damascus prison in a basket, finds himself caught up in the paradise of the third heaven, where he hears "unspeakable words, which it is not lawful for a man to utter" (2 Corinthians 12:4). Notwithstanding this reticence, the New Testament is saturated with words about heaven. In the Gospels, angels announce the nativity, a voice from heaven is heard at the baptism of Jesus, Jesus teaches in parables about the kingdom of heaven, heaven descends at the transfiguration, and the final words of Jesus to the thief on the cross are "Today shalt thou be with me in paradise" (Luke 23:43). Above all, the resurrection and ascension of Christ open up the heavens just as the crucifixion breaks down the gates of hell. Mary and the saints dwell in heaven, further humanizing this transcendent realm, and the holy souls in purgatory—heaven's antechamber—forge a link between the living and the dead.

Just as heaven is both a place (sky) and a state of being (union with God), so paradise, whose history intertwines with heaven's, is both a place—in the east, west, or center of the earth; atop a mountain; or translated to the sky—and a time—the golden age, the time of creation, and the future age, the time of resurrection. Beyond biblical Eden, paradise comprises the Elysian Fields, the Isles of the Blest, Arcadia, and all the other happy realms of Greek and Roman mythology. It is a land of saints and also a place of natural marvels (as in *The Voyage of Bran*), a lovers' bower (as in *The Romance of the Rose*), and a poor man's banquet (as in the legends of Cockaigne).

Enriching the stream of biblical thought about heaven, and at times diverting its course, are the myths and mysteries of the Greek and Roman gods, the solar and astral cults of the ancient Mediterranean world, and, above all, the philosophical and esoteric schools (Orphic, Pythagorean, Platonic) devoted to the art of transcending death. In graves scattered throughout southern Italy, Thessaly, and Crete, archaeologists have found golden tablets, instructing the dead in the stratagems they must use in order to be admitted to the highest heaven: Don't drink the water! Head for the fixed stars—don't stop at any of the moving planets! If anyone tries to send you back to earth, boldly claim your birthright: you are an immortal soul, a fallen divinity, returning to your native land in heaven. Plato and his followers would spiritualize this idea, telling us that our highest calling—our only chance at real happiness—is to turn from the shadow-world toward the eternal contemplation of the true, the good, and the beautiful. In this sense, philosophy itself—and all the arts and sciences into which philosophy has fragmented—is nothing less than the quest for heaven.

For Islam, the youngest great tradition of the West, heaven descends to earth at the moment that the angel Gabriel commands Muhammad to "Recite!" This reciting, or Qur'an, whose archetype is in heaven, speaks in unambiguous and glorious Arabic of a garden where believers will receive abundant reward. Islamic tradition recounts—as a further sign of divine favor—Muhammad's miraculous ascension through the seven heavens to God's own presence.

But heaven has always belonged as much to poets and painters as to philosophers and theologians. To describe this inherently indescribable realm takes what Dante calls *l'alta fantasia* ("high fantasy"), imagination on the threshold of vision. The great European poets of heaven—Dante, Spenser, Milton, Donne, Herbert, Vaughan, Traherne—have completely assimilated the Christian *mythos* and are therefore able to play with it more freely than most: to sustain extended metaphors, analogies, and "conceits"; deploy allegorical types without descending into stereotypes; integrate material from diverse sources; and personalize without trivializing their subject. Thus they quicken our own unformed imaginations and make heaven real, much as do the great painters of heaven—Fra Angelico, Luca Signorelli, Botticelli, Correggio, Van Eyck, Lochner.

Along with high fantasy, heaven is matter for high comedy (as in

Henry Fielding's *Journey from This World to the Next* and Mark Twain's *Extracts from Captain Stormfield's Visit to Heaven*), sentimental consolation (as in *The Gates Ajar* and *A Romance of Two Worlds*), wartime reflection (as in the heaven poem of Rupert Brooke), paranormal investigation (as in Emanuel Swedenborg's matter-of-fact observations of angelic society), speculative fiction (as in the fantasies of G. K. Chesterton and C. S. Lewis), and all manner of metaphysical adventures. In the mirror of heaven, we see ourselves as we are or we invent ourselves as we wish to be.

Beyond the West, heaven presents an aspect that cannot fail to dazzle, even as it instructs us in other ways of illuminating human nature and destiny. In Chou period China, heaven (*T'ien*) is not just a place, but an emperor-god whose mandate gives earthly rulers their authority. The *literati* traditions of Confucius and Lao Tzu tell us that the Way (*Tao*) of heaven—harmony within the nexus of natural and social relationships—is the means for attaining all the things we desire: longevity, prosperity, posterity, and peace; and the legendary Taoist immortals, masters of the Way, regularly travel to heaven to be recharged by the formless beginning of all things.

For the sages of classical Hinduism, heaven is the realm of the gods and a highly desirable place of rebirth, but it is not the ultimate goal. Better than rebirth in heaven, and better than return to earth, is union with the infinite and imperishable spirit by which one escapes the whole weary round of birth and death. Similarly, the Buddhist path is oriented toward awakening rather than toward heavenly bliss; enlightenment is the heaven beyond heaven. Yet Hindu and Buddhist heavens are as lush, as elaborate, and as soul-stirring as any that one could imagine. There is no end to the compassionate imagination of the celestial buddhas and bodhisattvas who mentally project heavens—or pure lands—in which to cultivate the spiritual welfare of sentient beings.

In all cultures where shamanism has flourished, heaven is very near to earth, and the folklore and fairy tales of the world abound in shamanic images of heaven. To reach heaven, one need only climb the tree, scale the ladder, cross the perilous bridge, ascend the mountain, or ford the river that separates the twin worlds. To plant an abundant crop, heal a serious illness, found a successful endeavor, or build a lasting edifice, one must secure heaven's favor, making sure that all earthly activities reflect their heavenly exemplars. We neglect heaven at our peril.

The Book of Heaven is an attempt to remedy this neglect, both through its focus on Western sources and through its inclusion of non-Western material. Only a global perspective can hope to do justice to the subject of heaven. And yet, by locating our exploration of heaven primarily—though not exclusively—in the West, we are able to probe more deeply than a generic study would permit, to see the enduring as well as the distinctive features of the changing face of heaven in literature, religion, and art. By concentrating on works written in English and other European languages, we are able to highlight the literary splendors of this material, often lost in translation from distant tongues, and demonstrate how such writings reflect a coherent literary and religious tradition with its own intentions, rules, and strategies.

Translations were chosen for their clarity, felicity, and fidelity to the original, as well as for their cultural significance. Recent translations are not always best for our purposes, even if they improve upon their predecessors in some details of scholarly reconstruction. Accordingly, all biblical passages come from the King James (Authorized) Version, as it is in this form that the English Bible has most profoundly shaped our heritage.

We include popular material along with classics, preferring vibrant expressions of genuine folk culture to products of commercial mass culture. Although a few selections have been chosen for their curiosity value, our overriding aim is to present works of enduring value and literary merit. Inevitably, though, there are great works we have been unable to include; no doubt you will think of some. Every anthology is necessarily incomplete—how much more so one whose subject is as inexhaustible as heaven.

The chapters are arranged thematically, after the pattern of a journey to heaven. Like most pilgrims, we saunter and circumambulate, rarely following a straight path. Within each chapter, we proceed by way of associated ideas, exploring affinities and contrasts, rather than pursuing a strictly chronological or historical scheme. The introductions and headnotes point out connections as a guide to the reader's own discovery.

Chapter 1 presents the entry into heaven—by way of death, visionary ascension, imaginative thought-experiment, or actual flight. The journey is a perilous one. Humans are easily distracted, ignorance and vice weigh them down, and hostile heavenly powers lie in ambush; hence the need for the protective prayers, spells, and magical formulae with which this chapter closes.

Chapter 2 explores the topography of heaven—the land of bliss—a land whose every feature is invested with allegorical significance. In its aspect as a garden, heaven is nature and culture synthesized, for heaven's nature is never raw wilderness. In its aspect as a city, heaven is culture and nature harmonized, the curse of Babel reversed. To survey the landscape of heaven is also to look back in time, for in heaven is the pristine exemplar after which our world was made.

Chapter 3 concerns the vision of God. Although it is said that no one can see God and live, the vision of God face to face is considered by many religious cultures to be the ultimate aim of human life. To see God is to pass beyond the sky-heavens to the heaven of heavens, to the transcendent mystery that founds all reality. And if the vision of God takes human form, the mystery is not overcome but deepened. Here is the center; everything else is periphery.

Chapter 4 takes one step outward from the center to encompass the surrounding celestial court. Here are the angels, gods, and demigods who dwell closest to the divine throne, where they wait upon the high God, argue among themselves, superintend the lower worlds, or intervene in human concerns. The imagery of city and kingdom predominates; the celestial court is the original model for sacral kingship, and next to God's throne lie the blueprints for a rightly ordered political and cultic life.

Chapter 5 takes a further step outward to mingle in heavenly society, the commonwealth of saints and spirits who have been translated to heaven after death. To the often-posed question "What do people actually do in heaven?" we offer an array of answers, ancient and modern, solemn and comic. Although peaceful, heaven is never static; people work, play, eat, pray, make love, pursue knowledge, intercede for the living, and settle the affairs of the dead.

Chapter 6 considers some of the many ways in which heaven can be found on earth, from earthly paradises to divine descents to utopian experiments. But utopias have a way of coming unraveled. Hence for those who would bring heaven down to earth, there is only one definitive solution: this worn-out earth must give way, so that a perfected world—surpassing even Eden restored—can take its place.

Chapter 7 presents the heaven of end times, the millennial kingdom, the general resurrection, the final judgment, and the ultimate conquest of evil and death.

Some readers may wonder why we have not allotted more space to the devil's—or the skeptic's—point of view. After all, there is a long and venerable tradition of skepticism about heaven, from the ancient Egyptian "Song of the Harper" to Stephen Hawking. There are anti-heaven poems (like Wallace Stevens's "Sunday Morning") and anti-heaven tracts (like Corliss Lamont's *The Illusion of Immortality*). Henry Fielding, Lord Byron, Rupert Brooke, Mark Twain, and Julian Barnes present their doubts in satiric fashion; we think that these are among the most elegant expressions of the case against heaven. But when it comes down to it, the literature of heaven is richer than the literature against it. In any case, the best satires of heaven have a purifying rather than a corrosive effect: they burn off the clichés and permit a fresh approach.

Is heaven, strictly speaking, inconceivable? Is perfect happiness a contradiction in terms? Perhaps so, but try this: Imagine the happiest moments of your childhood, the most genuinely gratifying experiences of your adult life. Add to these every glimpse of beauty, every act of creation, every awakening of insight. Subtract the anxiety that eats away at the core of even our best experiences, cancel the contradictions, and translate to eternity. Is this so difficult?

Without heaven, is earth bearable? Most societies have found it necessary to envision a future time of recompense in heaven or in the world to come. When the newspapers remind us daily that this world is one in which children are tortured, is it unreasonable to hope for another world, where tears will be dried and, as the English mystic Julian of Norwich puts it, "All well be well, and all will be well, and all manner of things will be well"?

Must you believe in heaven in order to enjoy this book? Hardly. You need only be curious about how human beings have responded to death, imagined the cosmos, and looked for ways to transcend their limits. You will surely be able to savor the comic elements in heaven, for indeed it is essentially comic to picture human beings divested of their mortal bodies, just as it is essentially tragic to picture the body's decline.

If you do believe in heaven, will it be discomfiting to encounter so many different views? We trust not. Not all versions of heaven are equally compelling, yet all have something to teach us. Whatever may finally be true about heaven is a secret that only heaven can disclose.

I

The Journey

Introduction

Heaven may be a distant country, a celestial sphere, a state of mind, a mode of being, a figment of the imagination. Whatever its nature, almost everyone agrees that it requires some effort to get there. This exertion usually takes the form of a journey, unfolding in multiple stages that may entail tests, dangers, discoveries, and unexpected encounters with beings human or divine. Success is rarely guaranteed. In many of the selections in this chapter, the protagonist never makes it as far as the heavenly realms, and in only a few does he or she penetrate to the very heart of heaven. Rather, these selections illuminate the preliminary steps in the heavenward trek: the departure from ordinary existence (by a magical chant, by death, by grasping onto the tail of a soaring elephant), the initial push into unknown realms, the adventurous approach to the heavenly precincts, entry into the sacred antechambers of heaven itself. These poems, folktales, scriptures, histories, laments, and spells remind us of how majestic are the routes to heaven, how perilous the ordeals, how exciting the prospects, how glorious the destination.

We begin with Dante, the world's preeminent poet of heaven. His masterpiece, *La commedia divina,* is an allegorical vision cast in the form of a pilgrimage. The journey begins on Good Friday 1300 with a descent through the subterranean circles of hell (*L'Inferno),* guided by the poet Virgil. In the *Purgatorio*, Dante struggles up the mountain of Purgatory, reaching the earthly paradise at its summit; here he undergoes the purification that will make him fit for heaven, bathing in Lethe for the forgetfulness of sins and drinking in the waters of Eunoe for the remembrance of good deeds. As the *Paradiso* opens,

Dante turns his gaze to his beloved Beatrice, who is Wisdom and Grace personified. Together, they look directly at the sun and Dante becomes "transhumanized"—a process that, as Dante explains, is beyond the reach of words. With Beatrice as his guide and intercessor, the pilgrim begins the long ascent through the heavenly spheres to the Empyrean where God dwells.

Christian, the protagonist of John Bunyan's *Pilgrim's Progress* is, like Dante, an Everyman figure on pilgrimage to the heavenly city. In Christian's case, however, progress is not a matter of ascending in a rarefied body, but rather of tramping, running, clambering, and swimming through an allegorical countryside that resembles seventeenth-century England. Nearly a century later, Henry Fielding's protagonist hops and coaches his way to the Elysian Fields, where he discovers, in lieu of a celestial city, an orange grove filled with the famous figures of history.

Dante, Bunyan, and a host of other authors—including the Taoist chronicler of "The Far-Off Journey" and the fashioner of the traditional Urdu tale "How the Weaver Went to Heaven"— have used devices such as vision, dream, pilgrimage, and magical flight to thrust their protagonists into heaven. But there exists another means of heavenly access, one with which we will all be familiar sooner or later: the doorway of death. Every world culture possesses its own peculiar map of the journey taken by the deceased, encoded in its burial practices and rites of mourning or made explicit in its guidebooks for death and dying. Various selections in this first chapter—the Tibetan Book of the Dead and the Vision of Drythelm among them—deal with the postmortem passage to heaven.

In St. Bede's account of the Vision of Drythelm, a Northumbrian man dies one night and returns to life the next morning. The journey he undertakes in the interim has a moral intent: "that the living might be saved from the death of the soul." Like Christian, Drythelm approaches the other world on foot; like Dante, his adventures begin with a vision of realms of punishment: a valley of fire and ice (which is, in fact, a purgatorial antechamber to heaven, although he mistakes it at first for hell) followed by a brief and harrowing glimpse into the black abyss of the damned, who attempt to seize him on the spot. Rescued by a luminous being, Drythelm finds himself miraculously transported across a vast wall to a fragrant garden (which he mistakes at first for heaven), where the souls of the "not so perfect" bide their time until they are ready for the vision of God.

Drythelm never makes it into heaven proper, although he is amazed by its radiance, its perfume, and the sweet singing that streams forth from it. He returns to life, repentant, to tell his tale, providing a map of the journey to which Dante himself—along with the whole genre of medieval vision literature—is clearly indebted, and which is echoed, with variations, in the short selections here from *The Book of the Craft of Dying* and Sir Walter Ralegh.

In the modern period, return-from-death narratives have caught the public eye again in the form of visionary near-death experiences, purporting to be eyewitness accounts of the other world. An eccentric example of this genre comes from C. G. Jung, whose close brush with death in 1944 allowed him to escape the "box system" of ordinary consciousness for a dazzling sequence of revelations.

Percy Bysshe Shelley's *Adonais*, by contrast, describes a death from which there is no return—that of John Keats, who passed away in Rome on 23 February 1821 at the age of 25. In Shelley's paradoxical vision, we are the dead, for we are consumed by the worms of fear and grief, while Keats "hath awakened from the dream of life" to be greeted by those other great poets who died in their youth—Thomas Chatterton, Philip Sidney, and Lucan among them—and who now dwell in "the abode where the Eternal are."

Dante and Jung, Bunyan and Bede, *The Book of the Craft of Dying* and the Tibetan Book of the Dead offer markedly different post-mortem itineraries, but they agree at least on one thing: to prepare for the journey is one of life's most pressing goals.

Dante Alighieri

(1265–1321)

The supreme poet of heaven, Dante composed La commedia *(later* La commedia divina*) while in exile from his beloved Florence. As the* Paradiso *opens, it is high noon on the spring equinox, and the pilgrim stands poised for his ascent through the nine heavenly spheres to the Empyrean.*

The glory of the One Who moves all things
penetrates all the universe, reflecting
in one part more and in another less.

I have been in His brightest shining heaven
and seen such things that no man, once returned
from there, has wit or skill to tell about;

for when our intellect draws near its goal
and fathoms to the depths of its desire,
the memory is powerless to follow;

but still, as much of Heaven's holy realm
as I could store and treasure in my mind
shall now become the subject of my song.

O great Apollo, for this final task,
make me a vessel worthy to receive
your genius and the longed-for laurel crown.

Thus far I have addressed my prayers to one
peak of Parnassus; now I need them both
to move into this heavenly arena.

Enter my breast, breathe into me as high
a strain as that which vanquished Marsyas
the time you drew him from his body's sheath.

O Power Divine, but lend me of yourself
so much as will make clear at least the shadow
of that high realm imprinted on my mind,

and you shall see me at your chosen tree,
crowning myself with those green leaves of which
my theme and you yourself will make me worthy.

So seldom, Father, are they plucked to crown
the triumph of a Caesar or a Poet
(the shame, the fault of mortal man's desires!)

that when a man yearns to achieve that goal,
then the Peneian frond should surely breed
a new joy in the joyous Delphic god.

From one small spark can come a mighty blaze:
so after me, perhaps, a better voice
may rise in prayer and win Cyrrha's response.

The lamp that lights the world rises for man
at different points, but from the place which joins
four circles with three crosses, it ascends

upon a happier course with happier stars
conjoined, and in this way it warms and seals
the earthly wax closer to its own likeness.

This glad union had made it morning there
and evening here: our hemisphere was dark,
while all the mountain bathed in white, when I

saw Beatrice turned round, facing left,
her eyes raised to the sun—no eagle ever
could stare so fixed and straight into such light!

As one descending ray of light will cause
a second one to rise back up again,
just as a pilgrim yearns to go back home,

so, like a ray, her act poured through my eyes
into my mind and gave rise to my own:
I stared straight at the sun as no man could.

In that place first created for mankind
much more is granted to the human senses
than ever was allowed them here on earth.

I could not look for long, but my eyes saw
the sun enclosed in blazing sparks of light
like molten iron as it pours from the fire.

And suddenly it was as if one day
shone on the next—as if the One Who Could
had decked the heavens with a second sun.

And Beatrice stood there, her eyes fixed
on the eternal spheres, entranced, and now
my eyes, withdrawn from high, were fixed on her.

Gazing at her, I felt myself becoming
what Glaucus had become tasting the herb
that made him like the other sea-gods there.

"Transhumanize"—it cannot be explained
per verba, so let this example serve
until God's grace grants the experience.

Whether it was the last created part
of me alone that rose, O Sovereign Love,
You know Whose light it was that lifted me.

When the great sphere that spins, yearning for You
eternally, captured my mind with strains
of harmony tempered and tuned by You,

I saw a great expanse of heaven ablaze
with the sun's flames: not all the rains and rivers
on earth could ever make a lake so wide.

The revelation of this light, this sound,
inflamed me with such eagerness to learn
their cause, as I had never felt before;

and she who saw me as I saw myself,
ready to calm my agitated mind,
began to speak before I asked my question:

"You have yourself to blame for burdening
your mind with misconceptions that prevent
from seeing clearly what you might have seen.

You may think you are still on earth, but lightning
never sped downward from its home as quick
as you are now ascending to your own."

As easily did these few and smiling words
release me from my first perplexity
than was my mind ensnared by yet another,

and I said: "Though I rest content concerning
one great wonder of mine, I wonder now
how I can rise through these light bodies here."

She sighed with pity when she heard my question
and looked at me the way a mother might
hearing her child in his delirium:

"Among all things, however disparate,
there reigns an order, and this gives the form
that makes the universe resemble God,"

she said; "therein God's higher creatures see
the imprint of Eternal Excellence—
that goal for which the system is created,

and in this order all created things,
according to their bent, maintain their place,
disposed in proper distance from their Source;

therefore, they move, all to a different port,
across the vast ocean of being, and each
endowed with its own instinct as its guide.

This is what carries fire toward the moon,
this is the moving force in mortal hearts,
this is what binds the earth and makes it one.

Not only living creatures void of reason
prove the impelling strength of instinct's bow,
but also those with intellect and love.

The Providence that regulates the whole
becalms forever with its radiance
the heaven wherein revolves the swiftest sphere;

to there, to that predestined place, we soar,
propelled there by the power of that bow
which always shoots straight to its Happy Mark.

But, it is true that just as form sometimes
may not reflect the artist's true intent,
the matter being deaf to the appeal,

just so, God's creature, even though impelled
toward the true goal, having the power to swerve,
may sometimes go astray along his course;

and just as fire can be seen as falling
down from a cloud, so too man's primal drive,
twisted by false desire, may bring him down.

You should, in all truth, be no more amazed
at your flight up than at the sight of water
that rushes down a mountain to its base.

If you, free as you are of every weight,
    had strayed below, then that would be as strange
    as living flame on earth remaining still.

And then she turned her gaze up toward the heavens.

St. Bede the Venerable

(672/673–735)

In this excerpt from The Ecclesiastical History of the English People, *the learned Anglo-Saxon Benedictine monk recounts the Vision of Drythelm, one of the earliest and most influential of medieval otherworld journeys.*

Of one among the Northumbrians, who rose from the dead, and related the things which he had seen, some exciting terror and others delight. [a.d. 696]

At this time a memorable miracle, and like to those of former days, was wrought in Britain; for, to the end that the living might be saved from the death of the soul, a certain person, who had been some time dead, rose again to life, and related many remarkable things he had seen; some of which I have thought fit here briefly to take notice of. There was a master of a family in that district of the Northumbrians which is called Cuningham, who led a religious life, as did also all that belonged to him. This man fell sick, and his distemper daily increasing, being brought to extremity, he died in the beginning of the night; but in the morning early, he suddenly came to life again, and sat up, upon which all those that sat about the body weeping, fled away in a great fright, only his wife, who loved him best, though in a great consternation and trembling, remained with him. He, comforting her, said, "Fear not, for I am now truly risen from death, and permitted again to live among men; however, I am not to live hereafter as I was wont, but from henceforward after a very different manner." Then rising immediately, he repaired to the oratory of the little town, and continuing in prayer till day, immediately divided all his substance into three parts; one whereof he gave to his wife, another to his children, and the third, belonging to himself, he instantly distributed among the poor. Not long after, he repaired to the monastery of Melrose, which is almost enclosed by the winding of the river Tweed, and having been shaven, went into a private dwelling, which the abbat had provided, where he continued till the day of his death, in such extraordinary contrition of mind and body, that though his tongue had been silent, his life declared that he had seen many things either to be dreaded or coveted, which others knew nothing of.

Thus he related what he had seen. "He that led me had a shining countenance and a bright garment, and we went on silently, as I thought, towards the north-east. Walking on, we came to a vale of great breadth and depth, but of infinite length; on the left it appeared full of dreadful flames, the other side was no less horrid for violent hail and cold snow flying in all directions; both places were full of men's souls, which seemed by turns to be tossed from one side to the other, as it were by a violent storm; for when the wretches could no longer endure the excess of heat, they leaped into the middle of the cutting cold; and finding no rest there, they leaped back again into the middle of the unquenchable flames. Now whereas an innumerable multitude of deformed spirits were thus alternately tormented far and near, as far as could be seen, without any intermission, I began to think that this perhaps might be hell, of whose intolerable flames I had often heard talk. My guide, who went before me, answered to my thought, saying, 'Do not believe so, for this is not the hell you imagine.'

"When he had conducted me, much frightened with that horrid spectacle, by degrees, to the farther end, on a sudden I saw the place begin to grow dusk and filled with darkness. When I came into it, the darkness, by degrees, grew so thick, that I could see nothing besides it and the shape and garment of him that led me. As we went on through the shades of night, on a sudden there appeared before us frequent globes of black flames, rising as it were out of a great pit, and falling back again into the same. When I had been conducted thither, my leader suddenly vanished, and left me alone in the midst of darkness and this horrid vision, whilst those same globes of fire, without intermission, at one time flew up and at another fell back into the bottom of the abyss; and I observed that all the flames, as they ascended, were full of human souls, which, like sparks flying up with smoke, were sometimes thrown on high, and again, when the vapour of the fire ceased, dropped down into the depth below. Moreover, an insufferable stench came forth with the vapors, and filled all those dark places.

"Having stood there a long time in much dread, not knowing what to do, which way to turn, or what end I might expect, on a sudden I heard behind me the noise of a most hideous and wretched lamentation, and at the same time a loud laughing, as of a rude multitude insulting captured enemies. When that noise, growing plainer, came up to me, I observed a gang of evil spirits dragging the howling and lamenting souls of men into the midst of the darkness, whilst they themselves laughed and rejoiced. Among those men, as I could discern, there was one shorn like a clergyman, a layman, and a woman. The evil spirits that dragged them went down into the midst of the burning pit; and as they went down deeper, I could no longer distinguish between the lamentation of the men and the laughing of the devils, yet I still had a confused sound in my ears. In the meantime, some of the dark spirits ascended from that flaming abyss, and running forward, beset me on all sides, and much perplexed me with their glaring eyes and the stinking fire which proceeded from their mouths and nostrils; and threatened to lay hold on me with burning tongs, which they had in their hands, yet they durst not touch me, though they frightened me. Being thus on all sides enclosed with enemies and darkness, and looking about on every side for assistance, there appeared behind me, on the way that I came, as it were, the brightness of a star shining amidst the darkness; which increased by degrees, and came rapidly towards me: when it drew near, all those evil spirits, that sought to carry me away with their tongs, dispersed and fled.

"He whose approach put them to flight, was the same that led me before; who, then turning towards the right, began to lead me, as it were, towards the south-east, and having soon brought me out of the darkness, conducted me into an atmosphere of clear light. While he thus led me in open light, I saw a vast wall before us, the length and height of which, in every direction, seemed to be altogether boundless. I began to wonder why we went up to the wall, seeing no door, window, or path through it. When we came to the wall, we were presently, I know not by what means, on the top of it, and within it was a vast and delightful field, so full of fragrant flowers that the odour of its delightful sweetness immediately dispelled the stink of the dark furnace, which had pierced me through and through. So great was the light in this place, that it seemed to exceed the brightness of the day, or the sun in its meridian height. In this field were innumerable assemblies of men in white, and many companies seated together rejoicing. As he led me through the midst of those happy inhabitants, I began to think that this might, perhaps, be the kingdom of heaven, of which I had often heard so much. He answered to my thought, saying, 'This is not the kingdom of heaven, as you imagine.'

"When we had passed those mansions of blessed souls and gone farther on, I discovered before me a much more beautiful light, and therein heard sweet voices of persons singing, and so wonderful a fragrancy proceeded from the place, that the other which I had before thought most delicious, then seemed to me but very indifferent; even as that extraordinary brightness of the flowery field, compared with this, appeared mean and inconsiderable. When I began to hope we should enter that delightful place, my guide, on a sudden stood still; and then turning back, led me back by the way we came.

"When we returned to those joyful mansions of the souls in white, he said to me, 'Do you know what all these things are which you have seen?' I answered, I did not; and then he replied, 'That vale you saw so dreadful for consuming flames and cutting cold, is the place in which the souls of those are tried and punished, who, delaying to confess and amend their crimes, at length have recourse to repentance at the point of death, and so depart this life; but nevertheless because they, even at their death, confessed and repented, they shall all be received into the kingdom of heaven at the day of judgment; but many are relieved before the day of judgment, by the prayers, alms, and fasting, of the living, and more especially by masses. That fiery and stinking pit, which you saw, is the mouth of hell, into which whosoever falls shall never be delivered to all eternity. This flowery place, in which you see these most beautiful young people, so bright and merry, is that into which the souls of those are received who depart the body in good works, but who are not so perfect as to deserve to be immediately admitted into the kingdom of heaven; yet they shall all, at the day of judgment, see Christ, and partake of the joys of his kingdom; for whoever are perfect in thought, word and deed, as soon as they depart the body, immediately enter into the kingdom of heaven; in the neighborhood whereof that place is, where you heard the sound of sweet singing, with the fragrant odour and bright light. As for you, who are now to return to your body, and live among men again, if you will endeavour nicely to examine your actions, and direct your speech and behaviour in righteousness and simplicity, you shall, after death, have a place or residence among these joyful troops of blessed souls; for when I left you for a while, it was to know how you were to be disposed of.' When he had said this to me, I much abhorred returning to my body, being delighted with the sweetness and beauty of the place I beheld, and with the company of those I saw in it. However, I durst not ask him any questions; but in the meantime, on a sudden, I found myself alive among men."

Now these and other things which this man of God saw, he would not relate to slothful persons and such as lived negligently; but only to those who, being terrified with the dread of torments, or delighted with the hopes of heavenly joys, would make use of his words to advance in piety. In the neighborhood of his cell lived one Hemgils, a monk, eminent in the priesthood, which he honored by his good works: he is still living, and leading a solitary life in Ireland, supporting his declining age with coarse bread and cold water. He often went to that man, and asking several questions, heard of him all the particulars of what he had seen when separated from his body; by whose relation we also came to the knowledge of those few particulars which we have briefly set down. He also related his vision to King Alfred, a man most learned in all respects, and was by him so willingly and attentively heard, that at his request he was admitted into the monastery above-mentioned, and received the monastic tonsure; and the said king, when he happened to be in those parts, very often went to hear him. At that time the religious and humble abbat and priest, Ethelwald, presided over the monastery, and now with worthy conduct possesses the episcopal see of the church of Lindisfarne.

He had a more private place of residence assigned him in that monastery, where he might apply himself to the service of his Creator in continual prayer. And as that place lay on the bank of the river, he was wont often to go into the same to do penance in his body, and many times to dip quite under the water, and to continue saying psalms or prayers in the same as long as he could endure it, standing still sometimes up to the middle, and sometimes to the neck in water; and when he went out from thence ashore, he never took off his cold and frozen garments till they grew warm and dry on his body. And when in the winter the half-broken pieces of ice were swimming about him, which he had himself broken, to make room to stand or dip himself in the river, those who beheld it would say, "It is wonderful, brother Drithelm, (for so he was called,) that you are able to endure such violent cold;" he simply answered, for he was a man of much simplicity and indifferent wit, "I have seen greater cold." And when they said, "It is strange that you will endure such austerity;" he replied, "I have seen more austerity." Thus he continued, through an indefatigable desire of heavenly bliss, to subdue his aged body with daily fasting, till the day of his being called away; and thus he forwarded the salvation of many by his words and example.

John Bunyan

(1628–1688)

An Anglican tinker's son turned Noncomformist minister, Bunyan composed The Pilgrim's Progress *while in prison for illegal preaching. Until the nineteenth century, this allegorical drama of a journey from the City of Destruction to the Heavenly City was the most popular English book after the Bible.*

Angels

Now I saw in my Dream, that by this time the Pilgrims were got over the Inchanted Ground, and entering into the Country of *Beulah*, whose air was very sweet and pleasant, the way lying directly through it, they solaced themselves there for a season. Yea, here they heard continually the singing of Birds, and saw every day the Flowers appear in the earth, and heard the voice of the Turtle in the land. In this Country the Sun shineth night and day; wherefore this was beyond the Valley of the *Shadow of Death*, and also out of the reach of Giant *Despair*, neither could they from this place so much as see *Doubting* Castle. Here they were within sight of the City they were going to, also here met them some of the inhabitants thereof; for in this land the Shining Ones commonly walked, because it was upon the borders of Heaven. In this land also the contract between the Bride and the Bridegroom was renewed; yea here, *as the Bridegroom rejoiceth over the Bride, so did their God rejoice over them.* Here they had no want of Corn and Wine; for in this place they met with abundance of what they had sought for in all their Pilgrimage. Here they heard voices from out of the City, loud voices, saying, *Say ye to the daughter of* Zion *Behold thy salvation cometh, behold his reward is with him*. Here all the inhabitants of the Country called them, *The holy People, The redeemed of the Lord, Sought out*, &c.

Now as they walked in this land, they had more rejoicing than in parts more remote from the Kingdom to which they were bound; and drawing near to the City, they had yet a more perfect view thereof. It was builded of Pearls and Precious Stones, also the Street thereof was paved with Gold; so that by reason of the natural glory of the City, and the reflections of the Sun-beams upon it, *Christian* with desire fell sick, *Hopeful* also had a fit or two of the same disease. Wherefore here they lay by it a while, crying out because of their pangs, *If you see my Beloved, tell him that I am sick of love*. But being a little strengthened, and better able to bear their sickness, they walked on their way, and came yet nearer and nearer, where were Orchards, Vineyards, and Gardens, and their gates opened into the High-way. Now as they came up to these places, behold the Gardener stood in the way, to whom the Pilgrims said, Whose goodly Vineyards and Gardens are these? He answered, They are the King's and are planted here for his own delights, and also for the solace of Pilgrims. So the Gardener had them into the Vineyards, and bid them refresh themselves with Dainties. He also shewed them there the King's walks, and the Arbors where he delighted to be; and here they tarried and slept.

Now I beheld in my Dream, that they talked more in their sleep at this time than ever they did in all their Journey; and being in a muse thereabout, the Gardener said even to me, Wherefore musest thou at the matter? It is the nature of the fruit of the Grapes of these Vineyards to go down so sweetly as to cause the lips of them that are asleep to speak.

So I saw that when they awoke, they addressed themselves to go up to the City. But, as I said, the reflection of the Sun upon the City (for the City was pure Gold) was so extremely glorious, that they could not as yet with open face behold it, but through an *Instrument* made for that purpose. So I saw that as they went on, there met them two men, in Raiment that shone like Gold, also their faces shone as the light.

These men asked the Pilgrims whence they came? and they told them. They also asked them where they had lodged, what difficulties and dangers, what comforts and pleasures they had met in the way? and they told them. Then said the men that met them, You have but two difficulties more to meet with, and then you are in the City.

Christian then and his Companion asked the men to go along with them, so they told them they would. But, said they, you must obtain it by your own Faith. So I saw in my Dream that they went on together till they came in sight of the Gate.

Now I further saw that betwixt them and the Gate was a River, but there was no Bridge to go over, the River was very deep: at the sight therefore of this River the Pilgrims were much stunned; but the men that went with them said, You must go through, or you cannot come at the Gate.

The Pilgrims then began to enquire if there was no other way to the Gate; to which they answered, Yes, but there hath not any, save two, to wit, *Enoch* and *Elijah*, been permitted to tread that path, since the foundation of the World, nor shall, until the last Trumpet shall sound. The Pilgrims then, especially *Christian*, began to dispond in his mind, and looked this way and that, but no way could be found by them by which they might escape the River. Then they asked the men if the Waters were all of a depth? They said, No; yet they could not help them in that case, for said they, *you shall find it deeper or shallower, as you believe in the King of the place.*

Death is not welcome to nature, though by it we pass out of this world in to glory

Angels help us not comfortably through death

They then addressed themselves to the Water; and entring, *Christian* began to sink, and crying out to his good friend *Hopeful*, he said, I sink in deep Waters; the Billows go over my head, all his Waves go over me, *Selah*.

Then said the other, Be of good cheer my Brother, I feel the bottom, and it is good. Then said *Christian*, Ah my friend, the sorrows of death have compassed me about, I shall not see the land that flows with milk and honey. And with that a great darkness and horror fell upon *Christian*, so that he could not see before him. Also here he in great measure lost his senses, so that he could neither remember, nor orderly talk of any of those sweet refreshments that he had met with in the way of his Pilgrimage. But all the words that he spake still tended to discover that he had horror of mind, and heart-fears that he should die in that River, and never obtain entrance in at the Gate. Here also, as they that stood by perceived, he was much in the

Christian's conflict at the hour of death

troublesome thoughts of the sins that he had committed, both since and before he began to be a Pilgrim. 'Twas also observed that he was troubled with apparitions of Hobgoblins and evil Spirits, for ever and anon he would intimate so much by words. *Hopeful* therefore here had much ado to keep his Brother's head above water; yea sometimes he would be quite gone down, and then ere a while he would rise up again half dead. *Hopeful* also would endeavour to comfort him, saying, Brother, I see the Gate, and men standing by to receive us. But *Christian* would answer, 'Tis you, 'tis you they wait for, you have been *hopeful* ever since I knew you. And so have you, said he to *Christian*. Ah Brother, said he, surely if I was right, he would now arise to help me; but for my sins he hath brought me into the snare, and hath left me. Then said *Hopeful*, My Brother, you have quite forgot the Text, where it is said of the wicked, *There is no band in their death, but their strength is firm, they are not troubled as other men, neither are they plagued like other men*. These troubles and distresses that you go through in these Waters are no sign that God hath forsaken you, but are sent to try you, whether you will call to mind that which heretofore you have received of his goodness, and live upon him in your distresses.

Christian delivered from his fears in death

Then I saw in my Dream, that *Christian* was as in a muse a while. To whom also *Hopeful* added this word, *Be of good cheer, Jesus Christ maketh thee whole*; and with that *Christian* brake out with a loud voice, Oh I see him again, and he tells me, *When thou passest through the Waters, I will be with thee; and through the Rivers, they shall not overflow thee*. Then they both took courage, and the Enemy was after that as still as a stone, until they were gone over. *Christian* therefore presently found ground to stand upon, and so it followed that the rest of the River was but shallow. Thus they got over. Now upon the bank of the River on the other side, they saw the two shining men again, who there waited for them; wherefore being come out of the River, they saluted them saying, *We are ministring Spirits, sent forth to minister for those that shall be heirs of salvation*. Thus they went along towards the Gate.

The angels do wait for them, so soon as they are passed out of this world

Now, now, look how the holy Pilgrims ride,
Clouds are their Chariots, Angels are their Guide:

Who would not here for him all hazards run,
That thus provides for his when this World's done?

Now you must note that the City stood upon a mighty Hill, but the Pilgrims went up that Hill with ease because they had these two men to lead them up by the arms; also they had left their *mortal Garments* behind them in the River, for though they went in with them, they came out without them. They therefore went up here with much agility and speed, though the foundation upon which the City was framed was higher than the Clouds. They therefore went up through the Regions of the Air, sweetly talking as they went, being comforted, because they safely got over the River, and had such glorious Companions to attend them.

They have put off mortality

The talk that they had with the Shining Ones was about the glory of the place, who told them that the beauty and glory of it was inexpressible. There, said they, is the Mount *Sion*, the heavenly *Jerusalem*, the innumerable company of Angels, and the Spirits of just men made perfect. You are going now, said they, to the Paradise of God, wherein you shall see the Tree of Life, and eat of the never-fading fruits thereof; and when you come there, you shall have white Robes given you, and your walk and talk shall be every day with the King, even all the days of Eternity. There you shall not see again such things as you saw when you were in the lower Region upon the earth, to wit, sorrow, sickness, affliction, and death, *for the former things are passed away.* You are now going to *Abraham*, to *Isaac*, and *Jacob*, and to the Prophets, men that God hath taken away from the evil to come, and that are now resting upon their beds, each one walking in his righteousness. The men then asked, What must we do in the holy place? To whom it was answered, You must there receive the comfort of all your toil, and have joy for all your sorrow; you must reap what you have sown, even the fruit of all your Prayers and Tears, and sufferings for the King by the way. In that place you must wear Crowns of Gold, and enjoy the perpetual sight and vision of the Holy one, *for there you shall see him as he is.* There also you shall serve him continually with praise, with shouting, and thanksgiving, whom you desired to serve in the

World, though with much difficulty, because of the infirmity of your flesh. There your eyes shall be delighted with seeing, and your ears with hearing the pleasant voice of the Mighty One. There you shall enjoy your friends again, that are gone thither before you; and there you shall with joy receive even every one that follows into the holy place after you. There also shall you be cloathed with Glory and Majesty, and put into an equipage fit to ride out with the King of Glory. When he shall come with sound of Trumpet in the Clouds, as upon the wings of the Wind, you shall come with him; and when he shall sit upon the Throne of Judgment, you shall sit by him; yea, and when he shall pass sentence upon all the workers of iniquity, let them be Angels or Men, you also shall have a voice in that Judgment, because they were his and your Enemies. Also when he shall again return to the City, you shall go too, with sound of Trumpet, and be ever with him.

Now while they were thus drawing towards the Gate, behold a company of the Heavenly Host came out to meet them; to whom it was said by the other two Shining Ones, These are the men that have loved our Lord when they were in the World, and that have left all for his Holy Name, and he hath sent us to fetch them, and we have brought them thus far on their desired Journey, that they may go in and look their Redeemer in the face with joy. Then the Heavenly Host gave a great shout, saying, *Blessed are they that are called to the Marriage Supper of the Lamb.* There came out also at this time to meet them, several of the King's Trumpeters, cloathed in white and shining Raiment, who with melodious noises and loud, made even the Heavens to echo with their sound. These Trumpeters saluted *Christian* and his fellow with ten thousand welcomes from the World, and this they did with shouting and sound of Trumpet.

This done, they compassed them round on every side; some went before, some behind, and some on the right hand, some on the left, (as 'twere to guard them through the upper Regions) continually sounding as they went with melodious noise, in notes on high: so that the very sight was to them that could behold it, as if Heaven itself was come down to meet them. Thus therefore they walked on together; and as they walked, ever and anon these Trumpeters, even with joyful sound, would, by mixing their musick with looks and gestures, still signify to *Christian* and his Brother, how welcome they were into their company, and with what gladness they came to meet them; and now were these two men as 'twere in Heaven before they came at it, being swallowed up with the sight of Angels, and with hearing of their melodious notes. Here also they had the City itself in view, and they thought they heard all the Bells therein ring to welcome them thereto. But above all, the warm and joyful thoughts that they had about their own dwelling there, with such company, and that for ever and ever. Oh, by what tongue or pen can their glorious joy be expressed! And thus they came up to the Gate.

Now when they were come up to the Gate, there was written over it in Letters of Gold, *Blessed are they that do his Commandments, that they may have right to the Tree of Life, and may enter in through the Gates into the City.*

Then I saw in my Dream, that the Shining Men bid them call at the Gate; the which when they did, some from above looked over the Gate, to wit, *Enoch, Moses*, and *Elijah, &c.*, to whom it was said, These Pilgrims are come from the City of *Destruction* for the love that they bear to the King of this place; and then the Pilgrims gave in unto them each man his Certificate, which they had received in the beginning; those therefore were carried in to the King, who when he had read them, said, Where are the men? To whom it was answered, They are standing without the Gate. The King then commanded to open the Gate, *That the righteous nation*, saith he, *that keepeth Truth may enter in.*

Now I saw in my Dream that these two men went in at the Gate: and lo, as they entered, they were transfigured, and they had Raiment put on that shone like Gold. There was also that met them with Harps and Crowns, and gave them to them, the Harps to praise withal, and the Crowns in token of honour. Then I heard in my Dream that all the Bells in the City rang again for joy, and that it was said unto them, *Enter ye into the joy of your Lord*. I also heard the men themselves, that they sang with a loud voice, saying, *Blessing, Honour, Glory, and Power, be to him that sitteth upon the Throne, and to the Lamb for ever and ever.*

Now just as the Gates were opened to let in the men, I looked in after them, and behold, the City shone like the Sun: the Streets also were paved with Gold, and in them walked many men, with Crowns on their heads, Palms in their hands, and golden Harps to sing praises withal.

There were also of them that had wings, and they answered one another without intermission, saying, *Holy, Holy, Holy, is the Lord.* And after that they shut up the Gates. Which when I had seen, I wished myself among them.

Ignorance comes up to the river

Vain-hope does ferry him over

Now while I was gazing upon all these things, I turned my head to look back, and saw *Ignorance* come up to the River-side; but he soon got over and that without half that difficulty which the other two men met with. For it happened that there was then in that place one *Vain-hope* a Ferry-man, that with his Boat helped him over; so he, as the other I saw, did ascend the Hill to come up to the Gate, only he came alone; neither did any man meet him with the least encouragement. When he was come up to the Gate, he looked up to the writing that was above, and then began to knock, supposing that entrance should have been quickly administered to him; but he was asked by the men that looked over the top of the Gate, Whence came you? and what would you have? He answered, I have eat and drank in the presence of the King, and he has taught in our Streets. Then they asked him for his Certificate, that they might go in and shew it to the King. So he fumbled in his bosom for one, and found none. Then said they, Have you none? But the man answered never a word. So they told the King, but he would not come down to see him, but commanded the two Shining Ones that conducted *Christian* and *Hopeful* to the City, to go out and take *Ignorance*, and bind him hand and foot, and have him away. Then they took him up, and carried him through the air to the door that I saw in the side of the Hill, and put him in there. Then I saw that there was a way to Hell even from the Gates of Heaven, as well as from the City of *Destruction*. So I awoke, and behold it was a Dream.

Henry Fielding

(1707–1754)

Fielding, an English satirist, journalist, and justice of the peace, was one of the founders of the English novel. These excerpts from A Journey from This World to the Next *(1743), published six years before his masterpiece,* Tom Jones, *present a rollicking portrait of the afterlife, where hopping is a popular mode of locomotion and the famous of all eras mingle with one another, exchanging witty remarks. The satire is unfinished; Fielding reports that the lost ending was "destroyed in rolling up pens, tobacco, etc."*

BOOK I

CHAPTER ONE

The author dies, meets with Mercury, and is by him conducted to the stage which sets out for the other world.

On the first day of December 1741[1] I departed this life at my lodgings in Cheapside. My body had been some time dead before I was at liberty to quit it, lest it should by any accident return to life: this is an injunction imposed on all souls by the eternal law of fate, to prevent the inconveniences which would follow. As soon as the destined period was expired (being no longer than till the body is become perfectly cold and stiff) I began to move; but found myself under a difficulty of making my escape, for the mouth or door was shut, so that it was impossible for me to go out at it; and the windows, vulgarly called the eyes, were so closely pulled down by the fingers of a nurse, that I could by no means open

1. Some doubt whether this should not be rather 1641, which is a date more agreeable to the account given of it in the introduction: but then there are some passages which seem to relate to transactions infinitely later, even within this year or two. To say the truth there are difficulties attending either conjecture; so the reader may take which he pleases.

them. At last I perceived a beam of light glimmering at the top of the house (for such I may call the body I had been inclosed in), whither ascending, I gently let myself down through a kind of chimney, and issued out at the nostrils.

No prisoner discharged from a long confinement ever tasted the sweets of liberty with a more exquisite relish than I enjoyed in this delivery from a dungeon wherein I had been detained upwards of forty years, and with much the same kind of regard I cast my eyes[1] backwards upon it.

My friends and relations had all quitted the room, being all (as I plainly overheard) very loudly quarrelling below stairs about my will; there was only an old woman left above to guard the body, as I apprehend. She was in a fast sleep, occasioned, as from her savour it seemed, by a comfortable dose of gin. I had no pleasure in this company, and, therefore, as the window was wide open, I sallied forth into the open air: but, to my great astonishment, found myself unable to fly, which I had always during my habitation in the body conceived of spirits: however, I came so lightly to the ground that I did not hurt myself; and, though I had not the gift of flying (owing probably to my having neither feathers nor wings), I was capable of hopping such a prodigious way at once, that it served my turn almost as well.

I had not hopped far before I perceived a tall young gentleman in a silk waistcoat, with a wing on his left heel, a garland on his head, and a caduceus in his right hand.[2] I thought I had seen this person before, but had not time to recollect where, when he called out to me and asked me how long I had been departed. I answered I was just come forth. "You must not stay here," replied he, "unless you had been murdered: in which case, indeed, you might have been suffered to walk some time; but if you died a natural death you must set out for the other world immediately." I desired to know the way. "O," cried the gentleman, "I will show you to the inn whence the stage proceeds; for I am the porter. Perhaps you never

---

1. Eyes are not perhaps so properly adapted to a spiritual substance; but we are here, as in many other places, obliged to use corporeal terms to make ourselves the better understood.

2. This is the dress in which the god appears to mortals at the theatres. One of the offices attributed to this god by the ancients, was to collect the ghosts as a shepherd doth a flock of sheep, and drive them with his wand into the other world.

heard of me—my name is Mercury." "Sure, sir," said I, "I have seen you at the playhouse." Upon which he smiled, and, without satisfying me as to that point, walked directly forward, bidding me hop after him. I obeyed him, and soon found myself in Warwick-lane; where Mercury, making a full stop, pointed at a particular house, where he had me enquire for the stage, and, wishing me a good journey, took his leave, saying he must go seek after other customers.

I arrived just as the coach was setting out, and found I had no reason for enquiry; for every person seemed to know my business the moment I appeared at the door: the coachman told me his horses were to, but that he had no place left; however, though there were already six, the passengers offered to make room for me. I thanked them, and ascended without much ceremony. We immediately began our journey. . . .

At length we arrived at the gate of Elysium. Here was a prodigious crowd of spirits waiting for admittance, some of whom were admitted, and some were rejected; for all were strictly examined by the porter, whom I soon discovered to be the celebrated judge Minos. . . .

CHAPTER SEVEN

The proceedings of Judge Minos at the gate of Elysium

I now got near enough to the gate to hear the several claims of those who endeavoured to pass. The first, among other pretensions, set forth that he had been very liberal to an hospital; but Minos answered, "Ostentation," and repulsed him. The second exhibited that he had constantly frequented his church, been a rigid observer of fast-days: he likewise represented the great animosity he had shewn to vice in others, which never escaped his severest censure; and as to his own behaviour, he had never been once guilty of whoring, drinking, gluttony, or any other excess. He said he had disinherited his son for getting a bastard. "Have you so?" said Minos; "then pray return into the other world and beget another; for such an unnatural rascal shall never pass this gate." A dozen others, who had advanced with very confident countenances, seeing him rejected, turned about of their own accord, declaring, if he could not pass, they had no expectation, and accordingly they followed him back to earth; which was the fate of all who were repulsed, they being obliged to take a further purification, unless those who were guilty of some very heinous crimes, who were hustled in at a little back gate, whence they tumbled immediately into the bottomless pit.

The next spirit that came up declared he had done neither good nor evil in the world; for that since his arrival at man's estate he had spent his whole time in search of curiosities; and particularly in the study of butterflies, of which he had collected an immense number. Minos made him no answer, but with great scorn pushed him back.

There now advanced a very beautiful spirit indeed. She began to ogle Minos the moment she saw him. She said she hoped there was some merit in refusing a great number of lovers, and dying a maid, though she had had the choice of a hundred. Minos told her she had not refused enow yet, and turned her back.

She was succeeded by a spirit who told the judge he believed his works would speak for him. "What works?" answered Minos. "My dramatic works," replied the other, "which have done so much good in recommending virtue and punishing vice." "Very well," said the judge; "if you please to stand by, the first person who passes the gate by your means shall carry you in with him; but, if you will take my advice, I think, for expedition sake, you had better return, and live another life upon earth." The bard grumbled at this, and replied that, besides his poetical works, he had done some other good things: for that he had once lent the whole profits of a benefit-night to a friend, and by that means had saved him and his family from destruction. Upon this the gate flew open, and Minos desired him to walk in, telling him, if he had mentioned this at first, he might have spared the remembrance of his plays. The poet answered, he believed if Minos had read his works, he would set a higher value on them. He was then beginning to repeat, but Minos pushed him forward, and, turning his back to him, applied himself to the next passenger, a very genteel spirit, who made a very low bow to Minos, and then threw himself into an erect attitude, and imitated the motion of taking snuff with his right hand. Minos asked him what he had to say for himself. He answered, he would dance a minuet with any spirit in Elysium: that he could likewise perform all his other exercise very well, and hoped he had in his life deserved the character of a perfect fine gentleman. Minos replied it would be great pity to rob the world of so fine a gentleman, and therefore desired him to take the other trip. The beau bowed, thanked the judge, and said he desired no better. . . .

The judge then addressed himself to me, who little expected to pass this fiery trial. I confessed I had indulged myself very freely with wine and women in my youth, but had never done an injury to any man living, nor avoided an opportunity of doing good; that I pretended to very little virtue more than general philanthropy and private friendship. I was proceeding, when Minos bid me enter the gate, and not indulge myself with trumpeting forth my virtues. I accordingly passed forward with my lovely companion, and, embracing her with vast eagerness, but spiritual innocence, she returned my embrace in the same manner, and we both congratulated ourselves on our arrival in this happy region, whose beauty no painting of the imagination can describe.

CHAPTER EIGHT

The adventures which the author met on his first entrance into Elysium

We pursued our way through a delicious grove of orange-tree, where I saw infinite numbers of spirits, every one of whom I knew, and was known by them (for spirits here know one another by intuition). I presently met a little daughter whom I had lost several years before. Good gods! what words can describe the raptures, the melting passionate tenderness, with which we kissed each other, continuing in our embrace, with the most ecstatic joy, a space which, if time had been measured here as on earth, could not be less than half a year.

The first spirit with whom I entered into discourse was the famous Leonidas of Sparta. I acquainted him with the honours which had been done him by a celebrated poet of our nation; to which he answered he was very much obliged to him.

We were presently afterwards entertained with the most delicious voice I had ever heard, accompanied by a violin, equal to Signior Piantinida. I presently discovered the musician and songster to be Orpheus and Sappho.

Old Homer was present at this concert (if I may so call it), and Madam Dacier sat in his lap. He asked much after Mr. Pope, and said he was very desirous of seeing him; for that he had read his Iliad in his translation with almost as much delight as he believed he had given others in the original. I had the curiosity to enquire whether he had really writ that poem in detached pieces, and sung it about as ballads all over Greece, according to the report which went of him. He smiled at my question, and asked me whether there appeared any connexion in the poem; for if there did he thought I might answer myself. I then importuned him to acquaint me in which of the cities which contended for the honour of his birth he was really born? To which he answered, "Upon my soul I can't tell."

Virgil then came up to me, with Mr. Addison under his arm. "Well, sir," said he, "how many translations have these few last years produced of my Æneid?" I told him I believed several, but I could not possibly remember; for that I had never read any but Dr. Trapp's. "Ay," said he, "that is a curious piece indeed!" I then acquainted him with the discovery made by Mr. Warburton of the Elusinian mysteries couched in his sixth book. "What mysteries?" said Mr. Addison. "The Elusinian," answered Virgil, "which I have disclosed in my sixth book." "How!" replied Addison. "You never mentioned a word of any such mysteries to me in all our acquaintance." "I thought it was unnecessary," cried the other, "to a man of your infinite learning: besides, you always told me you perfectly understood my meaning." Upon this I thought the critic looked a little out of countenance, and turned aside to a very merry spirit, one Dick Steele, who embraced him, and told him he had been the greatest man upon earth; that he readily resigned up all the merit of his own works to him. Upon which Addison gave him a gracious smile, and, clapping him on the back with much solemnity, cried out, "Well said, Dick!"

I then observed Shakspeare standing between Betterton and Booth, and deciding a difference between those two great actors concerning the placing an accent in one of his lines: this was disputed on both sides with a warmth which surprized me in Elysium, till I discovered by intuition that every soul retained its principal characteristic, being, indeed, its very essence. The line was that celebrated one in Othello—

Put out the light, and then put out the light.

according to Betterton. Mr. Booth contended to have it thus:—

Put out the light, and then put out THE *light.*

I could not help offering my conjecture on this occasion, and suggested it might perhaps be—

Put out the light, and then put out THY *light.*

Another hinted a reading very sophisticated in my opinion—

Put out the light, and then put out THEE, *light.*

making light to be the vocative case. Another would have altered the last word, and read—

Put out thy light, and then put out thy sight.

But Betterton said, if the text was to be disturbed, he saw no reason why a word might not be changed as well as a letter, and, instead of "put out thy light," you may read "put out thy eyes." At last it was agreed on all sides to refer the matter to the decision of Shakspeare himself, who delivered his sentiments as follows: "Faith, gentlemen, it is so long since I wrote the line, I have forgot my meaning. This I know, could I have dreamt so much nonsense would have been talked and writ about it, I would have blotted it out of my works; for I am sure, if any of these be my meaning, it doth me very little honour."

Percy Bysshe Shelley

(1792–1822)

The English Romantic poet Shelley was a freethinker, social reformer, and expatriate. "Adonais," an elegy in Spenserian stanzas on the death of John Keats, was published a year before Shelley's own death by drowning.

XXXIX.

Peace, peace! he is not dead, he doth not sleep—
He hath awakened from the dream of life—
'Tis we, who lost in stormy visions, keep
With phantoms an unprofitable strife,
And in mad trance, strike with our spirit's knife
Invulnerable nothings.—*We* decay
Like corpses in a charnel; fear and grief
Convulse us and consume us day by day,
And cold hopes swarm like worms within our living clay.

XL.

He has outsoared the shadow of our night;
Envy and calumny and hate and pain,
And that unrest which men miscall delight,
Can touch him not and torture not again;
From the contagion of the world's slow stain
He is secure, and now can never mourn
A heart grown cold, a head grown grey in vain;
Nor, when the spirit's self has ceased to burn,
With sparkless ashes load an unlamented urn.

XLI.

He lives, he wakes—'tis Death is dead, not he;
Mourn not for Adonais.—Thou young Dawn
Turn all thy dew to splendour, for from thee
The spirit thou lamentest is not gone;

Ye caverns and ye forests, cease to moan!
Cease ye faint flowers and fountains, and thou Air
Which like a mourning veil thy scarf hadst thrown
O'er the abandoned Earth, now leave it bare
Even to the joyous stars which smile on its despair!

XLII.

He is made one with Nature: there is heard
His voice in all her music, from the moan
Of thunder, to the song of night's sweet bird;
He is a presence to be felt and known
In darkness and in light, from herb and stone,
Spreading itself where'er that Power may move
Which has withdrawn his being to its own;
Which wields the world with never wearied love,
Sustains it from beneath, and kindles it above.

XLIII.

He is a portion of the loveliness
Which once he made more lovely: he doth bear
His part, while the one Spirit's plastic stress
Sweeps through the dull dense world, compelling there,
All new successions to the forms they wear;
Torturing th'unwilling dross that checks its flight
To its own likeness, as each mass may bear;
And bursting in its beauty and its might
From trees and beasts and men into the Heaven's light.

XLIV.

The splendours of the firmament of time
May be eclipsed, but are extinguished not;
Like stars to their appointed height they climb
And death is a low mist which cannot blot
The brightness it may veil. When lofty thought
Lifts a young heart above its mortal lair,
And love and life contend in it, for what
Shall be its earthly doom, the dead live there
And move like winds of light on dark and stormy air.

XLV.

The inheritors of unfulfilled renown
Rose from their thrones, built beyond mortal thought,
Far in the Unapparent. Chatterton
Rose pale, his solemn agony had not
Yet faded from him; Sidney, as he fought
And as he fell and as he lived and loved
Sublimely mild, a Spirit without spot,
Arose; and Lucan, by his death approved:
Oblivion as they rose shrank like a thing reproved.

XLVI.

And many more, whose names on Earth are dark
But whose transmitted effluence cannot die
So long as fire outlives the parent spark,
Rose, robed in dazzling immortality.
"Thou art become as one of us," they cry,
"It was for thee yon kingless sphere has long
"Swung blind in unascended majesty,
"Silent alone amid an Heaven of song.
"Assume thy winged throne, thou Vesper of our throng!"

XLVII.

Who mourns for Adonais? oh come forth
Fond wretch! and know thyself and him aright.
Clasp with thy panting soul the pendulous Earth;
As from a centre, dart thy spirit's light
Beyond all worlds, until its spacious might
Satiate the void circumference: then shrink
Even to a point within our day and night;
And keep thy heart light lest it make thee sink
When hope has kindled hope, and lured thee to the brink.

XLVIII.

Or go to Rome, which is the sepulchre
O, not of him, but of our joy: 'tis nought
That ages, empires, and religions there
Lie buried in the ravage they have wrought;
For such as he can lend,—they borrow not
Glory from those who made the world their prey;

And he is gathered to the kings of thought
Who waged contention with their time's decay,
And of the past are all that cannot pass away

XLIX.

Go thou to Rome,—at once the Paradise,
The grave, the city, and the wilderness;
And where its wrecks like shattered mountains rise,
And flowering weeds, and fragrant copses dress
The bones of Desolation's nakedness
Pass, till the Spirit of the spot shall lead
Thy footsteps to a slope of green access
Where, like an infant's smile, over the dead,
A light of laughing flowers along the grass is spread.

L.

And gray walls moulder round, on which dull Time
Feeds, like slow fire upon a hoary brand;
And one keen pyramid with wedge sublime,
Pavilioning the dust of him who planned
This refuge for his memory, doth stand
Like flame transformed to marble; and beneath,
A field is spread, on which a newer band
Have pitched in Heaven's smile their camp of death
Welcoming him we lose with scarce extinguished breath.

LI.

Here pause: these graves are all too young as yet
To have out grown the sorrow which consigned
Its charge to each; and if the seal is set,
Here, on one fountain of a mourning mind,
Break it not thou! too surely shalt thou find
Thine own well full, if thou returnest home,
Of tears and gall. From the world's bitter wind
Seek shelter in the shadow of the tomb.
What Adonais is, why fear we to become?

LII.

The One remains, the many change and pass;
Heaven's light forever shines, Earth's shadows fly;
Life, like a dome of many-coloured glass,

Stains the white radiance of Eternity,
Until Death tramples it to fragments.—Die,
If thou wouldst be with that which thou dost seek!
Follow where all is fled!—Rome's azure sky,
Flowers, ruins, statues, music, words, are weak
The glory they transfuse with fitting truth to speak.

LIII.

Why linger, why turn back, why shrink, my Heart?
Thy hopes are gone before: from all things here
They have departed; thou shouldst now depart!
A light is past from the revolving year,
And man, and woman; and what still is dear
Attracts to crush, repels to make thee wither
The soft sky smiles,—the low wind whispers near:
'Tis Adonais calls! oh, hasten thither,
No more let Life divide what Death can join together.

LIV.

That Light whose smile kindles the Universe,
That Beauty in which all things work and move,
That Benediction which the eclipsing Curse
Of birth can quench not, that sustaining Love
Which through the web of being blindly wove
By man and beast and earth and air and sea,
Burns bright or dim, as each are mirrors of
The fire for which all thirst; now beams on me,
Consuming the last clouds of cold mortality.

LV.

The breath whose might I have invoked in song
Descends on me; my spirit's bark is driven,
Far from the shore, far from the trembling throng
Whose sails were never to the tempest given;
The massy earth and sphered skies are riven!
I am borne darkly, fearfully, afar;
Whilst burning through the inmost veil of Heaven,
The soul of Adonais, like a star,
Beacons from the abode where the Eternal are.

"How the Weaver Went to Heaven"

A. K. Ramanujan here retells, from an Urdu version, a widespread North Indian folktale, belonging to the general category of "numskull tales."

There was once a weaver whose field used to be visited every night by an elephant of Indra, the king of heaven. It would come down from the sky and graze in his field, leaving it devastated. He asked his weaver friends what animal could be doing this to his field. "Perhaps it's the village grindstones. Maybe they get up in the night and visit your field," they said. So he had every grindstone in the village tied up, but the damage went on as before. He again consulted his friends and they said, "Maybe it's the village rice-pounders. Maybe they get up in the night and visit your field, when everybody is fast asleep." So he had all the rice-pounders tied up, but the damage continued. In fact, it got worse.

Then he went one night and lay in wait in the field. And what did he see? He saw an elephant fly down and graze on the crop. As it was about to fly away, he caught hold of its tail and went with it to Indra's court in heaven. There he sat in a corner and saw the celestial dancers dance and heard them sing. Nobody there seemed to take any notice of him, and he even had his fill of divine dishes in the gods' kitchen. Next night, when the elephant was flying back to earth, he held on to its tail and came home.

As soon as he landed, he told his friends of all the wonders he had seen and said, "What's the use of living in this wretched place? Let's all go to Indra's heaven." They agreed, and when the elephant was flying back after its nightly meal of earthly crops, first the weaver clung to its tail, his wife clung on to her husband's legs, and so all his kinsfolk held on too, in a long human chain. The elephant didn't seem to notice the human baggage it was carrying, and it flew away with them through the air. When they had got very high, the weaver began to think to himself, "What a fool I was not to bring my loom with me!" And with this thought, he felt like wringing his hands, and so he let go his hold and they all came tumbling down to earth again.

That's why they say a weaver has never made it to heaven.

The Tibetan Book of the Dead

The Tibetan Buddhist Bardo Thodol *(or* Bardo thos grol*), recited to the dying and the newly dead, is a manual for safe passage through the perilous interval (*bardo*) between death and rebirth. In this version, translator Edward Conze places himself ("E.C.") in the role of the deceased.*

This is what the Lama reads to the dying person:

Preamble

I now transmit to you the profound teachings which I have myself received from my Teacher, and, through him, from the long line of initiated Gurus. Pay attention to it now, and do not allow yourself to be distracted by other thoughts! Remain lucid and calm, and bear in mind what you hear! If you suffer, do not give in to the pain! If restful numbness overtakes you, if you swoon away into a peaceful forgetting—do not surrender yourself to that! Remain watchful and alert!

The factors which made up the person known as E.C. are about to disperse. Your mental activities are separating themselves from your body, and they are about to enter the intermediary state. Rouse your energy, so that you may enter this state self-possessed and in full consciousness!

I. The moment of death, and the clear light of Pure Reality

First of all there will appear to you, swifter than lightning, the luminous splendour of the colourless light of Emptiness, and that will surround you on all sides. Terrified, you will want to flee from the radiance, and you may well lose consciousness. Try to submerge yourself in that light, giving up all belief in a separate self, all attachment to your illusory ego. Recognize that the boundless Light of this true Reality is your own true self, and you shall be saved!

Few, however, are those who, having missed salvation during their life on earth, can attain it during this brief instant which passes so quickly. The overwhelming majority are shocked into unconsciousness by the terror they feel.

The emergence of a subtle body

If you miss salvation at that moment, you will be forced to have a number of further dreams, both pleasant and unpleasant. Even they offer you a chance to gain understanding, as long as you remain vigilant and alert. A few days after death there suddenly emerges a subtle illusory dream-body, also known as the 'mental body.' It is impregnated with the after-effects of your past desires, endowed with all sense-faculties, and has the power of unimpeded motion. It can go right through rocks, hills, boulders, and walls, and in an instant it can traverse any distance. Even after the physical sense-organs are dissolved, sights, sounds, smells, tastes, and touches will be perceived, and ideas will be formed. These are the result of the energy still residing in the six kinds of consciousness, the after-effects of what you did with your body and mind in the past. But you must know that all you perceive is a mere vision, a mere illusion, and does not reflect any really existing objects. Have no fear, and form no attachment! View it all evenmindedly, without like or dislike!

II. The experience of the spiritual realities

Three and a half days after your death, Buddhas and Bodhisattvas will for seven days appear to you in their benign and peaceful aspect. Their light will shine upon you, but it will be so radiant that you will scarcely be able to look at it. Wonderful and delightful though they are, the Buddhas may nevertheless frighten you. Do not give in to your fright! Do not run away! Serenely contemplate the spectacle before you! Overcome your fear, and feel no desire! Realize that these are the rays of the grace of the Buddhas, who come to receive you into their Buddha-realms. Pray to them with intense faith and humility, and, in a halo of rainbow light, you will merge into the heart of the divine Father-Mother, and take up your abode in one of the realms of the Buddhas. Thereby you may still at this moment win your salvation.

But if you miss it, you will next, for another seven days, be confronted with the angry deities, and the Guardians of the Faith, surrounded by their followers in tumultuous array, many of them in the form of animals which you have never seen in the life you left. Bathed in multicoloured light they stand before you, threatening you and barring your passage. Loud are their voices, with which they shout, 'Hit him! Hit him! Kill him! Kill him!' This is what you have to hear, because you turned a deaf ear to the saving truths of religion! All these forms are strange to you, you do not recognize them for what they are. They terrify you beyond words, and yet it is you who have created them. Do not give in to your fright, resist your mental confusion! All this is unreal, and what you see are the contents of your own mind in conflict with itself. All these terrifying deities, witches, and demons around you—fear them not, flee them not! They are but the benevolent Buddhas and Bodhisattvas, changed in their outward aspect. In you alone are the five wisdoms, the source of the benign spirits! In you alone are the five poisons, the source of the angry spirits! It is from your own mind therefore that all this has sprung. What you see here is but the reflection of the contents of your own mind in the mirror of the Void. If at this point you should manage to understand that, the shock of this insight will stun you, your subtle body will disperse into a rainbow, and you will find yourself in paradise among the angels.

III. Seeking rebirth

But if you fail to grasp the meaning of what you were taught, if you still continue to feel a desire to exist as an individual, then you are now doomed to again re-enter the wheel of becoming.

The judgment

You are now before Yama, King of the Dead. In vain will you try to lie, and to deny or conceal the evil deeds you have done. The Judge holds up before you the shining mirror of Karma, wherein all your deeds are reflected. But again you have to deal with dream images, which you yourself have made, and which you project outside, without recognizing them as your own work. The mirror in which Yama seems to read your past is your own memory, and also his judgement is your own. It is you yourself who pronounce your own judgement, which in its turn determines your next rebirth. No terrible God pushes you into it; you go there quite on your own. The shapes of the frightening monsters who take hold of you, place a rope round your neck and drag you along, are just an illusion which you create from the forces within you. Know that apart from these karmic forces there is no Judge of the Dead, no gods, and no demons. Knowing that, you will be free!

The desire for rebirth

At this juncture you will realize that you are dead. You will think, 'I am dead! What shall I do?' and you will feel as miserable as a fish out of water on red-hot embers. Your consciousness, having no object on which to rest, will be like a feather tossed about by the wind, riding on the horse of breath. At about that time the fierce wind of karma, terrific and hard to bear, will drive you onwards, from behind, in dreadful gusts. And after a while the thought will occur to you, 'O what would I not give to possess a body!' But because you can at first find no place for you to enter into, you will be disatisfied and have the sensation of being squeezed into cracks and crevices amidst rocks and boulders.

The dawning of the lights of the six places of rebirth

Then there will shine upon you lights of the six places of rebirth. The light of the place in which you will be reborn will shine most prominently, but it is your own karmic disposition which decides about your choice. The rays of lights which will guide you to the various worlds will seem to you restful and friendly compared with the blinding flash of light which met you at first.

If you have deserved it by your good deeds, a white light will guide you into one of the heavens, and for a while you will have some happiness among the gods. Habits of envy and ambition will attract you to the red light, which leads to rebirth among the warlike Asuras, forever agitated by anger and envy. If you feel drawn to a blue light, you will find yourself again a human being, and well you remember how little happiness that brought you! If you had a heavy and dull mind, you will choose the green light, which leads you to the world of animals, unhappy because insecure and excluded from the knowledge which brings salvation. A ray of dull yellow will lead you to the world of the ghosts, and, finally, a ray of the colour of darkish smoke into the hells. Try to desist, if you can! Think of the Buddhas and Bodhisattvas! Recall that all these visions are unreal, control your mind, feel amity towards all that lives! And do not be afraid! You alone are the source of all these different rays. In you alone they exist, and so do the worlds to which they lead. Feel not attracted or repelled, but remain evenminded and calm!

Reincarnation

If so far you have been deaf to the teaching, listen to it now! An overpowering craving will come over you for the sense-experiences which you remember having had in the past, and which through your lack of sense-organs you cannot now have. Your desire for rebirth becomes more and more urgent; it becomes a real torment to you. This desire now racks you; you do not, however, experience it for what it is, but feel it as a deep thirst which parches you as you wander along, harassed, among deserts of burning sands. Whenever you try to take some rest, monstrous forms rise up before you. Some have animal heads on human bodies, others are gigantic birds with huge wings and claws. Their howlings and their whips drive you on, and then a hurricane carries you along, with those demonic beings in hot pursuit. Greatly anxious, you will look for a safe place of refuge.

Everywhere around you, you will see animals and humans in the act of sexual intercourse. You envy them, and the sight attracts you. If your karmic coefficients destine you to become a male, you feel attracted to the females and you hate the males you see. If you are destined to become a female, you will feel love for the males and hatred for the females you see. Do not go near the couples you see, do not try to interpose yourself between them, do not try to take the place of one of them! The feeling which you would then experience would make you faint away, just at the moment when egg and sperm are about to unite. And afterwards you will find that you have been conceived as a human being or as an animal.

"The Far-off Journey"

This selection comes from the Ch'u Tz'u, *an anthology of songs and elegies traditionally attributed to China's first known poet, Ch'ü Yüan (343–289 B.C.). "The Far-Off Journey"* (Yüan Yu), *based in part on Ch'ü Yüan's allegorical lament,* Li Sao, *was probably written by a Han Taoist poet near the beginning of the first century B.C. Empowered by Taoist yogic techniques, the poet ascends to the stars, visits the legendary Immortals, enter the Palace of the Great Mystery, encounters gods, goddesses, and spirits, and finally attains purity in the "neighbourhood of the Great Beginning."*

1. Grieved at the parlous state of this world's ways,
I wanted to float up and away from them.
2. But my powers were too weak to give me support:
What could I ride on to bear me upwards?
3. Fallen on a time of foulness and impurity,
Alone with my misery, I had no one to confide in.
4. In the night-time I lay, wide-eyed, without sleeping;
My unquiet soul was active until the daylight.
5. I thought of the limitless vastness of the universe,
And wept for the long affliction of man's life.
6. Those that had gone before I should never see;
And those yet to come I could never know of.
7. Restless I paced, with my mind on distant things;
Despairing, frustrated, consumed with constant yearning.
8. My thoughts were wild and wandered distractedly;
My heart was melancholy with mounting sadness.
9. My spirit darted forth and did not return to me;
And my body, left tenantless, grew withered and lifeless.
10. Then I looked into myself to strengthen my resolution,
And sought to learn from where the primal spirit issues.

11. In emptiness and silence I found serenity;
In tranquil Inaction I gained true satisfaction.
12. I heard how Ch'ih Sung had washed the world's dust off:
I would model myself on the pattern he had left me.
13. I honoured the wondrous powers of the Pure Ones;
I admired those of past ages who had become
Immortals.
14. They departed in the flux of change and vanished from
men's sight,
Leaving a famous name that long endures after them.
15. I marvelled how Fu Yüeh lived on in a star;
I admired Han Chung for attaining Unity.
16. Their bodies grew dim and faded in the distance;
They left the crowd of men and withdrew themselves.
17. With the ether's transformations they rose upwards,
With godlike swiftness miraculously moving.
18. The world became hazy, viewed from the great distance;
The spirit essence dazzled as it flashed back and forth.
19. Leaving the dust behind, shedding their impurities,—
Never to return again to their old homes.
20. Escaping unafraid from all life's troubles:
No one in the world knows where they went to.
21. I was afraid at the passing of the seasons,
As the bright sun in splendour rode on his western
journey.
22. The fine frost descended and fell upon the earth,
And I feared the fragrant flowers would fade prematurely.
23. I wanted to roam about in leisurely enjoyment:
I had gone through the length of years with nothing yet
achieved.
24. With whom can I enjoy this fragrance that is left me?
Long I stand against the wind unburdening my heart.
25. But Kao Yang lived far from me in a distant time:
How can I. . . . . ?
. . . .
. . . .
26. Spring and autumn hurry by, never delaying:
How can I always stay in my old home?

27. Hsüan Yüan is too remote for me to aspire to;
I will follow Wang Ch'iao for my delight.
28. I supped the Six Essences; drank the Night Dew;
Rinsed my mouth in the Sun Mist; savoured the Morning Brightness;
29. Conserving the pure elements of the divine;
Absorbing the subtle essence and rejecting the grosser parts.
30. Drifting in the wake of the gentle south wind,
I travelled to Nan Ch'ao in a single journey.
31. There I saw Master Wang and made him salutation,
And asked him about the balance made by unifying essence.
32. He said: 'The Way can only be received, it cannot be given.
33. 'Small, it has no content; great, it has no bounds.
34. 'Keep your soul from confusion, and it will come naturally.
35. 'Unify the essences and control the spirit; preserve them inside you in the midnight hour.
36. 'Await it in emptiness, before even Inaction.
37. 'All other things proceed from this: this is the Door of Power.'
38. Having heard this precious teaching, I departed,
And swiftly prepared to start on my journey.
39. I met the Winged Ones on the Hill of Cinnabar;
I tarried in the ancient land of Immortality.
40. In the morning I washed my hair in the Valley of Morning;
In the evening I dried myself on the coasts of heaven.
41. I sipped the subtle liquor of the Flying Spring,
And held in my bosom the flower-bright *wan-yen* jewel.
42. My jade-like countenance flushed with radiant colour;
Purified, my vital essence started to grow stronger;
43. My corporeal parts dissolved to a soft suppleness;
And my spirit grew lissome and eager for movement.
44. How fine was the fiery nature of the south land!
How lovely the winter blooming of the cassia!

45. But the mountain was forlorn with no beasts upon it;
The moor was a lonely place with no man there.
. . . .
. . . .
46. I restrained my restless spirit and mounted the empyrean;
I clung to a floating cloud to ride aloft on.
47. I bade heaven's gate-keeper open up his doors,
And he pushed the portals open and looked out at me.
48. I summoned Feng Lung to lead the way ahead,
And asked where the Palace of the Great Mystery was.
49. I reached the walls of heaven and entered the house of God.
I came to the Week Star and looked on the Pure City.
50. In the morning I set off from the court of heaven;
In the evening Wei Lü came in sight below.
51. I marshalled together my ten thousand chariots:
Slowly and grandly we rode side by side.
52. I harnessed eight dragons, coiling and curveting,
And bore a cloud banner that flapped in the wind.
53. I set up a bright standard made of the rainbow,
The five colours dazzling the eye with their contrast.
54. Splendidly the yoke-horses bowed and tossed their heads;
Proudly the trace-horses arched and curved themselves.
55. The din and bustle rose confusedly
As our colourful, many-assorted train set out.
56. I held my reins and adjusted the whip,
And decided that I would go to visit Kou Mang.
57. We crossed the eastern heaven, wheeling to the right hand.
I sent Fei Lien on ahead to clear the way.
58. The sky was just flushing before the sunrise
As we forded the waters of the Pool of Heaven.
59. The Wind God drove on ahead for me,
To clear the dust away and make it clean and cool.
60. Phoenixes sweeping overhead bore up my pennant;
And so we met Ju Shou in the western heaven.
61. I seized the Broom Star for a banner,
And lifted the Dipper's Handle as my baton.

62. Up and down the long train went, plunging and soaring,
Drifting on the moving waves of the fleeting mist.
63. The daylight was fading in gathering darkness
As I summoned Hsüan Wu to serve in my train.
64. I made Wen Ch'ang follow in charge of the progress,
Disposing the gods in their places in my retinue.
65. Far, far the road stretched, endlessly onward:
We slowed down our pace and crossed the height of heaven.
66. The Rain God went on my left as guide;
The Thunder God went on my right as bodyguard.
67. I wanted to leave the world and forget about returning:
My thoughts were reckless with a heady freedom.
68. My heart, rejoicing, delighted in itself:
I would be merry and seek my own pleasure.
69. I crossed the blue clouds and was wandering freely,
When suddenly I glimpsed my old home below me.
70. My groom was homesick and my own heart downcast;
The trace-horses looked back and would not go forward.
71. I pictured my dear ones in imagination,
And, with a heavy sigh, I brushed the tears away.
72. Slowly I floated, rising even farther:
I must restrain my will and keep myself controlled.
73. Pointing to the Fiery God, I galloped straight towards him;
I wished to journey on to the world's southern shore.
74. I gazed on the wild world beyond the land's confines;
I floated onwards over the watery vastness.
75. Chu Jung stood in my way, warning me to turn back.
I sent word to the phoenix to invite Fu-fei.
76. I made the Hsiang goddesses play on their zithers,
And bade the Sea God dance with the River God.
77. They played the 'Pool of Heaven', then struck up 'To the Clouds',
Then the two goddesses performed the Nine Shao Songs.
78. They drew up water monsters to join them in the dance:
How their bodies coiled and writhed in undulating motion!

79. Gracefully the woman-rainbow made circles around
    them;
    The phoenixes soared up and hovered above.
80. The music swelled and swelled into infinity.
    Thereupon I left, and resumed my wandering.
81. Keeping step together, we galloped far away,
    Till, at the world's far end, we came to the Gate of
    Coldness.
82. There I raced the rushing wind to the Spring of Purity;
    I followed Chuan Hsü over the piled-up ice.
83. I turned from my path to cross the realm of Hsüan
    Ming;
    Bestriding the Dividers, I looked back behind me.
84. I summoned Ch'ien Lei to appear before me
    And caused him to go in front in the level way.
85. I toured the four outlands,
    Traversed the six regions,
86. Up to the lightning's fissure,
    And down to the Great Abyss.
87. In the sheer depths below, the earth was invisible;
    In the vastness above, the sky could not be seen.
88. When I looked, my startled eyes saw nothing;
    When I listened, no sound met my amazed ear.
89. Transcending Inaction, I came to Purity,
    And entered the neighbourhood of the Great Beginning.

C. G. Jung
(1875–1961)

The Swiss founder of analytical psychology, Jung introduced the concepts of the collective unconscious, the archetype, and the introvert and extrovert. He wrote at great length about his own dreams and visions. This excerpt from his posthumously published autobiography, Memories, Dreams, Reflections *(1973), describes his near-death experience.*

At the beginning of 1944 I broke my foot, and this misadventure was followed by a heart attack. In a state of unconsciousness I experienced deliriums and visions which must have begun when I hung on the edge of death and was being given oxygen and camphor injections. The images were so tremendous that I myself concluded that I was close to death. My nurse afterward told me, "It was as if you were surrounded by a bright glow." That was a phenomenon she had sometimes observed in the dying, she added. I had reached the outermost limit, and do not know whether I was in a dream or an ecstasy. At any rate, extremely strange things began to happen to me.

It seemed to me that I was high up in space. Far below I saw the globe of the earth, bathed in a gloriously blue light. I saw the deep blue sea and the continents. Far below my feet lay Ceylon, and in the distance ahead of me the subcontinent of India. My field of vision did not include the whole earth, but its global shape was plainly distinguishable and its outlines shone with a silvery gleam through that wonderful blue light. In many places the globe seemed colored, or spotted dark green like oxydized silver. Far away to the left lay a broad expanse—the reddish-yellow desert of Arabia; it was as though the silver of the earth had there assumed a reddish-gold hue. Then came the Red Seas, and far, far back—as if in the upper left of a map—I could just make out a bit of the Mediterranean. My gaze was directed chiefly toward that. Everything else appeared indistinct. I could also see the snow-covered Himalayas, but in that direction it was foggy or cloudy. I did not look to the right at all. I knew that I was on the point of departing from the earth.

Later I discovered how high in space one would have to be to have so extensive a view—approximately a thousand miles! The sight of the earth from this height was the most glorious thing I had ever seen.

After contemplating it for a while, I turned around. I had been standing with my back to the Indian Ocean, as it were, and my face to the north. Then it seemed to me that I made a turn to the south. Something new entered my field of vision. A short distance away I saw in space a tremendous dark block of stone, like a meteorite. It was about the size of my house, or even bigger. It was floating in space, and I myself was floating in space.

I had seen similar stones on the coast of the Gulf of Bengal. They were blocks of tawny granite, and some of them had been hollowed out into temples. My stone was one such gigantic dark block. An entrance led into a small antechamber. To the right of the entrance, a black Hindu sat silently in lotus posture upon a stone bench. He wore a white gown, and I knew that he expected me. Two steps led up to this antechamber, and inside, on the left, was the gate to the temple. Innumerable tiny niches, each with a saucer-like concavity filled with coconut oil and small burning wicks, surrounded the door with a wreath of bright flames. I had once actually seen this when I visited the Temple of the Holy Tooth at Kandy in Ceylon; the gate had been framed by several rows of burning oil lamps of this sort.

As I approached the steps leading up to the entrance into the rock, a strange thing happened: I had the feeling that everything was being sloughed away; everything I aimed at or wished for or thought, the whole phantasmagoria of earthly existence, fell away or was stripped from me—an extremely painful process. Nevertheless something remained; it was as if I now carried along with me everything I had ever experienced or done, everything that had happened around me. I might also say: it was with me, and I was it. I consisted of all that, so to speak. I consisted of my own history, and I felt with great certainty: this is what I am. "I am this bundle of what has been, and what has been accomplished."

This experience gave me a feeling of extreme poverty, but at the same time of great fullness. There was no longer anything I wanted or desired. I existed in an objective form; I was what I had been and lived. At first the sense of annihilation predominated, of having been stripped or pillaged;

but suddenly that became of no consequence. Everything seemed to be past; what remained was a *fait accompli*, without any reference back to what had been. There was no longer any regret that something had dropped away or been taken away. On the contrary: I had everything that I was, and that was everything.

Something else engaged my attention: as I approached the temple I had the certainty that I was about to enter an illuminated room and would meet there all those people to whom I belong in reality. There I would at last understand—this too was a certainty—what historical nexus I or my life fitted into. I would know what had been before me, why I had come into being, and where my life was flowing. My life as I lived it had often seemed to me like a story that has no beginning and no end. I had the feeling that I was a historical fragment, an excerpt for which the preceding and succeeding text was missing. My life seemed to have been snipped out of a long chain of events, and many questions had remained unanswered. Why had it taken this course? Why had I brought these particular assumptions with me? What had I made of them? What will follow? I felt sure that I would receive an answer to all these questions as soon as I entered the rock temple. There I would learn why everything had been thus and not otherwise. There I would meet the people who knew the answer to my question about what had been before and what would come after.

While I was thinking over these matters, something happened that caught my attention. From below, from the direction of Europe, an image floated up. It was my doctor, Dr. H.—or, rather, his likeness—framed by a golden chain or a golden laurel wreath. I knew at once: "Aha, this is my doctor, of course, the one who has been treating me. But now he is coming in his primal form, as a *basileus* of Kos. In life he was an avatar of this *basileus*, the temporal embodiment of the primal form, which had existed from the beginning. Now he is appearing in that primal form."

Presumably I too was in my primal form, though this was something I did not observe but simply took for granted. As he stood before me, a mute exchange of thought took place between us. Dr. H. had been delegated by the earth to deliver a message to me, to tell me that there was a protest against my going away. I had no right to leave the earth and must return. The moment I heard that, the vision ceased.

I was profoundly disappointed, for now it all seemed to have been for nothing. The painful process of defoliation had been in vain, and I was not to be allowed to enter the temple, to join the people in whose company I belonged.

In reality, a good three weeks were still to pass before I could truly make up my mind to live again. I could not eat because all food repelled me. The view of city and mountains from my sickbed seemed to me like a painted curtain with black holes in it, or a tattered sheet of newspaper full of photographs that meant nothing. Disappointed, I thought, "Now I must return to the 'box system' again." For it seemed to me as if behind the horizon of the cosmos a three-dimensional world had been artificially built up, in which each person sat by himself in a little box. And now I should have to convince myself all over again that this was important! Life and the whole world struck me as a prison, and it bothered me beyond measure that I should again be finding all that quite in order. I had been so glad to shed it all, and now it had come about that I—along with everyone else—would again be hung up in a box by a thread. While I floated in space, I had been weightless, and there had been nothing tugging at me. And now all that was to be a thing of the past!

I felt violent resistance to my doctor because he had brought me back to life. At the same time, I was worried about him. "His life is in danger, for heaven's sake! He has appeared to me in his primal form! When anybody attains this form it means he is going to die, for already he belongs to the 'greater company'!" Suddenly the terrifying thought came to me that Dr. H. would have to die in my stead. I tried my best to talk to him about it, but he did not understand me. Then I became angry with him. "Why does he always pretend he doesn't know he is a *basileus* of Kos? And that he has already assumed his primal form? He wants to make me believe that he doesn't know!" That irritated me. My wife reproved me for being so unfriendly to him. She was right; but at the time I was angry with him for stubbornly refusing to speak of all that had passed between us in my vision. "Damn it all, he ought to watch his step. He has no right to be so reckless! I want to tell him to take care of himself." I was firmly convinced that his life was in jeopardy.

In actual fact I was his last patient. On April 4, 1944—I still remember the exact date—I was allowed to sit up on the edge of my bed for the first time since the beginning of my illness, and on this same day Dr. H. took to his bed and did not leave it again. I heard that he was having intermittent attacks of fever. Soon afterward he died of septicemia. He was a good doctor; there was something of the genius about him. Otherwise he would not have appeared to me as a prince of Kos.

During those weeks I lived in a strange rhythm. By day I was usually depressed. I felt weak and wretched, and scarcely dared to stir. Gloomily, I thought, "Now I must go back to this drab world." Toward evening I would fall asleep, and my sleep would last until about midnight. Then I would come to myself and lie awake for about an hour, but in an utterly transformed state. It was as if I were in an ecstasy. I felt as though I were floating in space, as though I were safe in the womb of the universe—in a tremendous void, but filled with the highest possible feeling of happiness. "This is eternal bliss," I thought. "This cannot be described; it is far too wonderful!"

Everything around me seemed enchanted. At this hour of the night the nurse brought me some food she had warmed—for only then was I able to take any, and I ate with appetite. For a time it seemed to me that she was an old Jewish woman, much older than she actually was, and that she was preparing ritual kosher dishes for me. When I looked at her, she seemed to have a blue halo around her head. I myself was, so it seemed, in the Pardes Rimmonim, the garden of pomegranates, and the wedding of Tifereth with Malchuth was taking place. Or else I was Rabbi Simon ben Jochai, whose wedding in the afterlife was being celebrated. It was the mystic marriage as it appears in the Cabbalistic tradition. I cannot tell you how wonderful it was. I could only think continually, "Now this is the garden of pomegranates! Now this is the marriage of Malchuth with Tifereth!" I do not know exactly what part I played in it. At bottom it was I myself: I was the marriage. And my beatitude was that of a blissful wedding.

Gradually the garden of pomegranates faded away and changed. There followed the Marriage of the Lamb, in a Jerusalem festively bedecked. I cannot describe what it was like in detail. These were ineffable states of joy. Angels were present, and light. I myself was the "Marriage of the Lamb."

That, too, vanished, and there came a new image, the last vision. I walked up a wide valley to the end, where a gentle chain of hills began. The valley ended in a classical amphitheater. It was magnificently situated in the green landscape. And there, in this theater, the *hierosgamos* was being celebrated. Men and women dancers came onstage, and upon a flower-decked couch All-father Zeus and Hera consummated the mystic marriage, as it is described in the *Iliad*.

All these experiences were glorious. Night after night I floated in a state of purest bliss, "thronged round with images of all creation." Gradually, the motifs mingled and paled. Usually the visions lasted for about an hour; then I would fall asleep again. By the time morning drew near, I would feel: Now gray morning is coming again; now comes the gray world with its boxes! What idiocy, what hideous nonsense! Those inner states were so fantastically beautiful that by comparison this world appeared downright ridiculous. As I approached closer to life again, they grew fainter, and scarcely three weeks after the first vision they ceased altogether.

It is impossible to convey the beauty and intensity of emotion during those visions. They were the most tremendous things I have ever experienced. And what a contrast the day was: I was tormented and on edge; everything irritated me; everything was too material, too crude and clumsy, terribly limited both spatially and spiritually. It was all an imprisonment, for reasons impossible to divine, and yet it had a kind of hypnotic power, a cogency, as if it were reality itself, for all that I had clearly perceived its emptiness. Although my belief in the world returned to me, I have never since entirely freed myself of the impression that this life is a segment of existence which is enacted in a three-dimensional boxlike universe especially set up for it.

There is something else I quite distinctly remember. At the beginning, when I was having the vision of the garden of pomegranates, I asked the nurse to forgive me if she were harmed. There was such sanctity in the room, I said, that it might be harmful to her. Of course she did not understand me. For me the presence of sanctity had a magical atmosphere; I feared it might be unendurable to others. I understood then why one speaks of the odor of sanctity, of the "sweet smell" of the Holy Ghost. This was it. There was a *pneuma* of inexpressible sanctity in the room, whose manifestation was the *mysterium coniunctionis*.

I would never have imagined that any such experience was possible. It was not a product of imagination. The visions and experiences were utterly real; there was nothing subjective about them; they all had a quality of absolute objectivity.

We shy away from the word "eternal," but I can describe the experience only as the ecstasy of a non-temporal state in which present, past, and future are one. Everything that happens in time had been brought together into a concrete whole. Nothing was distributed over time, nothing could be measured by temporal concepts. The experience might best be defined as a state of feeling, but one which cannot be produced by imagination. How can I imagine that I exist simultaneously the day before yesterday, today, and the day after tomorrow? There would be things which would not yet have begun, other things which would be indubitably present, and others again which would already be finished—and yet all this would be one. The only thing that feeling could grasp would be a sum, an iridescent whole, containing all at once expectation of a beginning, surprise at what is now happening, and satisfaction or disappointment with the result of what has happened. One is interwoven into an indescribable whole and yet observes it with complete objectivity.

Poems, Prayers, and Spells

The Mithras Liturgy

The following selection, from a seventy-page papyrus now housed in the Bibliothèque nationale in Paris, belongs to a group of late antique texts from Greco-Roman Egypt, known collectively as the Greek Magical Papyri. This excerpt describes a portion of an initiation rite (the "Mithras Liturgy") whose purpose is to attain immortality in the presence of the sun-god Helios Mithras.

Draw breath from the rays [of sunlight] three times, breathing as deeply as you can, and you will see yourself becoming light and ascending on high, so that you seem to be in mid air. You will hear no sound of any creature, neither of man nor of any other animal, nor will you see at that time anything of the mortal things on earth, but you will see all immortal things. For you will see the divine constellation of that day and that hour, the presiding gods rising into heaven and others declining. The routs of the visible gods through the disc of the god, my father, will be seen, and likewise, too, the so-called tube, the source of the serviceable wind . . . And you will see the gods staring at you and rushing at you. You, then, immediately put your right index finger on your mouth and say, "Silence, Silence, symbol of the incorruptible living God, guard me, Silence!" Then give a long hiss, then smack your lips, saying [magical words], and then you will see the gods looking at you kindly and no longer rushing at you, but going to the proper order of their ranks. Accordingly, when you see the world above clear and revolving and none of the gods or angels rushing at you, expect to hear the crash of a thunderbolt so great as to terrify you. But again say, "Silence, Silence, [the spell], I am a star moving with you and rising radiant from the deep." At once, when you say these words, the disc [of the sun] will expand. And after you say the second spell in which is "Silence, Silence," and so on, hiss twice and smack your lips twice and forthwith you will see many five-rayed stars coming forth from the disc and filling all the air. But you again say, "Silence, Silence." And when the disc is opened you will see a circle free of fire and fiery doors, closed. And you immediately go on with the following spell, closing your eyes. Spell 3: "Hearken to me, hear me, N. N., Lord who hast bound together by spirit the fiery bars of the fourfold band [?], Thou who walkest in fire, creator of light, eternal sun, who breathest fire, fire-spirited Iao, spirit of light, oal, rejoicing in fire, beautiful in light, aeon, ruler of light, whose body is fire, giver of light, sower of fire, shaker of fire, strong of light, whirling fire, mover of light, thunderer, fame of light, increaser of light, who holdest light in fire, master of stars, open to me, for I call, because of the pressing and bitter and inexorable necessity, the immortal and living and honoured names which have never yet come into mortal nature nor been uttered in articulation by human tongue or mortal speech or mortal voice: [magical combinations of the vowels]." Say all this with fire and spirit, finishing the first recitation then similarly beginning the second until you finish the seven immortal gods of the world. When you have finished you will hear thunder and reverberation of the surrounding [heaven] and, in the same way, you will feel yourself shaken. And you say again, "Silence, [the spell]." Then open your eyes and you will see the doors opened and the world of the gods, which is inside the doors, so that from the pleasure and joy of the sight your spirit runs towards them and ascends. Then, standing still, gazing fixedly, at once draw your spirit from the divine into yourself. When, therefore, your soul has returned, say, "Come, Lord, [magical words]." When you say this, you will see a youthful god, well-favored, fiery-haired, in a white chiton and scarlet cloak, wearing a fiery crown. Forthwith greet him with the fiery greeting, "Hail, Lord, great in power, great ruler, king, greatest of the gods, Helios, the Lord of the heaven and the earth, god of gods, mighty is thy breath, mighty is thy power, O Lord. If thou seest fit, announce me to the greatest god, thy begetter and maker."

"Spell for Ascending through the Heavens"

This spell is from The Second Book of Jeu, *a fourth-century Coptic text in which a Gnostic Jesus teaches his disciples the magical formulae for getting past the hostile heavenly archons who block the ascent to the transcendent God.*

When you come out of the body and you reach the first of the aeons, and the archons of that aeon arrive before you, seal yourselves with this seal:

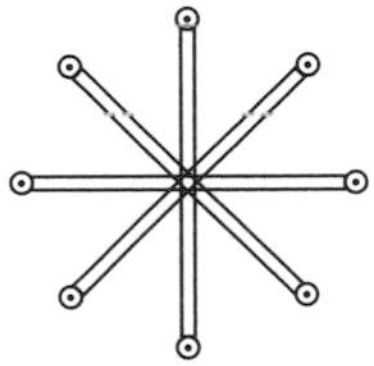

This is its name: Zozeze.

Say it one time only.

Grasp this pebble with both your hands: 1119, eleven hundred nineteen.

When you have finished sealing yourselves with this seal, and you recite its name one time only, say these protective spells also: "Retreat Prote (th), Persomphon, Chous, archons of the first aeon, for I invoke Eaza Zeozaz Zozeoz."

Whenever the archons of the first aeon hear these names, they will be very afraid, withdraw to themselves, and flee leftward to the west, while you journey on up.

When you reach the second of the aeons, Chouncheoch will arrive before you. Seal yourselves with this seal:

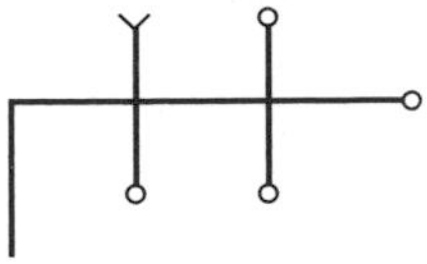

This is its name; say it one time only: Thozoaz.

Grasp this pebble with both your hands: 2219, twenty-two hundred nineteen.

When you have finished sealing yourselves with this seal, and you recite its name one time only, say these protective spells also: "Retreat Chouncheoch, archon of the second of the aeons, for I invoke Ezaoz Zoeza Zoozaz."

Yet again the archons of the second aeon will withdraw to themselves and flee westward to the left, while you journey on up.

When you reach the third of the aeons, Yaldabaoth and Choucho will be arriving before you. Seal yourselves with this seal:

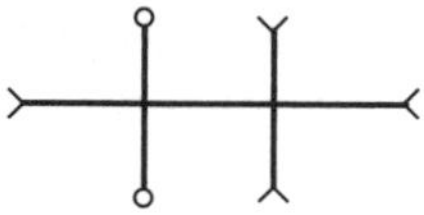

This is its name: Zozeaz.

Say it one time only.

Grasp this pebble with your hands: 3349, thirty-three hundred forty-nine.

When you have finished sealing yourselves with this seal, and have recited its name one time only, say these protective spells also: "Retreat Yaldabaoth and Choucho, archons of the third of the aeons, for I invoke Zozezaz Zaozoz Chozoz."

Yet again the archons of the third of the aeons will withdraw to themselves and flee westward to the left, while you journey on up.

Commendation of the Soul

This prayer for the moment of death comes from The Book of the Craft of Dying, *a fifteenth-century English tract on the art of dying well.*

Dear Brother, I commend thee to Almighty God, and commit thee to Him, Whose creature thou art, that when thy manhood hath paid his debt by the mean of death, that thou turn again to God thy creature, That made thee of the slime of the earth. When thy soul passeth out of thy body, glorious companies of angels come against thee: the victorious host, worthy judges, and senators of the holy apostles meet with thee: the fair, white, shining company of holy confessors, with the victorious number of glorious martyrs, come about thee: the joyful company of holy virgins receive thee: and the worthy fellowship of holy patriarchs open to thee the place of rest and joy, and deem thee to be among them that they be among, everlastingly.

Know thou never that (which) is horrible in darkness, that grinteth in flaming fire. They that punish in torments give place to thee, and grieve thee not. They that follow Sathanas with all his servants, in the coming against thee, be a-ghast at the presence of holy angels, and flee into darkness of everlasting night; into the great tribulous sea of hell. Our lord ariseth and His enemies he dispartled about; and Hee, they that hate Him, from His visage. Fail they as the smoke faileth, and as the wax melteth against the fire, so perish sinners from the face of God; and let rightful men eat and rejoice in the sight of God. All the contrary legions and ministers of Sathanas be not hardy to let thy journey. Christ deliver thee from torment, that vouchsafed to die for thee. Christ, God's Son, bring thee to the merry joys of Paradise, and the very Shepherd know thee among His sheep. He assoil thee from all thy sins, and put thee on His right side; in the sort of His chosen children, that thou may see thy Redemptor visage to visage, and presentially assisting to Him, see with (thine) eyes the blessed everlasting truth openly; and among the blessed company of the children of God have thou, and rejoice in the joy of the contemplation of God without end. AMEN.

Oratio

Go Christian Soul out of this world, in the name of the Almighty Father that made thee of nought; in the Name of Jesu Christ, His Son, that suffered His passion for thee; and in the Name of the Holy Ghost, that was infounded into thee. Holy angels, Thrones and Dominations, Princehoods, Potestates and Virtues, Cherubim and Seraphim, meet with thee. Patriarchs and prophets, apostles and evangelists, martyrs, confessors, monks and hermits, maidens and widows, children and innocents, help thee. The prayers of all priests and deacons, and all the degrees of Holy Church, help thee; that in peace be thy place, and thy dwelling in heavenly Jerusalem everlastingly; by the meditation of Our Lord Jesu Christ, that is Mediator between God and man. Amen.

Explicit Tractatus Utilissimus
De Arte Moriendi

Sir Walter Ralegh (1554–1618)

Poet, historian, explorer, and soldier, Ralegh was beheaded for treason by James I. "The Passionate Mans Pilgrimage" was purportedly written while Ralegh was incarcerated in the Tower of London under sentence of death.

THE PASSIONATE MANS PILGRIMAGE

Supposed to be Written by One at the Point of Death

Give me my Scallop shell of quiet,
My staffe of Faith to walke upon,
My Scrip of Joy, Immortall diet,
My bottle of salvation:
My Gowne of Glory, hopes true gage,
And thus Ile take my pilgrimage.

Blood must be my bodies balmer,
No other balme will there be given
Whilst my soule like a white Palmer
Travels to the land of heaven,
Over the silver mountaines,
Where spring the Nectar fountaines:
And there Ile kisse
The Bowle of blisse,
And drinke my eternall fill
On every milken hill.
My soule will be a drie before,
But after it, will nere thirst more.

And by the happie blisfull way
More peacefull Pilgrims I shall see,
That have shooke off their gownes of clay,
And goe appareld fresh like mee.

Ile bring them first
To slake their thirst,
And then to taste those Nectar suckets
At the cleare wells
Where sweetnes dwells,
Drawne up by Saints in Christall buckets.

And when our bottles and all we,
Are fild with immortalitie:
Then the holy paths weele travell
Strewde with Rubies thicke as gravell,
Seelings of Diamonds, Saphire floores,
High walles of Corall and Pearle Bowres.

From thence to heavens Bribeles hall
Where no corrupted voyces brall,
No Conscience molten into gold,
Nor forg'd accusers bought and sold,
No cause deferd, nor vaine spent Jorney,
For there Christ is the Kings Atturney:
Who pleades for all without degrees,
And he hath Angells, but no fees.

When the grand twelve million Jury,
Of our sinnes with sinfull fury,
Gainst our soules blacke verdicts give,
Christ pleades his death, and then we live,
Be thou my speaker taintles pleader,
Unblotted Lawyer, true proceeder,
Thou movest salvation even for almes:
Not with a bribed Lawyers palmes.

And this is my eternall plea,
To him that made Heaven, Earth and Sea,
Seeing my flesh must die so soone,
And want a head to dine next noone,
Just at the stroke when my vaines start and spred
Set on my soule an everlasting head.
Then am I readie like a palmer fit,
To tread those blest paths which before I writ.

Iroquois Mother's Lament

This late-nineteenth-century address by a Haudenosaunee (Iroquois) woman over the body of her son was recorded by Hasanoanda (Ely S. Parker), the famed Indian statesman and brigadier general in the U.S. Army, who was present at the occasion.

My son, listen once more to the words of thy mother. Thou wert brought into life with her pains. Thou wert nourished with her life. She has attempted to be faithful in raising thee up. When thou wert young, she loved thee as her life. Thy presence has been a source of great joy to her. Upon thee she depended for support and comfort in her declining days. She had ever expected to gain the end of the path of life before thee. But thou hast outstripped her, and gone before her. Our great and wise Creator has ordered it thus. By his will I am left to taste more of the miseries of this world. Thy friends and relatives have gathered about thy body, to look upon thee for the last time. They mourn, as with one mind, thy departure from among us. We, too, have but a few days more, and our journey shall be ended. We part now, and you are conveyed from our sight. But we shall soon meet again, and shall again look upon each other. Then we shall part no more. Our Maker has called you to his home. Thither will we follow. *Na-ho'*.

"The Hobo's Last Lament"

The following poem was published anonymously in the June 1917 issue of the St. Louis, Missouri, Hobo News.

Beside a Western water-tank
   One cold November day,
Inside an empty box-car,
   A dying hobo lay;

His old pal stood beside him,
   With low and dropping head,
Listening to the last words,
   As the dying hobo said;

"I am going to a better land,
   Where everything is bright,
Where beef-stews grow on bushes
   And you sleep out every night;

And you do not have to work at all,
   And never change your socks,
And streams of goodly whiskey
   Come trickling down the rocks.

"Tell the bunch around Market Street,
   That my face, no more, they'll view;
Tell them I've caught a fast freight,
   And that I'm going straight on through.
Tell them not to weep for me,
   No tears in their eyes must lurk;
For I'm going to a better land,
   Where they hate the word called work.

"Hark! I hear her whistling,
    I must catch her on the fly;
I would like one scoop of beer
    Once more before I die."

The hobo stopped, his head fell back,
    He'd sung his last refrain;
His old pal stole his coat and hat
    And caught an East-bound train.

II

Lands of Bliss

Introduction

The 1989 film *Field of Dreams,* in which a team of benevolent ghosts plays baseball in a midwest cornfield, contains the following memorable exchange:

> *Dead ballplayer*: It's so beautiful here. For me . . . well, for me it's like a dream come true. Can I ask you something? Is . . . is this heaven?
>
> *Living farmer*: It's Iowa.
>
> *Dead ballplayer*: Iowa? I could have sworn it was heaven.

Heaven may not be in the American cornbelt, but the deceased player had the right idea. Heavenly literature strongly agrees that, whatever else heaven may be, in one sense or another it must surely be an actual place: a realm of meadows, rivers, gardens, cities. The vision may vary from one text to the next, but the emphasis on heaven's visual concreteness is nearly universal.

Not surprisingly, the topography of heaven often reflects the desires of its inhabitants. In the poem "Where Is No More Sea," a weary mariner who wishes to escape the waves takes literally the promise made by the book of Revelation, imagining a heaven that is satisfyingly dry; while in Rupert Brooke's amusing inversion, a fish speculates that "somewhere, beyond Space and Time, / Is wetter water, slimier slime!"

One might think that heaven answers our wishes only after first purifying them, but the popular treatment of heaven requires that human needs be met in ways that are humanly familiar. This is the message of *The Gates Ajar*, the classic work of Victorian consolation literature. Here heaven is filled with all the homely things of earth—brooks and fields, houses and fountains—but improved, spiritualized, so that a mountain will be "the ideal of mountains which we catch in rare glimpses" and a house will be made not of oak and pine, but of a heavenly substance "that will be to us then what these are now."

To convey the beauty of heaven, most Western writers have relied upon the classical theme of the *locus amoenus*, or "lovely place," originally found in Greco-Roman myths of the Golden Age but later extended to cover all possible versions of paradise, both celestial and terrestrial. The *locus amoenus* is a place of perfectly harmonized sounds, sights, and scents, typically taking the form of a flowery meadow or enclosed garden, watered by streams or fountains. Topographic features are gently modulated and weather is perpetually springlike, yet never monotonous. The history of landscape architecture can be read as a series of efforts to realize this ideal, yet it is in the history of heaven that one finds its fullest expression. It has parallels throughout the heaven literature of the world.

In many accounts, the heavenly landscape is embellished by gems, mixing together the imagery of the garden with that of the palace and royal city. Thus in the western paradise (or Pure Land) of Amitabha Buddha, one finds a visionary landscape built of lapis-lazuli, coral, and other precious substances. The temperature is constant, the ground is laid with bejeweled tapestries, the breezes scatter petals in sublime patterns, and radiant light pervades the realm. Gratifying the senses without exciting the passions, these are the ideal conditions in which to attain full awakening or Buddhahood.

Heavenly music may be a natural part of the landscape. As Cicero tells us, following Pythagoras, it is produced by the mathematical proportion between the moving spheres. Or it may be, as in Howard Schwartz's "The Celestial Orchestra," the work of angels reciting the Torah in its musical form. In both cases, the music of heaven is divine speech, communicating wisdom that cannot be expressed in words alone. To hear it on earth is to be transported to heaven.

Although the *locus amoenus* is remarkably consistent across traditions, many other aspects of heaven's topography are specific to particular traditions. This stands to reason, for the landscape of heaven is never mere scenery: it is part of a larger world-picture, story of cosmic origins, and vision of human destiny. For example, "Rangi and Papatua," the Maori tale included here, is one of many accounts whose premise is that heaven and earth were originally wedded together, until forcibly separated to make room for human society. To this primeval divorce we owe both the blessings and the afflictions of our world. In other versions of this myth, the world derives from the aboriginal sexual union of heaven and earth. The implications are the same: There was a time when heaven and earth were joined and gods conversed freely with men. A rupture occurred, however, the result of human incompetence, disobedience, evolutionary necessity, or plain bad luck. The high god withdrew into remote regions of the sky; the several elements of the universe dispersed to their separate quarters; enmity developed between the sexes, among the species, and among the gods; and death entered the world. Henceforth any improvement of the human condition depends upon reconciling the two realms, either through ritual reenactment of the creation story or through shamanic practices (ecstasy, ascension, magical flight, possession) that reopen the channels of communication between heaven and earth.

A different conception of the relationship between heaven and earth emerges in cultures that envision a hierarchy of seven, nine, or ten astronomical spheres. Here a cosmic ladder joins earth to heaven, yet keeps the high god distant. According to a widespread Greco-Roman tradition, birth is a downward journey—a fall, even—in which the soul picks up from each sphere, by a kind of fatal attraction, the particular qualities that will mark its character and determine its destiny. (This may be the source of the ancient idea of seven deadly sins associated with the seven planets.) The return journey to heaven at death is a complicated and dangerous ordeal: at each of the spheres, a powerful astral guardian (like the Gnostic *archon* or the Byzantine toll-gate keeper) stands ready to block the soul's ascent. As the excerpt from Louis Ginzberg's *Legends of the Jews* demonstrates, Western religious thought adopted the hierarchical picture of heaven, yet sought to purge it of any astrological fatalism, reasserting God's prerogative to deal directly with the soul, to enter immediately into human history, to subdue the angelic powers, and thus to overcome the separation between the human and divine realms.

The topography and cosmology of heaven are always undergoing revision in the light of changing scientific conceptions of the universe, from Yggdrasil, the world-tree of the ancient Scandinavians (represented here by the selection from the Icelandic *Prose Edda*), to Dante's Ptolemaic cosmology, to the pseudoscientific speculations of the nineteenth-century chemist, inventor, and spiritualist Robert Hare. In a question-and-answer session with a convocation of deceased worthies (including George Washington, Isaac Newton, and Benjamin Franklin), Hare discovers that inhabitants of the seven spheres that make up the "country of spirits" glow by a means analogous to that of lightning-bugs and breathe an ethereal fluid whose gaseous by-product all living beings—especially fish!—need for spiritual sustenance.

Like much spiritualist literature of his time, Hare's cosmology relies upon a curious recycling of the ancient idea of *ether*. Originally the Greek *aither*, ether was the pure air at the summit of Mount Olympus, and the all-pervading celestial fifth element found in many ancient philosophical traditions, including Stoicism and classical Hinduism (*akasha*). But the term had an attractive scientific ring to it as well—until the 1881 Michelson-Morley experiment rendered implausible the hypothesis of a luminiferous ether through which light must pass.

The loss of ether has been something of a blow for spiritualist conceptions of heaven. As a substance midway between spirit and matter, ether seemed like the best candidate for a material from which spirit (or astral or subtle) bodies might be constructed, and through which mediumistic messages might be conducted. One does not like to think of heaven as empty of atmosphere, and it is natural to hope that such atmosphere as heaven possesses might somehow mingle with our own. However that may be, the scientific imagination, we suspect, will continue to play a part in our thinking about heaven.

"Where Is No More Sea"

Published in 1863 under the pseudonym "Fysh," this poem appeared in Lyra Coelestis: Hymns on Heaven, *an eccentric compilation by A. C. Thompson. The title comes from Revelation 21:1.*

When tempests toss, and billows roll,
And lightnings rend from pole to pole,
Sweet is the thought to me,
That one day it shall not be so;
In the bright world to which I go
The tempest shall forget to blow;
There shall be no more sea.

My little bark has suffered much
From adverse storms; nor is she such
As once she seemed to be;
But I shall shortly be at home,
No more a mariner to roam;
When once I to the port am come,
There will be no more sea.

Then let the waves run mountains high,
Confound the deep, perplex the sky,—
This shall not always be;
One day the sun will brightly shine
With life, and light, and heat divine;
And when that glorious land is mine,
There will be no more sea.

My Pilot tells me not to fear,
But trust entirely to his care,

  And he will guarantee,
If only I depend on him,
To land me safe, in his good time,
In yonder purer, happier clime,
  Where shall be no more sea.

Rupert Brooke

(1887–1915)

An English poet renowned for his World War I sonnets, Brooke died at age twenty-seven of blood poisoning aboard a hospital ship off the Greek island of Skyros. "Heaven" parodies the theme of "Where Is No More Sea" (see above) from a fish's perspective.

Fish (fly-replete, in depth of June,
Dawdling away their wat'ry noon)
Ponder deep wisdom, dark or clear,
Each secret fishy hope or fear.
Fish say, they have their Stream and Pond;
But is there anything Beyond?
This life cannot be All, they swear,
For how unpleasant, if it were!
One may not doubt that, somehow, Good
Shall come of Water and of Mud;
And, sure, the reverent eye must see
A Purpose in Liquidity.
We darkly know, by Faith we cry,
The future is not Wholly Dry.
Mud unto mud!—Death eddies near—
Not here the appointed End, not here!
But somewhere, beyond Space and Time,
Is wetter water, slimier slime!
And there (they trust) there swimmeth One
Who swam ere rivers were begun,
Immense, of fishy form and mind,
Squamous, omnipotent, and kind;
And under that Almighty Fin,
The littlest fish may enter in.

Oh! never fly conceals a hook,
Fish say, in the Eternal Brook,
But more than mundane weeds are there,
And mud, celestially fair;
Fat caterpillars drift around,
And Paradisal grubs are found;
Unfading moths, immortal flies,
And the worm that never dies.
And in that Heaven of all their wish,
There shall be no more land, say fish.

“Rangi and Papatua” or The Heavens and the Earth

This traditional Maori tale describes the primordial intimacy of Heaven and Earth, their forced separation, and how this led to the world as we know it today.

A long, long time ago, the god Rangi, the Heavens, and the goddess Papatua, the Earth, loved each other with a great love, and were so near together and so inseparable that the Heavens were ever near to the Earth, and only a dull twilight reigned between them. No stately forest trees could grow or bright flowers blossom, but low-growing vines and tender creeping plants spread over the earth. Some low shrubs tried to flourish and stretched out their branches like myriad uplifted hands, but their leaves were flattened, the sky pressed so heavily on them.

The water was not clear, but was of a thick red colour, for there was no light to purify it. No men lived on the earth then, only the children of the gods Rangi and Papatua. As these children grew up they began to grumble at the want of space, and they longed for more light; for once they had had a glimpse of the full light when their father, Rangi, lifted up his arms. So they wished much that he would go up higher and give them more room, and they tried to persuade him to do so. But Rangi refused, and said he would not leave his dear wife Papatua, the Earth.

Then the children became very angry, and, finding that their prayers were of no avail, they said to each other: “What shall we do?” Tu, the father of war, who was cruel and did not love his parents, said: “We will kill them.” The others would not agree to this; but all except Tawhiri, the father of the winds, said: “They must be separated by force.” Tawhiri did not wish them to be separated, for he was jealous even of his own mother, fearing lest she should become too beautiful when the full brightness of day should fall on her. But in spite of his opposition, Tané, the god of light and the father of the forests, who was anxious that trees should be able to rear their heads on high, and that birds and insects should increase, said: “Each of us shall in turn try to push our father high up above us, so that the light of day may fall on us all"; and Tawhiri dared not object longer, for Tané was much mightier than he was. So the children tried in turn to separate Rangi and Papatua, but they held so fast to each other that it was with great difficulty they were pushed even a little apart. Once Rangi was pushed up a short distance, but he was very heavy, and they thoughtlessly left him on the sharp pinnacles of the mountains. Now, this was not a comfortable resting-place for Rangi, and he reproached his children bitterly for their cruelty. At last Tané said to the others: "I will pick my father up higher, for I am the strongest; but we will keep Papatua, the Earth, close beside us—for is she not the mother who nursed us? and we need her love ever with us."

Tané then kicked out with violent strength, and sent Rangi, the Heavens, up so great a distance that he has stayed high up ever since.

But the cries and groans of Rangi and Papatua when they were thus violently separated were sad to hear. Tawihri, the father of the winds, followed his father up to the sky and there abode.

When the full light fell upon Papatua, the Earth, her numerous offspring crept from their places, and the creeping plants and shrubs began to grow.

Sometimes Tawhiri and his progeny would come down and attack his brother Tané and his children to destroy them. And Tané turned some of his offspring into fish and birds, and the earth hid them in her bosom. Yet Tawhiri and his children found and ate them; and, in later days, when men fed upon each other, they said, "Did not the gods teach us so to do?"

"The First Day"

This account of the creation of heaven and earth comes from a collection of Jewish lore related to Genesis, compiled from traditional Rabbinic sources by the great Talmud scholar Louis Ginzberg (1873–1953).

On the first day of creation God produced ten things: the heavens and the earth, Tohu and Bohu, light and darkness, wind and water, the duration of the day and the duration of the night.

Though the heavens and the earth consist of entirely different elements, they were yet created as a unit, "like the pot and its cover." The heavens were fashioned from the light of God's garment, and the earth from the snow under the Divine Throne. Tohu is a green band which encompasses the whole world, and dispenses darkness, and Bohu consists of stones in the abyss, the producers of the waters. The light created at the very beginning is not the same as the light emitted by the sun, the moon, and the stars, which appeared only on the fourth day. The light of the first day was of a sort that would have enabled man to see the world at a glance from one end to the other. Anticipating the wickedness of the sinful generations of the deluge and the Tower of Babel, who were unworthy to enjoy the blessing of such light, God concealed it, but in the world to come it will appear to the pious in all its pristine glory.

Several heavens were created, seven in fact, each to serve a purpose of its own. The first, the one visible to man, has no function except that of covering up the light during the night time; therefore it disappears every morning. The planets are fastened to the second of the heavens; in the third the manna is made for the pious in the hereafter; the fourth contains the celestial Jerusalem together with the Temple, in which Michael ministers as high priest, and offers the souls of the pious as sacrifices. In the fifth heaven, the angel hosts reside, and sing the praise of God, though only during the night, for by day it is the task of Israel on earth to give glory to God on high. The sixth heaven is an uncanny spot; there originate most of the trials and visitations ordained for the earth and its inhabitants. Snow lies heaped up there and hail; there are lofts full of noxious dew, magazines stocked with storms, and cellars holding reserves of smoke. Doors of fire separate these celestial chambers, which are under the supervision of the archangel Metatron. Their pernicious contents defiled the heavens until David's time. The pious king prayed God to purge His exalted dwelling of whatever was pregnant with evil; it was not becoming that such things should exist near the Merciful One. Only then they were removed to the earth.

The seventh heaven, on the other hand, contains naught but what is good and beautiful: right, justice, and mercy, the storehouses of life, peace, and blessing, the souls of the pious, the souls and spirits of unborn generations, the dew with which God will revive the dead on the resurrection day, and, above all, the Divine Throne, surrounded by the seraphim, the ofanim, the holy Hayyot, and the ministering angels.

Corresponding to the seven heavens, God created seven earths, each separated from the next by five layers. Over the lowest earth, the seventh, called Erez, lie in succession the abyss, the Tohu, the Bohu, a sea, and waters. Then the sixth earth is reached, the Adamah, the scene of the magnificence of God. In the same way the Adamah is separated from the fifth earth, the Arka, which contains Gehenna, and Sha'are Mawet, and Sha'are Zalmawet, and Beër Shahat, and Tit ha-Yawen, and Abaddon, and Sheol, and there the souls of the wicked are guarded by the Angels of Destruction. In the same way Arka is followed by Harabah, the dry, the place of brooks and streams in spite of its name, as the next, called Yabbashah, the mainland, contains the rivers and the springs. Tebel, the second earth, is the first mainland inhabited by living creatures, three hundred and sixty-five species, all essentially different from those of our own earth. Some have human heads set on the body of a lion, or a serpent, or an ox; others have human bodies topped by the head of one of these animals. Besides, Tebel is inhabited by human beings with two heads and four hands and feet, in fact with all their organs doubled excepting only the trunk. It happens sometimes that the parts of these double persons quarrel with each other, especially while eating and drinking, when each claims the best and largest portions for himself. This species of mankind is distinguished for great piety, another difference between it and the inhabitants of our earth.

Our own earth is called Heled, and, like the others, it is separated from the Tebel by an abyss, the Tohu, the Bohu, a sea, and waters.

Thus one earth rises above the other, from the first to the seventh, and over the seventh earth the heavens are vaulted, from the first to the seventh, the last of them attached to the arm of God. The seven heavens form a unity, the seven kinds of earth form a unity, and the heavens and the earth together also form a unity.

When God made our present heavens and our present earth, "the new heavens and the new earth" were also brought forth, yea, and the hundred and ninety-six thousand worlds which God created unto His own glory.

It takes five hundred years to walk from the earth to the heavens, and from one end of a heaven to the other, and also from one heaven to the next, and it takes the same length of time to travel from the east to the west, or from the south to the north. Of all this vast world only one-third is inhabited, the other two-thirds being equally divided between water and waste desert land.

Beyond the inhabited parts to the east is Paradise with its seven divisions, each assigned to the pious of a certain degree. The ocean is situated to the west, and it is dotted with islands upon islands, inhabited by many different peoples. Beyond it, in turn, are the boundless steppes full of serpents and scorpions, and destitute of every sort of vegetation, whether herbs or trees. To the north are the supplies of hell-fire, of snow, hail, smoke, ice, darkness, and windstorms, and in that vicinity sojourn all sorts of devils, demons, and malign spirits. Their dwelling-place is a great stretch of land, it would take five hundred years to traverse it. Beyond lies hell. To the south is the chamber containing reserves of fire, the cave of smoke, and the forge of blasts and hurricanes. Thus it comes that the wind blowing from the south brings heat and sultriness to the earth. Were it not for the angel Ben Nez, the Winged, who keeps the south wind back with his pinions, the world would be consumed. Besides, the fury of its blast is tempered by the north wind, which always appears as moderator, whatever other wind may be blowing.

In the east, the west, and the south, heaven and earth touch each other, but the north God left unfinished, that any man who announced himself as a god might be set the task of supplying the deficiency, and stand convicted as a pretender.

The construction of the earth was begun at the centre, with the foundation stone of the Temple, the Eben Shetiyah, for the Holy Land is at the central point of the surface of the earth, Jerusalem is at the central point of Palestine, and the Temple is situated at the centre of the Holy City. In the sanctuary itself the Hekal is the centre, and the holy Ark occupies the centre of the Hekal, built on the foundation stone, which thus is at the centre of the earth. Thence issued the first ray of light, piercing to the Holy Land, and from there illuminating the whole earth. The creation of the world, however, could not take place until God had banished the ruler of the dark. "Retire," God said to him, "for I desire to create the world by means of light." Only after the light had been fashioned, darkness arose, the light ruling in the sky, the darkness on the earth.

The power of God displayed itself not only in the creation of the world of things, but equally in the limitations which He imposed upon each. The heavens and the earth stretched themselves out in length and breadth as though they aspired to infinitude, and it required the word of God to call a halt to their encroachments.

Snorri Sturluson

(1179–1241)

Sturluson, Icelandic poet and politician, was the author of the Heimskringla, *a history of Norwegian kings, and of* The Prose Edda, *an introduction to Norse mythology and poetics. This selection, drawn from the latter work, offers a depiction of Yggdrasil, the world-tree where the gods dwell, and of Valhalla, the heavenly abode of slain warriors.*

"The Deluding of Gylfi"

Then Gangleri asked: 'Where is the chief place or sanctuary of the gods?'

High One replied: 'It is by the ash Yggdrasil. There every day the gods have to hold a court.'

Then Gangleri asked: 'In what way is that place famous?'

Then Just-as-high said: 'The ash is the best and greatest of all trees; its branches spread out over the whole world and reach up over heaven. The tree is held in position by three roots that spread far out; one is among the Æsir, the second among the frost ogres where once was Ginnungagap, and the third extends over Niflheim, and under that root is the well Hvergelmir; but Níðhögg[1] gnaws at the root from below. Under the root that turns in the direction of the frost ogres lies the spring of Mímir, in which is hidden wisdom and understanding; Mímir is the name of the owner of the spring. He is full of wisdom because he drinks [water] from the spring out of the horn Gjöll. All-father came there and asked for a single drink from the spring, but he did not get it until he had given one of his eyes as a pledge. As it says in the *Sibyl's Vision*:

1. Striker-that-destroys.

I know for certain Óðin
where you concealed your eye,
in the famous
spring of Mímir;
mead he drinks
every morning
from the pledge of the Father-of-the-slain.
Do you know any more or not?

The third root of the ash tree is in the sky, and under that root is the very sacred spring called the Spring of Urð.[1] There the gods hold their court of justice. The Æsir ride up to that place every day over the bridge of Bifröst, which is also known as the Bridge of the Æsir. The names of the horses of the gods are as follows: Sleipnir is the best, Óðin owns him, he has eight legs; the second is Glað;[2] the third, Gyllir; the fourth, Glen; the fifth, Skeiðbrimir;[3] the sixth, Silfr[in]topp;[4] the seventh, Sinir;[5] the eighth, Gils; the ninth, Falhófnir;[6] the tenth, Gulltopp;[7] the eleventh, Léttfet[i].[8] Baldr's horse was burned with him, and Thór walks to the court wading through the rivers that have these names:

Körmt and Örmt
and both the Kerlaugar
these must Thór wade through
every day,
when he goes to give judgment
at Yggdrasil's ash,
since the Bridge of the Æsir
is flaming with fire
the sacred waters glow.'

Then Gangleri asked: 'Does fire burn over Bifröst?'

High One replied: 'The red you see in the rainbow is flaming fire. If it were possible for all who wanted to go over Bifröst to do so, the frost

1. Destiny.

2. Shining One.

3. Fast-galloper.

4. Silver Forelock.

5. Strong-of-sinew.

6. Shaggy Fetlock.

7. Golden Forelock.

8. Lightfoot.

ogres and cliff giants would scale heaven. There are many beautiful places in heaven, and they are all under divine protection. There is a beautiful hall near the spring under the ash tree, and from it come three maidens whose names are Urð, Verðandi, Skuld.[1] These maidens shape the lives of men, and we call them Norns. There are, however, more Norns, those that come to every child that is born in order to shape its life, and these are beneficent, others belong to the family of the elves and a third group belongs to the family of the dwarfs, as it says here:

> Of different origins
> are the Norns, I think,
> not all of one kindred;
> some come from Æsir-kin,
> some from the elves
> and some are the daughters of Dvalin.'

Then Gangleri said: 'If the Norns decide the fates of men, they appoint very unequal destinies for them; for some have a good and abundant life, but others have little wealth or fame. Some have a long life and others a short one.'

High One said: 'The good Norns who come from good stock shape good lives, but those who meet with misfortune owe it to the evil Norns.'

Then Gangleri asked: 'In what other way is the ash tree remarkable?'

High One said: 'There is a great deal to tell about it. In the branches of the ash sits an eagle, and it is very knowledgeable, and between its eyes sits a hawk called Veðrfölnir.[2] A squirrel called Ratatosk[3] springs up and down the ash tree and conveys words of abuse exchanged between the eagle and Niðhögg. Four harts leap about the branches of the ash and eat the shoots; these are their names: Dáin, Dvalin, Duneyr, Durathrór. And along with Niðhögg in Hvergelmir there are so many serpents that no tongue can count them. As it says here:

> The ash Yggdrasil
> endures more pain

1. Past, Present and Future.

2. Weather-bleached One.

3. Gnaw-tooth.

than men perceive,
the hart devours it from above
and the sides of it decay,
Niðhögg is gnawing from below.

It is said:

There are more serpents
under the ash
Yggdrasil than fools imagine,
Góin[1] and Móin[2]
Grafvitnir's[3] sons,
Grábak[4] and Grafvölluð[5]
Ófnir and Sváfnir,
I think that they will destroy
for ever that ash-tree's branches.

It is said further that the Norns who live near the spring of Urð draw water from the spring every day, and along with it the clay that lies round about the spring, and they besprinkle the ash so that its branches shall not wither or decay. But that water is so sacred that everything that comes into the spring becomes as white as the film (which is called "skin") that lies within the eggshell. As it says here:

I know an ash-tree
known as Yggdrasil,
tall tree and sacred
besprent with white clay,
thence come the dews
that fall in the dales;
it stands ever green
over Urð's spring.

The dew which falls from it to the earth is called honey-dew by men, and

1. Living-deep-in-earth.

2. Dweller-on-a-moor.

3. Grave-wolf.

4. Grey-back.

5. Field-burrower.

the bees feed on it. Two birds are nourished in the spring of Urð; they are called swans, and from them have come the birds of this name.'

Then Gangleri said: 'You have a great deal to tell concerning heaven. Are there any other important places besides the spring of Urð?'

High One answered: 'There are many magnificent places there. There is one called Álfheim, and there live the people called the light elves, but the dark elves live down in the earth and they are unlike the others in appearance and much more so in character. The light elves are fairer than the sun to look upon, but the dark elves, blacker than pitch. Then there is Breiðablik,[1] there is no place there more beautiful. There is also one called Glitnir,[2] and its walls and posts and pillars are of red gold, but its roof is silver. Further there is that place called Himinbjörg;[3] it is at heaven's end by the bridge-head where Bifröst joins heaven. There is, moreover, a great dwelling called Valaskjálf[4] owned by Óðin, which the gods built and roofed with pure silver. The high seat known as Hliðskjálf is there in this hall, and when All-father sits on this seat he sees over the whole world. In the southern end of heaven is the most beautiful hall of all, brighter than the sun; it is called Gimlé;[5] it shall stand when both heaven and earth have passed away, and good and righteous men will inhabit that place for all time. As it says in the *Sibyl's Vision*:

> I know where stands a hall
> brighter than sunlight
> better than gold
> in Lee-of-flame, Gimlé;
> hosts of the righteous
> shall it inherit,
> live in delight
> everlastingly.'

Then Gangleri asked: 'What will protect this place when Surt's Fire is burning heaven and earth?'

High One replied: 'It is said that there is another heaven to the south of and above this one, and it is called Andlang;[6] and there is yet a third

---

1. Gleaming-far-and-wide.
2. Radiant Place.
3. Mount-of-heaven.
4. Hall-of-the-slain.
5. Lee-of-fire.
6. Outstretched.

heaven above these ones which is called Viðbláin,[1] and yet we think that this place [Gimlé] is there. At present, however, we think that it is inhabited only by white elves.' . . .

Then Gangleri said: 'You say that all the men who have fallen in battle since the beginning of the world have now come to Óðin in Valhalla—what has he got to feed them with? I imagine that there must be a huge crowd of them there.'

Then High One replied: 'What you say is true. There is a huge crowd there, and there will be many more still, and yet they will seem too few when the wolf comes. But there is never so big a crowd in Valhalla that they don't get enough pork from the boar called Saehrímnir. He is boiled every day, and comes alive every evening. But as for the question you are putting now, it seems to me that not many people would know enough to give you the correct answer. The cook's name is Andhrímnir,[2] and the cauldron is called Eldbrímnir,[3] as it is said here:

> Andhrímnir boils
> Valhalla's boar
> in the sooty cauldron,
> it's prime of pork
> but few men know
> on what Valhalla's champions feed.'

Then Gangleri asked: 'Does Óðin have the same food as the Einherjar?'

High One said: 'He gives what food is on his table to two wolves called Geri[4] and Freki[5]; but he himself needs nothing to eat. Wine is for him both food and drink, as it says here:

> Battle-wont and famous,
> Óðin war-glorious,
> sates Geri and Freki;
> the Father-of-armies

---

1. Wide Blue.
2. Sooty-face.
3. Fire-sooty.
4. Greedy.
5. Gluttonous.

himself lives always
only on wine.

'Two ravens sit on his shoulders and bring to his ears all the news that they see or hear; they are called Hugin[1] and Munin.[2] He sends them out at daybreak to fly over the whole world, and they come back at breakfast-time; by this means he comes to know a great deal about what is going on, and on account of this men call him the god-of-ravens. As it is said:

Over the world
every day
fly Hugin and Munin;
I fear that Hugin
will not come back,
though I'm more concerned about Munin.'

Then Gangleri asked: 'What do the Einherjar have to drink in as much abundance as their food? Is water drunk there?'

Then High One said: 'That is a queer question to ask now—whether All-father who invites kings and earls and other men of rank gives them water to drink! It is my belief that many a one coming to Valhalla would think a drink of water dearly paid for, if no better entertainment were to be found—and he after enduring wounds and smarting to death. I can tell you a very different story about that place. A goat called Heiðrún stands up [on its hind-legs] in Valhalla biting the buds off the branches of that very famous tree which is called Lærað. From her teats runs the mead with which every day she fills a cauldron, which is so big that all the Einherjar can drink their fill from it.'

Gangleri said: 'What an exceedingly convenient goat for them. It must be a mighty good tree she feeds on!'

Then High One said: 'Still more remarkable is the hart Eikthyrnir, which stands in Valhalla devouring the branches of this tree. Such a huge stream comes from its horns that it falls down into Hvergelmir and

1. Thought.

2. Memory.

thence flow the rivers called: Síð,[1] Víð,[2] Seken, Ekin, Svöl,[3] Gunnthró,[4] Fjörm, Fimbulthul,[5] Gipul, Göpul,[6] Gömul,[7] Geirvimul.[8] These flow about the dwellings of the gods. These are also mentioned: Thyn,[9] Vin, Thöll, Höll, Gráð[10] Gunnthráin, Nyt, Naut, Nön,[11] Hrön, Vína,[12] Vegsvin,[13] Thjóðnuma.'[14]

Then Gangleri remarked: 'This is wonderful news you are telling now. Valhalla must be an enormous house, and its doors must often be very crowded.'

Then High One answered: 'Why don't you ask how many doors the hall has, or how big they are? When you hear that you will say that it would be extraordinary if whoever wished could not go out and in; and in point of fact it is just as easy to find room inside as it is to enter it. You can hear this from the *Lay of Grímnir:*

> I think there are in Valhalla
> more than six hundred
> and forty doors;
> out of a single door at a time
> will tramp nine hundred and sixty men,
> champions advancing on the monster.'

Then Gangleri said: 'There is a great host in Valhalla, and, upon my word, Óðin is a very powerful chieftain to control so large an army. How do the Einherjar amuse themselves when they are not drinking?'

High One said: 'Every day after they have dressed, they put on their armour and go out into the courtyard and fight and lay one another low. That is their play and, when it is breakfast-time, they ride to the hall and sit down to drink, as it says here:

---

1. Slow.
2. Broad.
3. Cool.
4. Battle-defiant.
5. Loud-bubbling.
6. Forward-rushing.
7. Old.
8. Spear-teeming.
9. Frothing.
10. Greedy.
11. Strong.
12. Dwina.
13. Way-knowing.
14. Sweeping-people-away

All the champions
every day
contend in Óðin's courtyard;
they choose the slain
and ride from the field,
thenceforth sit reconciled.

What you say, however, is true; Óðin is very powerful and there are many proofs of this. As is said here in the words of the Æsir themselves:

The foremost of trees
is the ash Yggdrasil,
of ships Skíðblaðnir,
of Æsir Óðin,
Sleipnir of steeds,
Bifröst of bridges,
Bragi of poets,
Hábrók of hawks
and of hounds, Garm.'

The Sukhavativyuha Sutra

The Sutra of the Pure Land (or "Land of Bliss") describes the western paradise established by the compassionate vows of Amitabha, celestial Buddha of Measureless Light. In this excerpt from the longer Chinese version, the Lord Buddha Shakyamuni extols the wonders of this happy realm, where those who take refuge in Amitabha Buddha will be reborn.

Dharmakara as a Buddha

Ananda said to the Buddha: "This monk Treasure of Dharma, has he already attained buddhahood and experienced liberation, or is he yet to attain buddhahood and experience liberation, or does he remain now?"

The Buddha replied: "Ananda, the monk Treasure of Dharma has attained buddhahood and at present dwells in the western regions of the universe, a hundred thousand million buddha-fields away from here. This buddha's world system is called the 'Land of Peace and Happiness.'"

Ananda asked again: "Since this buddha realized the Way, how much time has passed?"

The Buddha replied: "Since he became a buddha, ten cosmic ages have passed."

Amitabha Buddha's Purified Field

"This buddha-field is naturally composed of the seven precious substances: gold, silver, lapis-lazuli, coral, amber, mother-of-pearl, and agate. The ground is vast and extensive, it is impossible to define its limits. The precious substances intermix everywhere, gradually coming together with one another to form different combinations. And these metals and gems are luminous, resplendent, exquisite, rare, and pure, so that this land surpasses all the worlds in the ten regions of the universe. Made from the essence of all the precious substances in the world, its jewels resemble those of the Sixth Heaven.

"Furthermore, in this land there is no Mount Sumeru, or any of the other mountains or land features of a world system down to the ring of Diamond Mountains. There are no great oceans, no small seas, no torrents, no canals, wells, or valleys. Through the majestic power of the Buddha, whatever one desires to see, one will see. Furthermore, there are no hells, hungry ghosts, animals, or any of the painful destinations of rebirth. Furthermore, this land does not have any of the four seasons: spring, fall, winter, or summer. It is neither cold nor hot. The temperature is always moderate, constant, and agreeable."

Then, Ananda addressed the Buddha, saying: "World Honored One, if there is no Mount Sumeru in that land, where would its gods dwell—the four Heavenly Guardian Kings and the others, up to the gods in Indra's Heaven of the Thirty-Three?"

The Buddha said to Ananda: "What about the gods of the Third Heaven, that is, the Realm of the Yama Gods, and all the others, up to the highest gods of the Realm of Pure Form, where do they dwell in this, our world system?"

Ananda said to the Buddha: "The fruits and retributions derived from actions are incomprehensible."

The Buddha said to Ananda: "If the fruits and retributions derived from actions are incomprehensible, every world system over which a buddha presides must be likewise incomprehensible. This is so because all living beings, by the power of their merits and their virtue, inhabit a place corresponding to their actions."

Ananda said to the Buddha: "Personally, I have no doubt with respect to this aspect of Dharma. If I have asked questions on this point, it is only because living beings of future generations will want to overcome these doubts." . . .

The Splendor of the Pure Land

The Buddha said to Ananda: "As to the gods and humans in the country of the Buddha of Measureless Life, the clothing, the meals, the flowers, the incense, the strings of gems, the parasols and banners, the wonderful sounds they enjoy, and the mansions, palaces, and towers where they live are in shape and size variously high or low, large or small. Or, again, these gods and humans obtain one precious substance, or two, or even as many as countless different kinds of precious substances the moment the wish comes to mind and exactly as they want them to be. And wonderful tapestries, studded with all kinds of gems, are spread on the ground all over, and every human and god walks on these. Nets studded with countless gems are stretched all over this buddha-land. All are decorated with golden laces, genuine pearls, and hundreds of thousands of various kinds of gems that are rare, wonderful, and unique. These ornaments extend everywhere into the four corners of that land, with jeweled bells, perfumes, and bright colors shining splendidly, in the most charming way.

"Breezes blow spontaneously, gently moving these bells, which swing gracefully. The breezes blow in perfect harmony. They are neither hot nor cold. They are at the same time calm and fresh, sweet and soft. They are neither fast nor slow. When they blow on the nets and the many kinds of jewels, the trees emit the innumerable sounds of the subtle and sublime Dharma and spread myriad sweet and fine perfumes. Those who hear these sounds spontaneously cease to raise the dust of tribulation and impurity. When the breezes touch their bodies they all attain a bliss comparable to that accompanying a monk's attainment of the samadhi of extinction.

"Moreover, when they blow, these breezes scatter flowers all over, filling this buddha-field. These flowers fall in patterns, according to their colors, without ever being mixed up. They have delicate hues and strong fragrance. When one steps on these petals the feet sink four inches. When one lifts the foot, the petals return to their original shape and position. When these flowers stop falling, the ground suddenly opens up, and they disappear as if by magic. They remain pure and do not decay, because, at a given time, the breezes blow again and scatter the flowers. And the same process occurs six times a day.

"Moreover, many jewel lotuses fill this world system. Each jewel blossom has a hundred thousand million petals. The radiant light emanating from their petals is of countless different colors. Blue colored flowers give out a blue light. White colored flowers give out a white light. Others have a deep color and light, and some are of yellow, red, and purple color and light. But the splendor of each of these lights surpasses the radiance of the sun and the moon. From every flower issue thirty-six hundred thousand million rays of light. From each one of these rays issue thirty-six hundred thousand million buddhas. Their bodies have the color of purple gold and in them the major marks and minor signs that adorn buddhas and bodhisattvas are rare and extraordinary. Moreover, each one of those buddhas emits hundreds of thousands of rays of light that spread out everywhere in the ten quarters and proclaim the subtle and sublime Dharma. In this way, each of these buddhas firmly establishes innumerable living beings in the Buddha's True Way."

Marcus Tullius Cicero

(106 B.C.–43 B.C.)

*Cicero, Roman orator, republican, and statesman, was the author of numerous works of philosophy, morals, history, and poetry. This excerpt from "The Dream of Scipio" (*De republica*, book 6), written in 52 B.C., discusses the music of the spheres.*

Scipio is speaking:] "When I went to Africa on the staff of the consul Manius Manilius with the rank, as you know, of military tribune of the Fourth Legion [i.e., in 149 B.C., at the beginning of the Third Punic War], my strongest desire was to meet King Masinissa, who for very good reason was a devoted friend of our family. When I entered the king's presence, that grand old man threw his arms around me and wept freely. After a little time he looked up to heaven and said, 'I give thee thanks, O Sun supreme, and you also, ye other heavenly beings, that before I depart this life I see within my kingdom and under my roof Publius Cornelius Scipio, the very sound of whose name refreshes me—so little can I forget that noble and invincible man!' [I.e., Scipio Africanus the Elder, Scipio's grandfather.]

"I then questioned him about his kingdom, while he in turn inquired about our Republic; thus we spent the whole day in conversation. After we had been entertained with royal hospitality, we continued our conversation until late in the night, the old king talking of nothing but Africanus, and recalling not only his every deed but also all his words. At last we parted for the night, and as I was tired from my journey, and also had sat up late, I fell at once into a much sounder sleep than usual. Then the following dream came to me, suggested no doubt by the subject of our conversation. For it often happens that our thoughts and words affect us during sleep somewhat in the way that Ennius records with reference to [the vision of] Homer, about whom, as you know, he was constantly thinking and speaking during his waking hours. In my case, Africanus appeared to me in the form with which I was familiar from his bust, rather than from my personal recollection. When I recognized him, I trembled with terror, but he said, 'Courage, Scipio; do not be afraid, but remember carefully what I am about to tell you.

"'Can you see that city yonder, which I forced to obey the Roman people, but which is now renewing its old hostility and cannot be at rest?' (He was pointing to Carthage, from a high starlit place, bathed in light.) 'That city,' he continued, 'you, now scarcely more than a common soldier, have come to lay siege to; but within two years, you, a consul, will lay it level with the ground. The surname [Africanus] to which you are now only an heir will then be your own through personal achievement. After destroying Carthage you will celebrate a triumph; then you will be censor, and will go on embassies to Egypt, Syria, Asia, and Greece. Finally, though absent from Rome, you will be elected consul for a second time and by the destruction of Numantia you will bring a great war to a close. However, after your triumphal entry into the Capitol you will find the Republic disturbed as the result of the schemes of my grandson [Tiberius Gracchus]. At that critical moment, Africanus, you must show forth in the service of your fatherland the light of your spirit, your abilities, your wise counsel.

"'Nevertheless, at that time, I see, two paths of destiny will confront you. For when your age has reached eight times seven solar circuits [i.e., 8 × 7 years], and when in the course of nature these two numbers—each of which is perfect, though for different reasons—have combined to produce the sum [= 56] so big with fate for you, then the whole State will turn to you and to your name alone. The Senate, all good citizens, the allies, the Latin peoples, will all look to you. You will be the only one who can save the nation. In a word, it will be your duty as dictator to restore order to the commonwealth—provided you escape the wicked hands of your kinsmen [the Gracchi].'"

(At this Laelius cried aloud, and the others uttered deep groans. But Scipio smiled gently and said: "Shh! I beg you, do not wake me from sleep, but listen for a little while and hear the rest.")

"'However, Africanus, in order to encourage you in your endeavors to safeguard the State, consider this: all those who have preserved, aided, or extended their fatherland have a special place assigned to them in heaven where they may enjoy an eternal life of happiness. For nothing done on earth more greatly pleases the supreme deity who rules the entire universe than assemblies or communities of men bound together by justice, which are called states. Their rulers and preservers go forth from here, and hither they return.'

"By this time I was thoroughly terrified, not so much fearing death as the treachery of my own kin. Nevertheless, I [went on and] inquired of Africanus whether he himself was still alive, and also whether my father Paulus was, and also the others whom we think of as having ceased to be.

"'Of course they are alive,' he replied: 'They have taken their flight from the bonds of the body as from a prison. Your so-called life [on earth] is really death. Do you not see your father Paulus coming to meet you?'

"At the sight of my father I broke down and cried. But he embraced me and kissed me and told me not to weep. As soon as I had controlled my grief and could speak, I began: 'Why, O best and saintliest of fathers, since here [only] is life worthy of the name, as I have just heard from Africanus, why must I live a dying life on earth? Why may I not hasten to join you here?'

"'No indeed,' he replied. 'Unless that God whose temple is the whole visible universe releases you from the prison of the body, you cannot gain entrance here. For men were given life for the purpose of cultivating that globe, called Earth, which you see at the center of this temple. Each has been given a soul, [a spark] from those eternal fires which you call stars and planets, which are globular and rotund and are animated by divine intelligences, and which with marvelous velocity revolve in their established orbits. Like all god-fearing men, therefore, Publius, you must leave the soul in the custody of the body, and must not quit the life on Earth unless you are summoned by the one who gave it to you; otherwise you will be seen to shirk the duty assigned by God to man.

"'But, Scipio, like your grandfather here, like myself, who was your father, cultivate justice and the sense of duty [*pietas*], which are of great importance in relation to parents and kindred but even more in relation to one's country. Such a life [spent in the service of one's country] is a highway to the skies, to the fellowship of those who have completed their earthly lives and have been released from the body and now dwell in that place which you see yonder' (it was the circle of dazzling brilliance which blazed among the stars), 'which you, using a term borrowed from the Greeks, call the Milky Way.'

"Looking about from this high vantage point, everything appeared to me to be marvelous and beautiful. There were stars which we never see from the Earth, and the dimensions of all of them were greater than we have ever suspected. The smallest among them was the one which, being farthest from Heaven and nearest the Earth, shone with a borrowed light [the Moon]. The size of the stars, however, far exceeded that of the Earth. Indeed, the latter seemed so small that I was humiliated with our empire, which is only a point where we touch the surface of the globe.

"As I gazed still more intently at the Earth, Africanus said: 'How long, I wonder, will your mind continue to be fastened to the soil? Do you not see what a temple you have entered? Here are the nine circles, or rather spheres, by which all things are held together. One of these, the outermost, is Heaven, which contains within it all the rest, and is itself the supreme deity, embracing all, enclosing all. Within it are fastened those [spheres] that revolve, the everlasting courses of the stars. Beneath it are seven spheres revolving the other way, in the direction opposite to that of Heaven. One sphere is occupied by that star which on earth they call Saturn. Next comes that of the bright light called Jupiter, bringing prosperity and health to mankind. Then there is one which you call Mars, of reddish hue and horrifying to the lands of men. Farther down, nearly midway between Heaven and Earth, is the region ruled by the Sun, who is the leader, prince, and governor of the other lights, the mind of the universe and its guiding principle, of such magnitude that he illumines and fills all things with his light. He is followed by two companions, so to speak, Venus and Mercury, in their courses. In the lowest sphere revolves the Moon, lighted up by the rays of the Sun. But below the Moon there is nothing but what is mortal and doomed to decay, except souls which are given by the gods to the human race. Above the Moon all things are eternal. The Earth, which is the ninth and central sphere, does not rotate, being at the lowest point of all; toward it all things are drawn by reason of their weight.'

"When I had recovered from my astonishment over this great panorama, and had come to myself, I asked: 'Tell me, what is this loud, sweet harmony that fills my ears?'

"He replied, 'This music is produced by the impulse and motion of these spheres themselves. The unequal intervals between them are arranged according to a strict proportion, and so the high notes blend agreeably with the low, and thus various sweet harmonies are produced. Such immense revolutions cannot, of course, be so swiftly carried out in silence, and it is only natural that one extreme should produce deep tones and the other high ones. Accordingly, this highest sphere of Heaven, which bears the stars, and whose revolution is swifter, produces a high shrill sound, whereas the lowest sphere, that of the Moon, rotates with the deepest sound. The Earth, of course, the ninth sphere, remains fixed and immovable in the center of the universe. But the other eight spheres, two of which move with the same speed, produce seven different sounds—a number, by the way, which is the key to almost everything. Skillful men reproducing this celestial music on stringed instruments have thus opened the way for their own return to this heavenly region, as other men of outstanding genius have done by spending their lives on Earth in the study of things divine.

"'Men's ears, being always filled with this music, have grown deaf to it. For it is a fact that none of your senses is so dull as that of hearing. Thus in the neighborhood of Catadupa, where the Nile comes rushing down [in a cataract] from high mountains, the people that live there have lost their sense of hearing as a result of the deafening noise. But this mighty music of the spheres, produced by the swift speed with which the whole universe spins round, is so overwhelming that no human ear can sense it, any more than you can look straight at the sun, whose rays would overpower the keenness of your sight.'"

Howard Schwartz

(b. 1945)

Schwartz is an American poet, story-teller, editor, and scholar of Jewish literature. In "The Celestial Orchestra," a Jewish treatment of the music of the spheres, the great Hasidic rebbe Nachman of Bratslav travels to the Celestial Temple to discover the source of the divine music that has troubled his sleep.

Once it happened that Reb Nachman woke up in the middle of the night, and instead of the deep silence that usually pervaded, he heard something like faint music. At first the sound seemed no more than an approaching wind, but soon he realized it actually was a kind of music. What could it be? He had no idea. But he continued to hear it ever so faintly, sometimes present, sometimes about to disappear. And as it did not grow any louder, he had to strain to listen. One thing was certain, though: Reb Nachman felt drawn to this music, as if it were a message coming to him from a great distance, which he was trying to receive.

Then Reb Nachman got up and went into his study and sat down by the window. And yes, from there the music seemed slightly louder, as if he were a little closer to its source, but it remained very faint. It did not seem to come from any instrument with which he was familiar, for it did not sound like a violin or a flute: not like a bass fiddle and not like a drum. Nor did it have the sound of voice or voices. If only he were able to hear it better, he thought, he might be able to identify its source.

Then Reb Nachman left the house and walked out into the field beyond the gate, under a sky crowded with stars. There he had no memory, except for questions that concerned the origin of the mysterious music. And while his eyes were fixed on the heavens, the ground remained unknown beneath his feet. And for that time he did not impose patterns on distant stars or imagine the life they might sustain. Nor did he count the gift of the stars as riches. Instead he listened for a long, long time.

At first Reb Nachman thought that what he heard was coming from a single instrument. But soon he was able to separate the instruments that wove their music together so well. Yet this new knowledge did not satisfy his longing and curiosity; in fact, it only served to whet it. Where was this distant music coming from? Surely it was not drifting there from any orchestra in Bratslav, or from anywhere else in this world. Of that Reb Nachman was certain. No, this was some kind of celestial music, music of the spheres. It was then Reb Nachman realized how much he wanted to follow that music and discover its source. And this longing grew so great that he became afraid his heart would break. Then, while he was staring upward, he saw a very large star fall from its place in the heavens and blaze across the sky like a comet. He followed that star as it fell, and shared its last journey. And somehow it seemed to Reb Nachman that he was falling with that star and was caught up in that same motion, as if he had been swept away by an invisible current, and he closed his eyes and let himself be carried.

Now it happened that when Reb Nachman opened his eyes again he found himself seated inside a chariot of fire that blazed its way across the heavens. And he did not have time to wonder how this had happened, or what it meant, but merely to marvel in awe as the wonders of the heavens passed before his eyes. Before him he saw two kinds of luminaries: those that ascended above were luminaries of light and those that descended below were luminaries of fire. And it was then, when his eyes had become adjusted to the sudden illuminations crossing his path, that Reb Nachman became aware of a presence beside him and began to perceive a dim body of light.

That is when the angel who drove the chariot first spoke to him, and said: "Reb Nachman, I am the angel Raziel. You should know that your calling and your prayers have not gone unheard in heaven. This chariot has been sent to bring you to the place you long for, the source you are seeking."

And with each word the angel Raziel spoke, the light surrounding his ethereal body grew brighter, until he appeared to Reb Nachman as a fully revealed human being. This was the first time Reb Nachman had ever been face-to-face with an angel. And yet, strange to say, he did not feel the fear he would have expected, but rather felt as if he had been reunited with a long-lost companion.

Just then the chariot approached some kind of parting of the heavens, which resembled a line drawn across the cosmos. As they drew closer, he saw it was actually an opening through which an ethereal light emerged. Raziel recognized the question taking form in Reb Nachman's mind, and he said: "We are approaching the place where the Upper Waters and the Lower Waters meet. This is where the Upper Worlds are separated from the Lower Worlds, and what belongs to the spheres above is divided from what belongs to the spheres below."

No sooner did the angel finish speaking than the chariot approached close enough to that place for Reb Nachman to catch a glimpse of what lay on the other side. And what he saw was a magnificent structure suspended in space. And from that one glimpse he knew that whatever it was, no human structure could begin to compare with it. But then, before he had time to question the angel, the chariot passed through that very aperture, to the complete astonishment of Reb Nachman, for it was no higher than a hand's breadth. It was at that moment that Reb Nachman grew afraid for the first time, for he realized he was flying through space at a great height and did not dare to look down. Then he said to the angel. "How is it possible that we have passed through that place which is no more than three finger-breadths?"

Raziel said, "In your world of men, Reb Nachman, it is possible to contain a garden in the world. But in this kingdom it is possible to contain the world in a garden. How can this be? Because here, whoever opens his heart to the Holy One, blessed be He, as much as the thickness of a needle, can pass through any portal."

Even as Raziel spoke these words Reb Nachman had already been captured by the radiant vision that loomed ahead. And again, without his having to ask, Raziel replied. "The place you are about to be taken to, Reb Nachman, is the very one you have been seeking. Yet since even this chariot is not permitted to approach much closer to that sacred place, you must soon depart from it and remain suspended in space, like the Sanctuary you see before you."

And without any other explanation, Reb Nachman realized that the wonderful structure he saw must be the Celestial Temple, after which the Temple in Jerusalem had been modeled, and with which it was identical in every aspect, except for the fire surrounding the heavenly Sanctuary. For the marble pillars of this heavenly miracle were illumined by red fire, the stones by green fire, the threshold by white fire, and the gates by blue fire. And angels entered and departed in a steady stream, intoning an unforgettable hymn to a melody Reb Nachman heard that day for the first time, but which he recognized as if it had been familiar to him all the days of his life.

That is when Reb Nachman realized he was no longer within the chariot but suspended in space without support for his hands or feet. And it was then, with his eyes fixed on that shimmering vision, that Reb Nachman was first able to distinguish the Divine Presence of the *Shekhinah* hovering above the walls and pillars of the Temple, illuminating them and wrapping them in a glowing light, which shone across all of heaven. It was this light he had seen from the other side of the aperture, before the chariot of fire had crossed into the Kingdom of Heaven. And so awestruck was Reb Nachman to witness the splendor of the *Shekhinah*, he suddenly experienced an overwhelming impulse to hide his face. He began to sway in that place and almost lost his balance. Had it not been for the angel Raziel speaking to him at that instant he might have fallen from that great height. The angel said, "Take care, Reb Nachman, and know that the Temple remains suspended by decree of the Holy One, blessed be He. And you must remember above all to keep your eyes fixed on its glory, if you are not to become lost in this place. For should you look away from the Temple for as long as a single instant, you would risk the danger of falling from this height. Even a mere distraction would take you to places unintended, from which you might never return. So too should you know that no living man may enter into that holy dwelling place and still descend to the world of men. For no man could survive the pure fire burning there, through which only angels and purified souls can pass."

And it was then, when he had regained his balance, that Reb Nachman finally discovered the source of the celestial music that had lured him from his house in a world so far removed, and yet so close. For as he followed that music to its source in the Celestial Temple, his eyes came to rest on concentric circles of angels in the Temple courtyard. Then he realized that the music he had been hearing was being played by an orchestra of angels. And when he looked still closer he saw that each of the angels played a golden vessel cast in the shape of a letter of the Hebrew alphabet. And each one had a voice of its own, and one angel in the center of the circle played an instrument in the shape of the letter Bet.

And as he listened to the music, Reb Nachman realized it was the long note of the letter Bet that served as its foundation and sustained all of the other instruments. He marveled at how long the angel was able to hold this note, drawing his breath back and forth like the Holy One Himself, who in this way brought the heavens and the earth into being. And at that moment Reb Nachman was willing to believe that the world only existed so that those secret harmonies could be heard. And he turned to the angel Raziel, who had never left his side, and once more the angel knew what he wished to know, and said. "The score of this symphony is the scroll of the Torah, which commences with the letter Bet, endless and eternal, and continues with each instrument playing in turn as it appears on the page, holding its note until the next letter has been sounded, and then breathing in and out a full breath."

And when Reb Nachman listened to that music he arrived at a new understanding of the Torah and realized that among its many mysteries there was one level on which it existed only as pure music. He was also aware that of all the instruments in that orchestra it was only the letter Bet that spoke to him and pronounced his name. Then the angel Raziel turned to him and said, "The souls of all men draw their strength from one of the instruments in this orchestra and thus from one of the letters of the alphabet. And that letter serves as the vessel through which the soul of a man may reveal itself. Your soul, Reb Nachman, is one of the thirty-six souls that draw their strength from the vessel of the letter Bet, which serves as their Foundation Stone and holds back the waters of the Abyss."

Then it happened that when the angel Raziel said the word "Abyss," Reb Nachman forgot all of his warnings for one instant and glanced down at the world so far below. And the next thing he knew, he felt like a falling star. That is when he realized he was still standing in the field beyond the gate. And the celestial music, though faint once more, still echoed in his ears.

The Passion of Saints Perpetua and Felicity

(Third Century)

Based on eyewitness accounts, this narrative tells of the martyrdom of five Christian companions in Carthage on 7 March 203, under the persecution of Septimus Severus. Here Perpetua and Saturus dream of visiting heaven, in anticipation of their deaths.

A few days after we were taken into prison, and I was much afraid because I had never known such darkness. O bitter day! There was a great heat because of the press, there was cruel handling of the soldiers. Lastly I was tormented there by care for the child. Then Tertius and Pomponius, the blessed deacons who ministered to us, obtained with money that for a few hours we should be taken forth to a better part of the prison and be refreshed. Then all of them going out from the dungeon took their pleasure; I suckled my child that was now faint with hunger. And being careful for him, I spoke to my mother and strengthened my brother and commended my son unto them. I pined because I saw they pined for my sake. Such cares I suffered for many days; and I obtained that the child should abide with me in prison; and straightway I became well, and was lightened of my labour and care for the child; and suddenly the prison was made a palace for me, so that I would sooner be there than anywhere else. . . .

Then said my brother to me: Lady my sister, thou art now in high honour, even such that thou mightest ask for a vision; and it should be shown thee whether this be a passion or else a deliverance. And I, as knowing that I conversed with the Lord, for Whose sake I had suffered such things, did promise him, nothing doubting; and I said: To-morrow I will tell thee. And I asked, and this was shown me.

I beheld a ladder of bronze, marvellously great, reaching up to heaven; and it was narrow, so that not more than one might go up at one time. And in the sides of the ladder were planted all manner of things of iron. There were swords there, spears, hooks, and knives; so that if any that went up took not good heed or looked not upward, he would be torn and his flesh cling to the iron. And there was right at the ladder's foot a serpent lying, marvellously great, which lay in wait for those that would go up, and frightened them that they might not go up. Now Saturus went up first (who afterwards had of his own will given up himself for our sakes, because it was he who had edified us; and when we were taken he had not been there). And he came to the ladder's head; and he turned and said: Perpetua, I await thee; but see that serpent bite thee not. And I said: It shall not hurt me, in the name of Jesus Christ. And from beneath the ladder, as though it feared me, it softly put forth its head; and as though I trod on the first step I trod on its head. And I went up, and I saw a very great space of garden, and in the midst a man sitting, white-headed, in shepherd's clothing, tall, milking his sheep; and standing around in white were many thousands. And he raised his head and beheld me and said to me: Welcome, child. And he cried to me, and from the curd he had from the milk he gave me as it were a morsel; and I took it with joined hands and ate it up; and all that stood around said, Amen. And at the sound of that word I awoke, yet eating I know not what of sweet.

And forthwith I told my brother, and we knew it should be a passion; and we began to have no hope any longer in this world. . . .

And blessed Saturus too delivered this vision which he himself wrote down.

We had suffered, saith he, and we passed out of the flesh, and we began to be carried towards the east by four angels whose hand touched us not. And we went not as though turned upwards upon our backs, but as though we went up an easy hill. And passing over the world's edge we saw a very great light; and I said to Perpetua (for she was at my side): This is that which the Lord promised us; we have received His promise. And while we were being carried by these same four angels, a great space opened before us, as it had been a pleasure garden, having rose-trees and all kinds of flowers. The height of the trees was after the manner of the cypress, and their leaves sang without ceasing. And there in the garden were four other angels, more glorious than the rest; who when they saw us gave us honour and said to the other angels: Lo, here are they, here are they: and marvelled. And the four angels who bore us set us down trembling; and we passed on foot by a broad way over a plain. There we found Jocundus and Saturninus and Artaxius who in the same persecution had suffered and had been burned alive; and Quintus, a martyr also, who in prison had departed this life; and we asked of them where were the rest. The other angels said to us: Come first, go in, and salute the Lord.

And we came near to a place, of which place the walls were such, they seemed built of light; and before the door of that place stood four angels who clothed us when we went in with white raiment. And we went in, and we heard as it were one voice crying *Sanctus, Sanctus, Sanctus* without any end. And we saw sitting in that same place as it were a man, white-headed, having hair like snow, youthful of countenance; whose feet we saw not. And on his right hand and on his left, four elders; and behind them stood many other elders. And we went in with wonder and stood before the throne; and the four angels raised us up; and we kissed him, and with his hand he passed over our faces. And the other elders said to us: Stand ye. And we stood, and gave the kiss of peace. And the elders said to us: Go ye and play. And I said to Perpetua: Thou hast that which thou desirest. And she said to me: Yea, God be thanked; so that I that was glad in the flesh am now more glad.

And we went out, and we saw before the doors, on the right Optatus the bishop, and on the left Aspasius the priest and teacher, being apart and sorrowful. And they cast themselves at our feet and said: Make peace between us, because ye went forth and left us thus. And we said to them: Art not thou our Father, and thou our priest, that ye should throw yourselves at our feet? And we were moved, and embraced them. And Perpetua began to talk with them in Greek; and we set them apart in the pleasure garden beneath a rose tree. And while we yet spoke with them, the angels said to them: Let these go and be refreshed; and whatsoever dissensions ye have between you, put them away from you each for each. And they made them to be confounded. And they said to Optatus: Correct thy people; for they come to thee as those that return from the games and wrangle concerning the parties there. And it seemed to us as though they would shut the gates. And we began to know many brothers there, martyrs also. And we were all sustained there with a savour inexpressible which satisfied us. Then in joy I awoke.

John G. Neihardt
(1881–1973)

An American poet, novelist, and historian, Neihardt recorded in Black Elk Speaks *(1932) the autobiographical reminiscences of the great Lakota holy man Nicholas Black Elk (1861–1950). In this passage Black Elk, nine years of age, undergoes his "Great Vision," encountering the Six Grandfathers, personifications of the six directions of the cosmos (east, west, north, south, sky, and earth) and of* wakan tanka, *the Great Mystery that underlies all things.*

Black Elk Continues:

I was four years old then, and I think it must have been the next summer that I first heard the voices. It was a happy summer and nothing was afraid, because in the Moon When the Ponies Shed (May) word came from the Wasichus that there would be peace and that they would not use the road any more and that all the soldiers would go away. The soldiers did go away and their towns were torn down; and in the Moon of Falling Leaves (November), they made a treaty with Red Cloud that said our country would be ours as long as grass should grow and water flow. You can see that it is not the grass and the water that have forgotten.

Maybe it was not this summer when I first heard the voices, but I think it was, because I know it was before I played with bows and arrows or rode a horse, and I was out playing alone when I heard them. It was like somebody calling me, and I thought it was my mother, but there was nobody there. This happened more than once, and always made me afraid, so that I ran home.

It was when I was five years old that my Grandfather made me a bow and some arrows. The grass was young and I was horseback. A thunder storm was coming from where the sun goes down, and just as I was riding into the woods along a creek, there was a kingbird sitting on a limb. This was not a dream, it happened. And I was going to shoot at the kingbird with the bow my Grandfather made, when the bird spoke and said: "The clouds all over are one-sided." Perhaps it meant that all the clouds were looking at me. And then it said: "Listen! A voice is calling you!" Then I looked up at the clouds, and two men were coming there, headfirst like arrows slanting down; and as they came, they sang a sacred song and the thunder was like drumming. I will sing it for you. The song and the drumming were like this:

> "Behold, a sacred voice is calling you;
> All over the sky a sacred voice is calling."

I sat there gazing at them, and they were coming from the place where the giant lives (north). But when they were very close to me, they wheeled about toward where the sun goes down, and suddenly they were geese. Then they were gone, and the rain came with a big wind and a roaring.

I did not tell this vision to any one. I liked to think about it, but I was afraid to tell it.

The Great Vision

What happened after that until the summer I was nine years old is not a story. There were winters and summers, and they were good; for the Wasichus had made their iron road along the Platte and traveled there. This had cut the bison herd in two, but those that stayed in our country with us were more than could be counted, and we wandered without trouble in our land.

Now and then the voices would come back when I was out alone, like someone calling me, but what they wanted me to do I did not know. This did not happen very often, and when it did not happen, I forgot about it; for I was growing taller and was riding horses now and could shoot prairie chickens and rabbits with my bow. The boys of my people began very young to learn the ways of men, and no one taught us; we just learned by doing what we saw, and we were warriors at a time when boys now are like girls.

It was the summer when I was nine years old, and our people were moving slowly towards the Rocky Mountains. We camped one evening in a valley beside a little creek just before it ran into the Greasy Grass, and there was a man by the name of Man Hip who liked me and asked me to eat with him in his tepee.

While I was eating, a voice came and said: "It is time; now they are calling you." The voice was so loud and clear that I believed it, and I thought I would just go where it wanted me to go. So I got right up and started. As I came out of the tepee, both my thighs began to hurt me, and suddenly it was like waking from a dream, and there wasn't any voice. So I went back into the tepee, but I didn't want to eat. Man Hip looked at me in a strange way and asked me what was wrong. I told him that my legs were hurting me.

The next morning the camp moved again, and I was riding with some boys. We stopped to get a drink from a creek, and when I got off my horse, my legs crumpled under me and I could not walk. So the boys helped me up and put me on my horse; and when we camped again that evening, I was sick. The next day the camp moved on to where the different bands of our people were coming together, and I rode in a pony drag, for I was very sick. Both my legs and both my arms were swollen badly and my face was all puffed up.

When we had camped again, I was lying in our tepee and my mother and father were sitting beside me. I could see out through the opening, and there two men were coming from the clouds, headfirst like arrows slanting down, and I knew they were the same that I had seen before. Each now carried a long spear, and from the points of these a jagged lightning flashed. They came clear down to the ground this time and stood a little way off and looked at me and said: "Hurry! Come! Your Grandfathers are calling you!"

Then they turned and left the ground like arrows slanting upward from the bow. When I got up to follow, my legs did not hurt me any more and I was very light. I went outside the tepee, and yonder where the men with flaming spears were going, a little cloud was coming very fast. It came and stooped and took me and turned back to where it came from, flying fast. And when I looked down I could see my mother and my father yonder, and I felt sorry to be leaving them.

Then there was nothing but the air and the swiftness of the little cloud that bore me and those two men still leading up to where white clouds were piled like mountains on a wide blue plain, and in them thunder beings lived and leaped and flashed.

Now suddenly there was nothing but a world of cloud, and we three were there alone in the middle of a great white plain with snowy hills and mountains staring at us; and it was very still; but there were whispers.

Then the two men spoke together and they said: "Behold him, the being with four legs!"

I looked and saw a bay horse standing there, and he began to speak: "Behold me!" he said. "My life-history you shall see." Then he wheeled about to where the sun goes down, and said: "Behold them! Their history you shall know."

I looked, and there were twelve black horses yonder all abreast with necklaces of bison hoofs, and they were beautiful, but I was frightened, because their manes were lightning and there was thunder in their nostrils.

Then the bay horse wheeled to where the great white giant lives (the north) and said: "Behold!" And yonder there were twelve white horses all abreast. Their manes were flowing like a blizzard wind and from their noses came a roaring, and all about them white geese soared and circled.

Then the bay wheeled round to where the sun shines continually (the east) and bade me look; and there twelve sorrel horses, with necklaces of elk's teeth, stood abreast with eyes that glimmered like the daybreak star and manes of morning light.

Then the bay wheeled once again to look upon the place where you are always facing (the south), and yonder stood twelve buckskins all abreast with horns upon their heads and manes that lived and grew like trees and grasses.

And when I had seen all these, the bay horse said: "Your Grandfathers are having a council. These shall take you; so have courage."

Then all the horses went into formation, four abreast—the blacks, the whites, the sorrels, and the buckskins—and stood behind the bay, who turned now to the west and neighed; and yonder suddenly the sky was terrible with a storm of plunging horses in all colors that shook the world with thunder, neighing back.

Now turning to the north the bay horse whinnied, and yonder all the sky roared with a mighty wind of running horses in all colors, neighing back.

And when he whinnied to the east, there too the sky was filled with glowing clouds of manes and tails of horses in all colors singing back. Then to the south he called, and it was crowded with many colored, happy horses, nickering.

Then the bay horse spoke to me again and said: "See how your horses all come dancing!" I looked, and there were horses, horses everywhere—a whole skyful of horses dancing round me.

"Make haste!" the bay horse said; and we walked together side by side, while the blacks, the whites, the sorrels, and the buckskins followed, marching four by four.

I looked about me once again, and suddenly the dancing horses without number changed into animals of every kind and into all the fowls that are, and these fled back to the four quarters of the world from whence the horses came, and vanished.

Then as we walked, there was a heaped up cloud ahead that changed into a tepee, and a rainbow was the open door of it; and through the door I saw six old men sitting in a row.

The two men with the spears now stood beside me, one on either hand, and the horses took their places in their quarters, looking inward, four by four. And the oldest of the Grandfathers spoke with a kind voice and said: "Come right in and do not fear." And as he spoke, all the horses of the four quarters neighed to cheer me. So I went in and stood before the six, and they looked older than men can ever be—old like hills, like stars.

The oldest spoke again: "Your Grandfathers all over the world are having a council, and they have called you here to teach you." His voice was very kind, but I shook all over with fear now, for I knew that these were not old men, but the Powers of the World. And the first was the Power of the West; the second, of the North; the third, of the East; the fourth, of the South; the fifth, of the Sky; the sixth, of the Earth. I knew this, and was afraid, until the first Grandfather spoke again: "Behold them yonder where the sun goes down, the thunder beings! You shall see, and have from them my power; and they shall take you to the high and lonely center of the earth that you may see; even to the place where the sun continually shines, they shall take you there to understand."

And as he spoke of understanding, I looked up and saw the rainbow leap with flames of many colors over me.

Now there was a wooden cup in his hand and it was full of water and in the water was the sky.

"Take this," he said. "It is the power to make live, and it is yours."

Now he had a bow in his hands. "Take this," he said. "It is the power to destroy, and it is yours."

Then he pointed to himself and said: "Look close at him who is your spirit now, for you are his body and his name is Eagle Wing Stretches."

And saying this, he got up very tall and started running toward where the sun goes down; and suddenly he was a black horse that stopped and turned and looked at me, and the horse was very poor and sick; his ribs stood out.

Then the second Grandfather, he of the North, arose with a herb of power in his hand, and said: "Take this and hurry." I took and held it toward the black horse yonder. He fattened and was happy and came prancing to his place again and was the first Grandfather sitting there.

The second Grandfather, he of the North, spoke again: "Take courage, younger brother," he said; "on earth a nation you shall make live, for yours shall be the power of the white giant's wing, the cleansing wing." Then he got up very tall and started running toward the north; and when he turned toward me, it was a white goose wheeling. I looked about me now, and the horses in the west were thunders and the horses of the north were geese. And the second Grandfather sang two songs that were like this:

> "They are appearing, may you behold!
> They are appearing, may you behold!
> The thunder nation is appearing, behold!
>
> They are appearing, may you behold!
> They are appearing, may you behold!
> The white geese nation is appearing, behold!"

And now it was the third Grandfather who spoke, he of where the sun shines continually. "Take courage, younger brother," he said, "for across the earth they shall take you!" Then he pointed to where the daybreak star was shining, and beneath the star two men were flying. "From them you shall have power," he said, "from them who have awakened all the beings of the earth with roots and legs and wings." And as he said this, he held in his hand a peace pipe which had a spotted eagle outstretched upon the stem; and this eagle seemed alive, for it was poised there, fluttering, and its eyes were looking at me. "With this pipe," the Grandfather said, "you shall walk upon the earth, and whatever sickens there you shall make well." Then he pointed to a man who was bright red all over, the color of good and of plenty, and as he pointed, the red man lay down and rolled and changed into a bison that got up and galloped toward the sorrel horses of the east, and they too turned to bison, fat and many.

And now the fourth Grandfather spoke, he of the place where you are always facing (the south), whence comes the power to grow. "Younger brother," he said, "with the powers of the four quarters you shall walk, a relative. Behold, the living center of a nation I shall give you, and with it many you shall save." And I saw that he was holding in his hand a bright red stick that was alive, and as I looked it sprouted at the top and sent forth branches, and on the branches many leaves came out and murmured and in the leaves the birds began to sing. And then for just a little while I thought I saw beneath it in the shade the circled villages of people and every living thing with roots or legs or wings, and all were happy. "It shall stand in the center of the nation's circle," said the Grandfather, "a cane to walk with and a people's heart; and by your powers you shall make it blossom."

Then when he had been still a little while to hear the birds sing, he spoke again: "Behold the earth!" So I looked down and saw it lying yonder like a hoop of peoples, and in the center bloomed the holy stick that was a tree, and where it stood there crossed two roads, a red one and a black. "From where the giant lives (the north) to where you always face (the south) the red road goes, the road of good," the Grandfather said, "and on it shall your nation walk. The black road goes from where the thunder beings live (the west) to where the sun continually shines (the east), a fearful road, a road of troubles and of war. On this also you shall walk, and from it you shall have the power to destroy a people's foes. In four ascents you shall walk the earth with power."

I think he meant that I should see four generations, counting me, and now I am seeing the third.

Then he rose very tall and started running toward the south, and was an elk; and as he stood among the buckskins yonder, they too were elks.

Now the fifth Grandfather spoke, the oldest of them all, the Spirit of the Sky. "My boy," he said, "I have sent for you and you have come. My power you shall see!" He stretched his arms and turned into a spotted eagle hovering. "Behold," he said, "all the wings of the air shall come to you, and they and the winds and the stars shall be like relatives. You shall go across the earth with my power." Then the eagle soared above my head and fluttered there; and suddenly the sky was full of friendly wings all coming toward me.

Now I knew the sixth Grandfather was about to speak, he who was the

Spirit of the Earth, and I saw that he was very old, but more as men are old. His hair was long and white, his face was all in wrinkles and his eyes were deep and dim. I stared at him, for it seemed I knew him somehow; and as I stared, he slowly changed, for he was growing backwards into youth, and when he had become a boy, I knew that he was myself with all the years that would be mine at last. When he was old again, he said: "My boy, have courage, for my power shall be yours, and you shall need it, for your nation on the earth will have great troubles. Come."

He rose and tottered out through the rainbow door, and as I followed I was riding on the bay horse who had talked to me at first and led me to that place.

Then the bay horse stopped and faced the black horses of the west, and a voice said: "They have given you the cup of water to make live the greening day, and also the bow and arrow to destroy." The bay neighed, and the twelve black horses came and stood behind me, four abreast.

The bay faced the sorrels of the east, and I saw that they had morning stars upon their foreheads and they were very bright. And the voice said: "They have given you the sacred pipe and the power that is peace, and the good red day." The bay neighed, and the twelve sorrels stood behind me, four abreast.

My horse now faced the buckskins of the south, and a voice said: "They have given you the sacred stick and your nation's hoop, and the yellow day; and in the center of the hoop you shall set the stick and make it grow into a shielding tree, and bloom." The bay neighed, and the twelve buckskins came and stood behind me, four abreast.

Robert Hare

(1781–1858)

Hare was a pioneering American chemist, inventor of the oxyhydrogen blowpipe, and ardent spiritualist. In this passage from Experimental Investigation of the Spirit Manifestations, Demonstrating the Existence of Spirits and Their Communion with Mortals *(1858), Hare summons, with the aid of a medium, a panoply of deceased American luminaries to confirm his research into the landscape and demographics of the spirit world.*

Convocation of Spirits

Sixty-four Queries addressed to a Convocation of Worthies from the Spirit World; also, the Replies given by them, and confirmed under conditions which no mortal could pervert.

Having received many pages of communication from my father, sister, brother, and certain other spirit friends, on the subject of the spirit world, and having been urged by him and other inhabitants of that world to publish the information thus communicated, I represented, at a time when this honoured being reported his presence, that I felt a reluctance at publishing solely on the authority of *my relations*; and requested that certain distinguished spirits, who, as I had been told, had attended one of my lectures at Boston, should sanction a synopsis of the facts which I had learned respecting the spirit world.

The propriety of my request being admitted, it was appointed that on Monday, the 18th of February, 1855, at nine o'clock, there should be a convocation of some of the worthies in question at the dwelling of the excellent medium employed. Accordingly, soon after my arrival there, at the appointed time, my father reported himself, and the following names were spelt out as being present:

George Washington,
J. Q. Adams,
Wm. H. Harrison,
A. Jackson,
Henry Clay,
Benjamin Franklin,
W. E. Channing,
H. K. White,
Isaac Newton,
Byron,
Martha Washington,
Besides relatives and friends.

The queries subjoined were when read successively, pausing, of course, for an answer to each in turn. . . .

(1.) Is it true that within a space lying between the earth and the lunar orbit there are seven concentric regions, denominated spheres, which may be called the country of spirits; that this country has all the features of terrestrial scenery, but with a much greater beauty, even in the third sphere, while the beauty of the other four spheres is greater in proportion as they are higher?

Ans. Yes.

(2.) Is it true that in those regions there are mountains, plains, rivers, lakes, brooks, rills, trees, flowers, birds, beasts, and every attribute of the most admired portions of this lower sphere?

Ans. Yes.

(3.) Is it true that, by the higher spirits, music, poetry, and all the sciences and fine arts, are highly and zealously cultivated, and that the pleasures of social intercourse are more highly enjoyed than upon earth?

Ans. Yes.

(4.) Are the narratives of their translation to the spirit world, which I have received from my sister, brother, William Wiggins, and the spirit Maria, to be relied on as coming from them, and as correct in their representations of the usual process of transference to the spiritual world after death?

Ans. Yes.

(5.) How many spheres are there, this world being the first in the series?

Ans. Seven.

(6.) How many inhabited by spirits?

Ans. Six.

(7.) Are there subdivisions? if so, how many in each sphere?

Ans. Six.

(8.) Are the subdivisions equidistant?

Ans. Yes.

(9.) How are they designated?

Ans. Either as circles or planes.

(10.) Are they concentric with each other and with this globe?

Ans. Yes.

(11.) At what distance from the terrestrial surface does the lower boundary of the second sphere, or first spiritual abode, commence?

Ans. Sixty miles.

(12.) Are the atmospheres of the spheres more rare in proportion as they are more elevated?

Ans. Yes.

(13.) Do they increase in beauty as they are higher in the series?

Ans. Yes.

(14.) How are they illuminated?

Ans. By a peculiar sun within the spiritual spheres.

(15.) Is our sun visible in the spirit world?

Ans. No.

(16.) If lighted by a peculiar spiritual sun invisible in our mundane region, do the rays of that sun consist of undulations of an all-pervading ethereal fluid, analogous to that assumed to exist by the undulationists?

Ans. Yes.

(17.) Or do they depend upon the last-mentioned fluid for existence?

Ans. No.

(18.) Are there not peculiar elementary principles appropriate, severally, to the spiritual world, and likewise to the material world?

Ans. Yes.

(19.) Is it not an error to suppose that any of the ponderable elements recognised by chemistry can contribute to the organization of the person of an imponderable spirit?

Ans. Of course, not without a loss of ponderosity, which involves a loss of identity or a transformation.

(20.) Is it not luminiferous matter which causes the effulgence of spirits, analogous in its effects to that of luminiferous insects, though consisting of a spiritual material entirely different from those which enter into the luminiferous matter of insects?

Ans. Yes.

(21.) Are spirits in the lowest level of the second sphere destitute of effulgence?

Ans. Yes.

(22.) Are they absolutely enveloped in a dark halo?

Ans. Yes.

(23.) Is reformation indicated first by diminished darkness, and subsequently by augmented effulgence?

Ans. Yes.

(24.) Is the sphere of a spirit known by the relative brightness or darkness of his halo?

Ans. Yes.

(25.) Is the lower circle of the second sphere disagreeable as to its scenery?

Ans. Yes.

(26.) Is spirit Maria's description of the spheres correct?

Ans. Yes.

(27.) Does this feature lessen as the circles are higher?

Ans. Yes.

(28.) Do the last-mentioned circles present an aspect less agreeable than that of our sphere?

Ans. Yes.

(29.) At what point does the scenery become superior to any in our world?

Ans. In the third sphere.

(30.) What designates the boundaries of the spheres, so as to make spirits perceive when they are passing through the partition between one and another?

Ans. Diversity of impression made upon the spirit.

(31.) What confines a spirit to his proper level, so that none can mount above it into a sphere to which he does not belong?

Ans. A moral specific gravity, in which the weight is inversely as the merit, prevents the spirit from rising above his proper level.

(32.) Are spirits of different densities rarer or more refined in constitution as they are higher in rank?

Ans. Yes.

(33.) Has the most dense or most undeveloped spirit any weight? if not, how are they denser than those who have progressed farther?

Ans. They are in the spheres heavy as compared with other spirits, but their weight would not influence a scale-beam in this mundane sphere.

(34.) If the lowest have no weight, wherefore are they more competent to give physical manifestations by moving ponderable bodies?

Ans. They do not act by weight, but all spirits, under favourable conditions and with certain means, possess, in a minute degree, a portion of that power possessed to an infinite extent by the Deity, of annulling gravitation and vis inertiæ; and though they cannot exercise such powers without the aid of a medium, the medium is to them as an implement in the hands of a human being.

(35.) How are such movements produced consistently with the law that action and reaction are equal and contrary?

Ans. Gravity and vis inertiæ being neutralized, the physical law of action and reaction does not prevail against the spirit volition.

(36.) Do spirits employ their limbs in effecting manifestations?

Ans. Not necessarily.

(37.) Have spirits a power of creating that which they desire?

Ans. Yes.

(38.) Like the genius of Aladdin's lamp, can spirits within their sphere create habitations at their bidding?

Ans. Yes.

(39.) Does this creative power exist in the spirits of each sphere, or is it denied, as I have been informed, to those of the second sphere?

Ans. It is denied.

(40.) Is this creative power more extensive as the sphere to which the spirit belongs is more elevated?

Ans. Yes.

(41.) Are the spirits of the third sphere happy?

Ans. Yes.

(42.) Does happiness become greater as the rank of the spirit becomes higher?

Ans. Yes.

(43.) Do spirits of infants go to the seventh sphere?

Ans. Yes.

(44.) Does an infant dying before noticing any thing go to that sphere?

Ans. Yes.

(45.) Does it require care analogous to that given to infants in this world?

Ans. It is carefully instructed.

(46.) Do infant spirits come down and reside among kindred more or less, visiting, as it grows older, those mundane scenes which may compensate it for its loss of opportunities by premature death?

Ans. Yes.

(47.) Does not the inability to communicate with its kindred cause it to be unhappy under these circumstances?

Ans. It is not rendered unhappy, in consequence of the peculiar manner in which such circumstances act upon the spirit mind.

(48.) Do such spirits, as for instance, those going to the other world while children, but having attained mature age, say forty, become companions for their parents and friends in the spheres who may have died after their maturity, or is there a too great simplicity or childishness?

Ans. In purity and simplicity they are contented to live.

(49.) Is the love of children, who have died very young, as great to their parents and relations who remain in this world as if they continued to live in their society?

Ans. Greater.

(50.) Is there a deference shown to spirits on the same plane commensurate with their superiority in learning, science, and wisdom?

Ans. Yes.

(51.) The object of marriage in this world being manifestly the perpetuation of the species, consistently with the preservation of refinement and the welfare of offspring, and there being no such motive in the spiritual world, how can there be any motive for any such indissoluble ties?

Ans. Between spirits joined by matrimony in the spheres there is a greater blending of mutual self-love into one common sentiment than in any other friendship.

(52.) Have spirits any fluid circulating through an arterial and venous system, which is subjected to a respiratory process, analogous to that which our blood undergoes?

Ans. Yes.

(53.) As spirits are weightless, is not this fluid devoid of weight?

Ans. Yes.

(54.) Has it any colour?

Ans. No.

(55.) Does the gaseous or ethereal matter respired by spirits pervade the mundane sphere?

Ans. Yes.

(56.) Do mortals breathe it as a means of sustenance to their spiritual organization while encased by this "mortal coil?"

Ans. Yes.

(57.) Does it supply the nervous system?

Ans. Yes.

(58.) Is it communicated to inferior animals?

Ans. Yes.

(59.) Do fishes require atmospheric oxygen while swimming, (water consisting of 8 parts in 9 of pure oxygen,) in order to get at the spiritual gas associated with the former?

Ans. The spiritual gas imperceptibly accompanying atmospheric air is especially necessary to fishes.

(60.) Creed is alleged to be productive of no obstruction to ascendency in the spiritual world.

Ans. Belief, being an *involuntary* act of the mind, has no merit or culpability attached to it, excepting so far as it is the consequence or is productive of prejudices; the advance of a spirit is retarded by these defects.

(61.) As in the spiritual world there is no necessity, desire, or passion which spirits can gratify by violence or fraud, on what is virtue founded? Where there is no motive or power to do wrong, where is the merit of doing right?

Ans. In the spheres, vice is displayed by the endurance of bad passions; virtue is manifested by love, purity, and the aspiration for improvement.

(62.) As the diversities of human character are clearly the results of organization and education, neither of which can be controlled by the human beings whose merit or demerit is the inevitable consequence, how can there be any culpability? It is true that a man can act as he wills; but is not his will the creature of his passions and reason jointly? If his passions be increased, will not reason be less capable of controlling them? and, *vice versâ*, if his passions be enfeebled or his reason strengthened, will not his passions have less sway? Does it not follow that while we must in self-defence resist or restrain those who cannot govern themselves, should we not commiserate all who have the misfortune to be so badly constituted?

Ans. We are no more able to answer that than you.

(63.) When a being virtuously constituted is murdered by one of the opposite character, who is most an object of commiseration? which is most favoured as a creature of God? Is not the difference between these beings analogous to that between the dog and the wolf? Both creatures of God—one is to be extirpated, the other cherished, as an inevitable consequence of the laws of creation?

Ans. The victim is most favoured.

(64.) Has not the analogy between a wicked or a savage man, and one who has the advantage of a good organization and education, a better exemplification in the case of a wild dog, and one brought up by a kind master, since the wild dog is reclaimable, may be reformed, and so may the bad or savage man. Hence, in the spheres, is not punishment or restraint made with a view to reformation rather than as a retribution for inevitable defects?

Ans. Correct.

Elizabeth Stuart Phelps

(1844–1911)

Phelps, an American author of over fifty popular books, dealt with life after death, women's issues, and the evils of alcohol and vivisection. Her sentimental allegory The Gates Ajar *(1868), an international bestseller in its day, was published when its author was only twenty-four. It presents the fictional diary of Mary Cabot, a young woman grieving over the death of her beloved brother. In these excerpts, Mary talks with her Aunt Winifred and others about the material conditions of the future life.*

June 20th

I wonder what it is going to look like," I said, as soon as I could put poor Dives out of my mind.

"Heaven? Eye hath not seen, but I have my fancies. I think I want some mountains, and very many trees."

"Mountains and trees!"

"Yes; mountains as we see them at sunset and sunrise, or when the maples are on fire and there are clouds enough to make great purple shadows chase each other into lakes of light, over the tops and down the sides,—the *ideal* of mountains which we catch in rare glimpses, as we catch the ideal of everything. Trees as they look when the wind cooes through them on a June afternoon; elms or lindens or pines as cool as frost, and yellow sunshine trickling through on moss. Trees in a forest so thick that it shuts out the world, and you walk like one in a sanctuary. Trees pierced by stars, and trees in a bath of summer moons to which the thrill of 'Love's young dream' shall cling forever—But there is no end to one's fancies. Some water, too, I would like."

"There shall be no more sea."

"Perhaps not; though, as the sea is the great type of separation and of destruction, that may be only figurative. But I'm not particular about the sea, if I can have rivers and little brooks, and fountains of just the right sort; the fountains of this world don't please me generally. I want a little brook to sit and sing to Faith by. O, I forgot! she will be a large girl probably, won't she?"

"Never too large to like to hear your mother sing, will you, Faith?"

"O no," said Faith, who bobbed in and out again like a canary, just then,—"not unless I'm *dreadful* big, with long dresses and a waterfall, you know. I s'pose, maybe, I'd have to have little girls myself to sing to, then. I hope they'll behave better'n Mary Ann does. She's lost her other arm, and all her sawdust is just running out. Besides, Kitty thought she was a mouse, and ran down cellar with her, and she's all shooken up, somehow. She don't look very pretty."

"Flowers, too," her mother went on, after the interruption. "*Not* all amaranth and asphodel, but of variety and color and beauty unimagined; glorified lilies of the valley, heavenly tea-rose buds, and spiritual harebells among them. O, how your poor mother used to say,—you know flowers were her poetry,—coming in weak and worn from her garden in the early part of her sickness, hands and lap and basket full: 'Winifred, if I only supposed I *could* have some flowers in heaven I shouldn't be half so afraid to go!' I had not thought as much about these things then as I have now, or I should have known better how to answer her. I should like, if I had my choice, to have day-lilies and carnations fresh under my windows all the time."

"Under your windows?"

"Yes. I hope to have a home of my own."

"Not a house?"

"Something not unlike it. In the Father's house are many mansions. Sometimes I fancy that those words have a literal meaning which the simple men who heard them may have understood better than we, and that Christ is truly 'preparing' my home for me. He must be there, too, you see,—I mean John."

I believe that gave me some thoughts that I ought not to have, and so I made no reply.

"If we have trees and mountains and flowers and books," she went on, smiling, "I don't see why not have houses as well. Indeed, (they seem to me as supposable as anything can be which is guess-work at the best;) for what a homeless, desolate sort of sensation it gives one to think of people wandering over the 'sweet fields beyond the flood' without a local habitation and a name. What could be done with the millions who, from the time of Adam, have been gathering there, unless they lived under the conditions of organized society? Organized society involves homes, not unlike the homes of this world.

"What other arrangement could be as pleasant, or could be pleasant at all? Robertson's definition of a church exactly fits. 'More united in each other, because more united in God.' A happy home is the happiest thing in the world. I do not see why it should not be in any world. I do not believe that all the little tendernesses of family ties are thrown by and lost with this life. In fact, Mary, I cannot think that anything which has in it the elements of permanency is to be lost, but sin. Eternity cannot be—it cannot be the great blank ocean which most of us have somehow or other been brought up to feel that it is, which shall swallow up, in a pitiless, glorified way, all the little brooks of our delight. So I expect to have my beautiful home, and my husband, and Faith, as I had them here; with many differences and great ones, but *mine* just the same. Unless Faith goes into a home of her own,—the little creature! I suppose she can't always be a baby.

"Do you remember what a pretty little wistful way Charles Lamb has of wondering about all this?

"'Shall I enjoy friendships there, wanting the smiling indications which point me to them here,—the "sweet assurance of a look"? Sun, and sky, and breeze, and solitary walks, and summer holidays, and the greenness of fields, and the delicious juices of meats and fish, and society, . . . and candle-light and fireside conversations, and innocent vanities, and jests, and *irony itself*,—do these things go out with life?'"

"Now, Aunt Winifred!" I said, sitting up straight, "what am I to do with these beautiful heresies? If Deacon Quirk *should* hear!"

"I do not see where the heresy lies. As I hold fast by the Bible, I cannot be in much danger."

"But you don't glean your conjectures from the Bible."

"I conjecture nothing that the Bible contradicts. I do not believe as truth indisputable anything that the Bible does not give me. But I reason from analogy about this, as we all do about other matters. Why should we not have pretty things in heaven? If this 'bright and beautiful economy' of skies and rivers, of grass and sunshine, of hills and valleys, is not too good for such a place as this world, will there be any less variety of the bright and beautiful in the next? There is no reason for supposing that the voice of God will speak to us in thunder-claps, or that it will not take to itself the thousand gentle, suggestive tongues of a nature built on the ruins of this, an unmarred system of beneficence.

"There is a pretty argument in the fact that just such sunrises, such opening of buds, such fragrant dropping of fruit, such bells in the brooks, such dreams at twilight, and such hush of stars, were fit for Adam and Eve, made holy man and woman. How do we know that the abstract idea of a heaven needs imply anything very much unlike Eden? There is some reason as well as poetry in the conception of a 'Paradise Regained.' A 'new earth wherein dwelleth righteousness.'"

"But how far is it safe to trust to this kind of argument?"

"Bishop Butler will answer you better than I. Let me see,—Isaac Taylor says something about that."

She went to the bookcase for his "Physical Theory of Another Life," and, finding her place, showed me this passage:—

"If this often repeated argument from analogy is to be termed, as to the conclusions it involves, a conjecture merely, we ought then to abandon altogether every kind of abstract reasoning; nor will it be easy afterwards to make good any principle of natural theology. In truth, the very basis of reasoning is shaken by a scepticism so sweeping as this."

And in another place:—

"None need fear the consequences of such endeavors who have well learned the prime principle of sound philosophy, namely, not to allow the most plausible and pleasing conjectures to unsettle our convictions of truth . . . resting upon positive evidence. If there be any who frown upon all such attempts, . . . they would do well to consider, that although individually, and from the constitution of their minds, they may find it very easy to abstain from every path of excursive meditation, it is not so with others who almost irresistibly are borne forward to the vast field of universal contemplation,—a field from which the human mind is not to be barred, and which is better taken possession of by those who reverently bow to the authority of Christianity, than left open to impiety."

"Very good," I said, laying down the book. "But about those trees and houses, and the rest of your 'pretty things'? Are they to be like these?"

"I don't suppose that the houses will be made of oak and pine and nailed together, for instance. But I hope for heavenly types of nature and of art. *Something that will be to us then what these are now.* That is the amount of it. They may be as 'spiritual' as you please; they will answer all the purpose to us. As we are not spiritual beings yet, however, I am under the necessity of calling them by their earthly names. You remember Plato's old theory, that the ideal of everything exists eternally in the mind of God. If that is so,—and I do not see how it can be otherwise,—then whatever of God is expressed to us in this world by flower, or blade of grass, or human face, why should not that be expressed forever in heaven by something corresponding to flower, or grass, or human face? I do not mean that the heavenly creation will be less real than these, but more so. Their 'spirituality' is of such a sort that our gardens and forests and homes are but shadows of them.

"You don't know how I amuse myself at night thinking this all over before I go to sleep; wondering what one thing will be like, and another thing; planning what I should like; thinking that John has seen it all, and wondering if he is laughing at me because I know so little about it! I tell you, Mary, there's a 'deal o' comfort in 't,' as Phoebe says about her cup of tea." . . .

July 25th.

To-day what should Deacon Quirk do but make a solemn call on Mrs. Forceythe, for the purpose of asking—and this with a hint that he wished he had asked before she became a member of the Homer First Congregational Church—whether there were truth in the rumors, now rife about town, that she was a Swedenborgian!

Aunt Winifred broke out laughing, and laughed merrily. The Deacon frowned.

"I used to fancy that I believed in Swedenborg," she said, as soon as she could sober down a little.

The Deacon pricked up his ears, with visions of excommunications and councils reflected on every feature.

"Until I read his books," she finished.

"Oh!" said the Deacon. He waited for more, but she seemed to consider the conversation at an end.

"So then you—if I understand—are *not* a Swedenborgian, ma'am?"

"If I were, I certainly should have had no inducement to join myself to your church," she replied, with gentle dignity. "I believe, with all my heart, in the same Bible and the same creed that you believe in, Deacon Quirk."

"And you *live* your creed, which all such genial Christians do not find it necessary to do," I thought, as the Deacon in some perplexity took his departure, and she returned with a smile to her sewing.

I suppose the call came about in this way. We had the sewing-circle here last week, and just before the lamps were lighted, and when people had dropped their work to group and talk in the corners, Meta Tripp came up with one or two other girls to Aunt Winifred, and begged "to hear some of those queer things people said she believed about heaven." Auntie is never obtrusive with her views on this or any other matter, but, being thus urged, she answered a few questions that they put to her, to the extreme scandal of one or two old ladies, and the secret delight of the rest.

"Well," said little Mrs. Bland, squeezing and kissing her youngest, who was at that moment vigorously employed in sticking very long darning-needles into his mother's waterfall, "I hope there'll be a great many babies there. I should be perfectly happy if I always could have babies to play with!"

The look that Aunt Winifred shot over at me was worth seeing.

She merely replied, however, that she supposed all our "highest aspirations,"—with an indescribable accent to which Mrs. Bland was safely deaf,—if good ones, would be realized; and added, laughing, that Swedenborg said that the babies in heaven—who outnumber the grown people—will be given into the charge of those women especially fond of them.

"Swedenborg is suggestive, even if you can't accept what seem to the uninitiated to be his natural impossibilities," she said, after we had discussed Deacon Quirk awhile. "He says a pretty thing, too, occasionally. Did I ever read you about the houses?"

She had not, and I wished to hear, so she found the book on Heaven and Hell, and read:—

"As often as I have spoken with the angels mouth to mouth, so often I have been with them in their habitations: their habitations are altogether like the habitations on earth which are called houses, but more beautiful; in them are parlors, rooms, and chambers in great numbers; there are also courts, and round about are gardens, shrubberies, and fields. Palaces of heaven have been seen, which were so magnificent that they could not be described; above, they glittered as if they were of pure gold, and below, as if they were of precious stones; one palace was more splendid than another; within, it was the same; the rooms were ornamented with such decorations as neither words nor sciences are sufficient to describe. On the side which looked to the south there were paradises, where all things in like manner glittered, and in some places the leaves were as of silver, and the fruits as of gold; and the flowers on their beds presented by colors as it were rainbows; at the boundaries again were palaces, in which the view terminated."

Aunt Winifred says that our hymns, taken all together, contain the worst and the best pictures of heaven that we have in any branch of literature.

"It seems to me incredible," she says, "that the Christian Church should have allowed that beautiful 'Jerusalem' in its hymnology so long, with the ghastly couplet,—

> 'Where congregations ne'er break up,
> And Sabbaths have no end.'

The dullest preachers are sure to give it out, and that when there are the greatest number of restless children wondering when it will be time to go home. It is only within ten years that modern hymn-books have altered it, returning in part to the original.

"I do not think we have chosen the best parts of that hymn for our 'service of song.' You never read the whole of it? You don't know how pretty it is! It is a relief from the customary palms and choirs. One's whole heart is glad of the outlet of its sweet refrain,—

> 'Would God that I were there!'

before one has half read it. You are quite ready to believe that

> 'There is no hunger, heat, nor cold,
> But *pleasure every way.*'

Listen to this:—

> 'Thy houses are of ivory,
> Thy windows crystal clear,
> Thy tiles are made of beaten gold;
> O God, that I were there!
>
> 'We that are here in banishment
> Continually do moan.

'Our sweet is mixed with bitter gall,
  Our pleasure is but pain,
Our joys scarce last the looking on,
  Our sorrows still remain.

'But there they live in such delight,
  Such pleasure and such play,
As that to them a thousand years
  Doth seem as yesterday.'

And this:—

'Thy gardens and thy gallant walks
  Continually are green;
There grow such sweet and pleasant flowers
  As nowhere else are seen.

'There cinnamon, there sugar grows,
  There nard and balm abound,
What tongue can tell, or heart conceive
  The joys that there are found?

'Quite through the streets, with silver sound,
  The flood of life doth flow,
Upon whose banks, on every side,
  The wood of life doth grow.'

I tell you we may learn something from that grand old Catholic singer. He is far nearer to the Bible than the innovators on his MSS. Do you not notice how like his images are to the inspired ones, and yet how pleasant and natural is the effect of the entire poem?

"There is nobody like Bonar, though, to sing about heaven. There is one of his, 'We shall meet and rest,'—do you know it?"

I shook my head, and knelt down beside her and watched her face,—it was quite unconscious of me, the musing face,—while she repeated dreamily:—

"Where the faded flower shall freshen,—
  Freshen nevermore to fade;
Where the shaded sky shall brighten,—

Brighten nevermore to shade;
Where the sun-blaze never scorches;
Where the star-beams cease to chill;
Where no tempest stirs the echoes
Of the wood, or wave, or hill; . . .
Where no shadow shall bewilder;
Where life's vain parade is o'er;
Where the sleep of sin is broken,
And the dreamer dreams no more
Where the bond is never severed,—
Partings, claspings, sob and moan,
Midnight waking, twilight weeping,
Heavy noontide,—all are done;
Where the child has found its mother;
Where the mother finds the child;
Where dear families are gathered,
That were scattered on the wild; . . .
Where the hidden wound is healed;
Where the blighted life reblooms;
Where the smitten heart the freshness
Of its buoyant youth resumes; . . .
Where we find the joy of loving,
As we never loved before,—
Loving on, unchilled, unhindered,
Loving once, forevermore." . . .

Monday night.

I saw as funny and as pretty a bit of a drama this afternoon as I have seen for a long time.

Faith had been rolling out in the hot hay ever since three o'clock, with one of the little Blands, and when the shadows grew long they came in with flushed cheeks and tumbled hair, to rest and cool upon the door-steps. I was sitting in the parlor, sewing energetically on some sun-bonnets for some of Aunt Winifred's people down town,—I found the heat to be more bearable if I kept busy,—and could see, unseen, all the little *tableaux* into which the two children grouped themselves; a new one every instant; in the shadow now,—now in a quiver of golden glow; the wind tossing their hair about, and their chatter chiming down the hall like bells.

"O what a funny little sunset there's going to be behind the maple-tree," said the blond-haired Bland, in a pause.

"Funny enough," observed Faith, with her superior smile, "but it's going to be a great deal funnier up in heaven, I tell you, Molly Bland."

"Funny in heaven? Why, Faith!" Molly drew herself up with a religious air, and looked the image of her father.

"Yes, to be sure. I'm going to have some little pink blocks made out of it when I go; pink and yellow and green and purple and—O, so many blocks! I'm going to have a little red cloud to sail round in, like that one up over the house, too, I should n't wonder."

Molly opened her eyes.

"O, I don't believe it!"

"*You* don't know much!" said Miss Faith, superbly. "I should n't s'pose you would believe it. P'r'aps I'll have some strawberries too, and some ginger-snaps,—I'm not going to have any old bread and butter up there,—O, and some little gold apples, and a lot of playthings; nicer playthings—why, nicer than they have in the shops in Boston, Molly Bland! God's keeping 'em up there a purpose."

"Dear me!" said incredulous Molly, "I should just like to know who told you that much. My mother never told it at me. Did your mother tell it at you?"

"O, she told me some of it, and the rest I thinked out myself."

"Let's go and play One Old Cat," said Molly, with an uncomfortable jump; "I wish I had n't got to go to heaven!"

"Why, Molly Bland! Why, I think heaven's splendid! I've got my papa up there, you know. 'Here's my little girl!' That's what he's going to say. Mamma, she'll be there, too, and we're all going to live in the prettiest house. I have dreadful hurries to go this afternoon sometimes when Phoebe's cross and won't give me sugar. They don't let you in, though, 'nless you're a good girl."

"Who gets it all up?" asked puzzled Molly.

"Jesus Christ will give me all these beautiful fings," said Faith, evidently repeating her mother's words,—the only catechism that she has been taught.

"And what will he do when he sees you?" asked her mother, coming down the stairs and stepping up behind her.

"Take me up in His arms and kiss me."

"And what will Faith say?"

"Fank—you!" said the child, softly.

In another minute she was absorbed, body and soul, in the mysteries of One Old Cat.

"But I don't think she will feel much like being naughty for half an hour to come," her mother said; "hear how pleasantly her words drop! Such a talk quiets her, like a hand laid on her head. Mary, sometimes I think it is His very hand, as much as when He touched those other little children. I wish Faith to feel at home with Him and His home. Little thing! I really do not think that she is conscious of any fear of dying; I do not think it means anything to her but Christ, and her father, and pink blocks, and a nice time, and never disobeying me, or being cross. Many a time she wakes me up in the morning talking away to herself, and when I turn and look at her, she says: 'O mamma, won't we go to heaven to-day, you fink? *When* will we go, mamma?'"

"If there had been any pink blocks and ginger-snaps for me when I was at her age, I should not have prayed every night to 'die out.' I think the horrors of death that children live through, unguessed and unrelieved, are awful. Faith may thank you all her life that she has escaped them."

"I should feel answerable to God for the child's soul, if I had not prevented that. I always wanted to know what sort of mother that poor little thing had, who asked, if she were *very* good up in heaven, whether they wouldn't let her go down to hell Saturday afternoons, and play a little while!"

"I know. But think of it,—blocks and ginger-snaps!"

"I treat Faith just as the Bible treats us, by dealing in *pictures* of truth that she can understand. I can make Clo and Abinadab Quirk comprehend that their pianos and machinery may not be made of literal rosewood and steel, but will be some synonyme of the thing, which will answer just such wants of their changed natures as rosewood and steel must answer now. There will be machinery and pianos in the same sense in which there will be pearl gates and harps. Whatever enjoyment any or all of them represent now, something will represent then.

"But Faith, if I told her that her heavenly ginger-snaps would not be made of molasses and flour, would have a cry, for fear that she was not going to have any ginger-snaps at all; so, until she is older, I give her unqualified ginger-snaps. The principal joy of a child's life consists in eating. Faith begins, as soon as the light wanes, to dream of that gum-drop which she is to have at bedtime. I don't suppose she can outgrow that at once by passing out of her little round body. She must begin where she left off,—nothing but a baby, though it will be as holy and happy a baby as Christ can make it. When she says: "Mamma, I shall be hungery and want my dinner, up there," I never hesitate to tell her that she shall have her dinner. She would never, in her secret heart, though she might not have the honesty to say so, expect to be otherwise than miserable in a dinnerless eternity."

"You are not afraid of misleading the child's fancy?"

"Not so long as I can keep the two ideas—that Christ is her best friend, and that heaven is not meant for naughty girls—pre-eminent in her mind. And I sincerely believe that He would give her the very pink blocks which she anticipates, no less than He would give back a poet his lost dreams, or you your brother. He has been a child; perhaps, incidentally to the unsolved mysteries of atonement, for this very reason,—that He may know how to 'prepare their places' for them, whose angels do always behold His Father. Ah, you may be sure that, if of such is the happy Kingdom, He will not scorn to stoop and fit it to their little needs.

"There was that poor little fellow whose guinea-pig died,—do you remember?"

"Only half; what was it?"

"'O mamma,'" he sobbed out, behind his handkerchief, 'don't great big elephants have souls?'

"'No, my son.'

"'Nor camels, mamma?'

"'No.'

"'Nor bears, nor alligators, nor chickens?'

"'O no, dear.'

"'O mamma, mamma! Don't little CLEAN—*white—guinea-pigs* have souls?'

"I never should have had the heart to say no to that; especially as we have no positive proof to the contrary.

"Then that scrap of a boy who lost his little red balloon the morning he bought it, and, broken-hearted, wanted to know whether it had gone to heaven. Don't I suppose if he had been taken there himself that very minute, that he would have found a little balloon in waiting for him? How can I help it?"

"It has a pretty sound. If people would not think it so material and shocking—"

"Let people read Martin Luther's letter to his little boy. There is the testimony of a pillar in good and regular standing! I don't think you need be afraid of my balloon, after that."

I remembered that there was a letter of his on heaven, but, not recalling it distinctly, I hunted for it to-night, and read it over. I shall copy it, the better to retain it in mind.

> "Grace and peace in Christ, my dear little son. I see with pleasure that thou learnest well, and prayed diligently. Do so, my son, and continue. When I come home I will bring thee a pretty fairing.
>
> "I know a pretty, merry garden wherein are many children. They have little golden coats, and they gather beautiful apples under the trees, and pears, cherries, plums, and wheatplums;—they sing, and jump, and are merry. They have beautiful little horses, too, with gold bits and silver saddles. And I asked the man to whom the garden belongs, whose children they were. And he said: 'They are the children that love to pray and to learn, and are good.' Then said I: 'Dear man, I have a son, too; his name is Johnny Luther. May he not also come into this garden and eat these beautiful apples and pears, and ride these fine horses?' Then the man said: 'If he loves to pray and to learn, and is good he shall come into this garden, and Lippus and Jost too; and when they all come together, they shall have fifes and trumpets, lutes and all sorts of music, and they shall dance, and shoot with little cross-bows.'
>
> "And he showed me a fine meadow there in the garden, made for dancing. There hung nothing but golden fifes, trumpets, and fine silver cross-bows. But it was early, and the children had not yet eaten; therefore I could not wait the dance, and I said to the man: 'Ah, dear sir! I will immediately go and write all this to my little son Johnny, and tell him to pray diligently, and to learn well, and to be good, so that he also may come to this garden. But he has an Aunt Lehne, he must bring her with him.' Then the man said: 'It shall be so; go, and write him so.'
>
> "Therefore, my dear little son Johnny, learn and pray away! and tell Lippus and Jost, too that they must learn and pray. And then you shall come to the garden together. Herewith I commend thee to Almighty God. And greet Aunt Lehne, and give her a kiss for my sake.
>
> "Thy dear Father,
>
> "Martinus Luther.
>
> "Anno 1530."

III

The Vision of God

Introduction

The journey to heaven, which we began to trace in chapters 1 and 2, has as its culminating moment a direct, naked encounter with God. St. Paul suggests that this experience lies in the future, at the end of life or time: "For now we see through a glass, darkly; but then face to face: now I know in part; but then shall I know even as also I am known" (1 Corinthians 13:12). Yet some few individuals report that they have, if only for a fleeting moment, experienced a glimpse of that incomparable bliss, while others have imagined, in poetry or fiction, what it may be like.

St. Augustine's description of the vision at Ostia, shared with his mother, Monica, stands alone in its compactness, its homely details, and its contemplative power. As they lean against a window overlooking a garden, the conversation of mother and son grows so filled with love and longing that they begin to ascend toward "that Wisdom by which all things are made," and then, "for one instant attain to touch it" before returning to the realities of the flesh. This brief account of a mystical ascension has an inherently social character; comrades in rapture, Monica and Augustine experience a foretaste not only of the beatific vision, but also of the communion of saints.

As a sure sign of his prophetic calling, Ezekiel is granted a vision of the Throne of Glory, the four living creatures who form its chariot, and, finally, "the appearance of the likeness of the glory of the Lord," to which he makes the prophet's characteristic response: "I fell upon my face." Similarly, Isaiah sees the Lord enthroned in his Temple, attended by the Seraphim, who cry out, "Holy, holy, holy." The author of Revelation, raised in spirit to the celestial court, sees the twenty-four elders and the four beasts, the right hand of the One enthroned, and the slain Lamb who alone can open the seven seals.

It is fitting that the Prophet Muhammad should enjoy a similar privilege. In as-Suyuti's account, Muhammad tells of experiencing the blinding radiance of his Lord's majesty, a radiance made bearable only because, in his great mercy, "He lowered somewhat for me His dignity and drew me near to Him." Touching Muhammad's heart with cold fingers, God burns away his fears, fills him with joy, and grants him instruction on such matters as the heavenly origins of the Qur'an, the merit of good deeds, and Muhammad's universal prophetic office, "to the white folk of the earth and the black folk and the red folk, to jinn and to men."

Perhaps the definitive account of the beatific vision is the last canto of Dante's *Paradiso*:

> And so my mind was totally entranced
> in gazing deeply, motionless, intent;
> the more it saw the more it burned to see.
>
> And one is so transformed within that Light
> that it would be impossible to think
> of ever turning one's eyes from that sight . . .

Finally, gazing upon the Trinity and striving to understand its mysteries, illumination floods into him and he writes, "like a wheel in perfect balance turning / I felt my will and my desire impelled / by the Love that moves the sun and the other stars." Jonathan Edwards, writing from his American Congregationalist pulpit, echoes the Italian Catholic Dante: "They shall see every thing in God that gratifies love. They shall see in him all that love desires. Love desires the love of the beloved. So the saints in glory shall see God's transcendent love to them; God will make ineffable manifestations of his love to them."

Yet in the midst of this boiling bliss, something remains—beyond. So many of the texts speak of this. Even as they are pouring out their impassioned descriptions of the ecstasies of the beatific vision, they assert that it is utterly indescribable. The Kausitaki Upanishad tells us that the soul's ultimate destination is God beyond the gods and their heavens, *brahman* itself beyond all attributes. Dante writes, "My vision rose to heights / higher than words, which fail before such sight, / and memory fails, too, at such extremes." Muhammad's vision of God is described as "a thing too stupendous for the tongue to tell of or the imagination to picture." Even Marie Corelli, in her Victorian occult ecstasies, is reticent. A journey begun on earth by drinking a tumbler of mysterious elixir ends at the outskirts of the "Electric Circle," God's abode. The narrator may proceed no further. Instead Christ, "majestic, unutterably grand and beautiful," rushes forward with a greeting worthy of a twentieth-century extraterrestrial encounter: "Mortal from the Star I saved from ruin, because thou hast desired Me, I come!"

In the words of the Pygmy hymn, "Who can make an image of God?" Nonetheless, images abound, yet none diminishes God's transcendence. The Jewish mystical text Shi'ur Qomah gives the exact measurements of God's body in a daring violation of the prohibition against pictorial representations of God. But the scale of these measurements is so preposterous, so unfathomable, as to leave the mystery intact. In all these accounts of the beatific vision, however laden with strange imagery, what is intended is the deification of man, not the domestication of God.

St. Augustine

(354–430)

Augustine, the Roman African rhetorician, became the greatest of the philosopher-theologians of Christian antiquity. Augustine's Confessions *have struck many readers as a literary miracle: the first genuinely self-revealing autobiography, cast in the form of a prayer-offering addressed directly to God. In this famous scene from book 9, Augustine and his mother experience a foretaste of the beatific vision.*

When the day was approaching on which she was to depart this life—a day that You knew though we did not—it came about, as I believe by Your secret arrangement, that she and I stood alone leaning in a window, which looked inwards to the garden within the house where we were staying, at Ostia on the Tiber; for there we were away from everybody, resting for the sea-voyage from the weariness of our long journey by land. There we talked together, she and I alone, in deep joy; and *forgetting the things that were behind and looking forward to those that were before,* we were discussing in the presence of Truth, which You are, what the eternal life of the saints could be like, *which eye has not seen nor ear heard, nor has it entered into the heart of man.* But with the mouth of our heart we panted for the high waters of Your fountain, the fountain of the life which is with You: that being sprinkled from that fountain according to our capacity, we might in some sense meditate upon so great a matter.

And our conversation had brought us to this point, that any pleasure whatsoever of the bodily senses, in any brightness whatsoever of corporeal light, seemed to us not worthy of comparison with the pleasure of that eternal Light, not worthy even of mention. Rising as our love flamed upward towards that Selfsame, we passed in review the various levels of bodily things, up to the heavens themselves, whence sun and moon and stars shine upon this earth. And higher still we soared, thinking in our minds and speaking and marvelling at Your works: and so we came to our own souls, and went beyond them to come at last to that region of richness unending, where You feed Israel forever with the food of truth: and there life is that Wisdom by which all things are made, both the things that have been and the things that are yet to be. But this Wisdom itself is not made: it is as it has ever been, and so it shall be forever: indeed "has ever been" and "shall be forever" have no place in it, but it simply is, for it is eternal: whereas "to have been" and "to be going to be" are not eternal. And while we were thus talking of His Wisdom and panting for it, with all the effort of our heart we did for one instant attain to touch it; then sighing, and leaving the first fruits of our spirit bound to it, we returned to the sound of our own tongue, in which a word has both beginning and ending. For what is like to your Word, Our Lord, who abides in Himself forever, yet grows not old and makes all things new!

So we said: If to any man the tumult of the flesh grew silent, silent the images of earth and sea and air: and if the heavens grew silent, and the very soul grew silent to herself and by not thinking of self mounted beyond self: if all dreams and imagined visions grew silent, and every tongue and every sign and whatsoever is transient—for indeed if any man could hear them, he should hear them saying with one voice: We did not make ourselves, but He made us who abides forever: but if, having uttered this and so set us to listening to Him who made them, they all grew silent, and in their silence He alone spoke to us, not by them but by Himself: so that we should hear His word, not by any tongue of flesh nor the voice of an angel nor the sound of thunder nor in the darkness of a parable, but that we should hear Himself whom in all these things we love, should hear Himself and not them: just as we two had but now reached forth and in a flash of the mind attained to touch the eternal Wisdom which abides over all: and if this could continue, and all other visions so different be quite taken away, and this one should so ravish and absorb and wrap the beholder in inward joys that his life should eternally be such as that one moment of understanding for which we had been sighing—would not this be: *Enter Thou into the joy of Thy Lord?* But when shall it be? Shall it be when *we shall all rise again and shall not all be changed?*

As-Suyuti

(1445–1505)

As-Suyuti, an Egyptian Muslim encyclopedist and philologist, was author of The History of the Caliphs *as well as commentaries on the Qur'an and compilations of prophetic tradition. This passage from* al-La'ālī al-maṣnū'a *recounts one of the key moments of the Prophet Muhammad's journey to heaven, as he floats upward on a silken cloth (*rafraf*) to meet his Lord face to face.*

Now when I was brought on my Night Journey to the [place of the] Throne and drew near to it, a green *rafraf* was let down to me, a thing too beautiful for me to describe to you, whereat Gabriel advanced and seated me on it. Then he had to withdraw from me, placing his hands over his eyes, fearing lest his sight be destroyed by the scintillating light of the Throne, and he began to weep aloud, uttering *tasbīḥ, taḥmīd* and *tathniya* to Allah. By Allah's leave, as a sign of His mercy toward me and the perfection of His favor to me, that *rafraf* floated me into the [presence of the] Lord of the Throne, a thing too stupendous for the tongue to tell of or the imagination to picture. My sight was so dazzled by it that I feared blindness. Therefore I shut my eyes, which was by Allah's good favor. When I thus veiled my sight Allah shifted my sight [from my eyes] to my heart, so with my heart I began to look at what I had been looking at with my eyes. It was a light so bright in its scintillation that I despair of ever describing to you what I saw of His majesty. Then I besought my Lord to complete His favor to me by granting me the boon of having a steadfast vision of Him with my heart. This my Lord did, giving me that favor, so I gazed at Him with my heart till it was steady and I had a steady vision of Him.

There He was, when the veil had been lifted from Him, seated on His Throne, in His dignity, His might, His glory, His exaltedness, but beyond that it is not permitted me to describe Him to you. Glory be to Him! How majestic is He! How bountiful are His works! How exalted is His position!

How brilliant is His light! Then He lowered somewhat for me His dignity and drew me near to Him, which is as He has said in His book, informing you of how He would deal with me and honor me: "One possessed of strength. He stood erect when He was at the highest point of the horizon. Then He drew near and descended, so that He was two bows' lengths off, or even nearer" (LIII, 6–9). This means that when He inclined to me He drew me as near to Him as the distance between the two ends of a bow, nay, rather, nearer than the distance between the crotch of the bow and its curved ends. "Then He revealed to His servant what he revealed" i.e., what matters He had decided to enjoin upon me. "His heart did not falsify what it saw" i.e., my vision of Him with my heart. "Indeed he was seeing one of the greatest signs of his Lord."

Now when He—glory be to Him—lowered His dignity for me He placed one of His hands between my shoulders and I felt the coldness of His finger tips for a while on my heart, whereat I experienced such a sweetness, so pleasant a perfume, so delightful a coolness, such a sense of honor in [being granted this] vision of Him, that all my terrors melted away and my fears departed from me, so my heart became tranquil. Then was I filled with joy, my eyes were refreshed, and such delight and happiness took hold of me that I began to bend and sway to right and left like one overtaken by slumber. Indeed, it seemed to me as though everyone in heaven and earth had died, for I heard no voices of angels, nor during the vision of my lord did I see any dark bodies. My lord left me there such time as he willed, then brought me back to my senses, and it was as though I had been asleep and had awakened. My mind returned to me and I was tranquil, realizing where I was and how I was enjoying surpassing favor and being shown manifest preference.

Then my Lord, glorified and praised be He, spoke to me, saying: "O Muhammad, do you know about what the Highest Council is disputing?" I answered: "O Lord, Thou Knowest best about that, as about all things, for Thou art the One who knows the unseen." "They are disputing," He said, "about the degrees (*darajāt*) and the excellences (*ḥasanāt*). Do you know, O Muhammad, what the degrees and the excellences are?" "Thou, O Lord," I answered, "knowest better and art more wise." Then He said: "The degrees are concerned with performing one's ablutions at times when that is disagreeable, walking on foot to religious assemblies, watching expectantly for the next hour of prayer when one time of prayer is over. As for the excellences, they consist of feeding the hungry, spreading peace, and performing the *Tahajjud* prayer at night when other folk are sleeping." Never have I heard anything sweeter or more pleasant than the melodious sound of His voice.

Such was the sweetness of His melodious voice that it gave me confidence, and so I spoke to Him of my need. I said: "O Lord, Thou didst take Abraham as a friend, Thou didst speak with Moses face to face, Thou didst raise Enoch to a high place, Thou didst give Solomon a kingdom such as none after him might attain, and didst give to David the Psalter. What then is there for me, O Lord?" He replied: "O Muhammad, I take you as a friend just as I took Abraham as a friend. I am speaking to you just as I spoke face to face with Moses. I am giving you the *Fātiḥa* (Sūra I) and the closing verses of *al-Baqara* (II, 284–286), both of which are from the treasuries of My Throne and which I have given to no prophet before you. I am sending you as a prophet to the white folk of the earth and the black folk and the red folk, to jinn and to men thereon, though never before you have I sent a prophet to the whole of them. I am appointing the earth, its dry land and its sea, for you and for your community as a place for purification and for worship. I am giving your community the right to booty which I have given as provision to no community before them. I shall aid you with such terrors as will make your enemies flee before you while you are still a month's journey away. I shall send down to you the Master of all Books and the guardian of them, a Qur'ān which We Ourselves have parceled out. I shall exalt your name for you, even to the extent of conjoining it with My name, so that none of the regulations of My religion will ever be mentioned without you being mentioned along with Me."

Then after this He communicated to me matters which I am not permitted to tell you, and when He had made His covenant with me and had left me there such time as He willed, He took His seat again upon His Throne. Glory be to Him in His majesty, His dignity, His might. Then I looked, and behold, something passed between us and a veil of light was drawn in front of Him, blazing ardently to a distance that none knows save Allah, and so intense that were it to be rent at any point it would burn up all Allah's creation. Then the green *rafraf* on which I was descended with me, gently rising and falling with me in 'Illiyūn . . . till it brought me back to Gabriel, who took me from it. Then the *rafraf* mounted up till it disappeared from my sight.

The Shi'ur Qomah

The Shi'ur Qomah ('Dimensions of the Body') represents Jewish Merkabah mysticism in its most intensely anthropomorphic form. In this selection the visionary beholds the hidden glory of God made manifest as a supernal Man.

Section A

The Book of the [Divine] Body [and] Varia Regarding the Chariot-Throne.

Blessed art Thou, O Lord, our God, the God of Abraham, the God of Isaac and the God of Jacob, the great mighty and awesome God, the exalted God, the Creator of heaven and earth. You are He who is the King of the kings of kings, God of gods and Lord of lords. Blessed be Your name, exalted be Your name and appelation forever and ever, for all eternity and for all time. And Your seat on the Throne of Glory; and the [celestial] creatures ascend to the Throne of Glory. You are fire and Your throne is fire, and Your [celestial] creatures and servants are fire. You are fire consuming fire. You are prince over the princes, and your *merkavot* are on the *'ofanim*. Send me! s-d-d-r-b-n. And he is appointed over the servants of God, and he will set the Torah in my heart, that they should cry out to me in my throat like a river that flows vigorously. Blessed art Thou, O Lord, Your great, mighty and awesome name is over [other] names. Be exalted in Your strength, O Lord, and we shall sing of Your mighty deeds and let them give thanks to Your great and awesome name; it is holy. . . .

Section D

R. Ishmael said: I saw the King of the kings of kings, the Holy One, blessed be He, as He was sitting on an exalted throne and His soldiers were standing before Him to the right and to the left. [Thereupon] spoke to me the angel, the prince of the presence, whose name is Metatron [*mṭṭrvn*], Ruah [*rvḥ*], Pisqonit [*pysqvnyt*], Itmon [*'yṭmvn*], Higron [*hygivn*], Sigron [*sygrvn*], Meton [*mṭvn*], Mitan [*myṭn*] and Neṭiṭ [*nṭyṭ*] and Netif [*nṭyp*]. R. Ishmael says: What is the measure of the body of the Holy One, blessed be He, who lives and exists for all eternity, may His name be blessed and His name exalted? The soles of His feet fill the entire universe, as it is stated [in Scripture]: The heavens are My seat, the earth, My footstool. The height of His soles is 30,000,000 parasangs; its name is Parmeseh [*prmsyyh*]. From His feet until His ankles is 10,000,500 parasangs. The name of His right ankle is Atarqam [*'ṭrqm*], and [the name] of the left [one] is Ava Tarqam [*'v' ṭrqm*]. From His ankles until His knees is 190,000,000 parasangs. Qanangi [*qnngy*] is its name. The name of His right calf is Qangi [*qngy*]; the name of the left [calf] is Mehariah [*mhryh*]. From His knees until His thighs is 120,000,000 parasangs. The name of His right knee is Setamnegatz [*stmngṣ*], and the name of the left [knee] is Pedangas [*pdngs*]. The name of the right thigh is Vihmai [*vyh-myy*], and the name of the left [thigh] is Partmai [*prṭmyy*]. From His thighs until His neck is 240,000,000 parasangs. The name of the innermost part of His loins is Asasnigiyahu [*'ssnygyhv*]. And on His heart are seventy names: ṣaṣ [*ṣṣ*], tzedeq [*ṣdq*], tzehu'el [*shv'l*], tzur [*ṣvr*], tzevi [*ṣby*], tzadiq [*ṣdyq*], sa^{c}af [*s^{c}p*], saḥan [*sḥn*], yyy, yehu [*yhv*], hhh, 'ahah [*'hh*], pa'af [*p'p*], ppp, yod [*yvd*], 'a'alef [*''lp*], tzah [*ṣḥ*], ve'edom [*v'dvm*], niṭar [*nyṭr*], niṭra [*nyṭr'*], hah [*hh*], yah [*yh*], yhvh, shadai [*shdy*], tzeva'ot [*sb'vt*],'ehyeh 'asher 'ehyeh [*'hyh 'ashr 'hyh*], hefetz [*ḥfṣ*], haṣaṣ [*hṣṣ*], rokhev ᶜaravot [*rvkb* ᶜrbvt], vihu [*vyhv*], hi [*hy*], hah [*hh*], mmm, nnn, qasheh [*qshh*], hadar [*hdr*], *va'el* [*v'l*], hahu [*hhv*], vehah [vhh], zakh [*zk*], veyashar [*vyshr*], 'a'a'a ['''], a'a'a ['''], pahah [*phh*], heḥai [*hḥy*], ram [*rm*], bakav [*bkb*], bbb, ṭṭṭ, 'amaṭ [*'mṭ*], 'el [*'l*], yah [*yh*], kelil [*klyl*], bekhakh [*bkk*],'i [*'y*], zeha' [*zh'*], tze^{c}a [*ṣ^{c}'*], 'ay'a [*'y'*], 'ahi [*'hy*], zi' [*zy'*], sis [*sys*], 'otiotav [*'vtyvtyv*]. Blessed and revered be the name of the glory of His kingdom forever. His neck is 130,000,000 parasangs tall. The name of His neck is Samanhu Vihteratz [*smnhv vyhtrṣ*]. The circumference of His head is 10,000,033 and a third [parasangs], that which the mouth cannot express, and that which the ear cannot hear. 'Atar Huriyah Va^{c}atasiyah [*'tr hvryh v^{c}ṭsyh*] is its name. His beard is 11,500 parasangs; its name is Hadarqamsiah [*hdrqmsyh*]. The appearance of the face and the appearance of the cheeks are in the image of the spirit [and in the form of the soul] and [as such,] no man is able to recognize it. His body is like *tarshish*. His splendor is luminous, [and] awesome from within [the] darkness; cloud and fog surround Him and all the princes of the presence [supplicate] before Him as [obedient as water] poured from a pitcher. We have naught in our hands save the names which are revealed alone. The nose, Mag Bag Ve'akhargag Tafia [*heḥai hashash; hḥy hshsh mg bg v'krgg tpy'*] is its name. His tongue [stretches] from one end of the universe to the other, as it is stated [in Scripture]: He tells His words to Jacob. The width of His forehead is 130,000,800 parasangs; the name of the width of His forehead is 'Istanyahu [*'stnyhv*; vocalization in text]. And on His forehead are written seventy letters: yh, yh', hh', hv', hyh, vyhh, 'hh, yhv, vhh, qv,'ehyeh 'asher 'ehyeh [*'hyh 'shr 'hyh*], 'h, hy, vyh, tzava' [ṣb'], hhv, hhv, hv, leh [*lyh*], vesam [*vsm*], hh. The black of His right eye is 10,000,500 parasangs. The name of its prince is Raḥmi'el [*rḥmy'l*]. The name of the white of His right eye is Paḥarkasiah [*pḥrksyh*], and the name of the left is Bazaqtzatqiah [*bzgstgyh*]. From His right shoulder to His left shoulder is 160,000,000 parasangs. The name of the right shoulder is Tatmehininiah [*ttmhynyny'*] and the name of the left is Shalmehinini'el [*shlmhynyny'l*]. From His right arm until His left arm is 120,000,000 parasangs. His arms are folded. The name of His right arm is Gevar Hodiah [*gbr hvdy'*] and the name of the left is Va^{c}ans [*v*^{c}ns]. His cheeks are like a bed of spices. And thus you begin to count from the big one. The palms of His hands are [a distance of] 40,000,000 parasangs; its name is 'Ashhuzia [*'shhvzy'*]. The fingers of His hands are 15,000,000 parasangs, 13,000,000 parasangs each finger. Its name is Tatmat [*ttmt*], Tatmetzatz [*ttmṣṣ*], Gagat [*ggt*], Menat [*mnt*], Gag [*gg*]. His toes are 100,000,000 parasangs; its name is 'Adarmatz [*'drmṣ*], Kakhmenat [*kkmnt*], Zu [*zv*], Zayin [*zyyn*], Menon [*mnvn*], Zayin [*zyyn*]. And thus you begin to count from the big one. Therefore is He called the great, mighty and awesome God as it is stated [in Scripture]: "For the Lord God is the God of gods etc." And it is [further] written: "And you shall know that the Lord your God is God, the faithful God, etc."

Kausitaki Upanishad

*This literary record of a sacred oral teaching conveys the classical Hindu prescription for a happy afterlife. There are two paths for the dead: one path returns to this perishing world and the other passes beyond all worlds, beyond heaven itself, to attain union with the infinite spirit (*brahman*).*

Once, when Citra Gāṅgāyani was preparing to perform a sacrifice, he chose Āruṇi as the officiating priest. But Āruṇi sent his son, Śvetaketu, instead, telling him: 'Go and officiate at his sacrifice.'

After Śvetaketu had taken his seat, Citra questioned him: 'Son of Gautama, is there a closed door in the world in which you will place me, or does it have another road? I fear that you will place me in a false world.' Śvetaketu replied: 'I don't know it, but I'll ask my teacher.'

So he went back to his father and asked him: 'Here are the questions he asked me. How should I answer him?' The father told him: 'Even I do not know the answer to them. Within the very sacrificial arena let us, after we have performed our vedic recitation, receive what outsiders may give us. Come, let us both go.'

Then, carrying firewood in his hands, Āruṇi went up to Citra Gāṅgāyani and said: 'Let me come to you as your pupil.' And Citra said to him: 'Gautama, you have proved yourself worthy of the formulation of truth (*brahman*), since you have not succumbed to pride. Come, I'll see to it that you perceive it clearly.'

2 Citra continued: 'When people depart from this world, it is to the moon that they all go. By means of their lifebreaths the moon swells up in the fortnight of waxing, and through the fortnight of waning it propels them to new birth. Now, the moon is the door to the heavenly world. It allows those who answer its question to pass. As to those who do not answer its question, after they have become rain, it rains them down here on earth, where they are born again in these various conditions—as a worm, an insect, a fish, a bird, a lion, a boar, a rhinoceros, a tiger, a man, or some other creature—each in accordance with his actions and his knowledge.'

When someone approaches it, the moon asks: 'Who are you?' And he should reply:

> The semen, O Seasons, is gathered,
>   from the radiant one,
>   from the one with fifteen parts,
>   from the one who is born,
>   from the one linked to the fathers.
> Then you sent me into a man, the agent;
>   and, through that man as the agent,
>   you poured me into a mother.
> Here I am born, given birth to as an addition,
>   as the thirteenth, the added month,
>   by a father of twelve parts.
>   I recognize it.
>   I understand it.
> So lead me, O Seasons, to immortality.
> By that truth, by that austerity—
>   I am the season!
>   I am the offspring of the season!
>   Who am I?
>   I am you!

The moon lets him pass.

3 He then gets on the path leading to the gods and reaches first the world of fire, then the world of wind, then the world of Varuṇa, then the world of Indra, then the world of Prajāpati, and finally the world of *brahman*.

Now, in this world are located the lake Āra, the watchmen Muhūrta, the river Vijarā, the tree Ilya, the plaza Sālajya, the palace Aparājita, the doorkeepers Indra and Prajāpati, the hall Vibhu, the throne Vicakṣaṇa, and the couch Amitaujas.

4a He first arrives at the lake Āra. He crosses it with his mind, but those who go into it without a complete knowledge drown in it. Then he arrives near the watchmen Muhūrta, but they flee from him. Then he arrives at the river Vijarā, which he crosses with just his mind. There he shakes off his good and bad deeds, which fall upon his relatives—the good deeds upon the ones he likes and the bad deeds upon the ones he dislikes. It is like this—as a man driving a chariot would look down and observe the two wheels of his chariot, so he looks down and observes the days and nights, the good and bad deeds, and all the pairs of opposite. Freed from his good and bad deeds, this man, who has the knowledge of *brahman*, goes on to *brahman*.

4b The beloved Mānasī and her twin Cākṣuṣī have picked flowers and bring them here—so also the two Jagatī, Ambā and Ambālī, and other celestial nymphs such as Ambikā. *Brahman* tells them: 'Run to him with my glory! He has already arrived at the river Vijarā! He will never grow old!' Five hundred celestial nymphs go out to meet him—one hundred carrying cosmetic powders, one hundred carrying clothes, and one hundred carrying fruits. And they adorn him with the ornaments of *brahman*. Then, decked with the ornaments of *brahman*, this man, who has the knowledge of *brahman*, goes on to *brahman*.

5 He then arrives at the tree Ilya, and the fragrance of *brahman* permeates him. Then he arrives at the plaza Sālajya, and the flavour of *brahman* permeates him. Then he arrives at the palace Aparājita, and the radiance of *brahman* permeates him. Then he arrives near the doorkeepers, Indra and Prajāpati, and they flee from him. Then he arrives at the hall Vibhu, and the glory of *brahman* permeates him.

Then he arrives at the throne Vicakṣaṇa. Its two front legs are the Sāman chants Bṛhat and Rathantara; its two back legs are the Sāman chants Śyaita and Naudhasa; its two lengthwise supports are the Sāman chants Vairūpa and Vairāja; and its two side supports are the Sāman chants Śākvara and Raivata. The throne itself is wisdom, for wisdom enables a man to be discerning.

Then he arrives at the couch Amitaujas. It is lifebreath. Its two front legs are the past and the present; its two back legs are prosperity and nourishment; its two lengthwise supports are the Sāman chants Bṛhat and Rathantara; its two head supports are the Sāman chants Bhadra and Yajñāyajñīya; the strings stretching lengthwise are the Ṛg verses and the Sāman chants; those stretching crosswise are the Yajus formulas; the coverlet is the Soma stalks; the second cover is the High Chant; and the pillow is prosperity.

On that couch sits *brahman*. A man who knows this mounts it, first with his foot. *Brahman* then asks him: 'Who are you?' He should reply—

6 'I am the season! I am the offspring of the season. I was born from the womb of space as the semen for the wife, as the radiance of the year, as the self (*ātman*) of every being! You are the self of every being. I am who you are.'

Brahman then asks him: 'Who am I?'

And he should reply: 'The real.'

'What is the real (*satyam*)?'

'Sat is whatever is other than the gods and the lifebreaths (*prāṇa*), while Tyam consists of the gods and the lifebreaths. All of that is comprehended by this word "real" (*satyam*). That is the full extent of this whole world. And you are this whole world.'

That is what he then said to *brahman*. This very point has been made in this verse:

7 Yajus is the belly, Sāman, the head;
The Ṛg is the body of this great seer;
He is imperishable,
He consists of *brahman*.
'He is *brahman*'—
So should he be known.

Brahman then asks him: 'By what means do you grasp my masculine names?'

He should reply: 'With my breath.'

'And my neuter names?'

'With my mind.'

'And my feminine names?'

'With my speech.'

'And my odours?'

'With my sense of smell.'

'And my visible appearances?'

'With my sight.'

'And my sounds?'

'With my hearing.'

'And my tasting of food?'

'With my tongue.'

'And my actions?'

'With my hands.'

'And my pleasure and pain?'

'With my body.'

'And my bliss, delight, and procreation?'

'With my sexual organ.'

'And my movements?'

'With my feet.'

'And my thoughts, objects of perception, and desires?'

'With my intellect.'

Brahman then tells him: 'I see that you have truly attained my world: It is yours, so-and-so!' Whatever victory and success belongs to *brahman*—the same victory he wins, the same success he attains, when a man comes to know this.

The Sukhavativyuha Sutra

In the context of his discourse on the Pure Land, the Buddha Shakyamuni describes the radiance of the celestial Buddha Amitabha.

Amita Buddha's Radiant Light

The Buddha said to Ananda: "Because of his majestic and celestial radiant light, the Buddha of Measureless Life is the first among the Most Honored Ones. The radiant light of all the buddhas cannot surpass the light of this buddha. His light radiates into the world systems of a hundred buddhas or into the world systems of a thousand buddhas—one would have to say even more, it radiates as far out as all the world systems of all the buddhas in the eastern regions of the universe, which are as numerous as the grains of sand in the Ganges, and one would have to say that it radiates into all the world systems to the south, to the west, to the north, and to the four intermediate cardinal points, and to the zenith and the nadir. Or the light of this buddha radiates to a distance of only one fathom, or radiates farther out to a distance of one league, or two, or three, or four, or five leagues. And it continues to increase again in this manner until it radiates into every corner of a buddha-land.

"This is why the Buddha of Measureless Life is called the Buddha of Measureless Light, the Buddha of Boundless Light, the Buddha of Unimpeded Light, the Buddha of Unopposed Light, the Buddha Monarch of Flaming Lights, the Buddha Pure Light, the Buddha Light of Joy, the Buddha Light of Wisdom, the Buddha of Uninterrupted Light, the Buddha of Inconceivable Light, the Buddha of Ineffable Light, and the Buddha of the Light that Surpasses Sun and Moon.

"When living beings come into contact with this light, the three kinds of defilements disappear in them. Their bodies and minds become supple and gentle. They become full of joy and enthusiasm and good thoughts arise in them. Even if they find themselves in one of the three impure realms or in the travail and sufferings of this world, if they see his radiant light, they all find repose and relief and never again are subject to sorrow and afflictions. After their life span comes to its end, they are all led to liberation.

"The radiant light of the Buddha of Measureless Life appears and shines in all the buddha-lands in the ten regions of the universe. No one is deprived of hearing and knowing about it. Not only do I praise now his radiant light, but all the buddhas, disciples and individual buddhas, and the host of all the bodhisattvas also praise it in unison in the same way.

"Any living beings who hear of his radiant light, his divine majesty, and his virtues, and single-mindedly praise him day and night, without interruption, will obtain, according to the resolution that they expressed in their vows, rebirth in his realm. And there the great host of bodhisattvas and disciples in unison sing, extol, and praise his virtues for the sake of those reborn there. Subsequently, when those reborn there attain the path of the buddhas, all the buddhas and all the bodhisattvas everywhere in the ten quarters will praise their radiant light, as I now am praising light of the Buddha of Measureless Life."

The Buddha said: "Even if I were to describe day and night for one whole cosmic age, the majestic power of the radiant light, sublime and extraordinary, of the Buddha of Measureless Life, I could never exhaust its praise."

Dante Alighieri

(1265–1321)

In the final canto of the Paradiso, *St. Bernard, personifying pure contemplation, entreats the Virgin Mary to purify Dante's desire and will so that he may at last behold "l'amor che move il sole e l'altre stelle." Briefly, Dante experiences the beatific vision, and the end of the* Paradiso *circles back to its beginning: "the glory of the One Who moves all things."*

Oh Virgin Mother, daughter of your son,
most humble, most exalted of all creatures
chosen of God in His eternal plan,

you are the one who ennobled human nature
to the extent that He did not disdain,
Who was its Maker, to make Himself man.

Within your womb rekindled was the love
that gave the warmth that did allow this flower
to come to bloom within this timeless peace.

For all up here you are the noonday torch
of charity, and down on earth, for men,
the living spring of their eternal hope.

Lady, you are so great; so powerful,
that who seeks grace without recourse to you
would have his wish fly upward without wings.

Not only does your loving kindness rush
to those who ask for it, but often times
it flows spontaneously before the plea.

In you is tenderness, in you is pity,
in you munificence—in you unites
all that is good in God's created beings.

This is a man who from the deepest pit
of all the universe up to this height
has witnessed, one by one, the lives of souls,

who begs you that you grant him through your grace
the power to raise his vision higher still
to penetrate the final blessedness.

And I who never burned for my own vision
more than I burn for his, with all my prayers
I pray you—and I pray they are enough—

that you through you own prayers dispel the mist
of his mortality, that he may have
the Sum of Joy revealed before his eyes.

I pray you also, Queen who can achieve
your every wish, keep his affections sound
once he has had the vision and returns.

Protect him from the stirrings of the flesh:
you see, with Beatrice, all the Blest,
hands clasped in prayer, are praying for my prayer."

Those eyes so loved and reverenced by God,
now fixed on him who prayed, made clear to us
how precious true devotion is to her;

then she looked into the Eternal Light,
into whose being, we must believe, no eyes
of other creatures pierce with such insight.

And I who was approaching now the end
of all man's yearning, strained with all the force
in me to raise my burning longing high.

Bernard then gestured to me with a smile
that I look up, but I already was
instinctively what he would have me be:

for now my vision as it grew more clear
was penetrating more and more the Ray
of that exalted Light of Truth Itself.

And from then on my vision rose to heights
higher than words, which fail before such sight,
and memory fails, too, at such extremes.

As he who sees things in a dream and wakes
to feel the passion of the dream still there
although no part of it remains in mind,

just such am I: my vision fades and all
but ceases, yet the sweetness born of it
I still can feel distilling in my heart:

so imprints on the snow fade in the sun,
and thus the Sibyl's oracle of leaves
was swept away and lost into the wind.

O Light Supreme, so far beyond the reach
of mortal understanding, to my mind
relend now some small part of Your own Self,

and give to my tongue eloquence enough
to capture just one spark of all Your glory
that I may leave for future generations;

for, by returning briefly to my mind
and sounding, even faintly, in my verse,
more of Your might will be revealed to men.

If I had turned my eyes away, I think,
from the sharp brilliance of the living Ray
which they endured, I would have lost my senses.

And this, as I recall, gave me more strength
to keep on gazing till I could unite
my vision with the Infinite Worth I saw.

O grace abounding and allowing me to dare
to fix my gaze on the Eternal Light,
so deep my vision was consumed in It!

I saw how it contains within its depths
all things bound in a single book by love
of which creation is the scattered leaves:

how substance, accident, and their relation
were fused in such a way that what I now
describe is but a glimmer of that Light.

I know I saw the universal form,
the fusion of all things, for I can feel,
while speaking now, my heart leap up in joy.

One instant brings me more forgetfulness
than five and twenty centuries brought the quest
that stunned Neptune when he saw Argo's keel.

And so my mind was totally entranced
in gazing deeply, motionless, intent;
the more it saw the more it burned to see.

And one is so transformed within that Light
that it would be impossible to think
of ever turning one's eyes from that sight,

because the good which is the goal of will
is all collected there, and outside it
all is defective that is perfect there.

Now, even in the things I do recall
my words have no more strength than does a babe
wetting its tongue, still at its mother's breast.

Not that within the Living Light there was
more than a sole aspect of the Divine
which always is what It has always been,

yet as I learned to see more, and the power
of vision grew in me, that single aspect
as I changed, seemed to me to change Itself.

Within Its depthless clarity of substance
I saw the Great Light shine into three circles
in three clear colors bound in one same space;

the first seemed to reflect the next like rainbow
on rainbow, and the third was like a flame
equally breathed forth by the other two.

How my weak words fall short of my conception,
which is itself so far from what I saw
that "weak" is much too weak a word to use!

O Light Eternal fixed in Self alone,
known only to Yourself, and knowing Self,
You love and glow, knowing and being known!

That circling which, as I conceived it, shone
in You as Your own first reflected light
when I had looked deep into It a while,

seemed in Itself and in Its own Self-color
to be depicted with man's very image.
My eyes were totally absorbed in It.

As the geometer who tries so hard
to square the circle, but cannot discover,
think as he may, the principle involved,

so did I strive with this new mystery:
I yearned to know how could our image fit
into that circle, how could it conform;

but my own wings could not take me so high—
then a great flash of understanding struck
my mind, and suddenly its wish was granted.

At this point power failed high fantasy
but, like a wheel in perfect balance turning,
I felt my will and my desire impelled

by the Love that moves the sun and the other stars.

Jonathan Edwards

(1703–1758)

Edwards—the preeminent early American philosopher and theologian, preacher of the Great Awakening, natural scientist, and psychologist of the religious affections—here explains, in a sermon on Romans 2:10, why the vision of God is the ultimate joy of the blessed.

They shall see every thing in God that tends to excite and inflame love, i.e. every thing that is lovely, every thing that tends to exalt their esteem and admiration, to warm and endear the heart. They shall behold the infinite excellency and glory of God, shall have a blessed making sight of his glorious Majesty and of his infinite holiness; shall see as those angels do, of whom we read in Isai. vi. 3. "That, standing before the throne, they cry 'Holy, holy, holy is the Lord of hosts,' and shall behold the infinite grace and goodness of God. Then shall that glorious fountain and ocean be opened fully to their view; then shall they behold all its excellency and loveliness, they shall have a clear sight of his immense glory and excellency.

They shall see every thing in God that gratifies love. They shall see in him all that love desires. Love desires the love of the beloved. So the saints in glory shall see God's transcendent love to them; God will make ineffable manifestations of his love to them. They shall see as much love in God towards them as they desire; they neither will nor can crave any more. This very manifestation that God will make of himself that will cause the beatific vision, will be an act of love in God: it will be from the exceeding love of God to them that he will give them this vision, which will add an immense sweetness to it. When they see God so glorious, and at the same time see how greatly this God loves them, what delight will it not cause in the soul! Love desires union. They shall therefore see this glorious God united to them, and see themselves united to him. They shall see that he is their Father, and that they are his children. They shall see God gloriously present with them; and God with them; and God in them; and they in God. Love desires the possession of its object. Therefore they shall see God, even their own God; when they behold this transcendent glory of God, they shall see him as their own. When they shall see that glory, power, and wisdom of God, they shall see it as altogether engaged for them; when they shall see the beauty of God's holiness, they shall see it as their own, for them to enjoy for ever; when they see the boundless ocean of God's goodness and grace, they shall see it to be all theirs.

The Manner in which they shall see and enjoy God; and that is as having communion with Christ therein. The saints shall enjoy God, as partaking with Christ of his enjoyment of God; for they are united to him, and are glorified and made happy in the enjoyment of God as his members. As the members of the body partake of the life and health of the head, so the saints in glory shall be happy as partaking of the blessedness of the Son of God; they being in Christ, shall partake of the love of God the Father to Christ. And as the Son knows the Father, so they shall partake with him in his sight of God, as being as it were parts of him. As he is in the bosom of the Father, so are they in the bosom of the Father; as he has immense joy in the love of the Father, so have they, every one of them in their measure, the same joy in the Father's love.

Herein they shall enjoy God in a more exalted and excellent manner than man would have done if he had never fallen; for doubtless that happiness, that Christ himself partakes of in his Father's bosom, is transcendently sweet and excellent; and how happy therefore are they who are admitted to partake of that portion of delight with him!

Marie Corelli

(1855–1924)

Mary Mackay, under the nom de plume Marie Corelli, became an immensely popular Victorian novelist. In this extract from Corelli's first work, A Romance of Two Worlds *(1886), the narrator ingests a magical elixir that propels her, with the help of a spirit named Azùl, into the celestial realms, where she meets her guardian angel and attains a vision of the "Last Circle."*

He held out to me a small tumbler filled with the sparkling volatile liquid he had poured from the flask. For one moment my courage almost forsook me, and an icy shiver ran through my veins. Then I bethought myself of all my boasted bravery; was it possible that I should fail now at this critical moment? I allowed myself no more time for reflection, but took the glass from his hand and drained its contents to the last drop. It was tasteless, but sparkling and warm on the tongue. Scarcely had I swallowed it, when a curiously light, dizzy sensation overcame me, and the figure of Heliobas standing before me seemed to assume gigantic proportions. I saw his hands extend—his eyes, like lamps of electric flame, burned through and through me—and like a distant echo, I heard the deep vibrating tones of his voice uttering the following words:

"Azùl! Azùl! Lift up this light and daring spirit unto thyself; be its pioneer upon the path it must pursue; suffer it to float untrammelled through the wide and glorious Continents of Air; give it form and force to alight on any of the vast and beautiful spheres it may desire to behold; and if worthy, permit it to gaze, if only for a brief interval, upon the supreme vision of the First and Last of worlds. By the force thou givest unto me, I free this soul; do thou, Azùl, quickly receive it!"

A dense darkness now grew thickly around me—I lost all power over my limbs—I felt myself being lifted up forcibly and rapidly, up, up, into some illimitable, terrible space of blackness and nothingness. I could not think, move, or cry out—I could only feel that I was rising, rising, steadily, swiftly, breathlessly. . . . A flashing opal brilliancy shot across the light in which I rested, and I beheld an Angel, grand, lofty, majestic, with a countenance in which shone the lustre of a myriad summer mornings. . . .

The Angel smiled and touched me.

"I am thy guardian," it said. "I have been with thee always. I can never leave thee so long as thy soul seeks spiritual things. Asleep or awake on the Earth, wherever thou art, I also am. There have been times when I have warned thee and thou wouldst not listen,—when I have tried to draw thee onward and thou wouldst not come; but now I fear no more thy disobedience, for thy restlessness is past. Come with me; it is permitted thee to see far off the vision of the Last Circle."

The glorious figure raised me gently by the hand, and we floated on and on, higher and higher, past little circles which my guide told me were all solar systems, though they looked nothing but slender garlands of fire, so rapidly did they revolve and so swiftly did we pass them. Higher and higher we went, till even to my untiring spirit the way seemed long. Beautiful creatures in human shape, but as delicate as gossamer, passed us every now and then, some in bands of twos and threes, some alone; and the higher we soared the more dazzlingly lovely these inhabitants of the air seemed to be.

"They are all born of the Great Circle," my guardian Angel explained to me; "and to them is given the power of communicating high thought or inspiration. Among them are the Spirits of music, of Poesy, of Prophecy, and of all Art ever known in all worlds. The success of their teaching depends on how much purity and unselfishness there is in the soul to which they whisper their divine messages—messages as brief as telegrams which must be listened to with entire attention and acted upon at once, or the lesson is lost and may never come again."

Just then I saw a Shape coming towards me as of a lovely fair-haired child, who seemed to be playing softly on a strange glittering instrument like a broken cloud strung through with sunbeams. Heedless of consequences, I caught at its misty robe in a wild effort to detain it. It obeyed my touch, and turned its deeply luminous eyes first upon me, and then upon the Angel who accompanied my flight.

"What seekest thou?" it asked in a voice like the murmuring of the wind among flowers.

"Music!" I answered. "Sing me thy melodies—fill me with harmonies divine and unreachable—and I will strive to be worthy of thy teachings!"

The young Shape smiled and drew closer towards me.

"Thy wish is granted, Sister Spirit!" it replied. "The pity I shall feel for thy fate when thou art again pent in clay, shall be taught thee in minor music—thou shalt possess the secret of unwritten sound, and I will sing to thee and bring thee comfort. On Earth, call but my name—Aeon! and thou shalt behold me. For thy longing voice is known to the Children of Music, and hath oft shaken the vibrating light wherein they dwell. Fear not! As long as thou dost love me, I am thine." And parting slowly, still smiling, the lovely vision, with its small radiant hands ever wandering among the starry things of its cloud-like lyre, floated onward.

Suddenly a clear voice said, "Welcome!" and looking up I saw my first friend Azùl. I smiled in glad recognition—I would have spoken—but lo! a wide immensity of blazing glory broke like many-coloured lightning around me—so dazzling, so overpowering, that I instinctively drew back and paused—I felt I could go no further.

"Here," said my guardian gently—"here ends thy journey. Would that it were possible, poor Spirit, for thee to pass this boundary! But that may not be—as yet! In the meanwhile thou mayest gaze for a brief space upon the majestic sphere which mortals dream of as Heaven. Behold and see how fair is the incorruptible perfection of God's World!"

I looked and trembled—I should have sunk yet further backward, had not Azùl and my Angel-guide held me with their light yet forcible clasp. My heart fails me now as I try to write of that tremendous, that sublime scene—the Centre of the Universe—the Cause of all Creation. How unlike Heaven such as we in our ignorance have tried to depict! though it is far better we should have a mistaken idea than none at all. What I beheld was a Circle, so huge that no mortal measurements could compass it—a wide Ring composed of seven colours, rainbow-like, but flashing with perpetual motion and brilliancy, as though a thousand million suns were for ever being woven into it to feed its transcendent lustre. From every part of this Ring darted long broad shafts of light, some of which stretched out so far that I could not see where they ended; sometimes a bubbling shower of lightning sparks would be flung out on the pure ether, and this would instantly form into circles, small or great, and whirl round and round the enormous girdle of flame from which they had been cast, with the most inconceivable rapidity. But wonderful as the Ring was, it encompassed a Sphere yet more marvellous and dazzling; a great Globe of opal-tinted light, revolving as it were upon its own axis, and ever surrounded by that scintillating, jewel-like wreath of electricity, whose only motion was to shine and burn within itself for ever. I could not bear to look upon the brightness of that magnificent central World—so large that multiplying the size of the sun by a hundred thousand millions, no adequate idea could be formed of its vast proportions. And ever it revolved—and ever the Rainbow Ring around it glittered and cast forth those rings which I knew now were living solar systems cast forth from that electric band as a volcano casts forth fire and lava. My Angel-guide motioned me to look towards that side of the Ring which was nearest to the position of the Earth. I looked, and perceived that there the shafts of descending light formed themselves as they fell into the shape of a Cross. At this, such sorrow, love, and shame overcame me, that I knew not where to turn. I murmured:

"Send me back again, dear Angel—send me back to that Star of Sorrow and Error! Let me hasten to make amends there for all my folly—let me try to teach others what now I know! I am unworthy to be here beside thee—I am unfit to look on yonder splendid World—let me return to do penance for my sins and shortcomings; for what am I that God should bless me? And though I should consume myself in labour and suffering, how can I ever hope to deserve the smallest place in that heavenly glory I now partly behold?" And could spirits shed tears, I should have wept with remorse and grief.

Azùl spoke, softly and tenderly:

"Now thou dost believe—henceforth thou must love! Love alone can pass yon flaming barrier—love alone can gain for thee eternal bliss. In love and for love were all things made—God loveth His creatures, even so let His creatures love Him, and so shall the twain be drawn together."

"Listen!" added my Angel-guide. "Thou hast not travelled so far as yet to remain in ignorance. That burning Ring thou seest is the result of the Creator's ever-working Intelligence; from it all the Universe hath sprung. It is exhaustless and perpetually creative; it is pure and perfect Light. The smallest spark of that fiery essence in a mortal frame is sufficient to form a soul or spirit, such as mine, or that of Azùl, or thine, when thou art perfected. The huge world rolling within the Ring is where God dwells. Dare not thou to question His shape, His look, His mien! Know that He is the Supreme Spirit in which all Beauty, all Perfection, all Love, find consummation. His breath is the fire of the Ring; His look, His pleasure, cause the motion of His World and all worlds. There, where He dwells, dwell also all pure souls; there all desires have fulfilment without satiety, and there all loveliness, wisdom or pleasure known in any or all of the other spheres are also known. Speak, Azùl, and tell this wanderer from Earth what she will gain in winning her place in Heaven."

Azùl looked tenderly upon me, and said:

"When thou hast slept the brief sleep of death,—when thou art permitted to throw off for ever thy garb of clay,—and when by thine own ceaseless love and longing thou hast won the right to pass the Great Circle, thou shalt find thyself in a land where the glories of the natural scenery alone shall overpower thee with joy—scenery that for ever changes into new wonders and greater beauty. Thou shalt hear music such as thou canst not dream of. Thou shalt find friends, beyond all imagination fair and faithful. Thou shalt read and see the history of all the planets, produced for thee in an ever-moving panorama. Thou shalt love and be beloved for ever by thine own Twin Soul; wherever that spirit may be now, it must join thee hereafter. The joys of learning, memory, consciousness, sleep, waking, and exercise shall all be thine. Sin, sorrow, pain, disease and death thou shalt know no more. Thou shalt be able to remember happiness, to possess it, and to look forward to it. Thou shalt have full and pleasant occupation without fatigue—thy food and substance shall be light and air. Flowers, rare and imperishable, shall bloom for thee; birds of exquisite form and tender voice shall sing to thee; angels shall be thy companions. Thou shalt have fresh and glad desires to offer to God with every portion of thy existence, and each one shall be granted as soon as asked, for then thou wilt not be able to ask anything that is displeasing to Him. But because it is a joy to wish, thou shalt wish; and because it is a joy to grant, so also will He grant. No delight, small or great, is wanting in that vast sphere; only sorrow is lacking, and satiety and disappointment have no place. Wilt thou seek for admittance there, or wilt thou faint by the way and grow weary?"

I raised my eyes full of ecstasy and reverence.

"My mere efforts must count as nothing," I said "but if love can help me, I will love and long for God's World until I die!"

My guardian Angel pointed to those rays of light I had before noticed, that slanted downwards towards Earth in the form of a Cross.

"That is the path by which thou must travel! Mark it well! All pilgrims from the Sorrowful Star must journey by that road. Woe to them that turn aside to roam 'mid spheres they know not of, to lose themselves in seas of light wherein they cannot steer! Remember my warning! And now, Spirit who art commended to my watchful care, thy brief liberty is ended. Thou hast been lifted up to the outer edge of the Electric Circle; further we dare not take thee. Hast thou aught else to ask before the veil of mortality again enshrouds thee?"

I answered not, but within myself I formed a wild desire. The Great Ring flashed fiercely on my uplifted eyes, but I kept them fixed hopefully and lovingly on its intensely deep brilliancy.

"If Love and Faith can avail me," I murmured, "I shall see what I have sought."

I was not disappointed. The fiery waves of light parted on either side of the spot where I with my companions rested; and a Figure,—majestic, unutterably grand and beautiful,—approached me. At the same moment a number of other faces and forms shone hoveringly out of the Ring; one I noticed like an exquisitely lovely woman with floating hair and clear, earnest, unfathomable eyes. Azùl and the Angel sank reverently down and drooped their radiant heads like flowers in hot sunshine. I alone, daringly, yet with inexpressible affection welling up within me, watched with unshrinking gaze the swift advance of that supreme Figure, upon whose broad brows rested the faint semblance of a Crown of Thorns. A voice penetratingly sweet addressed me:

"Mortal from the Star I saved from ruin, because thou hast desired Me, I come! Even as thy former unbelief, shall be now thy faith! Because thou lovest Me, I am with thee! For do I not know thee better than the Angels can? Have I not dwelt in thy clay, suffered thy sorrows, wept thy tears, died thy deaths? One with My Father, and yet one with thee, I demand thy love, and so through Me shalt thou attain immortal life!"

I felt a touch upon me like a scorching flame—a thrill rushed through my being—and then I knew that I was sinking down, down, further and further away. I saw that wondrous Figure standing serene and smiling between the retiring waves of radiance. I saw the great inner Sphere revolve, and glitter as it rolled, like an enormous diamond encircled with gold and sapphire, and then all suddenly the air grew dim and cloudy, and the sensation of falling became more and more rapid.

Songs of Adoration

Pygmy Hymn

This traditional Pygmy hymn, emphasizing the incorporeality of God, was first published in the 1930s by T. C. Young.

In the beginning was God,
Today is God,
Tomorrow will be God.
Who can make an image of God?
He has no body.
He is as a word which comes out of your mouth.
That word! It is no more,
It is past, and still it lives!
So is God.

Psalm 104: 1–4

Bless the Lord, O my soul. O Lord my God, thou art very great;
thou art clothed with honour and majesty.
2 Who coverest thyself with light as with a garment: who stretchest out
the heavens like a curtain:
3 Who layeth the beams of his chambers in the waters: who maketh
the clouds his chariot: who walketh upon the wings of the wind:
4 Who maketh his angels spirits; his ministers a flaming fire . . .

Ezekiel 1

Chapter 1

Now it came to pass in the thirtieth year, in the fourth month, in the fifth day of the month, as I was among the captives by the river of Chebar, that the heavens were opened, and I saw visions of God.

2 In the fifth day of the month, which was the fifth year of the king Jehoi'achin's captivity,

3 The word of the Lord came expressly unto Ezekiel the priest, the son of Buzi, in the land of the Chaldeans by the river Chebar; and the hand of the Lord was there upon him.

4 And I looked, and, behold, a whirlwind came out of the north, a great cloud, and a fire infolding itself, and a brightness was about it, and out of the midst thereof as the colour of amber, out of the midst of the fire.

5 Also out of the midst thereof came the likeness of four living creatures. And this was their appearance; they had the likeness of a man.

6 And every one had four faces, and every one had four wings.

7 And their feet were straight feet; and the sole of their feet was like the sole of a calf's foot: and they sparkled like the colour of burnished brass.

8 And they had the hands of a man under their wings on their four sides; and they four had their faces and their wings.

9 Their wings were joined one to another; they turned not when they went; they went every one straight forward.

10 As for the likeness of their faces, they four had the face of a man, and the face of a lion, on the right side: and they four had the face of an ox on the left side; they four also had the face of an eagle.

11 Thus were their faces: and their wings were stretched upward; two wings of every one were joined one to another, and two covered their bodies.

12 And they went every one straight forward: whither the spirit was to go, they went; and they turned not when they went.

13 As for the likeness of the living creatures, their appearance was like burning coals of fire, and like the appearance of lamps: it went up and

down among the living creatures; and the fire was bright, and out of the
fire went forth lightning.
14 And the living creatures ran and returned as the appearance of a
flash of lightning.
15 Now as I beheld the living creatures, behold one wheel upon the
earth by the living creatures, with his four faces.
16 The appearance of the wheels and their work was like unto the
colour of a beryl: and they four had one likeness: and their appearance
and their work was as it were a wheel in the middle of a wheel.
17 When they went, they went upon their four sides: and they turned
not when they went.
18 As for their rings, they were so high that they were dreadful; and
their rings were full of eyes round about them four.
19 And when the living creatures went, the wheels went by them: and
when the living creatures were lifted up from the earth, the wheels were
lifted up.
20 Whithersoever the spirit was to go, they went, thither was their spirit to go; and the wheels were lifted up over against them: for the spirit of
the living creature was in the wheels.
21 When those went, these went; and when those stood, these stood;
and when those were lifted up from the earth, the wheels were lifted up
over against them: for the spirit of the living creature was in the wheels.
22 And the likeness of the firmament upon the heads of the living creature was as the colour of the terrible crystal, stretched forth over their
heads above.
23 And under the firmament were their wings straight, the one toward
the other: every one had two, which covered on this side, and every one
had two, which covered on that side, their bodies.
24 And when they went, I heard the noise of their wings, like the noise
of great waters, as the voice of the Almighty, the voice of speech, as the
noise of an host: when they stood, they let down their wings.
25 And there was a voice from the firmament that was over their heads,
when they stood, and had let down their wings.
26 And above the firmament that was over their heads was the likeness
of a throne, as the appearance of a sapphire stone: and upon the likeness
of the throne was the likeness as the appearance of a man above upon it.
27 And I saw as the colour of amber, as the appearance of fire round
about within it, from the appearance of his loins even upward, and from

the appearance of his loins even downward, I saw as it were the appearance of fire, and it had brightness round about.

28 As the appearance of the bow that is in the cloud in the day of rain, so was the appearance of the brightness round about. This was the appearance of the likeness of the glory of the LORD. And when I saw it, I fell upon my face, and I heard a voice of one that spake.

Isaiah 6:1–7

In the year that king Uzzi'ah died I saw also the Lord sitting upon a throne, high and lifted up, and his train filled the temple.
2 Above it stood the seraphims: each one had six wings; with twain he covered his face, and with twain he covered his feet, and with twain he did fly.
3 And one cried unto another, and said, Holy, holy, holy, is the LORD of hosts: the whole earth is full of his glory.
4 And the posts of the door moved at the voice of him that cried, and the house was filled with smoke.
5 Then said I, Woe is me! for I am undone; because I am a man of unclean lips, and I dwell in the midst of a people of unclean lips: for mine eyes have seen the King, the LORD of hosts.
6 Then flew one of the seraphims unto me, having a live coal in his hand, which he had taken with the tongs from off the altar:
7 And he laid it upon my mouth, and said, Lo, this hath touched thy lips; and thine iniquity is taken away, and thy sin purged.

Revelation 4, 5

Chapter 4

After this I looked, and, behold, a door was opened in heaven: and the first voice which I heard was as it were of a trumpet talking with me; which said, Come up hither, and I will shew thee things which must be hereafter.

2 And immediately I was in the spirit; and, behold, a throne was set in heaven, and one sat on the throne.

3 And he that sat was to look upon like a jasper and a sardine stone: and there was a rainbow round about the throne, in sight like unto an emerald.

4 And round about the throne were four and twenty seats: and upon the seats I saw four and twenty elders sitting, clothed in white raiment; and they had on their heads crowns of gold.

5 And out of the throne proceeded lightnings and thunderings and voices: and there were seven lamps of fire burning before the throne, which are the seven Spirits of God.

6 And before the throne there was a sea of glass like unto crystal: and in the midst of the throne, and round about the throne, were four beasts full of eyes before and behind.

7 And the first beast was like a lion, and the second beast like a calf, and the third beast had a face as a man, and the fourth beast was like a flying eagle.

8 And the four beasts had each of them six wings about him; and they were full of eyes within: and they rest not day and night, saying, Holy, holy, holy, Lord God Almighty, which was, and is, and is to come.

9 And when those beasts give glory and honour and thanks to him that sat on the throne, who liveth for ever and ever,

10 The four and twenty elders fall down before him that sat on the throne, and worship him that liveth for ever and ever, and cast their crowns before the throne, saying,

11 Thou art worthy, O Lord, to receive glory and honour and power: for thou has created all things, and for thy pleasure they are and were created.

CHAPTER 5

And I saw in the right hand of him that sat on the throne a book written within and on the backside, sealed with the seven seals.

2 And I saw a strong angel proclaiming with a loud voice, Who is worthy to open the book, and to loose the seals thereof?

3 And no man in heaven, nor in earth, neither under the earth, was able to open the book, neither to look thereon.

4 And I wept much, because no man was found worthy to open and to read the book, neither to look thereon.

5 And one of the elders saith unto me, Weep not: behold, the Lion of the tribe of Juda, the Root of David, hath prevailed to open the book, and to loose the seven seals thereof.

6 And I beheld, and, lo, in the midst of the throne and of the four beasts, and in the midst of the elders, stood a Lamb as it had been slain, having seven horns and seven eyes, which are the seven Spirits of God sent forth into all the earth.

7 And he came and took the book out of the right hand of him that sat upon the throne.

8 And when he had taken the book, the four beasts and four and twenty elders fell down before the Lamb, having every one of them harps, and golden vials full of odours, which are the prayers of saints.

9 And they sung a new song, saying, Thou art worthy to take the book, and to open the seals thereof: for thou wast slain, and hast redeemed us to God by thy blood out of every kindred, and tongue, and people, and nation;

10 And hast made us unto our God kings and priests: and we shall reign on the earth.

11 And I beheld, and I heard the voice of many angels round about the throne and the beasts and the elders: and the number of them was ten thousand times ten thousand, and thousands of thousands;

12 Saying with a loud voice, Worthy is the Lamb that was slain to receive power, and riches, and wisdom, and strength, and honour, and glory, and blessing.

13 And every creature which is in heaven, and on the earth, and under the earth, and such as are in the sea, and all that are in them, heard I saying, Blessing, and honour, and glory, and power, be unto him that sitteth upon the throne, and unto the Lamb for ever and ever.
14 And the four beasts said, Amen. And the four and twenty elders fell down and worshipped him that liveth for ever and ever.

The Hekhalot Rabbati

According to this Jewish mystical treatise, these were the hymns Rabbi Akiba learned as he approached the Throne of Glory; like the seraphim's song in Isaiah, they form part of the celestial liturgy.

A quality of Holiness, a quality of power,
A quality of fearfulness, a quality of sublimity,
A quality of trembling, a quality of shaking,
A quality of terror, a quality of consternation,
Is the quality of the Garment of Zohorariel JHWH, God of Israel,
Who comes crowned to the throne of His glory.

And it [the *Ḥaluk*] is every part engraved from within and from without JHWH JHWH
And of no creature are the eyes able to behold it,
Not the eyes of flesh and blood, and not the eyes of His servants.
And as for him who does behold it, or sees or glimpses it,
Whirling gyrations grip the balls of his eyes.
And the balls of his eyes cast out and send forth torches of fire
And these enkindle him and these burn him.
For the fire which comes out from the man who beholds,
This enkindles him and this burns him.
Why is this? Because of [the quality] of the Garment of Zohorariel JHWH, the Lord of Israel,
Who comes crowned to the throne of His glory. . . .

Who is like unto our King? Who is like unto our Creator? Who is like unto the Lord our God?

The sun and the moon is cast out and sent forth by the crown
of His head.
The Pleiades and Orion and the Planet of Venus
Constellations and stars and zodiacal signs
Flow and issue forth from the garment of Him
Who is crowned and [shrouded] in it, sits upon the throne of
His glory. . . .

King of Kings, God of Gods and Lord of Lords
He who is surrounded with chains of crowns
Who is encompassed by the cluster of the rulers of radiance,
Who covers the Heavens with the wing of His magnificence,
And in His majesty appeared from the heights,
From His beauty the deeps were enkindled,
And from His stature the Heavens are sparkling
His stature sends out the lofty,
And His crown blazes out the mighty,
And His garment flows with the precious.
And all trees shall rejoice in His word,
And herbs shall exult in His rejoicing,
And His words shall drop as perfumes,
Flowing forth in flames of fire,
Giving joy to those who search them,
And quiet to those who fulfill them.

Edmund Spenser (1552/1553–1599)

Spenser is the English author of the great allegorical poem The Fairie Queene *(1590–1596). "An Hymne of Heavenly Beautie" appeared in* Fowre Hymnes *(1596); Spenser writes in his preface that this hymn and its twin sister, "An Hymne of Heavenly Love," were composed to counteract the arousal, in his readers, of passions brought about by two earlier hymns devoted to "Earthly or naturall love and beautie."*

An Hymne of Heavenly Beautie

Rapt with the rage of mine own ravisht thought,
Through contemplation of those goodly sights,
And glorious images in heaven wrought,
Whose wondrous beauty, breathing sweet delights,
Do kindle love in high conceipted sprights,
I faine to tell the things that I behold,
But feele my wits to faile, and tongue to fold.

Vouchsafe then, O Thou most Almightie Spright,
From whom all guifts of wit and knowledge flow,
To shed into my breast some sparkling light
Of thine eternal truth, that I may show
Some litle beames to mortall eyes below
Of that immortall Beautie, there with Thee,
Which in my weake distraughted mynd I see.

That with the glorie of so goodly sight,
The hearts of men, which fondly here admyre
Faire seeming shewes, and feed on vaine delight,
Transported with celestiall desyre

Of those faire formes, may lift themselves up hyer,
And learne to love with zealous humble dewty
Th' Eternall Fountaine of that heavenly Beauty.

Beginning then below, with th' easie vew
Of this base world, subject to fleshly eye,
From thence to mount aloft by order dew
To contemplation of th' immortall sky,
Of the soare faulcon so I learne to fly,
That flags awhile her fluttering wings beneath,
Till she her selfe for stronger flight can breath.

Then looke, who list thy gazefull eyes to feed
With sight of that is faire, looke on the frame
Of this wyde universe, and therein reed
The endlesse kinds of creatures, which by name
Thou canst not count, much lesse their natures aime:
All which are made with wondrous wise respect,
And all with admirable beautie deckt.

First th' earth, on adamantine pillers founded,
Amid the sea, engirt with brasen bands;
Then th' aire, still flitting, but yet firmely bounded
On everie side with pyles of flaming brands,
Never consum'd, nor quencht with mortall hands;
And last, that mightie shining christall wall,
Wherewith he hath encompassed this All.

By view whereof, it plainly may appeare,
That still as every thing doth upward tend,
And further is from earth, so still more cleare
And faire it growes, till to his perfect end
Of purest Beautie it at last ascend:
Ayre more then water, fire much more then ayre,
And heaven then fire appeares more pure and fayre.

Looke thou no further, but affixe thine eye
On that bright shynie round still moving masse,

The house of blessed gods, which men call skye,
All sowd with glistring stars more thicke then grasse,
Whereof each other doth in brightnesse passe;
But those two most, which, ruling night and day,
As king and queene, the heavens empire sway.

And tell me then, what hast thou ever seene
That to their beautie may compared bee?
Or can the sight that is most sharpe and keene
Endure their captains flaming head to see?
How much lesse those, much higher in degree,
And so much fairer, and much more then these,
As these are fairer then the land and seas?

For farre above these heavens which here we see,
Be others farre exceeding these in light,
Not bounded, not corrupt, as these same bee,
But infinite in largenesse and in hight,
Unmoving, uncorrupt, and spotlesse bright,
That need no sunne t' illuminate their spheres,
But their owne native light farre passing theirs.

And as these heavens still by degrees arize,
Until they come to their first movers bound,
That in his mightie compasse doth comprize
And carrie all the rest with him around,
So those likewise doe by degrees redound,
And rise more faire, till they at last arive
To the most faire, whereto they all do strive.

Faire is the heaven where happy soules have place,
In full enjoyment of felicitie,
Whence they doe still behold the glorious face
Of the Divine Eternal Majestie;
More faire is that where those Idees on hie
Enraunged be, which Plato so admyred,
And pure Intelligences from God inspyred.

Yet fairer is that heaven in which doe raine
The soveraine Powres and mightie Potentates,
Which in their high protections doe containe
All mortall princes and imperiall states;
And fayrer yet whereas the royall Seates
And heavenly Dominations are set,
From whom all earthly governance is fet.

Yet farre more faire be those bright Cherubins,
Which all with golden wings are overdight,
And those eternal burning Seraphins,
Which from their faces dart out fierie light;
Yet fairer then they both, and much more bright,
Be th' Angels and Archangels, which attend
On Gods owne person, without rest or end.

These thus in faire each other farre excelling,
As to the Highest they approach more neare,
Yet is that Highest farre beyond all telling,
Fairer then all the rest which there appeare,
Though all their beauties joynd together were:
How then can mortall tongue hope to expresse
The image of such endlesse perfectnesse?

Cease then, my tongue, and lend unto my mynd
Leave to bethinke how great that Beautie is,
Whose utmost parts so beautiful I fynd;
How much more those essentiall parts of His,
His truth, his love, his wisedome, and his blis,
His grace, his doome, his mercy, and his might,
By which he lends us of himselfe a sight!

John Henry Cardinal Newman (1801–1890)

Leader of the Anglican Tractarian Movement, Catholic convert, preacher, theologian, poet, and novelist, Cardinal Newman is best known for his autobiographical Apologia pro vita sua *(1864). Here he offers a meditation on God's plenitude and glory.*

God Is All in All

Unus deus et Pater omnium, qui est super omnes, et per omnia, et in omnibus nobis.
One God and Father of all, who is above all, and through all, and in us all.

God alone is in heaven; God is all in all. Eternal Lord, I acknowledge this truth, and I adore Thee in this sovereign and most glorious mystery. There is One God, and He fills Heaven; and all blessed creatures, though they ever remain in their individuality, are, as the very means of their blessedness, absorbed, and (as it were) drowned in the fullness of Him who is *super omnes, et per omnia, et in omnibus*. If ever, through Thy grace, I attain to see Thee in heaven, I shall see nothing else but Thee, because I shall see all whom I see in Thee, and seeing them I shall see Thee. As I cannot see things here below without light, and to see them is to see the rays which come from them, so in that Eternal City *claritas Dei illuminavit eam, et lucerna ejus est Agnus*—the glory of God hath enlightened it, and the Lamb is the lamp thereof. My God, I adore Thee now (at least I will do so to the best of my powers) as the One Sole True Life and Light of the soul, as I shall know and see Thee to be hereafter, if by Thy grace I attain to heaven.

2. Eternal, Incomprehensible God, I believe, and confess, and adore Thee, as being infinitely more wonderful, resourceful, and immense, than this universe which I see. I look into the depths of space, in which the stars are

scattered about, and I understand that I should be millions upon millions of years in creeping along from one end of it to the other, if a bridge were thrown across it. I consider the overpowering variety, richness, intricacy of Thy work; the elements, principles, laws, results which go to make it up. I try to recount the multitudes of kinds of knowledge, of sciences, and of arts of which it can be made the subject. And, I know, I should be ages upon ages in learning everything that is to be learned about this world, supposing me to have the power of learning it at all. And new sciences would come to light, at present unsuspected, as fast as I had mastered the old, and the conclusions of today would be nothing more than starting points of to-morrow. And I see moreover, and the more I examined it, the more I should understand, the marvellous beauty of these works of Thy hands. And so, I might begin again, after this material universe, and find a new world of knowledge, higher and more wonderful, in Thy intellectual creations, Thy angels and other spirits, and men. But all, all that is in these worlds, high and low, are but an atom compared with the grandeur, the height and depth, the glory, on which Thy saints are gazing in their contemplation of Thee. It is the occupation of eternity, ever new, inexhaustible, ineffably ecstatic, the stay and the blessedness of existence, thus to drink in and be dissolved in Thee.

3. My God, it was Thy supreme blessedness in the eternity past, as it is Thy blessedness in all eternities, to know Thyself, as Thou alone canst know Thee. It was by seeing Thyself in Thy Co-equal Son and Thy Coeternal Spirit, and in Their seeing Thee, that Father, Son, and Holy Ghost, Three Persons, One God, was infinitely blessed. O my God, what am I that Thou shouldst make my blessedness to consist in that which is Thy own! That Thou shouldst grant me to have not only the sight of Thee, but to share in Thy very own joy! O prepare me for it, teach me to thirst for it.

IV

The Celestial Court

Introduction

Nowhere do our images of heaven display such contrasting views as in depictions of the celestial court. At its best, the court—those personages dwelling in closest proximity to the divine throne—brightly reflects the splendor and goodness of God. One sees this in the seminal Christian work on the angelic ranks, the notoriously obscure *Celestial Hierarchy* of Pseudo-Dionysius. Here each angel fills its proper place in a "sacred, transcendent order." The seraphim, highest of all, circle endlessly around the divine throne and possess "the ability to hold unveiled and undiminished both the light they have and the illumination they give out." *The Vision of Adamnan* fills in this portrait of a harmonious court, as the saintly abbot of Iona sees God encircled by apostles, patriarchs, and prophets, the Virgin and all the saints, singing in adoration while bands of angels "do perpetual suit and service in the Royal presence." Just as words fail in describing the beatific vision (see chapter 3), so does St. Adamnan insist that "no man is there in this present life who may describe those assemblies, or who may tell of the very manner of them." God's court, no less than God himself, is too august for the poverties of the human tongue and perhaps too remote for human ken.

Still, there is much humanity in heaven. From a Christian perspective, this is accomplished by the presence in heaven of Christ himself, the divine man, and with him all those he has called to the divine presence, preeminently his own mother. In 1950, an important date in the Western understanding of heaven, Pope Pius XII made a matter of official doctrine what was already a widespread belief: that "Mary, the

Virgin Mother of God, was assumed, body and soul, into the glory of heaven." In the Assumption prayer composed by the Pope on that occasion and included here, Mary's exalted state as "the joy and gladness of all the Angels and of all the Saints" is matched by her compassion for suffering humanity, her eagerness to intercede on our behalf. Ineffable in her glory as Queen of Heaven, she is nonetheless completely reachable in her mercy. Thus John Henry Newman writes, "He is the Wisdom of God, she therefore is the Seat of Wisdom; His Presence is Heaven, she therefore is the Gate of Heaven; He is infinite Mercy, she then is the Mother of Mercy."

Not all depictions of the celestial court are so sanguine. Jonathan Swift's comment that "the two maxims of any great man at court are, always to keep his countenance, and never to keep his word" comes to mind. At its worst, the court is a breeding ground for deceit, envy, rebellion, and war. In the *Iliad*, the celestial court of Olympos is dominated by Zeus, who possesses a brooding temper and a wandering eye, yet seems more dignified than many in his retinue, including his hectoring wife, Hera, and the assorted gods and goddesses whose behavior seems at times astonishingly adolescent. In the Bhagavata Purana, a medieval Indian devotional work that blends scripture, myth, and epic, the heavenly climate is downright tumultuous, as the demon Bali and his great army storm and conquer the capital city of the gods. *Paradise Lost*, too, recounts a war in heaven: Satan, cast into the "darkness visible" of Hell, vows "revenge, immortal hate" against the tyranny of Heaven's king.

Although Satan has not prevailed, Western literature continues to envisage scenes of conflict in the heavens, especially when souls of uncertain merit come before the judgment seat and angels and demons must argue the case. For a memorable twist on such contested judgment scenes, we offer Robert Southey and Lord Byron, who make the postmortem judgment of King George the pretext for a poet's war in heaven. Finally, in a recent, curious variation on both our themes—the glory and meanness of the heavenly courtiers—G. K. Chesterton introduces us to a Edwardian English fantasy in which a group of seven police detectives, tracking down the World Anarchist Council, bumble and brave their way into a heavenly court in the midst of modern England. There each man finds his true identity, as each attempts to fathom the mystery of Sunday, a typically outsized and enigmatic Chestertonian hero who bears more than a passing resemblance to God.

Homer

(Eighth Century B.C.?*)*

In this passage from the first book of the Iliad, *Zeus, chief of the gods, quarrels on Mt. Olympos with Thetis, a Nereid, and with Hera, his wife, over the fate of Thetis's son, Achilles.*

But when the twelfth dawn after this day appeared, the gods who
live forever came back to Olympos all in a body
and Zeus led them; nor did Thetis forget the entreaties
of her son, but she emerged from the sea's waves early
in the morning and went up to the tall sky and Olympos.
She found Kronos' broad-browed son apart from the others
sitting upon the highest peak of rugged Olympos.
She came and sat beside him with her left hand embracing
his knees, but took him underneath the chin with her right hand
and spoke in supplication to lord Zeus son of Kronos:
'Father Zeus, if ever before in word or action
I did you favour among the immortals, now grant what I ask for.
Now give honour to my son short-lived beyond all other
mortals. Since even now the lord of men Agamemnon
dishonours him, who has taken away his prize and keeps it.
Zeus of the counsels, lord of Olympos, now do him honour.
So long put strength into the Trojans, until the Achaians
give my son his rights, and his honour is increased among them.'
She spoke thus. But Zeus who gathers the clouds made no answer
but sat in silence a long time. And Thetis, as she had taken
his knees, clung fast to them and urged once more her question:
'Bend your head and promise me to accomplish this thing,

or else refuse it, you have nothing to fear, that I may know
by how much I am the most dishonoured of all gods.'
Deeply disturbed Zeus who gathers the clouds answered her:
'This is a disastrous matter when you set me in conflict
with Hera, and she troubles me with recriminations.
Since even as things are, forever among the immortals
she is at me and speaks of how I help the Trojans in battle.
Even so, go back again now, go away, for fear she
see us. I will look to these things that they be accomplished.
See then, I will bend my head that you may believe me.
For this among the immortal gods is the mightiest witness
I can give, and nothing I do shall be vain nor revocable
nor a thing unfulfilled when I bend my head in assent to it.'
He spoke, the son of Kronos, and nodded his head with the dark brows,
and the immortally anointed hair of the great god
swept from his divine head, and all Olympos was shaken.
So these two who had made their plans separated, and Thetis
leapt down again from shining Olympos into the sea's depth,
but Zeus went back to his own house, and all the gods rose up
from their chairs to greet the coming of their father, not one had courage
to keep his place as the father advanced, but stood up to greet him.
Thus he took his place on the throne; yet Hera was not
ignorant, having seen how he had been plotting counsels
with Thetis the silver-footed, the daughter of the sea's ancient,
and at once she spoke revilingly to Zeus son of Kronos:
'Treacherous one, what god has been plotting counsels with you?
Always it is dear to your heart in my absence to think of
secret things and decide upon them. Never have you patience
frankly to speak forth to me the thing that you purpose.'
Then to her the father of gods and men made answer:
'Hera, do not go on hoping that you will hear all my
thoughts, since these will be too hard for you, though you are my wife.
Any thought that it is right for you to listen to, no one

neither man nor any immortal shall hear it before you.
But anything that apart from the rest of the gods I wish to
plan, do not always question each detail nor probe me.'
Then the goddess the ox-eyed lady Hera answered:
'Majesty, son of Kronos, what sort of thing have you spoken?
Truly too much in time past I have not questioned nor probed you,
but you are entirely free to think out whatever pleases you.
Now, though, I am terrible afraid you were won over
by Thetis the silver-footed, the daughter of the sea's ancient.
For early in the morning she sat beside you and took your
knees, and I think you bowed your head in assent to do honour
to Achilleus, and to destroy many beside the ships of the Achaians.'
Then in return Zeus who gathers the clouds made answer:
'Dear lady, I never escape you, you are always full of suspicion.
Yet thus you can accomplish nothing surely, but be more
distant from my heart than ever, and it will be the worse for you.
If what you say is true, then that is the way I wish it.
But go then, sit down in silence, and do as I tell you,
for fear all the gods, as many as are on Olympos, can do nothing
if I come close and lay my unconquerable hands upon you.'
He spoke, and the goddess the ox-eyed lady Hera was frightened
and went and sat down in silence wrenching her heart to obedience,
and all the Uranian gods in the house of Zeus were troubled.
Hephaistos the renowned smith rose up to speak among them,
to bring comfort to his beloved mother, Hera of the white arms:
'This will be a disastrous matter and not endurable
if you two are to quarrel thus for the sake of mortals
and bring brawling among the gods. There will be no pleasure
in the stately feast at all, since vile things will be uppermost.
And I entreat my mother, though she herself understands it,
to be ingratiating toward our father Zeus, that no longer
our father may scold her and break up the quiet of our feasting.
For if the Olympian who handles the lightning should be minded
to hurl us out of our places, he is far too strong for any.

Do you therefore approach him again with words made gentle,
and at once the Olympian will be gracious again to us.'
He spoke, and springing to his feet put a two-handled goblet
into his mother's hands and spoke again to her once more:
'Have patience, my mother, and endure it, though you be saddened,
for fear that, dear as you are, I see you before my own eyes
struck down, and then sorry though I be I shall not be able
to do anything. It is too hard to fight against the Olympian.
There was a time once before now I was minded to help you,
and he caught me by the foot and threw me from the magic threshold,
and all day long I dropped helpless, and about sunset
I landed in Lemnos, and there was not much life left in me.
After that fall it was the Sintian men who took care of me.'
He spoke, and the goddess of the white arms Hera smiled at him,
and smiling she accepted the goblet out of her son's hand.
Thereafter beginning from the left he poured drinks for the other
gods, dipping up from the mixing bowl the sweet nectar.
But among the blessed immortals uncontrollable laughter
went up as they saw Hephaistos bustling about the palace.
Thus thereafter the whole day long until the sun went under
they feasted, nor was anyone's hunger denied a fair portion,
nor denied the beautifully wrought lyre in the hands of Apollo
nor the antiphonal sweet sound of the Muses singing.
Afterwards when the light of the flaming sun went under
they went away each one to sleep in his home where
for each one the far-renowned strong-handed Hephaistos
had built a house by means of his craftsmanship and cunning.
Zeus the Olympian and lord of the lightning went to
his own bed, where always he lay when sweet sleep came on him.
Going up to the bed he slept and Hera of the gold throne beside him.

Pseudo-Dionysius

(Fifth or Sixth Century)

The Celestial Hierarchy *by this celebrated Christian Neoplatonist remains the classic text on the angelic orders.*

Chapter Six

What is the first rank of the heavenly beings, what is the middle, and what is the last?

How many ranks are there among the heavenly beings? What kind are they? How does each hierarchy achieve perfection?

Only the divine source of their perfection could really answer this, but at least they know what they have by way of power and enlightenment and they know their place in this sacred, transcendent order. As far as we are concerned, it is not possible to know the mystery of these celestial minds or to understand how they arrive at most holy perfection. We can know only what the Deity has mysteriously granted to us through them, for they know their own properties well. I have therefore nothing of my own to say about all this and I am content merely to set down, as well as I can, what it was that the sacred theologians contemplated of the angelic sights and what they shared with us about it.

2. The word of God has provided nine explanatory designations for the heavenly beings, and my own sacred-initiator has divided these into three threefold groups. According to him, the first group is forever around God and is said to be permanently united with him ahead of any of the others and with no intermediary. Here, then, are the most holy "thrones" and the orders said to possess many eyes and many wings, called in Hebrew the "cherubim" and "seraphim." Following the tradition of scripture, he says that they are found immediately around God and in a proximity enjoyed by no other. This threefold group, says my famous teacher, forms a single hierarchy which is truly first and whose members are of equal

status. No other is more like the divine or receives more directly the first enlightenments from the Deity.

The second group, he says, is made up of "authorities," "dominions," and "powers." And the third, at the end of the heavenly hierarchies, is the group of "angels," "archangels," and "principalities."

Chapter Seven

Concerning the seraphim, cherubim, and thrones, and theirs, the first hierarchy.

1. We accept that this is how the holy hierarchies are ordered and we agree that the designations given to these heavenly intelligences signify the mode in which they take on the imprint of God. Those with a knowledge of Hebrew are aware of the fact that the holy name "seraphim" means "fire-makers," that is to say, "carriers of warmth." The name "cherubim" means "fullness of knowledge" or "outpouring of wisdom." This first of the hierarchies is hierarchically ordered by truly superior beings, for this hierarchy possesses the highest order as God's immediate neighbor, being grounded directly around God and receiving the primal theophanies and perfections. Hence the descriptions "carriers of warmth" and "thrones." Hence, also, the title "outpouring of wisdom." These names indicate their similarity to what God is.

For the designation seraphim really teaches this—a perennial circling around the divine things, penetrating warmth, the overflowing heat of a movement which never falters and never fails, a capacity to stamp their own image on subordinates by arousing and uplifting in them too a like flame, the same warmth. It means also the power to purify by means of the lightning flash and the flame. It means the ability to hold unveiled and undiminished both the light they have and the illumination they give out. It means the capacity to push aside and to do away with every obscuring shadow.

The name cherubim signifies the power to know and to see God, to receive the greatest gifts of his light, to contemplate the divine splendor in primordial power, to be filled with the gifts that bring wisdom and to share these generously with subordinates as a part of the beneficent outpouring of wisdom.

The title of the most sublime and exalted thrones conveys that in them there is a transcendence over every earthly defect, as shown by their upward-bearing toward the ultimate heights, that they are forever separated from what is inferior, that they are completely intent upon remaining always and forever in the presence of him who is truly the most high, that, free of all passion and material concern, they are utterly available to receive the divine visitation, that they bear God and are ever open, like servants, to welcome God.

The Vision of Adamnan
(Tenth Century)

In this Irish-Gaelic otherworld vision, Saint Adamnan (c. 628–704), renowned scholar-abbot of Iona, journeys to heaven and visits the realms of bliss, purgation, and punishment.

Noble and wonderful is the Lord of the Elements, and great and marvellous are His might and His power. For He calleth to Himself in Heaven the charitable and merciful, the meek and considerate; but He consigns and casts down to Hell the impious and unprofitable host of the children of the curse. For upon the blessed He bestows the hidden treasures and the manifold wages of Heaven, while He inflicts a diversity of torments, in many kinds, upon the sons of death.

2. Now there are multitudes of the saints and righteous ones of the Lord of Creation, and of the apostles and disciples of Jesus Christ, unto whom have been revealed the secrets and the mysteries of the Heavenly Kingdom, and the golden wages of the righteous; likewise the divers pains of Hell, with them that are set in the midst thereof. For unto the Apostle Peter was shown the four-cornered vessel, let down from Heaven, with four cords to it, and they with sound as sweet as any music. Also, the Apostle Paul was caught up to Heaven, and heard the ineffable words of the angels, and the speech of them that dwell in Heaven. Moreover, on the day of Mary's death, all the apostles were brought to look upon the pains and miserable punishments of the unblest; for the Lord commanded the angels of the West to open up the earth before the face of the apostles, that they might see and consider Hell with all its torments, even as Himself had told them, long time before His Passion.

3. Finally, to Adamnán ua Thinne, the High Scholar of the Western World, were revealed the things which are here recorded; for his soul departed from out his body on the feast of John Baptist, and was conveyed to the celestial realm, where the heavenly angels are, and to Hell,

with its rabble rout. For no sooner had the soul issued from out the body, than there appeared to it the angel that had been its guardian while in the flesh, and bore it away with him to view, firstly, the Kingdom of Heaven.

4. Now the first land to which they come is the Land of Saints. A bright land of fair weather is that country. In it are diverse and wondrous companies, clad in cassocks of white linen, with hoods of radiant white upon their heads. The saints of the Eastern world form a company apart in the East of the Land of Saints; the saints of the Western world are to the West of the same land; the saints of the Northern world and of the South, in their great concourse, are to the South and North. For every one that is in the Land of Saints may freely listen to the music, and may contemplate the vault, wherein are the nine classes of Heaven, after their rank and order.

5. For one spell, then, the saints keep singing marvelous music in praise of God; for another, they are listening to the music of the heavenly host; for the saints have no other need than to listen to the music that they hear, and to contemplate the radiance that they see, and to sate themselves with the fragrance that there is in that land. The wonderful Lord is face to face with them, in the Southeast, and a crystal veil between; to the South is a golden portico, and through it they discern the form and adumbration of the people of Heaven. No veil, however, nor cloud is between the Host of Heaven and the Host of the Saints, but those are ever manifest and present unto these, in a place that is over against them. A circle of fire surrounds this place, yet do they all pass in and out, and it does scathe to none.

6. Now, the Twelve Apostles and Mary the pure Virgin form a band apart, about the mighty Lord. Next to the Apostles are the Patriarchs and Prophets, and the disciples of Jesus. On the other side are holy Virgins, at Mary's right hand, and with no great space between. Babes and striplings are about them on every side, and the bird-choirs of the heavenly folk, making their minstrelsy. And amid these companies, bands of angels, guardians of the souls, do perpetual suit and service in the Royal presence. No man is there in this present life who may describe those assemblies, or who may tell of the very manner of them. And the bands and companies which are in the land of saints abide continually in even such great glory as aforesaid, until the great Parliament of Doom, when the righteous Judge, on the Day of Judgment, shall dispose them in their stations and abiding places, where they shall contemplate God's countenance, with no veil nor shadow between, through ages everlasting.

7. But great and vast as are the splendour and the radiance in the Land of Saints, even as hath been said, more vast, a thousand times, the splendour which is in the region of the Heavenly Host, about the Lord's own throne. This throne is fashioned like unto a canopied chair, and beneath it are four columns of precious stone. Though one should have no minstrelsy at all, save the harmonious music of those four columns, yet would he have his fill of melody and delight. Three stately birds are perched upon that chair, in front of the King, their minds intent upon the Creator throughout all ages, for that is their vocation. They celebrate the eight [canonical] hours, praising and adoring the Lord, and the Archangels accompany them. For the birds and the Archangels lead the music, and then the Heavenly Host, with the Saints and Virgins, make response.

8. Over the head of the Glorious One that sitteth upon the royal throne is a great arch, like unto a wrought helmet, or a regal diadem. and the eye which should behold it would forthwith melt away. Three circles are round about it, separating it from the host, and by no explanation may the nature of them be known. Six thousand thousands, in guise of horses and of birds, surround the fiery chair, which still burns on, without end or term.

9. Now to describe the mighty Lord that is upon that throne is not for any, unless Himself should do so, or should so direct the heavenly dignitaries. For none could tell of his vehemence and might, His glow and splendour, His brightness and loveliness, His liberality and steadfastness, nor of the multitude of His Angels and Archangels, which chant their songs to Him. His messengers keep going to and from Him, ever and anon, with brief messages to each assemblage, telling to the one host of His mildness and mercy, and to the other of His sternness and harshness.

10. Whoso should stand facing about him, East and West, South and North, would behold on each side of him a majestic countenance, seven times as radiant as the sun. No human form thereto, with head or foot, may be discerned, but a fiery mass, burning on for ever, while one and all are filled with awe and trembling before Him. Heaven and earth are filled full with the light of Him, and a radiance as of a royal star encircles Him. Three thousand different songs are chanted by each several choir about Him, and sweeter than all the varied music of the world is each individual song of them.

11. Furthermore, in this wise is in the fashion of that city, wherein that

throne is set. Seven crystal walls of various hue surround it, each wall higher than the wall that is before it. The floor, moreover, and the lowest base of that city, is of fair crystal, with the sun's countenance upon it (?), shot with blue, and purple, and green, and every hue beside.

12. A gentle folk, most mild, most kindly, lacking in no goodly quality, are they that dwell within that city; for none come there, and none abide there ever, save holy youths, and pilgrims zealous for God. But as for their array and ordinance, hard is it to understand how it is contrived, for none turns back nor side to other, but the unspeakable power of God has set, and keeps, them face to face, in ranks and lofty coronels, all round the throne, circling it in brightness and bliss, their faces all towards God.

13. There is a chancel rail of silver between each two choirs, cunningly wrought upon with red gold and silver, and choice rows of precious stones, variegated with diverse gems, and against that lattice are seats and canopies of carbuncle. Between every two chief companies are three precious stones, softly vocal with sweet melody, and the upper halves of them are lighted lamps. Seven thousand angels, as it were great candles, shine and illumine that city round about; seven thousand others in the midst thereof are aflame for ever, throughout the royal city. The men of all the world, if gathered into one place, many as they are, would derive sustenance enough from the sweet savour of any one of those candles.

14. Now, such of the world's inhabitants as attain not to that city after their life is spent, and to whom a dwelling-place therein is allotted after the Words of Doom shall have been spoken, find a restless and unstable habitation, until the coming of Judgment, on heights and hilltops and in marshy places. Even so fare those hordes and companies, with the guardian angel of every soul in their midst, serving and tending them. In the main doorway of the city they are confronted by a veil of fire and a veil of ice, smiting perpetually one against the other. The noise and din of these veils, as they clash together, are heard throughout the world, and the seed of Adam, should they hear that din, would be seized thereat with trembling and intolerable dismay. Faint and dazed are the wicked at that din; howbeit, on the side of the Heavenly Host, nought is heard of that rude discord, save a very little only, and that sweeter than any music.

15. Awful is that city, and wonderful to describe; for a little out of much is that which we have told concerning its various orders, and the wonders of it. Seldom indeed may a spirit, after its converse and co-habitation with

the body, in slumber and repose, in freedom and luxury, win its way to the throne of the Creator, unguided of the angels; for hard of essay are the seven Heavens, nor is any one of them easier than the rest. Six guarded doors confront all those of mortal race who reach the Kingdom. There sits a porter and warder of the Heavenly Host, keeping guard over each door. At the door of that Heaven which is nearest on the hither side sits the Archangel Michael, and with him two youths, with iron rods in their laps to scourge and smite the sinners as they pass through this the first grief and torment of the path they have to tread.

16. At the door of the next Heaven, the Archangel Ariel is warder, and with him two youths, with fiery scourges in their hands, wherewith they scourge the wicked across the face and eyes. A river of fire, its surface an ever-burning flame, lies before that door. Abersetus is the angel's name who keeps watch over that river, and purges the souls of the righteous, and washes them in the stream, according to the amount of guilt that cleaves to them, until they become pure and shining as is the radiance of the stars. Hard by is a pleasant spring, flowery and fragrant, to cleanse and solace the souls of the righteous, though it annoys and scalds the souls of the guilty, and does away nought from them, but it is increase of pain and torment that comes upon them there. Sinners arise from out of it in grief and immeasurable sadness, but the righteous proceed with joy and great delight to the door of the third Heaven.

17. Above this, a fiery furnace keeps ever burning, its flames reaching a height of twelve thousand cubits; through it the righteous pass in the twinkling of an eye, but the souls of sinners are baked and scorched therein for twelve years, and then their guardian angel conveys them to the fourth door. About the entrance door of the fourth Heaven is a fiery stream, like the foregoing. It is surrounded by a wall of fire, in breadth twelve thousand measured cubits, through which the souls of the righteous pass as though it were not there, while the souls of the sinful tarry therein, amid pain and tribulation, for another twelve years, until their guardian angel bears them to the door of the fifth Heaven.

18. In that place is a fiery river, which is unlike all other rivers, for in the midst of it is a strange kind of whirlpool, wherein the souls of the wicked keep turning round and round, and there they abide for the space of sixteen years; the righteous, however, win through it straightway, without any hindrance. So soon as the due time cometh for the sinners to be released thereout, the angel strikes the water with a rod, hard as though

it were of stone, and uplifts the spirits with the end of that rod. Then Michael bears them up to the door of the sixth Heaven; but no pain nor torment is meted out to the spirits at that door, but there they are illumined with the lustre and the brilliancy of precious stones. Then Michael cometh to the Angel of the Trinity, and one on either side they usher the soul into the presence of God.

19. Infinite and beyond all telling is the welcome wherewith the Lord and the Heavenly Host then receive the soul, if he be a pure and righteous soul; if, however, he be an unrighteous and unprofitable soul, harsh and ungentle is the reception of him by the Mighty Lord. For He saith to the Heavenly Angels, 'Take, O Heavenly Angels, this unprofitable soul, and deliver him into the hand of Lucifer, that he may plunge him and utterly extinguish him in Hell's profound, through ages everlasting.'

20. Thereupon that wretched soul is parted, fearfully, sternly, awfully, from sight of the Heavenly Kingdom, and of God's countenance. Then utters he a groan, heavier than any groan, as he comes into the Devil's presence, after beholding the bliss of the Kingdom of Heaven. He is then deprived of the guidance of the Archangels, in whose company he had come unto Heaven. Twelve fiery dragons swallow up every spirit, one after the other, until the lowest dragon lands him in the Devil's maw. There doth he experience the consummation of all evil, in the Devil's own presence, throughout all ages.

Such then are the pains and torments which his guardian angel revealed to the spirit of Adamnán, after his journey towards the Heavenly Kingdom. After which he was borne in the twinkling of an eye through the golden forecourt, and through the crystal veil, to the Land of Saints, whereunto he had been brought at first, after his departure from the body. But when he bethought him to rest and tarry in that land, he heard, through the veil, the angel's voice enjoining him to return again into that body whence he had departed, and to rehearse in courts and assemblies, and in the great congregations of laymen and of clerics, the rewards of Heaven and the pains of Hell, even as his guardian angel had revealed them unto him. . . .

32. This, then, was the doctrine that Adamnán continually taught to the congregations, from that time forth, so long as he remained in life. This, too, is what he preached in the great assemblies of the men of Éire, wherein the Constitution of Adamnán was imposed upon the Gaels, and the women were emancipated by Adamnán and by Finnachta Fledach,

King of Éire, and the princes of Éire, of one accord. Such, too, were the tidings which Patrick, son of Calpurnius, at the Gospel-dawn, was ever wont to proclaim—to wit, the rewards of Heaven and the pains of Hell—to all them that would believe in the Lord, through his teaching, and would accept his guidance of their souls. That, too, is the doctrine most constantly taught by Peter and Paul, and the [other] apostles likewise, to wit, the enumeration of the rewards and pains which had been revealed to them in like manner. And so did Silvester, Abbot of Rome, teach Constantine, son of Helen, High King of the World, in the General Synod when he offered Rome to Paul and to Peter. Even so did Fabian, successor to Peter, teach Philip, son of Gordian, the King of Rome, whereby he believed in the Lord, and many thousands beside believed in that hour. For he was the first King of Rome that believed in the Saviour, Jesus Christ.

33. And these are the tidings which Elias declares continually unto the souls of the righteous, under the Tree of Life, which is in Paradise. So soon as Elias opens his book in order to instruct the spirits, the souls of the righteous, in form of bright white birds, repair to him from every side. Then he tells them, first, of the wages of the righteous, the joys and delights of the Heavenly Realm, and right glad thereat are all the throng. After that he tells them of the pains and torments of Hell, and the woes of Doomsday; and easy it is to mark the look of sorrow that is upon his face, and upon the face of Enoch; and these are the two sorrows of the Heavenly Kingdom. Then Elias shuts his book, and thereupon the birds make exceeding great lamentation, straining their wings against their bodies till streams of blood issue from them, in dismay of the woes of Hell and of the Day of Doom.

34. Now, seeing that they who make this moan are the Saints to whom have been allotted everlasting mansions in the Heavenly Realm, how much more fitting were it for the men that are yet on earth to ponder, even with tears of blood, upon the Judgment Day, and upon the pains of Hell. For at that time will the Lord render due recompense to every one on earth; that is to say, rewards to the righteous, and punishments to the guilty. And at that very time shall the guilty be set in the abyss of everlasting pain, and the book of the Word of God shall then be closed, under the curse of the Judge of Doom, for ever. But the saints and the righteous, the charitable and the merciful, shall be borne to the right hand of God, to a lasting habitation in the Kingdom of Heaven, there to abide without age or death, end or term, for ever and ever.

35. This, then, is the manner of that City: A kingdom without pride, or vanity, or falsehood, or outrage, or deceit, or pretence, or blushing, or shame, or reproach, or insult, or envy, or arrogance, or pestilence, or disease, or poverty, or nakedness, or death, or extinction, or hail, or snow, or wind, or rain, or din, or thunder, or darkness, or cold,—a noble, admirable, ethereal realm, endowed with the wisdom, and radiance, and fragrance of a plenteous land, wherein is the enjoyment of every excellence.

FINIT—AMEN—FINIT.

Bhagavata Purana

A sacred treasury of lore and teaching from South India (probably from the tenth century), this text encompasses the stories of the gods, the nature of the cosmos, the structure of society, and the ways to salvation, all seen in the light of devotion to the supreme beloved one, Lord Krishna. The following narrative concerns an ancient war in heaven. Bali, chief of the asuras *(demons), conquers Indra, chief of the* devas *(gods), and usurps his role as ruler of heaven.*

Book VIII

Chapter XV

Bali Ousts Indra as Ruler of Heaven

Srī Śuka said: Since Bali, defeated and deprived of all his prosperity and life by Indra, had been restored to life by the Bhṛgus, the generous pupil was devoted to them heart and soul, and propitiated them by bestowing on them all that they could desire. The Bhṛgus, eminent Brahmanas, who were pleased with him, consecrated him, according to the Śāstra, by giving him the great bath prescribed for him who would be Indra, since he wished to conquer heaven; and then conducted the Viśvajit sacrifice for him. From the fire in which sacrificial oblations were made, rose a chariot, plated with gold, with horses of the same hue as that of the horses that bear Indra, and a flag adorned with the figure of a lion; also a celestial bow, embellished with gold, two exhaustless quivers, and a celestial armour. His grandfather (Prahlāda) gave him an unfading garland and Śukra a conch. Being thus furnished with battle-equipment secured for him by the Brahmanas, and having got them to pronounce blessings on him, he circumambulated them in all reverence and prostrated himself before them. Then, making his reverence to Prahlāda, he took leave of him; and he, the mighty charioteer, got into the celestial chariot procured for him by the Bhṛgus. Wearing a beautiful garland, clad in armour, armed with bow and sword, and carrying his quivers, he, with his arms adorned with gold armlets, and his fish-shaped ear-pendants flashing, shone in his chariot like fire in the fire-pit. Accompanied by the great Daitya Chieftains, who were equal to him in splendour, strength and opulence, and who looked as if they would drink up the skies and burn the four quarters with their looks, the powerful warrior led a great army against Indra's prosperous capital city, shaking earth and heaven, as it were.

That city was delightful with its sumptuous woods and pleasure-gardens such as Nandana, filled with crooning birds in pairs and drunken bees humming, and with celestial trees whose branches were heavy with the burden of tender shoots, fruit and flower; there were lotus pools there, to which flocked swans, *sāras* cranes, *chakravākas* and *kārandavas*, and in them sported beautiful young women attended by the gods. That city, fashioned by Viśvakarmā, was encircled by the celestial Gangā as by a moat and lofty ramparts of gold blazing like fire, and provided with watch-towers. It had doorways with doors encased in sheeted gold and *gopura* gateways of crystal. Wide and well-aligned thoroughfares, courtyards and assembly halls and roads adorned it. There were numberless mansions in it, and its crossways, paved with brilliants, had raised seats of coral and diamond. Women who, with their eternal youth and beauty, look always like girls of sixteen, and are clad in spotless raiment and adorned with jewels, shine there like tongues of flame. In the streets the wind wafts the perfume of the wreaths of fresh-blown white lilies fallen from the tresses of the celestial damsels. The women, who are the favorites of the gods, walk along streets which are hidden from view by the fragrant, whitish smoke of burning aloes that issues through golden casements. There were to be seen everywhere canopies of pearl, flagstaffs made of gold and encrusted with gems, and balconies adorned with a variety of buntings. It resounded with the cries of peacock and pigeon and the hum of bees and the auspicious and sweet songs of the women in the mansions. It captivated the mind with the booming of *mṛdanga,* the sounds of conch and kettle-drum, the music of *vīnā* and tambourine, *ṛshti,* and flute, and cymbals, the dances with their musical accompaniments, and the singing of the demigods; and it out-dazzled all other luminous objects. That city is never gained by men wedded to unrighteousness or by blackguards, those who are guilty of cruelty to living creatures, or wicked, proud, licentious or avaricious men, while those who are free from such blemishes attain it.

The leader of the (invading) army invested the capital city of the gods with his forces on all sides. And he blew a mighty blare on the conch his preceptor had given him, rousing fear in the hearts of Indra's women. Indra, realizing that this was an all-out effort made by Bali (to oust him), waited on his preceptor, attended by the hosts of the gods, and said to him, 'This is a far more powerful attack than any previous one planned by our old enemy Bali. It seems irresistible to me. How has he become so strong? No one can withstand this attack or lead a counter-attack from anywhere. It has come upon us like the conflagration at the dissolution of the worlds, drinking up with its mouth the ten directions as it were, and smacking its lips, and burning them with its looks. Please tell me how my enemy became so formidable and wherefrom he got the vital and mental energy, physical strength and power, which have enabled him to launch this attack'.

His Guru told him, 'I know, O Maghavā, the cause of your foe's attaining this exalted position. The Bhṛgus, well-versed in the Vedas, have infused into their pupil their own spiritual energy. Neither you nor anyone like you, none in fact except Hari, the Supreme Lord, can make a stand against him, any more than men can stand up to death. Therefore, vacating heaven, you had better go, all of you, into hiding, and bide your time, which will be when the enemy's star sinks. He is benefiting in an ever-increasing degree from the strength of the Brahmanas, and his power is now at its height. It is by treating them with disrespect that he and his supporters will perish'.

Thus advised by their preceptor, who knew what was the proper thing to do at any time, the gods, who could take any form at will, abandoned heaven and went away. When the gods had disappeared, Bali, the son of Virochana, occupied the capital city of the gods and brought the three worlds under his control. The Bhṛgus, who loved their disciple, conducted a hundred horse sacrifices for him, who had conquered all the world. The greatness these sacrifices won for him spread his fame, already known to the three worlds, in all the ten directions, and he shone like the moon. Having realized as it seemed, the summit of his ambition, he enjoyed the affluence secured for him by the Brahmanas.

John Milton

(1608–1674)

Milton was an English poet, theologian, and political pamphleteer. His Paradise Lost, *the paramount English epic, re-creates in blank verse the biblical epic of the Fall. It begins before the creation of the visible heaven and earth, with a war in heaven provoked by Satan's revolt. When Milton wrote* Paradise Lost, *he had already gone blind and had barely escaped criminal prosecution by the Restoration government. The immense energy of Milton's Satan prompted William Blake to write, in* The Marriage of Heaven and Hell, *that "Milton wrote in fetters when he wrote of Angels & God, and at liberty when of Devils & Hell . . . because he was a true Poet and of the Devil's party without knowing it."*

Book 1

The Argument

This First Book proposes, first in brief, the whole subject—Man's disobedience, and the loss thereupon of Paradise, wherein he was placed: then touches the prime cause of his fall—the Serpent, or rather Satan in the Serpent; who, revolting from God, and drawing to his side many legions of Angels, was, by the command of God, driven out of Heaven, with all his crew, into the great Deep. Which action passed over, the Poem hastens into the midst of things; presenting Satan, with his Angels, now fallen into Hell—described here not in the Centre (for heaven and earth may be supposed as yet not made, certainly not yet accursed), but in a place of utter darkness, fitliest called Chaos. Here Satan, with his Angels lying on the burning lake, thunderstruck and astonished, after a certain space recovers, as from confusion; calls up him who, next in order and dignity, lay by him: they confer of their miserable fall. Satan awakens all his legions, who lay till then in the same manner confounded. They rise: their numbers; array of battle; their chief leaders named, according to the idols known afterwards in Canaan and the countries adjoining. To these Satan directs his speech; comforts them with hope yet of regaining Heaven; but tells them, lastly, of a new world and new kind of creature to be created, according to an ancient prophecy, or report, in Heaven—for that Angels were long before this visible creation was the opinion of many ancient Fathers. To find out the truth of this prophecy, and what to determine thereon, he refers to a full council. What his associates thence attempt. Pandemonium, the palace of Satan, rises, suddenly built out of the Deep: the infernal Peers there sit in council.

Of Man's first disobedience, and the fruit
Of that forbidden tree whose mortal taste
Brought death into the World, and all our woe,
With loss of Eden, till one greater Man
Restore us, and regain the blissful seat,
Sing, Heavenly Muse, that, on the secret top
Of Oreb, or of Sinai, didst inspire
That shepherd who first taught the chosen seed
In the beginning how the heavens and earth
Rose out of Chaos: or, if Sion hill
Delight thee more, and Siloa's brook that flowed
Fast by the oracle of God, I thence
Invoke thy aid to my adventurous song,
That with no middle flight intends to soar
Above the Aonian mount, while it pursues
Things unattempted yet in prose or rhyme.
And chiefly Thou, O Spirit, that dost prefer
Before all temples the upright heart and pure,
Instruct me, for Thou know'st; Thou from the first
Wast present, and, with mighty wings outspread,
Dove-like sat'st brooding on the vast Abyss,
And mad'st it pregnant: what in me is dark
Illumine, what is low raise and support;
That, to the highth of this great argument,
I may assert Eternal Providence,
And justify the ways of God to men.
    Say first—for Heaven hides nothing from thy view,
Nor the deep tract of Hell—say first what cause

Moved our grand Parents, in that happy state,
Favored of Heaven so highly, to fall off
From their Creator, and transgress his will
For one restraint, lords of the World besides.
Who first seduced them to that foul revolt?
    The infernal Serpent; he it was whose guile,
Stirred up with envy and revenge, deceived
The mother of mankind, what time his pride
Had cast him out from Heaven, with all his host
Of rebel Angels, by whose aid, aspiring
To set himself in glory above his peers.
He trusted to have equalled the Most High,
If he opposed, and, with ambitious aim
Against the throne and monarchy of God,
Raised impious war in Heaven and battle proud,
With vain attempt. Him the Almighty Power
Hurled headlong flaming from the ethereal sky,
With hideous ruin and combustion, down
To bottomless perdition, there to dwell
In adamantine chains and penal fire,
Who durst defy the Omnipotent to arms.
    Nine times the space that measures day and night
To mortal men, he, with his horrid crew,
Lay vanquished, rolling in the fiery gulf,
Confounded, though immortal. But his doom
Reserved him to more wrath; for now the thought
Both of lost happiness and lasting pain
Torments him: round he throws his baleful eyes,
That witnessed huge affliction and dismay,
Mixed with obdurate pride and steadfast hate.
At once, as far as Angel's ken, he views
The dismal situation waste and wild.
A dungeon horrible, on all sides round,
As one great furnace flamed; yet from those flames
No light; but rather darkness visible
Served only to discover sights of woe,
Regions of sorrow, doleful shades, where peace
And rest can never dwell, hope never comes

That comes to all, but torture without end
Still urges, and a fiery deluge, fed
With ever-burning sulphur unconsumed.
Such place Eternal Justice had prepared
For those rebellious; here their prison ordained
In utter darkness, and their portion set,
As far removed from God and light of Heaven
As from the centre thrice to the utmost pole.
Oh how unlike the place from whence they fell!
There the companions of his fall, o'erwhelmed
With floods and whirlwinds of tempestuous fire,
He soon discerns; and, weltering by his side,
One next himself in power, and next in crime,
Long after known in Palestine, and named
BEËLZEBUB. To whom the Arch-Enemy,
And thence in Heaven called SATAN, with bold words
Breaking the horrid silence, thus began:—
"If thou beest he—but Oh how fallen! how changed
From him!—who, in the happy realms of light,
Clothed with transcendent brightness, didst outshine
Myriads, though bright—if he whom mutual league,
United thoughts and counsels, equal hope
And hazard in the glorious enterprise,
Joined with me once, now misery hath joined
In equal ruin; into what pit thou seest
From what highth fallen: so much the stronger proved
He with his thunder: and till then who knew
The force of those dire arms? Yet not for those,
Nor what the potent Victor in his rage
Can else inflict, do I repent, or change,
Though changed in outward lustre, that fixed mind,
And high disdain from sense of injured merit,
That with the Mightiest raised me to contend,
And to the fierce contention brought along
Innumerable force of Spirits armed,
That durst dislike his reign, and, me preferring,
His utmost power with adverse power opposed
In dubious battle on the plains of Heaven,

And shook his throne. What though the field be lost?
All is not lost—the unconquerable will,
And study of revenge, immortal hate,
And courage never to submit or yield:
And what is else not to be overcome.
That glory never shall his wrath or might
Extort from me. To bow and sue for grace
With suppliant knee, and deify his power
Who, from the terror of this arm, so late
Doubted his empire—that were low indeed;
That were an ignominy and shame beneath
This downfall; since, by fate, the strength of Gods,
And this empyreal substance, cannot fail;
Since, through experience of this great event,
In arms not worse, in foresight much advanced,
We may with more successful hope resolve
To wage by force or guile eternal war,
Irreconcilable to our grand Foe,
Who now triumphs, and in the excess of joy
Sole reigning holds the tyranny of Heaven."

Robert Southey

(1774–1843)

Southey, English poet laureate, biographer, and historian, wrote A Vision of Judgment *(1820), excerpted here, as a stately, and at times pompous, account of heaven and the arrival there of the recently deceased King George III. An upholder of traditional morality, Southey had a long-standing quarrel with the profligate Lord Byron, and in the introduction to* A Vision, *he accuses Byron of belonging to the "Satanic School" of literature. Byron took his revenge with the hilarious parody* The Vision of Judgment *(1821), below.*

Overhead I beheld the infinite ether; beneath us
Lay the solid expanse of the firmament spread like a pavement:
Wheresoever I looked, there was light and glory around me.
Brightest it seemed in the East, where the New Jerusalem glittered.
Eminent on a hill, there stood the Celestial City:
Beaming afar it shone; its towers and cupolas rising
High in the air serene, with the brightness of gold in the furnace,
Where on their breadth the splendor lay intense and quiescent:
Part with a fierier glow, and a short, quick, tremulous motion,
Like the burning pyropus; and turrets and pinnacles sparkled,
Playing in jets of light, with a diamond-like glory coruscant.
Groves of all hues of green their foliage intermingled,
Tempering with grateful shade the else unendurable lustre.
Drawing near, I beheld what over the portal was written.
"This is the Gate of Bliss," it said: "through me is the passage
To the City of God, the abode of beatified Spirits.
Weariness is not there, nor change nor sorrow nor parting;
Time hath no place therein, nor evil. Ye who would enter,
Drink of the Well of Life, and put away all that is earthly."
O'er the adamantine gates an Angel stood on the summit.

"Ho!" he exclaimed, "King George of England cometh to judgment!
Hear, Heaven! Ye Angels, hear! Souls of the Good and the Wicked,
Whom it concerns, attend! Thou, Hell bring forth his accusers!"
As the sonorous summons was uttered, the Winds, who were waiting.
Bore it abroad through Heaven; and Hell in her nethermost caverns,
Heard, and obeyed in dismay.

Anon a body of splendor
Gathered before the gate, and veiled the Ineffable Presence,
Which, with a rushing of wings, came down. The sentient ether
Shook with that dread descent, and the solid firmament trembled.
Round the cloud were the Orders of Heaven.—Archangel and Angel,
Principality, Cherub and Seraph, Thrones, Dominations,
Virtues, and Powers. The Souls of the Good, whom Death hath made perfect,
Flocking on either hand, a multitudinous army,
Came at the awful call. In semicircle inclining,
Tier over tier they took place: aloft, in the distance
Far as the sight could pierce, that glorious company glistened.

George Gordon, Lord Byron

(1788–1824)

The English Romantic poet and social rebel, Byron was renowned for his elegant satirical verse, his brooding charisma, and his libertine moral views. The following excerpt from The Vision of Judgment *(1822), lampoons Southey's* A Vision of Judgment *(above) by describing the arrival of King George III in heaven from a decidedly skeptical point of view.*

I.

Saint Peter sat by the celestial gate:
  His keys were rusty, and the lock was dull,
So little trouble had been given of late;
  Not that the place by any means was full,
But since the Gallic era "eighty-eight"
  The devils had ta'en a longer, stronger pull,
And "a pull altogether," as they say
At sea—which drew most souls another way.

II.

The angels all were singing out of tune,
  And hoarse with having little else to do,
Excepting to wind up the sun and moon,
  Or curb a runaway young star or two,
Or wild colt of a comet, which too soon
  Broke out of bounds o'er the ethereal blue,
Splitting some planet with its playful tail,
As boats are sometimes by a wanton whale.

XVI.

Saint Peter sat by the celestial gate,
  And nodded o'er his keys; when, lo! there came

A wondrous noise he had not heard of late—
    A rushing sound of wind, and stream, and flame;
In short, a roar of things extremely great,
    Which would have made aught save a saint exclaim;
But he, with first a start and then a wink,
Said, "There's another star gone out, I think!"

XVII.

But ere he could return to his repose,
    A cherub flapp'd his right wing o'er his eyes—
At which Saint Peter yawn'd, and rubb'd his nose:
    "Saint porter," said the angel, "prithee rise!"
Waving a goodly wing, which glow'd, as glows
    An earthly peacock's tail, with heavenly dyes:
To which the saint replied, "Well, what's the matter?
"Is Lucifer come back with all this clatter?"

XVIII.

"No," quoth the cherub; "George the Third is dead."
    "And who is George the Third?" replied the apostle:
"What George? what Third?" "The king of England," said
The angel. "Well! he won't find kings to jostle
Him on his way; but does he wear his head?
Because the last we saw here had a tustle,
And ne'er would have got into heaven's good graces,
Had he not flung his head in all our faces.

XIX.

"He was, if I remember, king of France;
    That head of his, which could not keep a crown
On earth, yet ventured in my face to advance
    A claim to those of martyrs—like my own:
If I had had my sword, as I had once
    When I cut ears off, I had cut him down;
But having but my *keys*, and not my brand,
I only knock'd his head from out his hand.

XX.

"And then he set up such a headless howl,
    That all the saints came out and took him in;

And there he sits by St. Paul, cheek by jowl;
That fellow Paul—the parvenù! The skin
Of Saint Bartholomew, which makes his cowl
In heaven, and upon earth redeem'd his sin
So as to make a martyr, never sped
Better than did this weak and wooden head.

XXI.

"But had it come up here upon its shoulders,
There would have been a different tale to tell:
The fellow-feeling in the saints beholders
Seems to have acted on them like a spell;
And so this very foolish head heaven solders
Back on its trunk: it may be very well,
And seems the custom here to overthrow
Whatever has been wisely done below."

XXII.

The angel answer'd, "Peter! do not pout:
The king who comes has head and all entire,
And never knew much what it was about—
He did as doth the puppet—by its wire,
And will be judged like all the rest, no doubt:
My business and your own is not to enquire
Into such matters, but to mind our cue—
Which is to act as we are bid to do."

XXIII.

While thus they spake, the angelic caravan,
Arriving like a rush of mighty wind,
Cleaving the fields of space, as doth the swan
Some silver stream (say Ganges, Nile, or Inde,
Or Thames, or Tweed), and 'midst them an old man
With an old soul, and both extremely blind,
Halted before the gate, and in his shroud
Seated their fellow-traveller on a cloud.

XXIV.

But bringing up the rear of this bright host
A Spirit of a different aspect waved

His wings, like thunder-clouds above some coast
    Whose barren beach with frequent wrecks is paved;
His brow was like the deep when tempest-toss'd;
    Fierce and unfathomable thoughts engraved
Eternal wrath on his immortal face,
And *where* he gazed a gloom pervaded space.

XXV.

As he drew near, he gazed upon the gate
    Ne'er to be enter'd more by him or sin,
With such a glance of supernatural hate,
    As made Saint Peter wish himself within;
He patter'd with his keys at a great rate,
    And sweated through his apostolic skin:
Of course his perspiration was but ichor,
Or some such other spiritual liquor.

XXVI.

The very cherubs huddled all together,
    Like birds when soars the falcon; and they felt
A tingling to the tip of every feather,
    And form'd a circle like Orion's belt
Around their poor old charge; who scarce knew whither
    His guards had led him, though they gently dealt
With royal manes (for by many stories,
And true, we learn the angels all are Tories).

XXVII.

As things were in this posture, the gate flew
    Asunder, and the flashing of its hinges
Flung over space an universal hue
    Of many-colour'd flame, until its tinges
Reach'd even our speck of earth, and made a new
    Aurora borealis spread its fringes
O'er the North Pole; the same seen, when ice-bound,
By Captain Parry's crew, in "Melville's Sound."

XXVIII.

And from the gate thrown open issued beaming
    A beautiful and mighty Thing of Light,

Radiant with glory, like a banner streaming
    Victorious from some world-o'erthrowing fight:
My poor comparisons must needs be teeming
    With earth likenesses, for here the night
Of clay obscures our best conceptions, saving
Johanna Southcote, or Bob Southey raving.

John Henry Cardinal Newman

(1801–1890)

In this discourse "On the Fitness of the Glories of Mary," Newman commends belief in the Virgin Mary's assumption to heaven on the premise that "Nothing is too high for her to whom God owes His human life."

Discourse XVIII.

On the Fitness of the Glories of Mary

Now, as you know, it has been held from the first, and defined from an early age, that Mary is the Mother of God. She is not merely the Mother of our Lord's manhood, or our Lord's body, but she is to be considered the Mother of the Word Himself, the Word incarnate. God, in the person of the Word, the Second Person of the All-glorious Trinity, humbled Himself to become her Son. *Non horruisti Virginis uterum*, as the Church sings, "Thou didst not disdain the Virgin's womb". He took the substance of His human flesh from her, and clothed in it He lay within her; and He bore it about with Him after birth, as a sort of badge and witness that He, though God, was hers. He was nursed and tended by her; He was suckled by her; He lay in her arms. As time went on, He ministered to her, and obeyed her. He lived with her for thirty years, in one house, with an uninterrupted intercourse, and with only the saintly Joseph to share it with Him. She was the witness of His growth, of His joys, of His sorrows, of His prayers; she was blest with His smile, with the touch of His hand, with the whisper of His affection, with the expression of His thoughts and His feelings, for that length of time. Now, my brethren, what ought she to be, what is it *becoming* that she should be, who was so favoured?

Such a question was once asked by a heathen king, when he would place one of his subjects in a dignity becoming the relation in which the latter stood towards him. That subject had saved the king's life, and what was to be done to him in return? The king asked, "What should be done to the man whom the king desireth to honour?" And he received the following answer, "The man whom the king wisheth to honour ought to be clad in the king's apparel, and to be mounted on the king's saddle, and to receive the royal diadem on his head; and let the first among the king's princes and presidents hold his horse, and let him walk through the streets of the city, and say, Thus shall he be honoured, whom the king hath a mind to honour". So stands the case with Mary; she gave birth to the Creator, and what recompense shall be made her? what shall be done to her, who had this relationship to the Most High? what shall be the fit accompaniment of one whom the Almighty has deigned to make, not His servant, not His friend, not His intimate, but His superior, the source of His second being, the nurse of His helpless infancy, the teacher of His opening years? I answer, as the king was answered: Nothing is too high for her to whom God owes His human life; no exuberance of grace, no excess of glory, but is becoming, but is to be expected there, where God has lodged Himself, whence God has issued. Let her "be clad in the king's apparel," that is, let the fulness of the Godhead so flow into her that she may be a figure of the incommunicable sanctity, and beauty, and glory, of God Himself: that she may be the Mirror of Justice, the Mystical Rose, the Tower of Ivory, the House of Gold, the Morning Star. Let her "receive the king's diadem upon her head," as the Queen of heaven, the Mother of all living, the Health of the weak, the Refuge of sinners, the Comforter of the afflicted. And "let the first amongst the king's princes walk before her," let angels and prophets, and apostles, and martyrs, and all saints, kiss the hem of her garment and rejoice under the shadow of her throne. Thus is it that King Solomon has risen up to meet his mother, and bowed himself unto her, and caused a seat to be set for the king's mother, and she sits on his right hand.

We should be prepared then, my brethren, to believe that the Mother of God is full of grace and glory, from the very fitness of such a dispensation, even though we had not been taught it; and this fitness will appear still more clear and certain when we contemplate the subject more steadily. . . .

. . . As regards the Blessed Mary, a further thought suggests itself. She has no chance place in the Divine Dispensation; the Word of God did not merely come to her and go from her; He did not pass through her, as He visits us in Holy Communion. It was no heavenly body which the Eternal

Son assumed, fashioned by the angels, and brought down to this lower world: no; He imbibed, He absorbed into His Divine Person, her blood and the substance of her flesh; by becoming man of her, He received her lineaments and features, as the appropriate character in which He was to manifest Himself to mankind. The child is like the parent, and we may well suppose that by His likeness to her was manifested her relationship to Him. Her sanctity comes, not only of her being His mother, but also of His being her son. "If the first fruit be holy," says St. Paul, "the mass also is holy; if the mass be holy, so are the branches." And hence the titles which we are accustomed to give her. He is the Wisdom of God, she therefore is the Seat of Wisdom; His Presence is Heaven, she therefore is the Gate of Heaven; He is infinite Mercy, she then is the Mother of Mercy. She is the Mother of "fair love and fear, and knowledge and holy hope"; is it wonderful then that she has left behind her in the Church below "an odour like cinnamon and balm, and sweetness like to choice myrrh"?

Such, then, is the truth ever cherished in the deep heart of the Church, and witnessed by the keen apprehension of her children, that no limits but those proper to a creature can be assigned to the sanctity of Mary. . . .

It was surely fitting then, it was becoming, that she should be taken up into heaven and not lie in the grave till Christ's second coming, who had passed a life of sanctity and of miracle such as hers. All the works of God are in a beautiful harmony; they are carried on to the end as they begin. This is the difficulty which men of the world find in believing miracles at all; they think these break the order and consistency of God's visible word, not knowing that they do but subserve a higher order of things, and introduce a supernatural perfection. But at least, my brethren, when one miracle is wrought, it may be expected to draw others after it for the completion of what is begun. Miracles must be wrought for some great end; and if the course of things fell back again into a natural order before its termination, how could we but feel a disappointment? and if we were told that this certainly was to be, how could we but judge the information improbable and difficult to believe? Now this applies to the history of our Lady. I say, it would be a greater miracle if, her life being what it was, her death was like that of other men, than if it were such as to correspond to her life. Who can conceive, my brethren, that God should so repay the debt, which He condescended to owe to His Mother, for the elements of His human body, as to allow the flesh and blood from which it was taken to moulder in the grave? Do the sons of men thus deal with their mothers? do they not nourish and sustain them in their feebleness, and keep them in life while they are able? Or who can conceive that that virginal frame, which never sinned, was to undergo the death of a sinner? Why should she share the curse of Adam, who had no share in his fall? "Dust thou art, and into dust thou shalt return," was the sentence upon sin; she then, who was not a sinner, fitly never saw corruption. She died, then, as we hold, because even our Lord and Saviour died; she died, as she suffered, because she was in this world, because she was in a state of things in which suffering and death are the rule. She lived under their external sway; and, as she obeyed Caesar by coming for enrolment to Bethlehem, so did she, when God willed it, yield to the tyranny of death, and was dissolved into soul and body, as well as others. But though she died as well as others, she died not as others die; for, through the merits of her Son, by whom she was what she was, by the grace of Christ which in her had anticipated sin, which had filled her with light, which had purified her flesh from all defilement, she was also saved from disease and malady, and all that weakens and decays the bodily frame. Original sin had not been found in her, by the wear of her senses, and the waste of her frame, and the decrepitude of years, propagating death. She died, but her death was a mere fact, not an effect; and, when it was over, it ceased to be. She died that she might live, she died as a matter of form or (as I may call it) an observance, in order to fulfil, what is called, the debt of nature,—not primarily for herself or because of sin, but to submit herself to her condition, to glorify God, to do what her Son did; not however as her Son and Saviour, with any suffering for any special end; not with a martyr's death, for her martyrdom had been in living; not as an atonement, for man could not make it, and One had made it, and made it for all; but in order to finish her course, and to receive her crown.

Pope Pius XII

(1876–1958)

Pius XII composed the following prayer to commemorate one of the most important acts of his pontificate, the definition on 1 November 1950 of the dogma of the Virgin Mary's bodily assumption into heaven.

Assumption Prayer

O Immaculate Virgin, Mother of God and Mother of Men.

We believe with all the fervor of our Faith in your triumphal Assumption, both in body and soul, into Heaven, where you are acclaimed as Queen by all the choirs of Angels and all the legions of the Saints; And we unite with them to praise and bless the Lord Who has exalted you above all other pure creatures, and to offer you the tribute of our devotion and our love.

We know that your gaze, which on earth watched over the humble and suffering humanity of Jesus, in Heaven is filled with the vision of that Humanity glorified, and with the vision of uncreated Wisdom, and that the joy of your soul in the direct contemplation of the adorable Trinity causes your heart to throb with overwhelming tenderness;

And we, poor sinners, whose body weighs down the flight of the soul, beg you to purify our hearts so that, while we remain here below, we may learn to see God and God alone in the beauties of His creatures.

We trust that your merciful eyes may deign to glance down upon our miseries and our sorrows; upon our struggles and our weaknesses; that your countenance may smile upon our joys and our victories; that you may hear the voice of Jesus saying to you of each one of us, as He once said to you of His beloved disciple: behold thy son.

And we, who call upon you as our Mother, we like John, take you as the guide, strength and consolation of our mortal life.

We are inspired by the certainty that your eyes, which wept over the earth watered by the blood of Jesus, are yet turned toward this world, held in the clutches of wars, persecutions, oppression of the just and the weak;

And from the shadows of this vale of tears, we seek in your Heavenly assistance and tender mercy comfort for our aching hearts and help in the trials of the Church and of our fatherland.

We believe, finally, that in the glory where you reign, clothed with the sun and crowned with the stars, you are, after Jesus, the joy and gladness of all the Angels and of all the Saints;

And from this earth, over which we tread as pilgrims, comforted by our faith in future resurrection, we look to you, our life, our sweetness and our hope; draw us onward with the sweetness of your voice that one day, after our exile, you may show us Jesus, the Blessed Fruit of your womb, O Clement, O Loving, O Sweet Virgin Mary.

G. K. Chesterton

(1874–1936)

Chesterton was an English journalist, novelist, poet, literary critic, religious essayist, and ebullient aphorist. As this excerpt from The Man Who Was Thursday *(1908) opens, a band of detectives, led by the poet-policeman Syme, cross London in pursuit of a giant balloon that carries the mysterious Sunday, the target of their madcap investigation. Sunday's identity is uncertain. He may be a madman, the president of the Central Anarchist Council, or God himself, about to greet the guests at his celestial court.*

Syme's eyes were still fixed upon the errant orb, which, reddened in the evening light, looked like some rosier and more innocent world.

"Have you noticed an odd thing," he said, "about all your descriptions? Each man of you finds Sunday quite different, yet each man of you can only find one thing to compare him to—the universe itself. Bull finds him like the earth in spring, Gogol like the sun at noonday. The Secretary is reminded of the shapeless protoplasm, and the Inspector of the carelessness of virgin forests. The Professor says he is like a changing landscape. This is queer, but it is queerer still that I also have had my odd notion about the President, and I also find that I think of Sunday as I think of the whole world."

"Get on a little faster, Syme," said Bull; "never mind the balloon."

"When I first saw Sunday," said Syme slowly, "I only saw his back; and when I saw his back, I knew he was the worst man in the world. His neck and shoulders were brutal, like those of some apish god. His head had a stoop that was hardly human, like the stoop of an ox. In fact, I had at once the revolting fancy that this was not a man at all, but a beast dressed up in men's clothes."

"Get on," said Dr. Bull.

"And then the queer thing happened. I had seen his back from the street, as he sat in the balcony. Then I entered the hotel, and coming round the other side of him, saw his face in the sunlight. His face frightened me, as it did every one; but not because it was brutal, not because it was evil. On the contrary, it frightened me because it was so beautiful, because it was so good."

"Syme," exclaimed the Secretary, "are you ill?"

"It was like the face of some ancient archangel, judging justly after heroic wars. There was laughter in the eyes, and in the mouth honour and sorrow. There was the same white hair, the same great, grey-clad shoulders that I had seen from behind. But when I saw him from behind I was certain he was an animal, and when I saw him in front I knew he was a god."

"Pan," said the Professor dreamily, "was a god and an animal."

"Then, and again and always," went on Syme, like a man talking to himself, "that has been for me the mystery of Sunday, and it is also the mystery of the world. When I see the horrible back, I am sure the noble face is but a mask. When I see the face but for an instant, I know the back is only a jest. Bad is so bad, that we cannot but think good an accident; good is so good, that we feel certain that evil could be explained. But the whole came to a kind of crest yesterday when I raced Sunday for the cab, and was just behind him all the way."

"Had you time for thinking then?" asked Ratcliffe.

"Time," replied Syme, "for one outrageous thought. I was suddenly possessed with the idea that the blind, blank back of his head really was his face—an awful, eyeless face staring at me! And I fancied that the figure running in front of me was really a figure running backwards, and dancing as he ran."

"Horrible!" said Dr. Bull, and shuddered.

"Horrible is not the word," said Syme. "It was exactly the worst instant of my life. And yet ten minutes afterwards, when he put his head out of the cab and made a grimace like a gargoyle, I knew that he was only like a father playing hide-and-seek with his children."

"It is a long game," said the Secretary, and frowned at his broken boots.

"Listen to me," cried Syme with extraordinary emphasis. "Shall I tell you the secret of the whole world? It is that we have only known the back of the world. We see everything from behind, and it looks brutal. That is not a tree, but the back of a tree. That is not a cloud, but the back of a cloud. Cannot you see that everything is stooping and hiding a face? If we could only get round in front—"

"Look!" cried out Bull clamorously, "the balloon is coming down!"

There was no need to cry out to Syme, who had never taken his eyes off it. He saw the great luminous globe suddenly stagger in the sky, right itself, and then sink slowly behind the trees like a setting sun.

The man called Gogol, who had hardly spoken through all their weary travels, suddenly threw up his hands like a lost spirit.

"He is dead!" he cried. "And now I know he was my friend—my friend in the dark!"

"Dead!" snorted the Secretary. "You will not find him dead easily. If he has been tipped out of the car, we shall find him rolling as a colt rolls in a field, kicking his legs for fun."

"Clashing his hoofs," said the Professor. "The colts do, and so did Pan."

"Pan again!" said Dr. Bull irritably. "You seem to think Pan is everything."

"So he is," said the Professor, "in Greek. He means everything."

"Don't forget," said the Secretary, looking down, "that he also means Panic."

Syme had stood without hearing any of the exclamations.

"It fell over there," he said shortly. "Let us follow it!"

Then he added with an indescribable gesture—

"Oh, if he has cheated us all by getting killed! It would be like one of his larks."

He strode off towards the distant trees with a new energy, his rags and ribbons fluttering in the wind. The others followed him in a more footsore and dubious manner. And almost at the same moment all six men realised that they were not alone in the little field.

Across the square of turf a tall man was advancing towards them, leaning on a strange long staff like a sceptre. He was clad in a fine but old-fashioned suit with knee-breeches; its colour was that shade between blue, violet and grey which can be seen in certain shadows of the woodland. His hair was whitish grey, and at the first glance, taken along with his knee-breeches, looked as if it was powdered. His advance was very quiet; but for the silver frost upon his head, he might have been one of the shadows of the wood.

"Gentlemen," he said, "my master has a carriage waiting for you in the road just by."

"Who is your master?" asked Syme, standing quite still.

"I was told you knew his name," said the man respectfully.

There was a silence, and then the Secretary said—

"Where is this carriage?"

"It has been waiting only a few moments," said the stranger. "My master has only just come home."

Syme looked left and right upon the patch of green field in which he found himself. The hedges were ordinary hedges, the trees seemed ordinary trees; yet he felt like a man entrapped in fairy-land.

He looked the mysterious ambassador up and down, but he could discover nothing except that the man's coat was the exact colour of the purple shadows, and that the man's face was the exact colour of the red and brown and golden sky.

"Show us the place," Syme said briefly, and without a word the man in the violet coat turned his back and walked towards a gap in the hedge, which let in suddenly the light of a white road.

As the six wanderers broke out upon this thoroughfare, they saw the white road blocked by what looked like a long row of carriages, such a row of carriages as might close the approach to some house in Park Lane. Along the side of these carriages stood a rank of splendid servants, all dressed in the grey-blue uniform, and all having a certain quality of stateliness and freedom which would not commonly belong to the servants of a gentleman, but rather to the officials and ambassadors of a great king. There were no less than six carriages waiting, one for each of the tattered and miserable band. All the attendants (as if in court-dress) wore swords, and as each man crawled into his carriage they drew them, and saluted with a sudden blaze of steel.

"What can it all mean?" asked Bull of Syme as they separated. "Is this another joke of Sunday's?"

"I don't know," said Syme as he sank wearily back in the cushions of his carriage; "but if it is, it's one of the jokes you talk about. It's a good-natured one."

The six adventurers had passed through many adventures, but not one had carried them so utterly off their feet as this last adventure of comfort. They had all become inured to things going roughly; but things suddenly going smoothly swamped them. They could not even feebly imagine what the carriages were; it was enough for them to know that they were carriages, and carriages with cushions. They could not conceive who the old man was who had led them; but it was quite enough that he had certainly led them to the carriages.

Syme drove through a drifting darkness of trees in utter abandonment. It was typical of him that while he had carried his bearded chin forward fiercely so long as anything could be done, when the whole business was taken out of his hands he fell back on the cushions in a frank collapse.

Very gradually and very vaguely he realised into what rich roads the carriage was carrying him. He saw that they passed the stone gates of what might have been a park, that they began gradually to climb a hill which, while wooded on both sides, was somewhat more orderly than a forest. Then there began to grow upon him, as upon a man slowly waking from a healthy sleep, a pleasure in everything. He felt that the hedges were what hedges should be, living walls; that a hedge is like a human army, disciplined, but all the more alive. He saw high elms behind the hedges, and vaguely thought how happy boys would be climbing there. Then his carriage took a turn of the path, and he saw suddenly and quietly, like a long, low, sunset cloud, a long, low house, mellow in the mild light of sunset. All the six friends compared notes afterwards and quarrelled; but they all agreed that in some unaccountable way the place reminded them of their boyhood. It was either this elm-top or that crooked path, it was either this scrap of orchard or that shape of a window; but each man of them declared that he could remember this place before he could remember his mother.

When the carriages eventually rolled up to a large, low, cavernous gateway, another man in the same uniform, but wearing a silver star on the grey breast of his coat, came out to meet them. This impressive person said to the bewildered Syme—

"Refreshments are provided for you in your room."

Syme, under the influence of the same mesmeric sleep of amazement, went up the large oaken stairs after the respectful attendant. He entered a splendid suite of apartments that seemed to be designed specially for him. He walked up to a long mirror with the ordinary instinct of his class, to pull his tie straight or to smooth his hair; and there he saw the frightful figure that he was—blood running down his face from where the bough had struck him, his hair standing out like yellow rags of rank grass, his clothes torn into long, wavering tatters. At once the whole enigma sprang up, simply as the question of how he had got there, and how he was to get out again. Exactly at the same moment a man in blue, who had been appointed as his valet, said very solemnly—

"I have put out your clothes, sir."

"Clothes!" said Syme sardonically. "I have no clothes except these," and he lifted two long strips of his frock-coat in fascinating festoons, and made a movement as if to twirl like a ballet girl.

"My master asks me to say," said the attendant, "that there is a fancy dress ball to-night, and that he desires you to put on the costume that I have laid out. Meanwhile, sir, there is a bottle of Burgundy and some cold pheasant, which he hopes you will not refuse, as it is some hours before supper."

"Cold pheasant is a good thing," said Syme reflectively, "and Burgundy is a spanking good thing. But really I do not want either of them so much as I want to know what the devil all this means, and what sort of costume you have got laid out for me. Where is it?"

The servant lifted off a kind of ottoman a long peacock-blue drapery, rather of the nature of a domino, on the front of which was emblazoned a large golden sun, and which was splashed here and there with flaming stars and crescents.

"You're to be dressed as Thursday, sir," said the valet somewhat affably.

"Dressed as Thursday!" said Syme in meditation. "It doesn't sound a warm costume."

"Oh, yes, sir," said the other eagerly, "the Thursday costume is quite warm, sir. It fastens up to the chin."

"Well, I don't understand anything," said Syme, sighing. "I have been used so long to uncomfortable adventures that comfortable adventures knock me out. Still, I may be allowed to ask why I should be particularly like Thursday in a green frock spotted all over with the sun and moon. Those orbs, I think, shine on other days. I once saw the moon on Tuesday, I remember."

"Beg pardon, sir," said the valet, "Bible also provided for you," and with a respectful and rigid finger he pointed out a passage in the first chapter of Genesis. Syme read it wondering. It was that in which the fourth day of the week is associated with the creation of the sun and moon. Here, however, they reckoned from a Christian Sunday.

"This is getting wilder and wilder," said Syme, as he sat down in a chair. "Who are these people who provide cold pheasant and Burgundy, and green clothes and Bibles? Do they provide everything?"

"Yes, sir, everything," said the attendant gravely. "Shall I help you on with your costume?"

"Oh, hitch the bally thing on!" said Syme impatiently.

But though he affected to despise the mummery, he felt a curious freedom and naturalness in his movements as the blue and gold garment fell about him; and when he found that he had to wear a sword, it stirred a boyish dream. As he passed out of the room he flung the folds across his shoulder with a gesture, his sword stood out at an angle, and he had all the swagger of a troubadour. For these disguises did not disguise, but reveal.

As Syme strode along the corridor he saw the Secretary standing at the top of a great flight of stairs. The man had never looked so noble. He was draped in a long robe of starless black, down the centre of which fell a band or broad stripe of pure white, like a single shaft of light. The whole looked like some very severe ecclesiastical vestment. There was no need for Syme to search his memory or the Bible in order to remember that the first day of creation marked the mere creation of light out of darkness. The vestment itself would alone have suggested the symbol; and Syme felt also how perfectly this pattern of pure white and black expressed the soul of the pale and austere Secretary, with his inhuman veracity and his cold frenzy, which made him so easily make war on the anarchists, and yet so easily pass for one of them. Syme was scarcely surprised to notice that, amid all the ease and hospitality of their new surroundings, this man's eyes were still stern. No smell of ale or orchards could make the Secretary cease to ask a reasonable question.

If Syme had been able to see himself, he would have realised that he, too, seemed to be for the first time himself and no one else. For if the Secretary stood for that philosopher who loves the original and formless light, Syme was a type of the poet who seeks always to make the light in special shapes, to split it up into sun and star. The philosopher may sometimes love the infinite; the poet always loves the finite. For him the great moment is not the creation of light, but the creation of the sun and moon.

As they descended the broad stairs together they overtook Ratcliffe, who was clad in spring green like a huntsman, and the pattern upon whose garment was a green tangle of trees. For he stood for that third day on which the earth and green things were made, and his square, sensible face, with its not unfriendly cynicism, seemed appropriate enough to it.

They were led out of another broad and low gateway into a very large old English garden, full of torches and bonfires, by the broken light of which a vast carnival of people were dancing in motley dress. Syme seemed to see every shape in Nature imitated in some crazy costume.

There was a man dressed as a windmill with enormous sails, a man dressed as an elephant, a man dressed as a balloon; the two last, together, seemed to keep the thread of their farcical adventures. Syme even saw, with a queer thrill, one dancer dressed like an enormous hornbill, with a beak twice as big as himself—the queer bird which had fixed itself on his fancy like a living question while he was rushing down the long road at the Zoological Gardens. There were a thousand other such objects, however. There was a dancing lamp-post, a dancing apple tree, a dancing ship. One would have thought that the untamable tune of some mad musician had set all the common objects of field and street dancing an eternal jig. And long afterwards, when Syme was middle-aged and at rest, he could never see one of those particular objects—a lamp-post, or an apple tree, or a windmill—without thinking that it was a strayed reveller from that revel of masquerade.

On one side of this lawn, alive with dancers, was a sort of green bank, like the terrace in such old-fashioned gardens.

Along this, in a kind of crescent, stood seven great chairs, the thrones of the seven days. Gogol and Dr. Bull were already in their seats; the Professor was just mounting to his. Gogol, or Tuesday, had his simplicity well symbolised by a dress designed upon the division of the waters, a dress that separated upon his forehead and fell to his feet, grey and silver, like a sheet of rain. The Professor, whose day was that on which the birds and fishes—the ruder forms of life—were created, had a dress of dim purple, over which sprawled goggle-eyed fishes and outrageous tropical birds, the union in him of unfathomable fancy and of doubt. Dr. Bull, the last day of Creation, wore a coat covered with heraldic animals in red and gold, and on his crest a man rampant. He lay back in this chair with a broad smile, the picture of an optimist in his element.

One by one the wanderers ascended the bank and sat in their strange seats. As each of them sat down a roar of enthusiasm rose from the carnival, such as that with which crowds receive kings. Cups were clashed and torches shaken, and feathered hats flung in the air. The men for whom these thrones were reserved were men crowned with some extraordinary laurels. But the central chair was empty.

Syme was on the left hand of it and the Secretary on the right. The Secretary looked across the empty throne at Syme, and said, compressing his lips—

"We do not know yet that he is not dead in a field."

Almost as Syme heard the words, he saw on the sea of human faces in front of him a frightful and beautiful alternation, as if heaven had opened behind his head. But Sunday had only passed silently along the front like a shadow, and had sat in the central seat. He was draped plainly, in a pure and terrible white, and his hair was like a silver flame on his forehead.

For a long time—it seemed for hours—that huge masquerade of mankind swayed and stamped in front of them to marching and exultant music. Every couple dancing seemed a separate romance; it might be a fairy dancing with a pillar-box, or a peasant girl dancing with the moon; but in each case it was, somehow, as absurd as Alice in Wonderland, yet as grave and kind as a love story. At last, however, the thick crowd began to thin itself. Couples strolled away into the garden-walks, or began to drift towards that end of the building where stood smoking, in huge pots like fish-kettles, some hot and scented mixtures of old ale or wine. Above all these, upon a sort of black framework on the roof of the house, roared in its iron basket a gigantic bonfire, which lit up the land for miles. It flung the homely effect of firelight over the face of vast forests of grey or brown, and it seemed to fill with warmth even the emptiness of upper night. Yet this also, after a time, was allowed to grow fainter; the dim groups gathered more and more round the great cauldrons, or passed, laughing and clattering, into the inner passages of that ancient house. Soon there were only some ten loiterers in the garden; soon only four. Finally the last stray merry-maker ran into the house whooping to his companions. The fire faded, and the slow, strong stars came out. And the seven strange men were left along, like seven stone statues on their chairs of stone. Not one of them had spoken a word.

They seemed in no haste to do so, but heard in silence the hum of insects and the distant song of one bird. Then Sunday spoke, but so dreamily that he might have been continuing a conversation rather than beginning one.

"We will eat and drink later," he said. "Let us remain together a little, we who have loved each other so sadly, and have fought so long. I seem to remember only centuries of heroic war, in which you were always heroes—epic on epic, iliad on iliad, and you always brothers in arms. Whether it was but recently (for time is nothing), or at the beginning of the world, I sent you out to war. I sat in the darkness, where there is not any created thing, and to you I was only a voice commanding valour and an unnatural virtue. You heard the voice in the dark, and you never heard it again. The sun in heaven denied it, the earth and sky denied it, all human wisdom denied it. And when I met you in the daylight I denied it myself."

Syme stirred sharply in his seat, but otherwise there was silence, and the incomprehensible went on.

"But you were men. You did not forget your secret honour, though the whole cosmos turned an engine of torture to tear it out of you. I knew how near you were to hell. I know how you, Thursday, crossed swords with King Satan, and how you, Wednesday, named me in the hour without hope."

There was complete silence in the starlit garden, and then the black-browed Secretary, implacable, turned in his chair towards Sunday, and said in a harsh voice—

"Who and what are you?"

"I am the Sabbath," said the other without moving. "I am the peace of God."

The Secretary started up, and stood crushing his costly robe in his hand.

"I know what you mean," he cried, "and it is exactly that that I cannot forgive you. I know you are contentment, optimism, what do they call the thing, an ultimate reconciliation. Well, I am not reconciled. If you were the man in the dark room, why were you also Sunday, an offence to the sunlight? If you were from the first our father and our friend, why were you also our greatest enemy? We wept, we fled in terror; the iron entered into our souls—and you are the peace of God! Oh, I can forgive God His anger, though it destroyed nations; but I cannot forgive Him His peace."

Sunday answered not a word, but very slowly he turned his face of stone upon Syme as if asking a question.

"No," said Syme, "I do not feel fierce like that. I am grateful to you, not only for wine and hospitality here, but for many a fine scamper and free fight. But I should like to know. My soul and heart are as happy and quiet here as this old garden, but my reason is still crying out. I should like to know."

Sunday looked at Ratcliffe, whose clear voice said—

"It seems so *silly* that you should have been on both sides and fought yourself."

Bull said—

"I understand nothing, but I am happy. In fact, I am going to sleep."

"I am not happy," said the Professor with his head in his hands, "because I do not understand. You let me stray a little too near to hell."

And then Gogol said, with the absolute simplicity of a child—

"I wish I know why I was hurt so much."

Still Sunday said nothing, but only sat with his mighty chin upon his hand, and gazed at the distance. Then at last he said—

"I have heard your complaints in order. And here, I think, comes another to complain, and we will hear him also."

The falling fire in the great cresset threw a last long gleam, like a bar of burning gold, across the dim grass. Against this fiery band was outlined in utter black the advancing legs of a black-clad figure. He seemed to have a fine close suit with knee-breeches such as that which was worn by the servants of the house, only that it was not blue, but of this absolute sable. He had, like the servants, a kind of sword by his side. It was only when he had come quite close to the crescent of the seven and flung up his face to look at them, that Syme saw, with thunderstruck clearness, that the face was the broad, almost ape-like face of his old friend Gregory, with its rank red hair and its insulting smile.

"Gregory!" gasped Syme, half-rising from his seat. "Why, this is the real anarchist!"

"Yes," said Gregory, with a great and dangerous restraint, "I am the real anarchist."

"'And there came a day,'" murmured Bill, who seemed really to have fallen asleep, "'when the sons of God came before the Lord, and Satan also came with them.'"

"You are right," said Gregory, and gazed all round. "I am a destroyer. I would destroy the world if I could."

A sense of pathos far under the earth stirred up in Syme, and he spoke brokenly and without sequence.

"Oh, most unhappy man," he cried, "try to be happy! You have red hair like your sister."

"My red hair, like red flames, shall burn up the world," said Gregory. "I thought I hated everything more than common men can hate anything; but I find that I do not hate everything so much as I hate you!"

"I never hated you," said Syme very sadly.

Then out of this unintelligible creature the last thunders broke.

"You!" he cried. "You never hated because you never lived. I know what you are all of you, from first to last—you are the people in power! You are the police—the great, fat, smiling men in blue and buttons! You are the Law, and you have never been broken. But is there a free soul alive that does not long to break you, only because you have never been broken? We in revolt talk all kind of nonsense doubtless about this crime or that crime of the Government. It is all folly! The only crime of the Government is that it governs. The unpardonable sin of the supreme power is that it is supreme. I do not curse you for being cruel. I do not curse you (though I might) for being kind. I curse you for being safe! You sit in your chairs of stone, and have never come down from them. You are the seven angels of heaven, and you have had no troubles. Oh, I could forgive you everything, you that rule all mankind, if I could feel for once that you had suffered for one hour a real agony such as I——"

Syme sprang to his feet, shaking from head to foot.

"I see everything," he cried, "everything that there is. Why does each thing on the earth war against each other thing? Why does each small thing in the world have to fight against the world itself? Why does a fly have to fight the whole universe? Why does a dandelion have to fight the whole universe? For the same reason that I had to be alone in the dreadful Council of the Days. So that each thing that obeys law may have the glory and isolation of the anarchist. So that each man fighting for order may be as brave and good a man as the dynamiter. So that the real lie of Satan may be flung back in the face of this blasphemer, so that by tears and torture we may earn the right to say to this man, 'You lie!' No agonies can be too great to buy the right to say to this accuser, 'We also have suffered.'

"It is not true that we have never been broken. We have been broken upon the wheel. It is not true that we have never descended from these thrones. We have descended into hell. We were complaining of unforgettable miseries even at the very moment when this man entered insolently to accuse us of happiness. I repel the slander; we have not been happy. I can answer for every one of the great guards of Law whom he has accused. At least——"

He had turned his eyes so as to see suddenly the great face of Sunday, which wore a strange smile.

"Have you," he cried in a dreadful voice, "have you ever suffered?"

As he gazed, the great face grew to an awful size, grew larger than the colossal mask of Memnon, which had made him scream as a child. It grew larger and larger, filling the whole sky; then everything went black. Only in the blackness before it entirely destroyed his brain he seemed to hear a distant voice saying a commonplace text that he had heard somewhere, "Can ye drink of the cup that I drink of?"

V

Heavenly Society

Introduction

In chapter 5, we move beyond the immediate precincts of the divine throne to explore the far-flung social life of the heavenly kingdom. The tone of the material changes dramatically, from solemn to satirical, from rhapsodic to matter-of-fact. As attention shifts from God to his creatures, heaven takes on a new role as a foil for human foibles.

The champion of this material, appropriately, is the great American humorist Mark Twain. He relishes the problems intrinsic to heaven: How does one handle crowd control for billions of spirits, assembled not only from earth but from myriad other celestial worlds? How do the recently deceased adapt to having wings? (It turns out that wings, harp, and halo are a uniform worn only on ceremonial occasions.) Is the social hierarchy of heaven the same as that on earth? (Not in the least; in heaven, "Shakespeare and the rest have to walk behind a common tailor from Tennessee, by the name of Billings.")

Twain's narrator, a wizened sea captain brimming with Yankee common sense, retains the nineteenth century's interest in the traditional inhabitants of heaven: patriarchs and prophets, angels and archangels. By the time we arrive at the end of the twentieth century and the satire of Julian Barnes, all that is swept away and the narrator becomes a middle-class hedonist who asks nothing more of heaven than great shopping, sex, and golf. He finds all three and then wonders what happened to the old-fashioned heaven, the one with God and angelic choirs. "Heaven is democratic these days," he is told. "We don't impose Heaven on people anymore." Instead, people "get the sort of Heaven they want."

Emanuel Swedenborg brings to his study of heaven the mind and training of an accomplished scientist. He approaches heaven as an anthropologist might. Indeed, by his own account, he has made numerous field trips into the celestial realm. Heaven has a structure that can be scrutinized and catalogued down to the most intricate details. The stuff of high fantasy—for example, the clothing, speech, and pastimes of angels—receives sober, minute analysis. Everything on earth has a heavenly counterpart; thus angels live in houses much like our own, with parlors and bedrooms, only "more beautiful." This is, perhaps, not so different from Barnes's account of how the things of heaven are the things of earth exquisitely improved: "Now, you know what a grapefruit's like: the way it spurts juice down your shirt and keeps slipping out of your hand. . . . Now let me tell you about *this* grapefruit. Its flesh was pink for a start, not yellow, and each segment had already been carefully freed from its clinging membrane." One finds the same literalness in Sir Arthur Conan Doyle's fictional account of spiritualist rescue circles in England in the 1920s. Heaven has seven spheres; the highest is home for "the Christs"; the third is Summerland, "the first really happy sphere"; the lowest—the subject of our excerpt—is the abode of confused or angry spirits, many of whom are not even aware that they are dead.

A third approach to heavenly society comes from Hildegard of Bingen, who celebrates the lyricism of heaven, relating the delights of the virgins in an incantatory style reminiscent of her musical compositions. There is no hint of satire in these passages, nor of labored exactitude; heaven is a realm where serene contemplation and easy sociability combine.

A new element appears in this chapter: the traffic between heaven and earth becomes two-way. We include four accounts, from Christian, Jewish, and Islamic sources, of celestial intercession in earthly affairs. These accounts range from Sufi poetry to medieval legend to late nineteenth-century vision. They accord in suggesting that the saints of heaven have their eyes on human beings as well as on God, and that in their love and concern for us, they are willing to quit their bright, heavenly stations and make the return trip down to the shadowy lands of earth.

Mark Twain

(1835–1910)

Twain—the American humorist, pseudonym of Samuel Langhorne Clemens—wrote Extract from Captain Stormfield's Visit to Heaven *as a riposte to Elizabeth Stuart Phelps's phenomenally popular* The Gates Ajar *(see chapter 2, above). The title character, thirty years dead and zooming around space at "a million miles a minute," spots "a tremendous long row of blinking lights away on the horizon ahead." The lights turn out to be heaven's portals; Stormfield enters one, and his madcap adventures begin.*

II

I had been having considerable trouble with my wings. The day after I helped the choir I made a dash or two with them, but was not lucky. First off, I flew thirty yards, and then fouled an Irishman and brought him down—brought us both down, in fact. Next, I had a collision with a Bishop—and bowled him down, of course. We had some sharp words, and I felt pretty cheap, to come banging into a grave old person like that, with a million strangers looking on and smiling to themselves.

I saw I hadn't got the hang of the steering, and so couldn't rightly tell where I was going to bring up when I started. I went afoot the rest of the day, and let my wings hang. Early next morning I went to a private place to have some practice. I got up on a pretty high rock, and got a good start, and went swooping down, aiming for a bush a little over three hundred yards off; but I couldn't seem to calculate for the wind, which was about two points abaft my beam. I could see I was going considerable to looard of the bush, so I worked my starboard wing slow and went ahead strong on the port one, but it wouldn't answer; I could see I was going to broach to, so I slowed down on both, and lit. I went back to the rock and took another chance at it. I aimed two or three points to starboard of the bush—yes, more than that—enough so as to make it nearly a head-wind. I done well enough, but made pretty poor time. I could see, plain enough, that on a head-wind, wings was a mistake. I could see that a body could sail pretty close to the wind, but he couldn't go in the wind's eye. I could see that if I wanted to go a-visiting any distance from home, and the wind was ahead, I might have to wait days, maybe, for a change; and I could see, too, that these things could not be any use at all in a gale; if you tried to run before the wind, you would make a mess of it, for there isn't any way to shorten sail—like reefing, you know—you have to take it *all* in—shut your feathers down flat to your sides. That would *land* you, of course. You could lay to, with your head to the wind—that is the best you could do, and right hard work you'd find it, too. If you tried any other game, you would founder, sure.

I judge it was about a couple of weeks or so after this that I dropped old Sandy McWilliams a note one day—it was a Tuesday—and asked him to come over and take his manna and quails with me next day; and the first thing he did when he stepped in was to twinkle his eye in a sly way, and say,—

"Well, Cap, what you done with your wings?"

I saw in a minute that there was some sarcasm done up in that rag somewhere, but I never let on. I only says,—

"Gone to the wash."

"Yes," he says, in a dry sort of way, "they mostly go to the wash—about this time—I've often noticed it. Fresh angels are powerful neat. When do you look for 'em back?"

"Day after to-morrow," says I.

He winked at me, and smiled.

Says I,—

"Sandy, out with it. Come—no secrets among friends. I notice you don't ever wear wings—and plenty others don't. I've been making an ass of myself—is that it?"

"That is about the size of it. But it is no harm. We all do it at first. It's perfectly natural. You see, on earth we jump to such foolish conclusions as to things up here. In the pictures we always saw the angels with wings on—and that was all right; but we jumped to the conclusion that that was their way of getting around—and that was all wrong. The wings ain't anything but a uniform, that's all. When they are in the field—so to speak,—they always wear them; you never see an angel going with a message anywhere without his wings, any more than you would see a military officer presiding at a courtmartial without his uniform, or a postman delivering letters, or a policeman walking his beat, in plain clothes. But they ain't to *fly* with! The wings are for show, not for use. Old experienced angels are like officers of the regular army—they dress plain, when they are off duty. New angels are like the militia—never shed the uniform—always fluttering and floundering around in their wings, butting people down, flapping here, and there, and everywhere, always imagining they are attracting the admiring eye—well, they just think they are the very most important people in heaven. And when you see one of them come sailing around with one wing tipped up and t'other down, you make up your mind he is saying to himself: 'I wish Mary Ann in Arkansaw could see me now. I reckon she'd wish she hadn't shook me.' No, they're just for show, that's all—only just for show."

"I judge you've got it about right, Sandy," says I.

"Why, look at it yourself," says he. "*You* ain't built for wings—no man is. You know what a grist of years it took you to come here from the earth—and yet you were booming along faster than any cannon-ball could go. Suppose you had to fly that distance with your wings—wouldn't eternity have been over before you got here? Certainly. Well, angels have to go to the earth every day—millions of them—to appear in visions to dying children and good people, you know—it's the heft of their business. They appear with their wings, of course, because they are on official service, and because the dying persons wouldn't know they were angels if they hadn't wings—but do you reckon they fly with them? It stands to reason they don't. The wings would wear out before they got half-way; even the pin-feathers would be gone; the wing frames would be as bare as kite sticks before the paper is pasted on. The distances in heaven are billions of times greater; angels have to go all over heaven every day; could they do it with their wings alone? No, indeed; they wear the wings for style, but they travel any distance in an instant by *wishing*. The wishing-carpet of the Arabian Nights was a sensible idea—but our earthly idea of angels flying these awful distances with their clumsy wings was foolish.

"Our young saints, of both sexes, wear wings all the time—blazing red ones, and blue and green, and gold, and variegated, and rainbowed, and ring-streaked-and-striped ones—and nobody finds fault. It is suitable to their time of life. The things are beautiful, and they set the young people off. They are the most striking and lovely part of their outfit—a halo don't *begin*."

"Well," says I, "I've tucked mine away in the cupboard, and I allow to let them lay there till there's mud."

"Yes—or a reception."

"What's that?"

"Well, you can see one to-night if you want to. There's a barkeeper from Jersey City going to be received."

"Go on—tell me about it."

"This barkeeper got converted at a Moody and Sankey meeting, in New York, and started home on the ferryboat, and there was a collision and he got drowned. He is of a class that think all heaven goes wild with joy when a particularly hard lot like him is saved; they think all heaven turns out hosannahing to welcome them; they think there isn't anything talked about in the realms of the blest but their case, for that day. This barkeeper thinks there hasn't been such another stir here in years, as his coming is going to raise.—And I've always noticed this peculiarity about a dead barkeeper—he not only expects all hands to turn out when he arrives, but he expects to be received with a torchlight procession."

"I reckon he is disappointed, then."

"No, he isn't. No man is allowed to be disappointed here. Whatever he wants, when he comes—that is, any reasonable and unsacrilegious thing—he can have. There's always a few millions or billions of young folks around who don't want any better entertainment than to fill up their lungs and swarm out with their torches and have a high time over a barkeeper. It tickles the barkeeper till he can't rest, it makes a charming lark for the young folks, it don't do anybody any harm, it don't cost a rap, and it keeps up the place's reputation for making all comers happy and content."

"Very good. I'll be on hand and see them land the barkeeper."

"It is manners to go in full dress. You want to wear your wings, you know, and your other things."

"Which ones?"

"Halo, and harp, and palm branch, and all that."

"Well," says I, "I reckon I ought to be ashamed of myself, but the fact is I left them laying around that day I resigned from the choir. I haven't got a rag to wear but this robe and the wings."

"That's all right. You'll find they've been raked up and saved for you. Send for them."

"I'll do it, Sandy. But what was it you was saying about unsacrilegious things, which people expect to get, and will be disappointed about?"

"Oh, there are a lot of such things that people expect and don't get. For instance, there's a Brooklyn preacher by the name of Talmage, who is laying up a considerable disappointment for himself. He says, every now and then in his sermons, that the first thing he does when he gets to heaven, will be to fling his arms around Abraham, Isaac and Jacob, and kiss them and weep on them. There's millions of people down there on earth that are promising themselves the same thing. As many as sixty thousand people arrive here every single day, that want to run straight to Abraham, Isaac and Jacob, and hug them and weep on them. Now mind you, sixty thousand a day is a pretty heavy contract for those old people. If they were a mind to allow it, they wouldn't ever have anything to do, year in and year out, but stand up and be hugged and wept on thirty-two hours in the twenty-four. They would be tired out and as wet as muskrats all the time. What would heaven be, to *them?* It would be a mighty good place to get out of—you know that, yourself. Those are kind and gentle old Jews, but they ain't any fonder of kissing the emotional highlights of Brooklyn than you be. You mark my words, Mr. T.'s endearments are going to be declined, with thanks. There are limits to the privileges of the elect, even in heaven. Why, if Adam was to show himself to every new comer that wants to call and gaze at him and strike him for his autograph, he would never have time to do anything else but just that. Talmage has said he is going to give Adam some of his attentions, as well as A., I. and J. But he will have to change his mind about that."

"Do you think Talmage will really come here?"

"Why, certainly, he will; but don't you be alarmed; he will run with his own kind, and there's plenty of them. That is the main charm of heaven—there's all kinds here—which wouldn't be the case if you let the preachers tell it. Anybody can find the sort he prefers, here, and he just lets the others alone, and they let him alone. When the Deity builds a heaven, it is built right, and on a liberal plan."

Sandy sent home for his things, and I sent for mine, and about nine in the evening we begun to dress. Sandy says,—

"This is going to be a grand time for you, Stormy. Like as not some of the patriarchs will turn out."

"No, but will they?"

"Like as not. Of course they are pretty exclusive. They hardly ever show themselves to the common public. I believe they never turn out except for an eleventh-hour convert. They wouldn't do it then, only earthly tradition makes a grand show pretty necessary on that kind of an occasion."

"Do they all turn out, Sandy?"

"Who?—all the patriarchs? Oh, no—hardly ever more than a couple. You will be here fifty thousand years—maybe more—before you get a glimpse of all the patriarchs and prophets. Since I have been here, Job has been to the front once, and once Ham and Jeremiah both at the same time. But the finest thing that has happened in my day was a year or so ago; that was Charles Peace's reception—him they called 'the Bannercross Murderer'—an Englishman. There were four patriarchs and two prophets on the Grand Stand that time—there hasn't been anything like it since Captain Kidd came; Abel was there—the first time in twelve hundred years. A report got around that Adam was coming; well, of course, Abel was enough to bring a crowd, all by himself, but there is nobody that can draw like Adam. It was a false report, but it got around, anyway, as I say, and it will be a long day before I see the like of it again. The reception was in the English department, of course, which is eight hundred and eleven million miles from the New Jersey line. I went, along with a good many of my neighbors, and it was a sight to see, I can tell you. Flocks came from all the departments. I saw Esquimaux there, and Tartars, negroes, Chinamen—people from everywhere. You see a mixture like that in the Grand Choir, the first day you land here, but you hardly ever see it again. There were billions of people; when they were singing or hosannahing, the noise was wonderful; and even when their tongues were still the drumming of the wings was nearly enough to burst your head, for all the sky was as thick as if it was snowing angels. Although Adam was not there, it was a great time anyway, because we had three archangels on the Grand Stand—it is a seldom thing that even one comes out."

"What did they look like, Sandy?"

"Well, they had shining faces, and shining robes, and wonderful rainbow wings, and they stood eighteen feet high, and wore swords, and held their heads up in a noble way, and looked like soldiers."

"Did they have halos?"

"No—anyway, not the hoop kind. The archangels and the upper-class patriarchs wear a finer thing than that. It is a round, solid, splendid glory of gold, that is blinding to look at. You have often seen a patriarch in a picture, on earth, with that thing on—you remember it?—he looks as if he had his head in a brass platter. That don't give you the right idea of it at all—it is much more shining and beautiful."

"Did you talk with those archangels and patriarchs, Sandy?"

"Who—I? Why, what can you be thinking about, Stormy? I ain't worthy to speak to such as they."

"Is Talmage?"

"Of course not. You have got the same mixed-up idea about these things that everybody has down there. I had it once, but I got over it. Down there they talk of the heavenly King—and that is right—but then they go right on speaking as if this was a republic and everybody was on a dead level with everybody else, and privileged to fling his arms around anybody he comes across, and be hail-fellow-well-met with all the elect, from the highest down. How tangled up and absurd that is! How are you going to have a republic under a king? How are you going to have a republic at all, where the head of the government is absolute, holds his place forever, and has no parliament, no council to meddle or make in his affairs, nobody voted for, nobody elected, nobody in the whole universe with a voice in the government, nobody asked to take a hand in its matters, and nobody *allowed* to do it? Fine republic, ain't it?"

"Well, yes—it *is* a little different from the idea I had—but I thought I might go around and get acquainted with the grandees, anyway—not exactly splice the main-brace with them, you know, but shake hands and pass the time of day."

"Could Tom, Dick and Harry call on the Cabinet of Russia and do that?—on Prince Gortschakoff, for instance?"

"I reckon not, Sandy."

"Well, this is Russia—only more so. There's not the shadow of a republic about it anywhere. There are ranks, here. There are viceroys, princes, governors, sub-governors, sub-sub-governors, and a hundred orders of nobility, grading along down from grand-ducal archangels, stage by stage, till the general level is struck, where there ain't any titles. Do you know what a prince of the blood is, on earth?"

"No."

"Well, a prince of the blood don't belong to the royal family exactly, and he don't belong to the mere nobility of the kingdom; he is lower than the one, and higher than t'other. That's about the position of the patriarchs and prophets here. There's some mighty high nobility here—people that you and I ain't worthy to polish sandals for—and *they* ain't worthy to polish sandals for the patriarchs and prophets. That gives you a kind of an idea of their rank, don't it? You begin to see how high up they are, don't you? Just to get a two-minute glimpse of one of them is a thing for a body to remember and tell about for a thousand years. Why, Captain, just think of this: if Abraham was to set his foot down here by this door, there would be a railing set up around that foot-track right away, and a shelter put over it, and people would flock here from all over heaven, for hundreds and hundreds of years, to look at it. Abraham is one of the parties that Mr. Talmage, of Brooklyn, is going to embrace, and kiss, and weep on, when he comes. He wants to lay in a good stock of tears, you know, or five to one he will go dry before he gets a chance to do it."

"Sandy," says I, "I had an idea that *I* was going to be equals with everybody here, too, but I will let that drop. It don't matter, and I am plenty happy enough anyway."

"Captain, you are happier than you would be, the other way. These old patriarchs and prophets have got ages the start of you; they know more in two minutes than you know in a year. Did you ever try to have a sociable improving-time discussing winds, and currents and variations of compass with an undertaker?"

"I get your idea, Sandy. He couldn't interest me. He would be an ignoramus in such things—he would bore me, and I would bore him."

"You have got it. You would bore the patriarchs when you talked, and when they talked they would shoot over your head. By and by you would say, 'Good morning, your Eminence, I will call again'—but you wouldn't. Did you ever ask the slush-boy to come up in the cabin and take dinner with you?"

"I get your drift again, Sandy. I wouldn't be used to such grand people as the patriarchs and prophets, and I would be sheepish and tongue-tied in their company, and mighty glad to get out of it. Sandy, which is the highest rank, patriarch or prophet?"

"Oh, the prophets hold over the patriarchs. The newest prophet, even, is of a sight more consequence than the oldest patriarch. Yes, sir, Adam himself has to walk behind Shakespeare."

"Was Shakespeare a prophet?"

"Of course he was; and so was Homer, and heaps more. But Shakespeare and the rest have to walk behind a common tailor from Tennessee, by the name of Billings; and behind a horse-doctor named Sakka, from Afghanistan. Jeremiah, and Billings and Buddha walk together, side by side, right behind a crowd from planets not in our astronomy; next come a dozen or two from Jupiter and other worlds; next come Daniel, and Sakka and Confucius; next a lot from systems outside of ours; next come Ezekiel, and Mahomet, Zoroaster, and a knife-grinder from ancient Egypt; then there is a long string, and after them, away down toward the bottom, come Shakespeare and Homer, and a shoemaker named Marais, from the back settlements of France."

"Have they really rung in Mahomet and all those other heathens?"

"Yes—they all had their message, and they all get their reward. The man who don't get his reward on earth, needn't bother—he will get it here, sure."

"But why did they throw off on Shakespeare, that way, and put him away down there below those shoe-makers and horse-doctors and knife-grinders—a lot of people nobody ever heard of?"

"That is the heavenly justice of it—they warn't rewarded according to their deserts, on earth, but here they get their rightful rank. That tailor Billings, from Tennessee, wrote poetry that Homer and Shakespeare couldn't begin to come up to; but nobody would print it, nobody read it but his neighbors, an ignorant lot, and they laughed at it. Whenever the village had a drunken frolic and a dance, they would drag him in and crown him with cabbage leaves, and pretend to bow down to him; and one night when he was sick and nearly starved to death, they had him out and crowned him, and then they rode him on a rail about the village, and everybody followed along, beating tin pans and yelling. Well, he died before morning. He wasn't ever expecting to go to heaven, much less that there was going to be any fuss made over him, so I reckon he was a good deal surprised when the reception broke on him."

"Was you there, Sandy?"

"Bless you, no!"

"Why? Didn't you know it was going to come off?"

"Well, I judge I did. It was the talk of these realms—not for a day, like this barkeeper business, but for twenty years before the man died."

"Why the mischief didn't you go, then?"

"Now how you talk! The like of me go meddling around at the reception of a prophet? A mudsill like me trying to push in and help receive an awful grandee like Edward J. Billings? Why, I should have been laughed at for a billion miles around. I shouldn't ever heard the last of it."

"Well, who did go, then?"

"Mighty few people that you and I will ever get a chance to see, Captain. Not a solitary commoner ever has the luck to see a reception of a prophet, I can tell you. All the nobility, and all the patriarchs and prophets—every last one of them—and all the archangels, and all the princes and governors and viceroys, were there,—and *no* small fry—not a single one. And mind you, I'm not talking about only the grandees from *our* world, but the princes and patriarchs and so on from *all* the worlds that shine in our sky, and from billions more that belong in systems upon systems away outside of the one our sun is in. There were some prophets and patriarchs there that ours ain't a circumstance to, for rank and illustriousness and all that. Some were from Jupiter and other worlds in our own system, but the most celebrated were three poets, Saa, Bo and Soof, from great planets in three different and very remote systems. There three names are common and familiar in every nook and corner of heaven, clear from one end of it to the other—fully as well known as the eighty Supreme Archangels, in fact—whereas our Moses, and Adam, and the rest, have not been heard of outside of our world's little corner of heaven, except by a few very learned men scattered here and there—and they always spell their names wrong, and get the performances of one mixed up with the doings of another, and they almost always locate them simply *in our solar system*, and think that is enough without going into little details such as naming the particular world they are from. It is like a learned Hindoo showing off how much he knows by saying Longfellow lives in the United States—as if he lived all over the United States, and as if the country was so small you couldn't throw a brick there without hitting him. Between you and me, it does gravel me, the cool way people from those monster worlds outside our system snub our little world, and even our system. Of course we think a good deal of Jupiter, because our world is only a potato to it, for size; but then there are worlds in other systems that Jupiter isn't even a mustard-seed to—like the planet Goobra, for instance, which you couldn't squeeze inside the orbit of Halley's comet without straining the rivets. Tourists from Goobra (I mean parties that lived and died there—natives) come here, now and then, and inquire about our world, and when they find out it is so little that a streak of lightning can flash clear around it in the eighth of a second, they have to lean up against something to laugh. Then they screw a glass into their eye and go to examining *us*, as if we were a curious kind of foreign bug, or something of that sort. One of them asked me how long our day was; and when I told him it was twelve hours long, as a general thing, he asked me if people where I was from considered it worth while to get up and wash for such a day as that. That is the way with those Goobra people—they can't seem to let a chance go by to throw it in your face that their day is three hundred and twenty-two of our years long. This young snob was just of age—he was six or seven thousand of his days old—say two million of our years—and he had all the puppy airs that belong to that time of life—that turning-point when a person has got over being a boy and yet ain't quite a man exactly. If it had been anywhere else but in heaven, I would have given him a piece of my mind. Well, anyway, Billings had the grandest reception that has been seen in thousands of centuries, and I think it will have a good effect. His name will be carried pretty far, and it will make our system talked about, and maybe our world, too, and raise us in the respect of the general public of heaven. Why, look here—Shakespeare walked backwards before that tailor from Tennessee, and scattered flowers for him to walk on, and Homer stood behind his chair and waited on him at the banquet. Of course that didn't go for much *there*, amongst all those big foreigners from other systems, as they hadn't heard of Shakespeare or Homer either, but it would amount to considerable down there on our little earth if they could know about it. I wish there was something *in* that miserable spiritualism, so we could send them word. That Tennessee village would set up a monument to Billings, then, and his autograph would outsell Satan's. Well, they had grand times at that reception—a small-fry noble from Hoboken told me all about it—Sir Richard Duffer, Baronet."

"What, Sandy, a nobleman from Hoboken? How is that?"

"Easy enough. Duffer kept a sausage-shop and never saved a cent in his life because he used to give all his spare meat to the poor, in a quiet way. Not tramps,—no, the other sort—the sort that will starve before they will beg—honest square people out of work. Dick used to watch hungry-looking men and women and children, and track them home, and find out all about them from the neighbors, and then feed them and find them work. As nobody ever *saw* him give anything to anybody, he had the reputation of being mean; he died with it, too, and everybody said it was a good riddance; but the minute he landed here, they made him a baronet, and the very first words Dick the sausage-maker of Hoboken heard when he stepped upon the heavenly shore were, 'Welcome, Sir Richard Duffer!' It surprised him some, because he thought he had reasons to believe he was pointed for a warmer climate than this one."

Emanuel Swedenborg

(1688–1772)

Prodigious natural scientist of the spiritual world, Swedenborg published widely in the fields of chemistry, geology, cosmology, and physiology, all foreshadowing his later theological work, which yielded some thirty volumes of scriptural exegesis and visionary investigation of the other world. Swedenborg's revelations about the harmonious ordering of marriage, friendship, work, leisure, and education in heaven profoundly influenced eighteenth- and nineteenth-century social critics. Equally significant are the trenchant satires he inspired, from Immanuel Kant's Dreams of a Spirit Seer *(1766) to William Blake's ironic apocalypse* The Marriage of Heaven and Hell *(1790), which counters Swedenborg's rationalistic spiritualism with the exuberant creed, Energy is Eternal Delight. This excerpt comes from* Heaven and Its Wonders and Hell *(1758).*

XXI.

The Places of Abode and Dwellings of Angels

As there are societies in heaven and the angels live as men they have also places of abode, and these differ in accordance with each one's state of life. They are magnificent for those in higher dignity, and less magnificent for those in lower condition. I have frequently talked with angels about the places of abode in heaven, saying that scarcely any one will believe at the present day that they have places of abode and dwellings; some because they do not see them, some because they do not know that angels are men, and some because they believe that the angelic heaven is the heaven that is seen with their eyes around them, and as this appears empty and they suppose that angels are ethereal forms, they conclude that they live in ether. Moreover, they do not comprehend how there can be such things in the spiritual world as there are in the natural world, because they know nothing about the spiritual. The angels replied that they are aware that such ignorance prevails at this day in the world, and to their astonishment, chiefly within the church, and more with the intelligent than with those who are called simple. They said also that it might be known from the Word that angels are men, since those that have been seen have been seen as men; and the Lord, who took all His Human with Him, appeared in like manner. It might be known also that as angels are men they have dwellings and places of abode, and do not fly about in air, as some think in their ignorance, which the angels call insanity, and that although they are called spirits they are not winds. This they said might be apprehended if men would only think independently of their acquired notions about angels and spirits, as they do when they are not canvassing the subject and bringing to direct thought the question whether it is so. For every one has a general idea that angels are in the human form, and have homes which are called the mansions of heaven, which surpass in magnificence earthly dwellings; but this general idea, which flows in from heaven, at once falls to nothing when it is brought under direct scrutiny and inquiry whether it is so, as happens especially with the learned, who by their own intelligence have closed up heaven to themselves and the entrance of heavenly light. The same is true of the belief in the life of man after death. When one speaks of it, not thinking at the same time about the soul from the light of worldly learning or from the doctrine of its reunion with the body, he believes that after death he is to live a man, and among angels if he has lived well, and that he will then see magnificent things and perceive joys; but as soon as he turns his thoughts to the doctrine of reunion with the body, or to his theory about the soul, and the question arises whether the soul be such, and thus whether this can be true, his former idea is dissipated.

184. But it is better to present the evidence of experience. Whenever I have talked with angels face to face, I have been with them in their abodes. These abodes are precisely like abodes on the earth which we call houses, but more beautiful. In them there are chambers, parlors, and bedrooms in great number; there are also courts, and there are gardens and flower-beds and lawns round about. Where they live together their houses are near each other, arranged one next to the other in the form of a city, with avenues, streets, and public squares, exactly like cities on the earth. I have been permitted to pass through them, looking about on every side, and sometimes entering the house. This occurred when my inner sight was opened, and I was fully awake.

185. I have seen palaces in heaven of such magnificence as cannot be described. Above they glittered as if made of pure gold, and below as if made of precious stones, some more splendid than others. It was the same within. Both words and knowledge are inadequate to describe the decorations that adorned the rooms. On the side looking to the south there were parks, where, too, everything shone, in some places the leaves glistening as if made of silver, and fruit as if made of gold; while the flowers in their beds formed rainbows with their colors. Beyond the borders, where the view terminated, were seen other palaces. Such is the architecture of heaven that you would say that art there is in its art; and no wonder, because the art is itself from heaven. The angels said that such things and innumerable others still more perfect are set forth before their eyes by the Lord; and yet these things are more pleasing to their minds than to their eyes, because in every one of them they see a correspondence, and through the correspondences what is Divine.

186. As to these correspondences I have also been told that not only the palaces and houses, but all things and each thing, both inside and outside of them, correspond to the interior things which they have from the Lord, the house itself in general corresponding to their good, the particular things inside of a house to the various things of which their good consists, and the things outside to truths derived from good, and also to their perceptions and knowledges; and as these things correspond to the goods and truths they have from the Lord they correspond to their love, and to their wisdom and intelligence from love, since love belongs to good, wisdom to good and truth together, and intelligence to truth from good. These are what the angels perceive when they behold what is around them, and thus their minds are more delighted and moved by them than their eyes.

187. All this makes clear why the Lord called Himself the temple at Jerusalem (*John* ii. 19, 21), namely, because the temple represented His Divine Human; also why the New Jerusalem was seen to be of pure gold, its gates of pearls, and its foundations of precious stones (*Apoc.* xxi.), namely, because the New Jerusalem signifies the church which was afterwards to be established, the twelve gates its truths leading to good, and the foundations the truths on which the church is founded.

188. The angels of whom the Lord's celestial kingdom consists dwell for the most part in elevated places that appear as mountains of soil; the angels of whom the Lord's spiritual kingdom consists dwell in less elevated places that appear like hills; while the angels in the lowest parts of heaven dwell in places that appear like ledges of stone. All these things spring from correspondence, for interior things correspond to higher things, and exterior things to lower things, and this is why in the Word "mountains" signify celestial love, "hills" spiritual love, and "rocks" faith.

189. There are also angels who do not live associated together, but apart, house by house. These dwell in the midst of heaven, since they are the best of angels.

190. The houses in which angels dwell are not erected, as houses in the world are, but are given to them gratuitously by the Lord, to every one in accordance with his perception of good and truth. They also change a little in accordance with changes of the state of interiors of the angels. Every thing whatsoever that the angels possess they hold as received from the Lord; and every thing they have need of is given them.

XLI.

The Employment of Angels in Heaven

387. It is impossible to enumerate the employments in the heavens, still less to describe them in detail, but something may be said about them in a general way; for they are numberless, and vary in accordance with the functions of the societies. Each society has its peculiar function, for as societies are distinct in accordance with goods, so they are distinct in accordance with uses, because with all in the heavens goods are goods in act, which are uses. Every one there performs a use, for the Lord's kingdom is a kingdom of uses.

388. In the heavens as on earth there are many forms of service, for there are ecclesiastical affairs, there are civil affairs and there are domestic affairs. Ecclesiastical affairs are referred to in what has been said and shown above, where Divine worship is treated of; civil affairs where governments in heaven are treated of; and domestic affairs where the dwellings and homes of angels are treated of, and marriages in heaven; all of which show that in every heavenly society there are many employments and services.

389. All things in the heavens are organized in accordance with Divine order, which is everywhere guarded by the services performed by angels, those things that pertain to the general good or use by the wiser angels, those that pertain to particular uses by the less wise, and so on. They are subordinated just as uses are subordinated in the Divine order; and for this reason a dignity is connected with every function according to the dignity of the use. Nevertheless, an angel does not claim dignity to himself, but ascribes all dignity to the use; and as the use is the good that he accomplishes, and all good is from the Lord, so he ascribes all dignity to the Lord. Therefore he that thinks of honor for himself and subsequently for the use, and not for the use and subsequently for himself, can perform no function in heaven, because this is looking away backwards from the Lord, and putting self in the first place and use in the second. When use is spoken of the Lord also is meant, because, as has just been said, use is good, and good is from the Lord.

390. From this it may be inferred what subordinations in the heavens are, namely, that as any one loves, esteems, and honors the use he also loves, esteems, and honors the person with whom the use is connected; also that the person is loved, esteemed, and honored in the measure in which he ascribes the use to the Lord and not to himself; for to that extent he is wise, and the uses he performs he performs from good. Spiritual love, esteem, and honor are nothing else than the love, esteem, and honor of the use in the person, together with the honor to the person because of the use, and not honor to the use because of the person. This is the way, moreover, in which men are regarded when they are regarded from spiritual truth, for one man is then seen to be the same as another, whether he be in great or in little dignity, the only perceptible difference being a difference in wisdom; and wisdom is loving use, that is, loving and good of a fellow citizen, of society, of one's country, and of the church. It is this that constitutes love to the Lord, because every good that is a good of use is from the Lord; and it constitutes also love towards the neighbor, because the neighbor means the good that is to be loved in a fellow citizen, in society, in one's country, and in the church, and that is to be done in their behalf.

391. As all the societies in the heavens are distinct in accordance with their goods so they are distinct in accordance with their uses, goods being goods in act, that is, goods of charity which are uses. Some societies are employed in taking care of little children; others in teaching and training them as they grow up; others in teaching and training in like manner the boys and girls that have acquired a good disposition from their education in the world, and in consequence have come into heaven. There are other societies that teach the simple good from the Christian world, and lead them into the way to heaven; there are others that in like manner teach and lead the various heathen nations. There are some societies that defend from infestations by evil spirits the newly arrived spirits that have just come from the world; there are some that attend upon the spirits that are in the lower earth; also some that attend upon spirits that are in the hells, and restrain them from tormenting each other beyond prescribed limits; and there are some that attend upon those who are being raised from the dead. In general, angels from each society are sent to men to watch over them and to lead them away from evil affections and consequent thoughts, and to inspire them with good affections so far as they will receive them in freedom; and by means of these they direct the deeds or works of men by removing as far as possible evil intentions. When angels are with men they dwell as it were in their affections; and they are near to man just in the degree in which he is in good from truths, and are distant from him just in the degree in which his life is distant from good. But all these employments of angels are employments of the Lord through the angels, for the angels perform them from the Lord and not from themselves. For this reason, in the Word in its internal sense "angels" mean, not angels, but something belonging to the Lord; and for the same reason angels are called "gods" in the Word.

392. These employments of the angels are their general employments; but each one has his particular charge; for every general use is composed of innumerable uses which are called mediate, ministering, and subservient uses, all and each coordinated and subordinated in accordance with Divine order, and taken together constituting and perfecting the general use, which is the general good.

393. Those are concerned with ecclesiastical affairs in heaven who in the world loved the Word and eagerly sought in it for truths, not with honor or gain as an end, but uses of life both for themselves and for others. These in heaven are in enlightenment and the light of wisdom in the measure of their love and desire for use; and this wisdom they receive from the Word in heaven, which is not a natural Word, as it is in the world, but a spiritual Word. These minister in the preaching office; and in accordance with Divine order those are in higher positions who from enlightenment excel others in wisdom. Those are concerned with civil affairs who in the world loved their country, and loved its general good more than their own, and did what is just and right from a love for what is just and right. So far as these from the eagerness of love have investigated the laws of justice and have thereby become intelligent, they have the ability to perform such functions in heaven, and they perform these in that position or degree that accords with their intelligence, their intelligence being in equal degree with their love of use for the general good. Furthermore, there are in heaven more functions and services and occupations than can be enumerated; while in the world there are few in comparison. But however many there may be that are so employed, they are all in the delight of their work and labor from a love of use, and no one from a love of self or of gain; and as all the necessaries of life are furnished them gratuitously they have no love or gain for the sake of a living. They are housed gratuitously, clothed gratuitously, and fed gratuitously. Evidently, then, those that have loved themselves and the world more than use have no lot in heaven; for his love or affection remains with every one after his life in the world, and is not extirpated to eternity.

394. In heaven every one comes into his own occupation in accordance with correspondence, and the correspondence is not with the occupation but with the use of each occupation; for there is a correspondence of every thing. He that in heaven comes into the employment or occupation corresponding to his use is in just the same condition of life as when he was in the world; since what is spiritual and what is natural make one by correspondences; yet there is this difference, that he then comes into an interior delight, because into spiritual life, which is an interior life, and therefore more receptive of heavenly blessedness.

Sir Arthur Conan Doyle

(1859–1930)

The British novelist and short story writer—and creator of Sherlock Holmes—Doyle was also a zealous spiritualist. In this selection from his novel The Land of Mist *(1926), a spiritualist rescue circle guided by the medium John Terbane and a long-dead Chinese philosopher named Mr. Chang, helps the newly dead find their way in the land beyond the grave.*

Chapter X

De Profundis

They were still having tea when Mr. Charles Mason was ushered in. Nothing draws people together into such intimate soul-to-soul relationship as psychic quest, and thus it was that Roxton and Malone, who had only known him in the one episode, felt more near to this man than to others with whom they had associated for years. This close vital comradeship is one of the outstanding features of such communion. When his loosely built, straggling, lean, clerical figure appeared, with that gaunt, worn face illuminated by its human grin and dignified by its earnest eyes, through the doorway, they both felt as if an old friend had entered. His own greeting was equally cordial.

"Still exploring!" he cried, as he shook them by the hand. "We will hope your new experiences will not be so nerve-racking as our last."

"By Jove, padre!" said Roxton. "I've worn out the brim of my hat taking it off to you since then."

"Why, what did he do?" asked Mrs. Mailey.

"No, no!" cried Mason. "I tried in my poor way to guide a darkened soul. Let us leave it at that. But that is exactly what we are here for now, and what these dear people do every week of their lives. It was from Mr. Mailey here that I learned how to attempt it."

"Well, certainly we have plenty of practice," said Mailey. "You have seen enough of it, Mason, to know that."

"But I can't get the focus of this at all!" cried Malone. "Could you clear my mind a little on the point? I accept for the moment your hypothesis, that we are surrounded by material earth-bound spirits who find themselves under strange conditions which they don't understand, and who want counsel and guidance. That more or less expresses it, does it not?"

The Maileys both nodded their agreement.

"Well, their dead friends and relatives are presumably on the other side and cognizant of their benighted condition. They know the truth. Could they not minister to the wants of these afflicted ones far better than we can?"

"It is a most natural question," Mailey answered. "Of course we put that objection to them and we can only accept their answer. They appear to be actually anchored to the surface of this earth, too heavy and gross to rise. The others are, presumably, on a spiritual level and far separated from them. They explain that they are much nearer to us and that they are cognizant of us, but not of anything higher. Therefore it is we who can reach them best."

"There was one poor dear dark soul—"

"My wife loves everybody and everything," Mailey explained. "She is capable of talking of the poor dear devil."

"Well, surely they are to be pitied and loved!" cried the lady. "This poor fellow was nursed along by us week by week. He had really come from the depths. Then one day he cried in rapture, 'My mother has come! My mother is here!' We naturally said, 'But why did she not come before?' 'How could she,' said he, 'when I was in so dark a place that she could not see me?'"

"That's very well," said Malone, "but so far as I can follow your methods it is some guide or control or higher spirit who regulates the whole matter and brings the sufferer to you. If he can be cognizant, one would think other higher spirits could also be."

"No, for it is his particular mission," said Mailey. "To show how marked the divisions are I can remember one occasion when we had a dark soul here. Our own people came through and did not know he was there until we called their attention to it. When we said to the dark soul, 'Don't you see our friends beside you?' he answered, 'I can see a light but nothing else.'"

At this point the conversation was interrupted by the arrival of Mr. John Terbane from Victoria Station, where his mundane duties lay. He was dressed now in civil garb and appeared as a pale, sad-faced, clean-shaven, plump-featured man with dreamy, thoughtful eyes, but no other indication of the remarkable uses to which he was put.

"Have you my record?" was his first question.

Mrs. Mailey, smiling, handed him an envelope. "We kept it all ready for you but you can read it at home. You see," she explained, "poor Mr. Terbane is in trance and knows nothing of the wonderful work of which he is the instrument, so after each sitting my husband and I draw up an account for him."

"Very much astonished I am when I read it," said Terbane.

"And very proud, I should think," added Mason.

"Well, I don't know about that," Terbane answered humbly. "I don't see that the tool need be proud because the worker happens to use it. Yet it is a privilege, of course."

"Good old Terbane!" said Mailey, laying his hand affectionately on the railwayman's shoulder. "The better the medium the more unselfish. That is my experience. The whole conception of a medium is one who gives himself up for the use of others, and that is incompatible with selfishness. Well, I suppose we had better get to work or Mr. Chang will scold us."

"Who is he?" asked Malone.

"Oh, you will soon make the acquaintance of Mr. Chang! We need not sit round the table. A semi-circle round the fire does very well. Lights half-down. That is all right. You'll make yourself comfortable, Terbane. Snuggle among the cushions."

The medium was in the corner of a comfortable sofa, and had fallen at once into a doze. Both Mailey and Malone sat with notebooks upon their knees awaiting developments.

They were not long in coming. Terbane suddenly sat up, his dreamy self transformed into a very alert and masterful individuality. A subtle change had passed over his face. An ambiguous smile fluttered upon his lips, his eyes seemed more oblique and less open, his face projected. The two hands were thrust into the sleeves of his blue lounge jacket.

"Good-evening," said he, speaking crisply and in short staccato sentences. "New faces! Who these?"

"Good-evening, Chang," said the master of the house. "You know Mr.

Mason. This is Mr. Malone who studies our subject. This is Lord Roxton who has helped me today."

As each name was mentioned, Terbane made a sweeping Oriental gesture of greeting, bringing his hand down from his forehead. His whole bearing was superbly dignified and very different from the humble little man who had sat down a few minutes before.

"Lord Roxton!" he repeated. "An English milord! I knew Lord—Lord Macart—No! I cannot say it. Alas! I called him 'foreign devil' then. Chang, too, had much to learn."

"He is speaking of Lord Macartney. That would be over a hundred years ago. Chang was a great living philosopher then," Mailey explained.

"Not lose time!" cried the control. "Much to do today! Crowd waiting. Some new, some old. I gather strange folk in my net. Now I go." He sank back among the cushions.

A minute elapsed, then he suddenly sat up.

"I want to thank you," he said, speaking perfect English. "I came two weeks ago. I have thought over all you said. The path is lighter."

"Were you the spirit who did not believe in God?"

"Yes, yes! I said so in my anger. I was so weary—so weary. Oh, the time, the endless time, the gray mist, the heavy weight of remorse! Hopeless! Hopeless! And you brought me comfort, you and this great Chinese spirit. You gave me the first kind words I have had since I died!"

"When was it that you died?"

"Oh! It seems an eternity. We do not measure as you do. It is a long, horrible dream without change or break."

"Who was king in England?"

"Victoria was queen. I had attuned my mind to matter and so it clung to matter. I did not believe in a future life. Now I know that I was all wrong, but I could not adapt my mind to new conditions."

"Is it bad where you are?"

"It is all—all gray. That is the awful part of it. One's surroundings are so horrible."

"But there are many more. You are not alone."

"No, but they know no more than I. They, too, scoff and doubt and are miserable."

"You will soon get out."

"For God's sake, help me to do so!"

"Poor soul!" said Mrs. Mailey in her sweet, caressing voice, a voice which could bring every animal to her side. "You have suffered much. But do not think of yourself. Think of these others. Try to bring one of them up and so you will best help yourself."

"Thank you, lady, I will. There is one here whom I brought. He has heard you. We will go on together. Perhaps some day we may find the light."

"Do you like to be prayed for?"

"Yes, yes, indeed I do!"

"I will pray for you," said Mason. "Could you say the 'Our Father' now?" He uttered the old universal prayer, but before he had finished Terbane had collapsed again among the cushions. He sat up again as Chang.

"He come on well," said the control. "He give up time for others who wait. That is good. Now I have hard case. Ow!"

He gave a comical cry of disapprobation and sank back.

Next moment he was up, his face long and solemn, his hands palm to palm.

"What is this?" he asked in a precise and affected voice. "I am at a loss to know what right this Chinese person has to summon me here. Perhaps you can enlighten me."

"It is that we may perhaps help you."

"When I desire help, sir, I ask for it. At present I do not desire it. The whole proceeding seems to me to be a very great liberty. So far as this Chinaman can explain it, I gather that I am the involuntary spectator of some sort of religious service."

"We are a spiritualistic circle."

"A most pernicious sect. A most blasphemous proceeding. As a humble parish priest I protest against such desecrations."

"You are held back, friend, by those narrow views. It is you who suffer. We want to relieve you."

"Suffer? What do you mean, sir?"

"You realize that you have passed over?"

"You are talking nonsense!"

"Do you realize that you are dead?"

"How can I be dead when I am talking to you?"

"Because you are using this man's body."

"I have certainly wandered into an asylum."

"Yes, an asylum for bad cases. I fear you are one of them. Are you happy where you are?"

"Happy? No, sir. My present surroundings are perfectly inexplicable to me."

"Have you any recollection of being ill?"

"I was very ill indeed."

"So ill that you died."

"You are certainly out of your senses."

"How do you know you are not dead?"

"Sir, I must give you some religious instruction. When one dies and has led an honourable life, one assumes a glorified body and one associates with the angels. I am now in exactly the same body as in life, and I am in a very dull, drab place. Such companions as I have are not such as I have been accustomed to associate with in life, and certainly no one could describe them as angels. Therefore your absurd conjecture may be dismissed."

"Do not continue to deceive yourself. We wish to help you. You can never progress until you realize your position."

"Really you try my patience too far. Have I not said—?"

The medium fell back among the cushions. An instant later the Chinese control, with his whimsical smile and his hands tucked away in his sleeves, was talking to the circle.

"He good man—fool man—learn sense soon. Bring him again. Not waste more time. Oh, my God! My God! Help! Mercy! Help!"

He had fallen full length upon the sofa, face upward, and his cries were so terrible that the little audience all sprang to their feet. "A saw! A saw! Fetch a saw!" yelled the medium. His voice sank into a moan.

Even Mailey was agitated. The rest were horrified.

"Someone has obsessed him. I can't understand it. It may be some strong evil entity."

"Shall I speak to him?" asked Mason.

"Wait a moment! Let it develop. We shall soon see."

The medium writhed in agony. "Oh, my God! Why don't you fetch a saw!" he cried. "It's here across my breast-bone. It is cracking! I feel it! Hawkin! Hawkin! Pull me from under! Hawkin! Push up the beam! No, no, that's worse! And it's on fire! Oh, horrible! Horrible!"

His cries were blood-curdling. They were all chilled with horror. Then in an instant the Chinaman was blinking at them with his slanting eyes.

"What you think of that, Mister Mailey?"

"It is terrible, Chang. What was it?"

"It was for him," nodding towards Malone. "He want newspaper story, I give him newspaper story. He will understand. No time 'splain now. Too many waiting. Sailor man come next. Here he comes!"

The Chinaman was gone, and a jovial, puzzled grin passed over the face of the medium. He scratched his head.

"Well, damn me," said he. "I never thought I would take orders from a Chink, but he says 'hist!' and by crums you've got to hist and no back talk either. Well, here I am. What did you want?"

"We wanted nothing."

"Well, the Chink seemed to think you did, for he slung me in here."

"It was you that wanted something. You wanted knowledge."

"Well, I've lost my bearings, that's true. I know I am dead 'cause I've seen the gunnery lootenant, and he was blown to bits before my eyes. If he's dead I'm dead and all the rest of us, for we are over to the last man. But we've got the laugh on our sky pilot, for he's as puzzled as the rest of us. Damned poor pilot, I call him. We're all taking our own sounding now."

"What was your ship?"

"The *Monmouth*."

"She that went down in battle with the German?"

"That's right. South American waters. It was clean hell. Yes, it was hell." There was a world of emotion in his voice. "Well," he added more cheerfully, "I've heard our mates got level with them later. That is so, sir, is it not?"

"Yes, they all went to the bottom."

"We've seen nothing of them this side. Just as well, maybe. We don't forget nothing."

"But you must," said Mailey. "That's what is the matter with you. That is why the Chinese control brought you through. We are here to teach you. Carry our message to your mates."

"Bless your heart, sir, they are all here behind me."

"Well, then, I tell you and them that the time for hard thoughts and worldly strife is over. Your faces are to be turned forward, not back. Leave this earth which still holds you by the ties of thought and let all your desire be to make yourself unselfish and worthy of a higher, more peaceful, more beautiful life. Can you understand?"

"I hear you, sir. So do they. We want steering, sir, for, indeed, we've had wrong instructions, and we never expected to find ourselves cast away like this. We had heard of heaven and we had heard of hell, but this don't seem to fit in with either. But this Chinese gent says time is up, and we can report again next week. I thank you, sir, for self and company. I'll come again."

There was silence.

"What an incredible conversation!" gasped Malone. "If I were to put down that man's sailor talk and slang as emanating from a world of spirits, what would the public say?"

Mailey shrugged his shoulders.

"Does it matter what the public says? I started as a fairly sensitive person, and now a tank takes as much notice of small shot as I do of newspaper attacks. They honestly don't even interest me. Let us just stick fast to truth as near as we can get it, and leave all else to find its own level."

"I don't pretend to know much of these things," said Roxton, "but what strikes me most is that these folk are very decent ordinary people. What? Why should they be wanderin' about in the dark, and hauled up here by this Chinaman when they've done no partic'lar harm in life?"

"It is the strong earth tie and the absence of any spiritual nexus in each case," Mailey explained. "Here is a clergy-man with his mind entangled with formulas and ritual. Here is a materialist who has deliberately attuned himself to matter. Here is a seaman brooding over revengeful thoughts. They are there by the million million."

"Where?" asked Malone.

"Here," Mailey answered. "Actually on the surface of the earth. Well, you saw it for yourself, I understand, when you went down to Dorsetshire. That was on the surface, was it not? That was a very gross case, and that made it more visible and obvious, but it did not change the general law. I believe that the whole globe is infested with the earthbound, and that when a great cleansing comes, as is prophesied, it will be for their benefit as much as for that of the living."

Malone thought of the strange visionary Miromar and his speech at the Spiritualistic Church on the first night of his quest.

"Do you then believe in some impending event?" he asked.

Mailey smiled. "That is rather a large subject to open up," he said. "I believe—But here is Mr. Chang again!"

The control joined in the conversation.

"I heard you. I sit and listen," said he. "You speak now of what is to come. Let it be! Let it be! The Time is not yet. You will be told when it is good that you know. Remember this. All is best. Whatever come all is best. God makes no mistakes. Now others here who wish your help, I leave you."

Several spirits came through in quick succession. One was an architect who said that he had lived at Bristol. He had not been an evil man, but had simply banished all thoughts of the future. Now he was in the dark and needed guidance. Another had lived in Birmingham. He was an educated man but a materialist. He refused to accept the assurances of Mailey, and was by no means convinced that he was really dead. Then came a very noisy and violent man of a crudely religious and narrowly intolerant type, who spoke repeatedly of "the blood."

"What is this ribald nonsense?" he asked several times.

"It is not nonsense. We are here to help," said Mailey.

"Who wants to be helped by the devil?"

"Is it likely that the devil would wish to help souls in trouble?"

"It is part of his deceit. I tell you it is of the devil! Be warned! I will take no further part in it."

The placid, whimsical Chinaman was back like a flash. "Good man. Foolish man," he repeated once more. "Plenty time. He learn better some day. Now I bring bad case—very bad case. Ow!"

He reclined his head in the cushion and did not raise it as the voice, a feminine voice, broke out:

"Janet! Janet!"

There was a pause.

"Janet! I say! Where is the morning tea? Janet! This is intolerable! I have called you again and again! Janet!" The figure sat up, blinking and rubbing his eyes.

"What is this?" cried the voice. "Who are you? What right have you here? Are you aware that this is my house?"

"No, friend, this is my house."

"Your house! How can it be your house when this is my bedroom? Go away this moment!"

"No, friend. You do not understand your position."

"I will have you put out. What insolence! Janet! Janet! Will no one look after me this morning?"

"Look round you, lady. Is this your bedroom?"

Terbane looked round with a wild stare.

"It is a room I never saw in my life. Where am I? What is the meaning of it? You look like a kind lady. Tell me, for God's sake, what is the meaning of it? Oh, I am so terrified! So terrified! Where are John and Janet?"

"What do you last remember?"

"I remember speaking severely to Janet. She is my maid, you know. She has become so very careless. Yes, I was very angry with her. I was so angry that I was ill. I went to bed feeling very ill. They told me that I should not get excited. How can one help getting excited? Yes, I remember being breathless. That was after the light was out. I tried to call Janet. But why should I be in another room?"

"You passed over in the night?"

"Passed over? Do you mean I died?"

"Yes, lady, you died."

There was a long silence. Then there came a shrill scream. "No, no, no! It is a dream! A nightmare! Wake me! Wake me! How can I be dead? I was not ready to die! I never thought of such a thing. If I am dead, why am I not in heaven or hell? What is this room? This room is a real room."

"Yes, lady, you have been brought here and allowed to use this man's body—"

"A man?" She convulsively felt the coat and passed her hand over the face. "Yes, it is a man. Oh, I am dead! I am dead! What shall I do?"

"You are here that we may explain to you. You have been, I judge, a worldly woman—a society woman. You have lived always for material things."

"I went to church. I was at St. Saviour's every Sunday."

"That is nothing. It is the inner daily life that counts. You were material. Now you are held down to the world. When you leave this man's body you will be in your own body once more and in your old surroundings. But no one will see you. You will remain there unable to show yourself. Your body of flesh will be buried. You will still persist, the same as ever."

"What am I to do? Oh, what can I do?"

"You will take what comes in a good spirit and understand that it is for your cleansing. We only clear ourselves of matter by suffering. All will be well. We will pray for you."

"Oh, do! Oh, I need it so! Oh my God! . . . " The voice trailed away.

"Bad case," said the Chinaman, sitting up. "Selfish woman! Bad woman! Live for pleasure. Hard on those around her. She have much to suffer. But you put her feet on the path. Now my medium tired. Plenty waiting, but no more to-day."

"Have we done good, Chang?"

"Plenty good. Plenty good."

"Where are all these people, Chang?"

"I tell you before."

"Yes, but I want these gentlemen to hear."

"Seven spheres round the world, heaviest below, lightest above. First sphere is on the earth. These people belong to that sphere. Each sphere is separate from the other. Therefore it is easier for you to speak with these people than for those in any other sphere."

"And easier for them to speak to us?"

"Yes. That why you should be plenty careful when you do not know to whom you talk. Try the spirits."

"What sphere do you belong to, Chang?"

"I came from Number Four sphere."

"Which is the first really happy sphere?"

"Number Three. Summerland. Bible book called it the third heaven. Plenty sense in Bible book, but people do not understand."

"And the seventh heaven?"

"Ah! That is where the Christs are. All come there at last—you, me, everybody."

"And after that?"

"Too much question, Mr. Mailey. Poor old Chang not know so much as that. Now good-bye! God bless you! I go."

It was the end of the sitting of the rescue circle. A few minutes later Terbane was sitting up smiling and alert, but with no apparent recollection of anything which had occurred. He was pressed for time and lived afar, so that he had to make his departure, unpaid save by the blessing of those whom he had helped. Modest little unvenal man, where will he stand when we all find our real places in the order of creation upon the further side?

The circle did not break up at once. The visitors wanted to talk and the Maileys to listen.

"What I mean," said Roxton, "it's doosed interestin' and all that, but there is a sort of variety-show element in it. What! Difficult to be sure it's really real, if you take what I mean."

"That is what I feel also," said Malone. "Of course on its face value it is simply unspeakable. It is a thing so great that all ordinary happenings become commonplace. That I grant. But the human mind is very strange. I've read the case Moreton Prince examined, and Miss Beauchamp and the rest; also the results of Charcot, the great Nancy hypnotic school. They could turn a man into anything. The mind seems to be like a rope which can be unravelled into its various threads. Then each thread is a different personality which may take dramatic form, and act and speak as such. That man is honest, and he could not normally produce these effects. But how do we know that he is not self-hypnotized, and that under those conditions one strand of him becomes Mr. Chang and another becomes a sailor and another a society lady, and so forth?"

Mailey laughed. "Every man his own Cinquevalli," said he, "but it is a rational objection and has to be met."

"We have traced some of the cases," said Mrs. Mailey. "There is not a doubt of it—names, addresses, everything."

"Well, then we have to consider the question of Terbane's normal knowledge. How can you possibly know what he has learned? I should think a railway-guard is particularly able to pick up such information."

"You have seen one sitting," Mailey answered. "If you had been present at as many as we and noted the cumulative effect of the evidence you would not be sceptical."

"That is very possible," Malone answered. "And I dare-say my doubts are very annoying to you. And yet one is bound to be brutally honest in a case like this. Anyhow, whatever the ultimate cause, I have seldom spent so thrilling an hour. Heavens! If it only *is* true, and if you had a thousand circles instead of one, what regeneration would result!"

"That will come," said Mailey in his patient, determined fashion. "We shall live to see it. I am sorry that thing has not forced conviction upon you. However, you must come again."

But it so chanced that a further experience became unnecessary. Conviction came in a full flood and in a strange fashion that very evening. Malone had hardly got back to the office, and was seated at his desk drawing up some sort of account from his notes of all that had happened in the afternoon, when Mailey burst into the room, his yellow beard bristling with excitement. He was waving an *Evening News* in his hand.

Without a word he seated himself beside Malone and turned the paper over. Then he began to read:

"ACCIDENT IN THE CITY

"This afternoon shortly after five o'clock, an old house, said to date from the fifteenth century, suddenly collapsed. It was situated between Lesser Colman Street and Elliott Square and next door to the Veterinary Society's Headquarters. Some preliminary crackings warned the occupants and most of them had time to escape. Three of them, however, James Beale, William Moorson, and a woman whose name has not been ascertained, were caught by the falling rubbish. Two of these seem to have perished at once, but the third, James Beale, was pinned down by a large beam and loudly demanded help. A saw was brought, and one of the occupants of the house, Samuel Hawkin, showed great gallantry in an attempt to free the unfortunate man. Whilst he was sawing the beam, however, a fire broke out among the débris around him, and though he persevered most manfully, and continued until he was himself badly scorched, it was impossible for him to save Beale, who probably died from suffocation. Hawkin was removed to the London Hospital, and it is reported to-night that he is in no immediate danger."

"That's that!" said Mailey, folding up the paper. "Now, Mr. Thomas Didymus, I leave you to your conclusions," and the enthusiast vanished out of the office as precipitately as he had entered.

Julian Barnes

(b. 1949)

Barnes is a contemporary English novelist and essayist. A History of the World in 10½ Chapters *(1989) begins with a comic retelling of the myth of Noah's Ark and ends with a visit to heaven, from which the following excerpt is taken.*

I dreamt that I woke up. It's the oldest dream of all, and I've just had it. I dreamt that I woke up.

I was in my own bed. That seemed a bit of a surprise, but after a moment's thought it made sense. Who else's bed should I wake up in? I looked around and I said to myself, Well, well, well. Not much of a thought, I admit. Still, do we ever find the right words for the big occasions?

There was a knock on the door and a woman came in, sideways and backwards at the same time. It should have looked awkward but it didn't, no, it was all smooth and stylish. She was carrying a tray, which was why she'd come in like that. As she turned, I saw she was wearing a uniform of sorts. A nurse? No, she looked more like a stewardess on some airline you've never heard of. 'Room service,' she said with a bit of a smile, as if she wasn't used to providing it, or I wasn't used to expecting it; or both.

'Room service?' I repeated. Where I come from something like that only happens in films. I sat up in bed, and found I didn't have any clothes on. Where'd my pyjamas gone? That was a change. It was also a change that when I sat up in bed and realized she could see me bollock-naked to the waist, if you understand me, I didn't feel at all embarrassed. That was good.

'Your clothes are in the cupboard,' she said. 'Take your time. You've got all day. And,' she added with more of a smile, 'all tomorrow as well.'

I looked down at my tray. Let me tell you about that breakfast. It was the breakfast of my life and no mistake. The grapefruit, for a start. Now, you know what a grapefruit's like: the way it spurts juice down your shirt and keeps slipping out of your hand unless you hold it down with a fork or something, the way the flesh always sticks to those opaque membranes and then suddenly comes loose with half the pith attached, the way it always tastes sour yet makes you feel bad about piling sugar on the top of it. That's what a grapefruit's like, right? Now let me tell you about *this* grapefruit. Its flesh was pink for a start, not yellow, and each segment had already been carefully freed from its clinging membrane. The fruit itself was anchored to the dish by some prong or fork through its bottom, so that I didn't need to hold it down or even touch it. I looked around for the sugar, but that was just out of habit. The taste seemed to come in two parts—a sort of awakening sharpness followed quickly by a wash of sweetness; and each of those little globules (which were about the size of tadpoles) seemed to burst separately in my mouth. That was the grapefruit of my dreams, I don't mind telling you.

Like an emperor, I pushed aside the gutted hull and lifted a silver dome from a crested plate. Of course I knew what would be underneath. Three slices of grilled streaky bacon with the gristle and rind removed, the crispy fat all glowing like a bonfire. Two eggs, fried, the yolk looking milky because the fat had been properly spooned over it in the cooking, and the outer edges of the white trailing off into filigree gold braid. A grilled tomato I can only describe in terms of what it wasn't. It wasn't a collapsing cup of stalk, pips, fibre and red water, it was something compact, sliceable, cooked equally all the way through and tasting—yes, this is the thing I remember—tasting of tomato. The sausage: again, not a tube of lukewarm horsemeat stuffed into a French letter, but dark umber and succulent . . . a . . . a sausage, that's the only word for it. All the others, the ones I'd thought I'd enjoyed in my previous life, were merely practising to be like this; they'd been auditioning—and they wouldn't get the part, either. There was a little crescent-shaped side-plate with a crescent-shaped silver lid. I raised it: yes, there were my bacon rinds, separately grilled, waiting to be nibbled.

The toast, the marmalade—well, you can imagine those, you can dream what they were like for yourselves. But I must tell you about the teapot. The tea, of course, was the real thing, tasting as if it had been picked by some rajah's personal entourage. As for the teapot . . . Once, years ago, I went to Paris on a package holiday. I wandered off from the others and walked around where the smart people live. Where they shop and eat, anyway. On a corner I passed a café. It didn't look particularly grand, and just for a minute I thought of sitting down there. But I didn't, because at one of the tables I saw a man having tea. As he poured himself a fresh cup, I spotted a little gadget which seemed to me almost a definition of luxury: attached to the teapot's spout, and dangling by three delicate silver chains, was a strainer. As the man raised the pot to its pouring angle, this strainer swung outwards to catch the leaves. I couldn't believe that serious thought had once gone into the matter of how to relieve this tea-drinking gentleman of the incredible burden of picking up a normal strainer with his free hand. I walked away from that café feeling a bit self-righteous. Now, on my tray, I had a teapot bearing the insignia of some chic Parisian café. A strainer was attached to its spout by three silver chains. Suddenly, I could see the point of it.

After breakfast, I put the tray down on my bedside table, and went to the cupboard. Here they all were, my favourite clothes. That sports jacket I still liked even after people started saying, how unusual, did you buy it secondhand, another twenty years and it'll be back in fashion. That pair of corduroy trousers my wife threw out because the seat was beyond repair; but someone had managed to repair it, and the trousers looked almost new, though not so new you weren't fond of them. My shirts held out their arms to me, and why not, as they'd never been pampered like this in their lives before—all in ranks on velvet-covered hangers. There were shoes whose deaths I'd regretted; socks now deholed again; ties I'd seen in shop windows. It wasn't a collection of clothes you'd envy, but that wasn't the point. I was reassured. I would be myself again. I would be more than myself.

By the side of the bed was a tasselled bell-pull I hadn't previously noticed. I tugged it, then felt a bit embarrassed, and climbed under the sheets again. When the nurse-stewardess came in, I slapped my stomach and said, 'You know, I could eat that all over again.'

'I'm not surprised,' she replied. 'I was half expecting you to say so.' . . .

I didn't get up all day. I had breakfast for breakfast, breakfast for lunch, and breakfast for dinner. It seemed like a good system. I would worry about lunch tomorrow. Or rather, I wouldn't worry about lunch tomorrow. I wouldn't worry about anything tomorrow. Between my breakfast-lunch and my breakfast-dinner (I was really beginning to appreciate that strainer system—you can carry on eating a croissant with your free hand while you pour) I had a long sleep. Then I took a shower. I could have had a bath, but I seem to have spent decades in the bath, so instead I took a shower. I found a quilted dressing-gown with my initials in gilt cord on the breast pocket. It fitted well, but I thought those initials were farting higher than my arse-hole. I hadn't come here to swank around like a film star. As I was staring at these golden squiggles, they disappeared from before my eyes. I blinked and they were gone. The dressing-gown felt more comfortable with just a normal pocket.

The next day I woke up—and had another breakfast. It was as good as the previous three. Clearly the problem of breakfast had now been solved.

When Brigitta came to clear the tray, she murmured, 'Shopping?'

'Of course.' It was exactly what had been on my mind.

'Do you want to go shopping or stay shopping?'

'Go shopping,' I said, not really understanding the difference.

'Sure.'

My wife's brother once came back from ten days in Florida and said, 'When I die, I don't want to go to Heaven, I want to go shopping in America.' That second morning I began to understand what he meant. . . .

I did all sorts of other things:

—I went on several cruises;
—I learned canoeing, mountaineering, ballooning;
—I got into all sorts of danger and escaped;
—I explored the jungle;
—I watched a court case (didn't agree with the verdict);
—I tried being a painter (not as bad as I thought!) and a surgeon;
—I fell in love, of course, lots of times;
—I pretended I was the last person on earth (and the first).

None of this meant that I stopped doing what I'd always done since I got here. I had sex with an increasing number of women, sometimes simultaneously; I ate rarer and stranger foods; I met famous people all the way to the edges of my memory. For instance, I met every footballer there ever was. I started with the famous ones, then the ones I admired but weren't particularly famous, then the average ones, then the ones whose names I remembered without remembering what they looked like or played like; finally I asked for the only ones I hadn't met, the nasty, boring, violent players that I didn't admire at all. I didn't enjoy meeting them—they were just as nasty, boring and violent off the pitch as on—but I didn't want to run out of footballers. Then I ran out of footballers. I asked to see Margaret again.

'I've met all the footballers,' I said.

'I'm afraid I don't know much about football, either.'

'And I don't have any dreams,' I added, in a tone of complaint.

'What would they be for,' she replied. 'What *would* they be for?'

I sensed that in a way she was testing me, seeing how serious I was. Did it all add up to more than a mere adjustment problem?

'I think I'm owed an explanation,' I announced—a little pompously, I have to admit.

'Ask anything you like.' She settled back in her office chair.

'Look, I want to get things straight.'

'An admirable ambition.' She talked a bit posh, like that.

I thought I'd better start at the beginning. 'Look, this is Heaven, isn't it?'

'Oh yes.'

'Well, what about Sundays?'

'I don't follow you.'

'On Sundays,' I said, 'as far as I can work out, because I don't follow the days too closely any more, I play golf, go shopping, eat dinner, have sex and don't feel bad.'

'Isn't that . . . perfect?'

'I don't want to sound ungrateful,' I said cautiously, 'but where's God?'

'God. Do you want God? Is that what you want?'

'Is it a question of what I want?'

'That's exactly what it's a question of. Do you want God?'

'I suppose I thought it wasn't that way round. I suppose I thought either there would be one or there wouldn't be one. I'd find out what the case was. I didn't think it depended on me in any way.'

'Of course it does.'

'Oh.'

'Heaven is democratic these days,' she said. Then added, 'Or at least, it is if you want it to be.'

'What do you mean, democratic?'

'We don't impose Heaven on people any more,' she said. 'We listen to their needs. If they want it, they can have it; if not, not. And then of course they get the sort of Heaven they want.'

'And what sort do they want on the whole?'

'Well, they want a continuation of life, that's what we find. But . . . better, needless to say.'

'Sex, golf, shopping, dinner, meeting famous people and not feeling bad?' I asked, a bit defensively.

'It varies. But if I were being honest, I'd say that it doesn't vary all that much.'

'Not like the old days.'

'Ah, the old days.' She smiled. 'That was before my time, of course, but yes, dreams of Heaven used to be a lot more ambitious.'

'And Hell?' I asked.

'What about it?'

'Is there Hell?'

'Oh no,' she replied. 'That was just necessary propaganda.'

'I was wondering, you see. Because I met Hitler.'

'Lots of people do. He's a sort of . . . tourist site, really. What did you make of him?'

'Oh, I didn't *meet* him,' I said firmly. 'He's a man I wouldn't shake the hand of. I watched him go by from behind the bushes.'

'Ah, yes. Quite a lot of people prefer to do it that way.'

'So I thought, if he's here, there can't be Hell.'

'A reasonable deduction.'

'Just out of interest,' I said, 'what does *he* do all day?' I imagined him going to the 1936 Berlin Olympics every afternoon, watching the Germans win everything while Jesse Owens fell over, then back for some sauerkraut, Wagner and a romp with a busty blonde of pure Aryan blood.

'I'm afraid we do respect people's confidentiality.'

'Naturally.' That was right. I wouldn't want everyone knowing what I got up to, come to think of it.

'So there isn't any Hell?'

'Well, there's something we *call* Hell. But it's more like a theme park. You know, skeletons popping out and frightening you, branches in your face, stink bombs, that sort of thing. Just to give you a good scare.'

'A good scare,' I remarked, 'as opposed to a bad scare?'

'Exactly. We find that's all people want nowadays.'

'Do you know about Heaven in the old days?'

'What, Old Heaven? Yes, we know about Old Heaven. It's in the records.'

'What happened to it?'

'Oh, it sort of closed down. People didn't want it any more. People didn't need it any more.'

'But I knew a few people who went to church, had their babies christened, didn't use rude words. What about them?'

'Oh, we get those,' she said. 'They're catered for. They pray and give thanks rather as you play golf and have sex. They seem to enjoy themselves, to have got what they wanted. We've built them some very nice churches.'

'Does God exist for them?' I asked.

'Oh, surely.'

'But not for me?'

'It doesn't seem so. Unless you want to change your requirements of Heaven. I can't deal with that myself. I could refer you.'

'I've probably got enough to think about for the moment.'

'Fine. Well, until the next time.'

I slept badly that night. My mind wasn't on the sex, even though they all did their very best. Was it indigestion? Had I bolted my sturgeon? There I was, worrying about my health again.

The next morning I shot a 67 on the golf course. My caddy Severiano reacted as if it was the best round he'd seen me play, as if he didn't know I could do 20 shots better. Afterwards, I asked for certain directions, and drove towards the only visible patch of bad weather. As I'd expected, Hell was a great disappointment: the thunderstorm in the car-park was probably the best bit. There were out-of-work actors prodding other out-of-work actors with long forks, pushing them into vats labelled 'Boiling Oil'. Phoney animals with strap-on plastic beaks pecked at foam-rubber corpses. I saw Hitler riding on the Ghost Train with his arm round a Mädchen with pigtails. There were bats and creaking coffin lids and a smell of rotting floorboards. Is that what people wanted?

'Tell me about Old Heaven,' I said to Margaret the following week.

'It was much like your accounts of it. I mean, that's the principle of Heaven, that you get what you want, what you expect. I know some people imagine it's different, that you get what you deserve, but that's never been the case. We have to disabuse them.'

'Are they annoyed?'

'Mostly not. People prefer to get what they want rather than what they deserve. Though some of them did get a little irritated that others weren't sufficiently maltreated. Part of their expectation of Heaven seemed to be that other people would go to Hell. Not very Christian.'

'And were they . . . disembodied? Was it all spirit life and so on?'

'Yes indeed. That's what they wanted. Or at any rate, in certain epochs. There has been a lot of fluctuation over the centuries about decorporealization. At the moment, for instance, there's quite an emphasis on retaining your own body and your own personality. This may just prove a phase, like any other.'

'What are you smiling for?' I asked. I was rather surprised. I thought Margaret was there just to give information, like Brigitta. Yet she obviously had her own opinions, and didn't mind telling you them.

'Only because it sometimes seems odd how tenaciously people want to stick with their own bodies. Of course, they occasionally ask for minor surgery. But it's as if, say, a different nose or a tuck in the cheek or a handful of silicone is all that stands between them and their perfect idea of themselves.'

'What happened to Old Heaven?'

'Oh, it survived for a while, after the new Heavens were built. But there was increasingly little call for it. People seemed keener on the new Heavens. It wasn't all that surprising. We take the long view here.'

'What happened to the Old Heaveners?'

Margaret shrugged, rather complacently, like some corporate planner whose predictions had been borne out to the tiniest decimal point. 'They died off.'

'Just like that? You mean, you closed down their Heaven and so they died off?'

'No, not at all, on the contrary. That's not how it works. Constitutionally, there would have been an Old Heaven for as long as the Old Heaveners wanted it.'

'Are there any Old Heaveners around?'

'I think there are a few left.'

'Can I meet one?'

'They don't take visits, I'm afraid. They used to. But the New Heaveners tended to behave as if they were at a freak-show, kept pointing and asking silly questions. So the Old Heaveners declined to meet them any more. They gave up speaking to anyone but other Old Heaveners. Then they began to die off. Now there aren't many left. We have them tagged, of course.'

'Are they disembodied?'

'Some of them are, some of them aren't. It depends on the sect. Of course the ones that are disembodied don't have much trouble avoiding the New Heaveners.'

Well, that made sense. In fact, it all made sense except for the main thing. 'And what do you mean, the others died off?'

'Everyone has the option to die off if they want to.'

'I never knew that.'

'No. There are bound to be a few surprises. Did you really want to be able to predict it all?'

'And how do they die? Do they kill themselves? Do you kill them?'

Margaret looked a bit shocked at the crassness of my idea. 'Goodness, no. As I said, it's democratic nowadays. If you want to die off, you do. You just have to want to for long enough and that's it, it happens. Death isn't a matter of hazard or gloomy inevitability, the way it is the first time round. We've got free will sorted out here, as you may have noticed.'

Hildegard of Bingen

(1098–1179)

The German Benedictine abbess of Bingen, Hildegard was a monastic and political reformer and a prolific author whose legacy includes scientific and medical treatises, hymns and sequences, and visionary writings such as the following depiction of heavenly joys, from The Book of the Rewards of Life.

Concerning the Heavenly Joys of Virgins

I also saw air in the brightness in a similar manner, as if in a mirror. This air was purer than the clearest water and shone with a brightness beyond the brightness of the sun. This air was blowing. It contained all the greenness of the herbs and flowers of both paradise and the earth, and its aroma was also full of all greenness, just as the summer has the sweetest aroma of herbs and flowers. In this air, I saw certain ones, as if through a mirror, who were clothed with the whitest garment interwoven with gold and embellished with the most precious stones from their breast to their feet, in the manner of a hanging sash. Their garment emitted a very strong aroma, like perfume. And they were girdled with a girdle embellished with gold and gems and pearls beyond human understanding.

On their head they wore crowns intertwined with gold and roses and lilies and surrounded with pipes of most precious stones. Whenever the Lamb of God used his voice, this sweetest blowing of the wind coming from the secret place of the Divinity touched these pipes so that they resounded with every type of sound that a harp and organ make. No one was playing this song, except these who wore these crowns, but the others who heard this song rejoiced in it, just like a man who could not see previously, now sees the brightness of the sun.

They wore foot coverings that shone through, as if they had been taken from the fountain of living water. They sometimes walked as if they were upon golden wheels. They carried lyres in their hands, which they played.

And they knew and spoke and understood a foreign language. I was not, however, strong enough to see the rest of their many embellishments.

Because they had filled their faith with good works since they had known their Creator while they had been alive, they rested with blessedness and joy in the brightness. Because they had ignored the airy variety of fleshly desires in the purity of their minds and because they had gone beyond the requirements of the legal precepts out of love of the true fiery sun, they have this air that was purer than the clearest water and that shone with a brightness beyond the brightness of the sun. Because of their very sweet desire that they had shown to God and to men in the greenness of their virginity and in the flower of their mind and body, as a result rising up in the love of the Holy Spirit when they had sent out the good aroma of many virtues everywhere, they felt that this air was blowing. It contained all the greenness of the herbs and flowers of both paradise and the earth, and its aroma was also full of all the greenness, just as the summer has the sweetest aroma of herbs and flowers.

Because with a most chaste heart they had won the trials of the flesh wisely with the holy virtues in the devotion of their hearts right up to the consummation of good perseverance, they were clothed with the whitest garment interwoven with gold and embellished with the most precious stones from their breast to their feet, in the manner of a hanging sash. Because they had done this in the praiseworthy and lovable name of virginity, their garment emitted a very strong aroma, like perfume. They had also restrained their will against perilous rashness by taming their own flesh. Because they had abstained with the sweetness of honesty, changing neither here nor there in many different directions, they were girdled with a girdle embellished with gold and gems and pearls beyond human understanding. Wisely giving glory and honor to God in their hearts and competently denying themselves youthful playfulness with the mortification of their bodies, they had given signs of their vow of chastity to men beyond the precepts of the law, fortifying themselves with the sighs of celestial desires and with the strength and firmness of the virtues, just as if they did not have flesh and blood. Because they had been modest with their bodies and had shown modesty in their faces while they fulfilled their various duties, on their head they wore crowns intertwined with gold and roses and lilies and surrounded with pipes of most precious stones.

Because they had inclined themselves to the gentleness of the incarnate Son of God and had lifted their minds to a great height since they had vowed virginity to God and because they had kept their vow worthily and holily, the Lamb of God uses his voice, and this sweetest blowing of the wind coming from the secret place of the Divinity touches the signs of their crowned virginity so that they resound the song of the Lamb that was not in the others who did not have these same signs, although the others can rejoice when they hear this song. Because they had followed in the footsteps God had shown man in his ancient counsel, they wore foot coverings that shone through, as if they had been taken from the fountain of living water.

Because they had always walked wisely and humbly and had offered the movements of their bodies with the purest chastity to the sight of the Divinity and because they had piously and mercifully helped those in need with generous alms, they had transcended human nature with the denial of their fleshly desires, giving praise to God with voice and heart and contemplating his divine miracles and professing him in their contemplation, they sometimes walked as if they were upon golden wheels. They carried lyres in their hands, which they played. And they knew and spoke and understood a foreign language. For while they had been alive, they had imitated the angels and had served God in the singularity of their virginity. They had also given themselves completely in good and holy works as an offering to God. The rest of their embellishments and their significance were truly hidden from my sight and understanding.

Tales of Heavenly Intercession

St. Thérèse of Lisieux (1873–1897)

Thérèse is the saint who promised to spend her heaven doing good on earth. Her autobiography, Story of a Soul *(1898), is an incomparable melange of passionate devotion, sentimentality, and surrender to God's will. Here she describes a vision of three Carmelite saints, whose visit assures her of heaven's solicitude.*

J.M.J.T.

September 8, 1896

(To my dear Sister Marie of the Sacred Heart)

Jesus, my Beloved, who could express the tenderness and sweetness with which You are guiding my soul! It pleases You to cause the rays of Your grace to shine through even in the midst of the darkest storm! Jesus, the storm was raging very strongly in my soul ever since the beautiful feast of Your victory, the radiant feast of Easter; one Saturday in the month of May, thinking of the mysterious dreams which are granted at times to certain souls, I said to myself that these dreams must be very sweet consolation, and yet I wasn't asking for such a consolation. In the evening, considering the clouds which were covering her heaven, my little soul said again within herself that these beautiful dreams were not for her. And then she fell asleep in the midst of the storm. The next day was May 10, the second SUNDAY of Mary's month, and perhaps the anniversary of the day when the Blessed Virgin deigned to smile upon her little flower.

At the first glimmerings of dawn I was (in a dream) in a kind of gallery and there were several other persons, but they were at a distance. Our

Mother was alone near me. Suddenly, without seeing how they had entered, I saw three Carmelites dressed in their mantles and long veils. It appeared to me they were coming for our Mother, but what I did understand clearly was that they came from heaven. In the depths of my heart I cried out: "Oh! how happy I would be if I could see the face of one of these Carmelites!" Then, as though my prayer were heard by her, the tallest of the saints advanced towards me; immediately I fell to my knees. Oh! what happiness! the Carmelite *raised her veil or rather she raised it and covered me with it.* Without the least hesitation, I recognized *Venerable Anne of Jesus,* Foundress of Carmel in France. Her face was beautiful but with an immaterial beauty. No ray escaped from it and still, in spite of the veil which covered us both, I saw this heavenly face suffused with an unspeakably gentle light, a light it didn't receive from without but was produced from within.

I cannot express the joy of my soul since these things are experienced but cannot be put into words. Several months have passed since this sweet dream, and yet the memory it has left in my soul has lost nothing of its freshness and heavenly charms. I still see Venerable Mother's glance and smile which was FILLED WITH LOVE. I believe I can still feel the caresses she gave me at this time.

Seeing myself so tenderly loved, I dared to pronounce these words: "O Mother! I beg you, tell me whether God will leave me for a long time on earth. Will He come soon to get me?" Smiling tenderly, the saint whispered: *"Yes, soon, soon, I promise you."* I added: "Mother, tell me further if God is not asking something more of me than my poor little actions and desires. Is He content with me?" The saint's face took on an expression *incomparably more tender* than the first time she spoke to me. Her look and her caresses were the sweetest of answers. However, she said to me: "God asks no other thing from you. He is content, very content!" After again embracing me with more love than the tenderest of mothers has ever given to her child, I saw her leave. My heart was filled with joy, and then I remembered my Sisters, and I wanted to ask her some favors for them, but alas, I awoke!

O Jesus, the storm was no longer raging, heaven was calm and serene. I *believed,* I *felt* there was a *heaven* and that this *heaven* is peopled with souls who actually love me, who consider me their child. This impression remains in my heart, and this all the more because I was, up until then, *absolutely indifferent to Venerable Mother Anne of Jesus.* I never invoked her in prayer and the thought of her never came to my mind except when I heard others speak of her which was seldom. And when I understood to what a degree *she loved me,* how *indifferent* I had been towards her, my heart was filled with love and gratitude, not only for the Saint who had visited me but for all the blessed inhabitants of heaven.

Evelyn Underhill
(1875–1941)

Underhill was an English poet and scholar of mysticism. "The Window of Paradise" from The Miracles of Our Lady Saint Mary *(1905) is one of the "Mary-legends" of medieval Europe. As Underhill writes, these stories "do in literature that which the Gothic sculptors do in art; make a link between heaven and earth, give actual and familiar significance to the most awful mysteries of faith, and set the Queen of Angels in the midst of her faithful friends."*

The Window of Paradise

Here we tell how a certain sacristan had great comfort of Our Lady, because of these words: Coeli Fenestra Facta Es.

Verily it is a great matter to have Our Lady's friendship, and little need they fear that possess this sovereign grace; for neither man, nor the Enemy in Hell, nor the very Saints that are in Paradise can hurt them, so great a power and subtlety hath the glorious Virgin in her children's help and defence. And that ye may know somewhat of the manner in which she guards us, I will here set in writing the adventure of a certain poor Christian that was sacristan in the church of the Blessed Apostle Saint Peter that is in the city of Rome.

Now amongst the many offices wherewith this sacristan was charged, one devoir he had of great import, namely, to tend and nourish with pure oil the lamps that burned before the altars of the Saints; for these lamps should burn for ever with an unchanging light, being indeed the emblem of the Church's prayers. And because he had a special love for our dear Lady Saint Mary, this sacristan had exceeding care of the lamp that was before her altar, and trimmed it very often, and kept it always filled with oil and burning brightly. But one day it chanced that this lamp wanted for oil, so that its light grew dim and was like to be extinguished; and when he saw it he was much vexed, and cast about to see what he might do to replenish it as quickly as he could.

Now the lamp that burned before the shrine of the Blessed Apostle Saint Peter was full of oil even to the brim; and it burned with a great light, exceeding all other in the church. Therefore this sacristan, for that he was old and somewhat slothful, bethought him that he would take a little oil from Saint Peter's lamp, and therefrom replenish that of the Blessed Virgin Mary, the which was like to be extinguished. This he did, thinking no harm of it, for he held that even the Prince of the Apostles should find it a pleasant thing and just to give to God's Mother those things of which she stood in need. And not on this day only, but on many others, he fed the lamp of his Lady from out the superfluity of oil which Saint Peter's suppliants offered at his shrine.

Nevertheless, that holy Apostle was greatly vexed at it; for he was of opinion that in this church, wherein his confession was, he stood higher than all other saints, yea, even than the Queen of Angels herself. And he could not endure that the oil of his lamp should be taken in order that a brighter flame might burn before that Lady's shrine. Therefore one night he came from Paradise and appeared in vision before that sacristan whiles he slept, and with angry looks he saith to him:

"Wherefore, oh sacristan, have you taken the oil from my lamp? Is it for this that my shrine has been given into your keeping?"

Said the sacristan, "Messire Saint Peter, I did but borrow a little that the lamp of Our Lady Saint Mary might be fed."

The Apostle replied, "God's Mother hath much honour in many lands, and many shrines and pilgrimages there are established in her name: but this is my house, wherein my body lies, that is the very Rock on which the Church is built, and here I can in no wise suffer that you do the Lady Mary this courtesy at my expense. Oil has been provided wherewith to light her altar, and this must suffice. Here am I accustomed to be honoured above all other saints, and ill shall it be for them that fail to give me my due. Behold, I keep the key of Heaven, and none can enter in save them to whom I open; and if you be so hardy to come thither, that have given me less oil that the Blessed Virgin may have more, very surely I shall shut the door in your face."

Then the sacristan awoke, full of dread, and he rose up swiftly and went into the church; and there he made haste to tend the lamp of the

Blessed Apostle Saint Peter and show him every courtesy he could. But little hope did he have of it, for he knew him to be a hasty and a vengeful man.

And when he had done all he might for Saint Peter's lamp, then did he give oil to the one that burned before Saint Mary's altar, and, "Ah, dearest Lady," he said, "how dearly have I paid for my love! For the Blessed Apostle Saint Peter is very wrathful because I have dared to prefer your service before his; and since I have earned his enmity, he will not open the door of Heaven to let me in. Alas, Madame, what shall I do? Because of my devotion I am like to be damned, for very surely none shall enter Paradise that have not the goodwill of him that keeps the keys."

But behold, that night as he lay on his bed, Madame Saint Mary came and stood beside that poor sacristan, and spoke comfortable words to him, saying:

"My very dear friend and faithful servant, be joyful and fear not, for none can harm you whiles you have my love. Therefore continue firmly in all that you have aforetime done, honouring me at my altar and tending my lamp before all else. If this you do, greatly shall it profit you; for though the Apostle Saint Peter refuse to open the door of Heaven to let you in, yet is he powerless to keep you from the Celestial City so long as you do call upon my name. Very truly he keeps the keys of the door of Paradise, but so soon as he hath shut it against you, I, of whom my anthem saith, "Coeli fenestra facta es," shall open the window, that thereby you may come in. This will I ever do for my friends that fail not in my service; for the door of Heaven is a very narrow gate, and Saint Peter keepeth it exceeding straitly, but the window of my love is very wide."

Then was the poor sacristan greatly comforted by the words that the Queen of Heaven had said; and he rose up full of joy to give her thanks, repeating much devoutly the anthem that was an earnest of her grace. Ever after he tended her lamp before all others, so that it burned day and night with exceeding splendour, the brightest in all that church. No heed did he give to the wrath that the Blessed Apostle Saint Peter might feel at it, that was so greatly jealous for the honour of his shrine; for he knew that all the Saints that are in Paradise, yea, and the very hosts of highest Heaven, are powerless to do hurt to those poor Christians that do serve God's Mother zealously and with love.

Elijah

From Louis Ginzberg's Legends of the Jews, *these tales recount Elijah's service to mankind after his translation to heaven.*

About three years later, Elijah was taken up into heaven, but not without first undergoing a struggle with the Angel of Death. He refused to let Elijah enter heaven at his translation, on the ground that he exercised jurisdiction over all mankind, Elijah not excepted. God maintained that at the creation of heaven and earth He had explicitly ordered the Angel of Death to grant entrance to the living prophet, but the Angel of Death insisted that by Elijah's translation God had given just cause for complaint to all other men, who could not escape the doom of death. Thereupon God: "Elijah is not like other men. He is able to banish thee from the world, only thou dost not recognize his strength." With the consent of God, a combat took place between Elijah and the Angel of Death. The prophet was victorious, and, if God had not restrained him, he would have annihilated his opponent. Holding his defeated enemy under his feet, Elijah ascended heavenward.

In heaven he goes on living for all time. There he sits recording the deeds of men and the chronicles of the world. He has another office besides. He is the Psychopomp, whose duty is to stand at the cross-ways in Paradise and guide the pious to their appointed places; who brings the souls of sinners up from Gehenna at the approach of the Sabbath, and leads them back again to their merited punishment when the day of rest is about to depart; and who conducts these same souls, after they have atoned for their sins, to the place of everlasting bliss.

Elijah's miraculous deeds will be better understood if we remember that he had been an angel from the very first, even before the end of his earthly career. When God was about to create man, Elijah said to Him: "Master of the world! If it be pleasing in Thine eyes, I will descend to earth, and make myself serviceable to the sons of men." Then God changed his angel name, and later, under Ahab, He permitted him to abide among men on earth, that he might convert the world to the belief that "the Lord is God." His mission fulfilled, God took him again into heaven, and said to him: "Be thou the guardian spirit of My children forever, and spread the belief in Me abroad in the whole world."

His angel name is Sandalphon, one of the greatest and mightiest of the fiery angel host. As such it is his duty to wreathe garlands for God out of the prayers sent aloft by Israel. Besides, he must offer up sacrifices in the invisible sanctuary, for the Temple was destroyed only apparently; in reality, it went on existing, hidden from the sight of ordinary mortals.

After His Translation

Elijah's removal from earth, so far from being an interruption to his relations with men, rather marks the beginning of his real activity as a helper in time of need, as a teacher and as a guide. At first his intervention in sublunar affairs was not frequent. Seven years after his translation, he wrote a letter to the wicked king Jehoram, who reigned over Judah. The next occasion on which he took part in an earthly occurrence was at the time of Ahasuerus, when he did the Jews a good turn by assuming the guise of the courtier Harbonah, in a favorable moment inciting the king against Haman.

It was reserved for later days, however, for Talmudic times, the golden age of the great scholars, the Tannaim and the Amoraim, to enjoy Elijah's special vigilance as protector of the innocent, as a friend in need, who hovers over the just and the pious, ever present to guard them against evil or snatch them out of danger. With four strokes of his wings Elijah can traverse the world. Hence no spot on earth is too far removed for his help. As an angel he enjoys the power of assuming the most various appearances to accomplish his purposes. Sometimes he looks like an ordinary man, sometimes he takes the appearance of an Arab, sometimes of a horseman, now he is a Roman court-official, now he is a harlot.

Once upon a time it happened that when Nahum, the great and pious teacher, was journeying to Rome on a political mission, he was without his knowledge robbed of the gift he bore to the Emperor as an offering from the Jews. When he handed the casket to the ruler, it was found to contain common earth, which the thieves had substituted for the jewels they had abstracted. The Emperor thought the Jews were mocking at him, and their representative, Nahum, was condemned to suffer death. In his piety the Rabbi did not lose confidence in God; he only said: "This too is for good." And so it turned out to be. Suddenly Elijah appeared, and, assuming the guise of a court-official, he said: "Perhaps the earth in this casket is like that used by Abraham for purposes of war. A handful will do the work of swords and bows." At his instance the virtues of the earth were tested in the attack upon a city that had long resisted Roman courage and strength. His supposition was verified. The contents of the casket proved more efficacious than all the weapons of the army, and the Romans were victorious. Nahum was dismissed, laden with honors and treasures, and the thieves, who had betrayed themselves by claiming the precious earth, were executed, for, naturally enough, Elijah works no wonders for evil-doers.

Another time, for the purpose of rescuing Rabbi Shila, Elijah pretended to be a Persian. An informer had denounced the Rabbi with the Persian Government, accusing him of administering the law according to the Jewish code. Elijah appeared as witness for the Rabbi and against the informer, and Shila was honorably dismissed.

When the Roman bailiffs were pursuing Rabbi Meïr, Elijah joined him in the guise of a harlot. The Roman emissaries desisted from their pursuit, for they could not believe that Rabbi Meir would choose such a companion.

A contemporary of Rabbi Meïr, Rabbi Simon ben Yohai, who spent thirteen years in a cave to escape the vengeance of the Romans, was informed by Elijah of the death of the Jew-baiting emperor, so that he could leave his hiding-place.

Equally characteristic is the help Elijah afforded the worthy poor. Frequently he brought them great wealth. Rabbi Kahana was so needy that he had to support himself by peddling with household utensils. Once a lady of high standing endeavored to force him to commit an immoral act, and Kahana, preferring death to iniquity, threw himself from a loft. Though Elijah was at a distance of four hundred parasangs, he hastened to the spot in time to catch the Rabbi before he touched the ground. Besides, he gave him means enough to enable him to abandon an occupation beset with perils.

Rabba bar Abbahu likewise was a victim of poverty. He admitted to Elijah that on account of his small means he had no time to devote to his studies. Thereupon Elijah led him into Paradise, bade him remove his mantle, and fill it with leaves grown in the regions of the blessed. When the Rabbi was about to quit Paradise, his garment full of leaves, a voice was heard to say: "Who desires to anticipate his share in the world to come during his earthly days, as Rabba bar Abbahu is doing?" The Rabbi quickly cast the leaves away; nevertheless he received twelve thousand denarii for his upper garment, because it retained the wondrous fragrance of the leaves of Paradise.

Elijah's help was not confined to poor teachers of the law; all who were in need, and were worthy of his assistance, had a claim upon him. A poor man, the father of a family, in his distress once prayed to God: "O Lord of the world, Thou knowest, there is none to whom I can tell my tale of woe, none who will have pity upon me. I have neither brother nor kinsman nor friend, and my starving little ones are crying with hunger. Then do Thou have mercy and be compassionate, or let death come and put an end to our suffering." His words found a hearing with God, for, as he finished, Elijah stood before the poor man, and sympathetically inquired why he was weeping. When the prophet had heard the tale of his troubles, he said: "Take me and sell me as a slave; the proceeds will suffice for thy needs." At first the poor man refused to accept the sacrifice, but finally he yielded, and Elijah was sold to a prince for eighty denarii. This sum formed the nucleus of the fortune which the poor man amassed and enjoyed until the end of his days. The prince who had purchased Elijah intended to build a palace, and he rejoiced to hear that his new slave was an architect. He promised Elijah liberty if within six months he completed the edifice. After nightfall of the same day, Elijah offered a prayer, and instantaneously the palace stood in its place in complete perfection. Elijah disappeared. The next morning the prince was not a little astonished to see the palace finished. But when he sought his slave to reward him, and sought him in vain, he realized that he had had dealings with an angel. Elijah meantime repaired to the man who had sold him, and related his story to him, that he might know he had not cheated the purchaser out of his price; on the contrary, he had enriched him, since the palace was worth a hundred times more than the money paid for the pretended slave.

A similar thing happened to a well-to-do man who lost his fortune, and became so poor that he had to do manual labor in the field of another. Once, when he was at work, he was accosted by Elijah, who had assumed the appearance of an Arab: "Thou art destined to enjoy seven good years. When dost thou want them—now, or as the closing years of thy life?" The man replied: "Thou art a wizard; go in peace, I have nothing for thee."

Three times the same question was put, three times the same reply was given. Finally the man said: "I shall ask the advice of my wife." When Elijah came again, and repeated his question, the man, following the counsel of his wife, said: "See to it that seven good years come to us at once." Elijah replied: "Go home. Before thou crossest thy threshold, thy good fortune will have filled thy house." And so it was. His children had found a treasure in the ground, and, as he was about to enter his house, his wife met him and reported the lucky find. His wife was an estimable, pious woman, and she said to her husband: "We shall enjoy seven good years. Let us use this time to practice as much charity as possible; perhaps God will lengthen out our period of prosperity." After the lapse of seven years, during which man and wife used every opportunity of doing good, Elijah appeared again, and announced to the man that the time had come to take away what he had given him. The man responded: "When I accepted thy gift, it was after consultation with my wife. I should not like to return it without first acquainting her with what is about to happen." His wife charged him to say to the old man who had come to resume possession of his property: "If thou canst find any who will be more conscientious stewards of the pledges entrusted to us than we have been, I shall willingly yield them up to thee." God recognized that these people had made a proper use of their wealth, and He granted it to them as a perpetual possession.

If Elijah was not able to lighten the poverty of the pious, he at least sought to inspire them with hope and confidence. Rabbi Akiba, the great scholar, lived in dire poverty before he became the famous Rabbi. His rich father-in-law would have nothing to do with him or his wife, because the daughter had married Akiba against her father's will. On a bitter cold winter night, Akiba could offer his wife, who had been accustomed to the luxuries wealth can buy, nothing but straw as a bed to sleep upon, and he tried to comfort her with assurances of his love for the privations she was suffering. At that moment Elijah appeared before their hut, and cried out in supplicating tones: "O good people, give me, I pray you, a little bundle of straw. My wife has been delivered of a child, and I am so poor I haven't even enough straw to make a bed for her." Now Akiba could console his wife with the fact that their own misery was not so great as it might have been, and thus Elijah had attained his end, to sustain the courage of the pious.

In the form of an Arab, he once appeared before a very poor man, whose piety equalled his poverty. He gave him two shekels. These two coins brought him such good fortune that he attained great wealth. But in his zeal to gather worldly treasures, he had no time for deeds of piety and charity. Elijah again appeared before him and took away the two shekels. In a short time the man was as poor as before. A third time Elijah came to him. He was crying bitterly and complaining of his misfortune, and the prophet said: "I shall make thee rich once more, if thou wilt promise me under oath thou wilt not let wealth ruin thy character." He promised, the two shekels were restored to him, he regained his wealth, and he remained in possession of it for all time, because his piety was not curtailed by his riches.

Poverty was not the only form of distress Elijah relieved. He exercised the functions of a physician upon Rabbi Shimi bar Ashi, who had swallowed a noxious reptile. Elijah appeared to him as an awe-inspiring horseman, and forced him to apply the preventives against the disease to be expected in these circumstances.

He also cured Rabbi Judah ha-Nasi of long-continued toothache by laying his hand on the sufferer, and at the same time he brought about the reconciliation of Rabbi Judah with Rabbi Hayyah, whose form he had assumed. Rabbi Judah paid the highest respect to Rabbi Hayyah after he found out that Elijah had considered him worthy of taking his appearance.

On another occasion, Elijah re-established harmony between a husband and his wife. The woman had come home very late one Friday evening, having allowed herself to be detained by the sermon preached by Rabbi Meïr. Her autocratic husband swore she should not enter the house until she had spat in the very face of the highly-esteemed Rabbi. Meantime Elijah went to Rabbi Meïr, and told him a pious woman had fallen into a sore predicament on his account. To help the poor woman, the Rabbi resorted to a ruse. He announced that he was looking for one who knew how to cast spells, which was done by spitting into the eye of the afflicted one. When he caught sight of the woman designated by Elijah, he asked her to try her power upon him. Thus she was able to comply with her husband's requirement without disrespect to the Rabbi; and through the instrumentality of Elijah conjugal happiness was restored to an innocent wife.

Elijah's versatility is shown in the following occurrence. A pious man bequeathed a spice-garden to his three sons. They took turns in guarding it against thieves. The first night the oldest son watched the garden. Elijah appeared to him and asked him: "My son, what wilt thou have—knowledge of the Torah, or great wealth, or a beautiful wife?" He chose wealth, great wealth. Accordingly Elijah gave him a coin, and he became rich. The second son, to whom Elijah appeared the second night, chose knowledge of the Torah. Elijah gave him a book, and "he knew the whole Torah." The third son, on the third night, when Elijah put the same choice before him as before his brothers, wished for a beautiful wife. Elijah invited this third brother to go on a journey with him. Their first night was passed at the house of a notorious villain, who had a daughter. During the night Elijah overheard the chickens and the geese say to one another: "What a terrible sin that young man must have committed, that he should be destined to marry the daughter of so great a villain!" The two travellers journeyed on. The second night the experiences of the first were repeated. The third night they lodged with a man who had a very pretty daughter. During the night Elijah heard the chickens and the geese say to one another. "How great must be the virtues of this young man, if he is privileged to marry so beautiful and pious a wife." In the morning, when Elijah arose, he at once became a matchmaker, the young man married the pretty maiden, and husband and wife journeyed homeward in joy.

If it became necessary, Elijah was ready to do even the services of a sexton. When Rabbi Akiba died in prison Elijah betook himself to the dead man's faithful disciple Rabbi Joshua, and the two together went to the prison. There was none to forbid their entrance; a deep sleep had fallen upon the turnkeys and the prisoners alike. Elijah and Rabbi Joshua took the corpse with them. Elijah bearing it upon his shoulder. Rabbi Joshua in astonishment demanded how he, a priest, dared defile himself upon a corpse. The answer was: "God forbid! the pious can never cause defilement." All night the two walked on with their burden. At break of day they found themselves near Caesarea. A cave opened before their eyes, and within they saw a bed, a chair, a table, and a lamp. They deposited the corpse upon the bed, and left the cave, which closed up behind them. Only the light of the lamp, which had lit itself after they left, shone through the chinks. Whereupon Elijah said: "Hail, ye just, hail to you who devote yourself to the study of the law. Hail to you, ye God-fearing men, for your places are set aside, and kept, and guarded, in Paradise, for the time to come. Hail to thee, Rabbi Akiba, that thy lifeless body found lodgment for a night in a lovely spot."

Jalal ad-Din ar-Rumi
(1207–1273)

From the angelic Sufi master of Persian mystical poetry, this selection is a meditation on the saints as channels of divine regenerative power.

The Spirit of the Saints

There is a Water that flows down from Heaven
To cleanse the world of sin by grace Divine.
At last, its whole stock spent, its virtue gone,
Dark with pollution not its own, it speeds
Back to the Fountain of all purities;
Whence, freshly bathed, earthward it sweeps again,
Trailing a robe of glory bright and pure.

This Water is the Spirit of the Saints,
Which ever sheds, until itself is beggared,
God's balm on the sick soul; and then returns
To Him who made the purest light of Heaven.

VI

Heaven on Earth

Introduction

The most celebrated gates to heaven hinge on death or vision. But what if there were another way to enter? For thousands of years it has been rumored in poetry, song, travel narratives, and social manifestos that heaven may exist right here on earth, accessible to those with the courage or sanctity to seek it out.

One of the most curious expressions of this idea comes in our first selection, from Plato's *Phaedo*. Socrates begins by describing the earth as "a round body in the centre of the heavens," so vast that those who dwell in the region around Greece "inhabit a small portion only about the sea, like ants or frogs about a marsh." But in believing that we dwell on the earth's surface and that the sky above us is heaven, we are deceived, Socrates suggests. In fact, we live in the earth's hollows, where the sediment of the upper world collects; we breathe an impure mixture of mist and air, drink brackish water, and feed on slimy vegetation. The real earth is what we call heaven; there above, air is true ground and ether is true air. If we could climb high enough, we would discover that this land is inhabited by people who live long, disease-free lives; converse freely with the gods; and "see the sun, moon, and stars as they truly are." Socrates is speaking allegorically, of course, but if we are immortal, he explains, then either this or something like it must be true.

The eighth-century *Voyage of Bran* describes an attempt to reach heaven by sail. A mysterious woman appears in court, bearing a magical apple branch and singing of the Land of the Living, a western paradise of 150 isles unvisited by sorrow, disease, or death. Bran sets sail with thirty men; his exploits constitute perhaps the finest of the Irish *imramha*, or voyages of adventure, a genre that also includes numerous accounts of actual westward voyages by Irish monks. Fact or legend, most *imramha* describe the same motive for travel: the search for paradise. Nor is this quest limited to Irish religions; many of the great explorers set out in search not only of earthly gold but of the golden ramparts of paradise. Indeed Columbus, in his third voyage to the Americas, was convinced that he had discovered, near the Gulf of Paria between Venezuela and Trinidad, the outskirts of this long-sought goal. In an entirely different cultural setting, we find the Tibetan story of Shambhala (the original for the Shangri-La of James Hilton's 1948 best-seller, *Lost Horizon*). There are fantastical elements here as well—jeweled cities, shape-shifting witches, great serpents—but nonetheless Shambhala is conceived as a real paradise, "gleaming among ranges of snow mountains like stars on the waves of the Ocean of Milk."

The paradise of *The Romance of the Rose*, by contrast, is strictly literary, a walled garden teeming with allegorical figures such as Idleness, Beauty, Courtesy, and a God of Love with a quiver packed with arrows. Also not meant to be taken literally are the wonderful medieval legends of Cockaigne, later renamed Lubberland (see "The Hobo's Last Lament" in chapter 1), a city of fantastical largesse where the rivers run with claret, hot roasted pigs scamper down the streets squealing "Come eat me," and neither law nor labor exists to impede the inhabitants' perfect freedom.

One must travel far to arrive at Cockaigne, Shambhala, or the Land of the Living, but sometimes heaven can be found close at hand, as in our excerpt from the Bhagavata Purana, in which Krishna's revels with the cowherd wives (the *gopis*) transform Vrindavana, on the banks of the holy river Yamuna, into a divine bower of love and thus into one of the great sacred sites of India, that preeminent land of pilgrims.

Even a clod of mud may be an image of heaven, if it marks the site of a divine visitation. Jacob was sleeping on a stone pillow, in an undistinguished spot, when he dreamed of the ladder of heaven. On awakening, he exclaimed, "How dreadful is this place! this is none other but the house of God, and this is the gate of heaven" (Genesis 28:17). That crude stone on which Jacob slept foreshadowed the Temple where his descendants would celebrate the liturgy of heaven. It's a universal idea: All houses of worship symbolize heaven, whether by their heaven-shaped domes or soaring transepts, their images of heavenly beings or scrolls of divine words, or by the heavenly fragrance, music, and light with which they are filled. Heaven also touches earth in certain places reputed to be the center of the world—Jerusalem, Banaras, Mecca, Black Elk's Harney Peak—and at certain times, as well: when the star of Bethlehem passes overhead, when the year of jubilee arrives, when a child is born, when a good person dies.

In Hans Christian Andersen's "A Leaf from Heaven," a "very little leaf" dropped by an angel takes root in the middle of a wood, where it attracts the attention of a young girl, a professor, a swineherd, and a king. Only the girl benefits from its presence, for she alone has the purity of heart that enables her to find it and put it to good use. Mikhail Lermontov writes of another angel who brings to earth a newborn soul, all the while singing a heavenly song that the soul will remember during its terrestrial sojourn: "And that heavenly music was never usurped / By the wearisome songs of the earth." The idea that infants retain a vivid memory of heaven, epitomized in Wordsworth's description of newborns "trailing clouds of glory" ("Ode: Intimations of Immortality"), finds ecstatic expression in the memories of Thomas Traherne, who reports that at birth, "My Knowledg was Divine. I knew by Intuition those things which since my Apostasie, I Collected again, by the Highest Reason . . . I saw all in the Peace of Eden . . . All Time was Eternity, and a Perpetual Sabbath."

How can this divine state be regained? For Traherne, the task entails "unlearning" the "Dirty Devices of this World" with the grace of God; for others, it is a matter of social engineering. Heaven can be ours in this lifetime, if we rearrange our customs. Charles Fourier's rearrangement—or derangement, one is tempted to say—involved the creation of "phalanxes," small socialist agricultural communities. So far so reasonable, but Fourier believed that if his theories were followed, we would witness "the most spectacular historical change which can take place in all the universes," including not only universal peace, but the transformation of the ocean from salt water into lemonade. Despite these bizarre claims, Fourier found many followers, including Nathaniel Hawthorne and Charles Dana, stockholders in the Fourier-inspired utopia of Brook Farm in Massachusetts. Life at Brook Farm was pleasant enough during the few years of its existence, but it suffered, one suspects, from the same malaise that William James found in the quasi-utopian educational community by Chatauqua Lake: a life without crime, drunkenness, or discord; a life "so refined that ice-cream soda-water is the utmost offering it can make to the brute animal in man." A middle-class heaven, James discovered, is no heaven at all.

In our excerpt from *Paradise Lost*, John Milton provides, from a Satan's-eye view, a glimpse of the first utopia:

> From this Assyrian garden, where the Fiend
> Saw undelighted all delight, all kind
> Of living creatures, new to sight and strange.
> Two of far nobler shape, erect and tall,
> God-like erect, with native honor clad
> In naked majesty, seemed lords of all,
> And worthy seemed; for in their looks divine
> The image of their glorious Maker shone . . .

Remembering what happened to Adam and Eve, we should not be surprised at any utopian experiment that runs afoul; even so, there is something of heaven in the persistent desire to live, as in the Shaker song, "in the valley of love and delight."

Plato

(428/427–348/347 B.C.)

In the Phaedo, *Plato's memorial tribute to Socrates, we see the master on the verge of martyrdom, encouraging his disciples by engaging in a philosophic quest for reasons to believe in immortality. In this parable, Socrates proposes that we are living in the hollows of the earth; the real earth is what we call heaven, and the philosopher who awakens to this truth is already halfway there.*

Well then, he said, my conviction is, that the earth is a round body in the centre of the heavens, and therefore has no need of air or of any similar force to be a support, but is kept there and hindered from falling or inclining any way by the equability of the surrounding heaven and by her own equipoise. For that which, being in equipoise, is in the centre of that which is equably diffused, will not incline any way in any degree, but will always remain in the same state and not deviate. And this is my first notion.

Which is surely a correct one, said Simmias.

Also I believe that the earth is very vast, and that we who dwell in the region extending from the river Phasis to the Pillars of Heracles inhabit a small portion only about the sea, like ants or frogs about a marsh, and that there are other inhabitants of many other like places; for everywhere on the face of the earth there are hollows of various forms and sizes, into which the water and the mist and the lower air collect. But the true earth is pure and situated in the pure heaven—there are the stars also; and it is the heaven which is commonly spoken of by us as the ether, and of which our own earth is the sediment gathering in the hollows beneath. But we who live in these hollows are deceived into the notion that we are dwelling above on the surface of the earth, which is just as if a creature who was at the bottom of the sea were to fancy that he was on the surface of the water, and that the sea was the heaven through which he saw the sun and the other stars, he having never come to the surface by reason of his feebleness and sluggishness, and having never lifted up his head and seen, nor ever heard from one who had seen, how much purer and fairer the world above is than his own. And such is exactly our case: for we are dwelling in a hollow of the earth, and fancy that we are on the surface; and the air we call the heaven, in which we imagine that the stars move. But the fact is, that owing to our feebleness and sluggishness we are prevented from reaching the surface of the air: for if any man could arrive at the exterior limit, or take the wings of a bird and come to the top, then like a fish who puts his head out of the water and sees this world, he would see a world beyond; and, if the nature of man could sustain the sight, he would acknowledge that this other world was the place of the true heaven and the true light and the true earth. For our earth, and the stones, and the entire region which surrounds us, are spoilt and corroded, as in the sea all things are corroded by the brine, neither is there any noble or perfect growth, but caverns only, and sand, and an endless slough of mud; and even the shore is not to be compared to the fairer sights of this world. And still less is this our world to be compared with the other. Of that upper earth which is under the heaven, I can tell you a charming tale, Simmias, which is well worth hearing.

And we, Socrates, replied Simmias, shall be charmed to listen to you.

The tale, my friend, he said, is as follows:—In the first place, the earth, when looked at from above, is in appearance streaked like one of those balls which have leather coverings in twelve pieces, and is decked with various colours, of which the colours used by painters on earth are in a manner samples. But there the whole earth is made up of them, and they are brighter far and clearer than ours; there is a purple of wonderful lustre, also the radiance of gold, and the white which is in the earth is whiter than any chalk or snow. Of these and other colours the earth is made up, and they are more in number and fairer than the eye of man has ever seen; the very hollows (of which I was speaking) filled with air and water have a colour of their own, and are seen like light gleaming amid the diversity of the other colours, so that the whole presents a single and continuous appearance of variety in unity. And in this fair region everything that grows—trees, and flowers, and fruits—are in a like degree fairer than any here; and there are hills, having stones in them in a like degree smoother, and more transparent, and fairer in colour than our highly valued emeralds and sardonyxes and jaspers, and other gems, which are but minute fragments of them: for there all the stones are like our precious stones, and fairer still. The reason is, that they are pure, and not, like our precious stones, infected or corroded by the corrupt briny elements which coagulate among us, and which breed foulness and disease both in earth and stones, as well as in animals and plants. They are the jewels of the upper earth, which also shines with gold and silver and the like, and they are set in the light of day and are large and abundant and in all places, making the earth a sight to gladden the beholder's eye. And there are animals and men, some in a middle region, others dwelling about the air as we dwell about the sea; others in islands which the air flows round, near the continent; and in a word, the air is used by them as the water and the sea are by us, and the ether is to them what the air is to us. Moreover, the temperament of their seasons is such that they have no disease, and live much longer than we do, and have sight and hearing and smell, and all the other senses, in far greater perfection, in the same proportion that air is purer than water or the ether than air. Also they have temples and sacred places in which the gods really dwell, and they hear their voices and receive their answers, and are conscious of them and hold converse with them; and they see the sun, moon, and stars as they truly are, and their other blessedness is of a piece with this.

The Voyage of Bran
(Eighth Century)

The old Irish Imram Brain *has Bran and his companions traveling by sea to the Land of the Living, an archipelago beyond the reach of time and death. Their last sojourn is in the Land of the Women, where the delights are such that years pass in a moment.*

The Voyage of Bran son of Febal, and his Expedition here below

'Twas fifty quatrains the woman from unknown lands sang on the floor of the house to Bran son of Febal, when the royal house was full of kings, who knew not whence the woman had come, since the ramparts were closed.

2. This is the beginning of the story. One day, in the neighbourhood of his stronghold, Bran went about alone, when he heard music behind him. As often as he looked back, 'twas still behind him the music was. At last he fell asleep at the music, such was its sweetness. When he awoke from his sleep, he saw close by him a branch of silver with white blossoms, nor was it easy to distinguish its bloom from that branch. Then Bran took the branch in his hand to his royal house. When the hosts were in the royal house, they saw a woman in strange raiment on the floor of the house. 'Twas then she sang the fifty quatrains to Bran, while the host heard her, and all beheld the woman.

And she said:

3. 'A branch of the apple-tree from Emain
I bring, like those one knows;
Twigs of white silver are on it,
Crystal brows with blossoms.

4. 'There is a distant isle,
Around which sea-horses glisten:
A fair course against the white-swelling surge,
Four feet uphold it.

5. 'A delight of the eyes, a glorious range,
Is the plain on which the hosts hold games:
Coracle contends against chariot
In southern Mag Findargat.

6. 'Feet of white bronze under it
Glittering through beautiful ages.
Lovely land throughout the world's age,
On which the many blossoms drop.

7. 'An ancient tree there is with blossoms,
On which birds call to the Hours.
'Tis in harmony it is their wont
To call together every Hour.

8. 'Splendours of every colour glisten
Throughout the gentle-voiced plains.
Joy is known, ranked around music,
In southern Mag Argatnél.

9. 'Unknown is wailing or treachery
In the familiar cultivated land,
There is nothing rough or harsh,
But sweet music striking on the ear.

10. 'Without grief, without sorrow, without death,
Without any sickness, without debility,
That is the sign of Emain—
Uncommon is an equal marvel.

11. 'A beauty of a wondrous land,
Whose aspects are lovely,

Whose view is a fair country,
Incomparable is its haze.

12. 'Then if Aircthech is seen
On which dragonstones and crystals drop
The sea washes the wave against the land,
Hair of crystal drops from its mane.

13. 'Wealth, treasures of every hue,
Are in Ciuin, a beauty of freshness,
Listening to sweet music,
Drinking the best of wine.

14. 'Golden chariots in Mag Réin,
Rising with the tide to the sun,
Chariots of silver in Mag Mon,
And of bronze without blemish.

15. 'Yellow golden steeds are on the sward there,
Other steeds with crimson hue,
Others with wool upon their backs
Of the hue of heaven all-blue.

16. 'At sunrise there will come
A fair man illumining level lands;
He rides upon the fair sea-washed plain,
He stirs the ocean till it is blood.

17. 'A host will come across the clear sea,
To the land they show their rowing;
Then they row to the conspicuous stone,
From which arise a hundred strains.

18. 'It sings a strain unto the host
Through long ages, it is not sad,
Its music swells with choruses of hundreds—
They look for neither decay nor death.

19. 'Many-shaped Emne by the sea,
Whether it be near, whether it be far,
In which are many thousands of motley women,
Which the clear sea encircles.

20. 'If he has heard the voice of the music,
The chorus of the little birds from Imchiuin,
A small band of women will come from a height
To the plain of sport in which he is.

21. 'There will come happiness with health
To the land against which laughter peals,
Into Imchiuin at every season
Will come everlasting joy.

22. 'It is a day of lasting weather
That showers silver on the lands,
A pure-white cliff on the range of the sea,
Which from the sun receives its heat.

23. 'The host race along Mag Mon,
A beautiful game, not feeble,
In the variegated land over a mass of beauty
They look for neither decay nor death.

24. 'Listening to music at night,
And going into Ildathach,
A variegated land, splendour on a diadem of beauty,
Whence the white cloud glistens.

25. 'There are thrice fifty distant isles
In the ocean to the west of us;
Larger than Erin twice
Is each of them, or thrice.

26. 'A great birth will come after ages,
That will not be in a lofty place,

The son of a woman whose mate will not be known,
He will seize the rule of the many thousands.

27. 'A rule without beginning, without end,
He has created the world so that it is perfect,
Whose are earth and sea,
Woe to him that shall be under His unwill!

28. ' 'Tis He that made the heavens,
Happy he that has a white heart,
He will purify hosts under pure water,
'Tis He that will heal your sicknesses.

29. 'Not to all of you is my speech,
Though its great marvel has been made known:
Let Bran hear from the crowd of the world
What of wisdom has been told to him.

30. 'Do not fall on a bed of sloth,
Let not thy intoxication overcome thee,
Begin a voyage across the clear sea,
If perchance thou mayst reach the land of women.'

31. Thereupon the woman went from them, while they knew not whither she went. And she took her branch with her. The branch sprang from Bran's hand into the hand of the woman, nor was there strength in Bran's hand to hold the branch.

32. Then on the morrow Bran went upon the sea. The number of his men was three companies of nine. One of his foster-brothers and mates was set over each of the three companies of nine. When he had been at sea two days and two nights, he saw a man in a chariot coming towards him over the sea. That man also sang thirty other quatrains to him, and made himself known to him, and said that he was Manannan the son of Ler, and said that it was upon him to go to Ireland after long ages, and that a son would be born to him, even Mongan son of Fiachna—that was the name which would be upon him.

So he sang these thirty quatrains to him:

33. 'Bran deems it a marvellous beauty
In his coracle across the clear sea:
While to me in my chariot from afar
It is a flowery plain on which he rides about.

34. 'What is a clear sea
For the prowed skiff in which Bran is,
That is a happy plain with profusion of flowers
To me from the chariot of two wheels.

35. 'Bran sees
The number of waves beating across the clear sea:
I myself see in Mag Mon
Red-headed flowers without fault.

36. 'Sea-horses glisten in summer
As far as Bran has stretched his glance:
Rivers pour forth a stream of honey
In the land of Manannan son of Ler.

37. 'The sheen of the main, on which thou art,
The white hue of the sea, on which thou rowest about,
Yellow and azure are spread out,
It is land, and is not rough.

38. 'Speckled salmon leap from the womb
Of the white sea, on which thou lookest:
They are calves, they are coloured lambs
With friendliness, without mutual slaughter.

39. 'Though (but) one chariot-rider is seen
In Mag Mell of many flowers,
There are many steeds on its surface,
Though them thou seest not.

40. 'The size of the plain, the number of the host,
Colours glisten with pure glory,

A fair stream of silver, cloths of gold,
Afford a welcome with all abundance.

41. 'A beautiful game, most delightful,
They play (sitting) at the luxurious wine,
Men and gentle women under a bush,
Without sin, without crime.

42. 'Along the top of a wood has swum
Thy coracle across ridges,
There is a wood of beautiful fruit
Under the prow of thy little skiff.

43. 'A wood with blossom and fruit,
On which is the vine's veritable fragrance,
A wood without decay, without defect,
On which are leaves of golden hue.

44. 'We are from the beginning of creation
Without old age, without consummation of earth,
Hence we expect not that there should be frailty,
The sin has not come to us.

45. 'An evil day when the Serpent went
To the father to his city!
She has perverted the times in this world,
So that there came decay which was not original.

46. 'By greed and lust he has slain us,
Through which he has ruined his noble race:
The withered body has gone to the fold of torment,
And everlasting abode of torture.

47. 'It is a law of pride in this world
To believe in the creatures, to forget God,
Overthrow by diseases, and old age,
Destruction of the soul through deception.

48. 'A noble salvation will come
From the King who has created us,
A white law will come over seas,
Besides being God, He will be man.

49. 'This shape, he on whom thou lookest,
Will come to thy parts;
'Tis mine to journey to her house,
To the woman in Line-mag.

50. 'For it is Moninnan, the son of Ler,
From the chariot in the shape of a man,
Of his progeny will be a very short while
A fair man in a body of white clay.

51. 'Monann, the descendant of Ler, will be
A vigorous bed-fellow to Caintigern
He shall be called to his son in the beautiful world,
Fiachna will acknowledge him as his son.

52. 'He will delight the company of every fairy-knoll,
He will be the darling of every goodly land,
He will make known secrets—a course of wisdom—
In the world, without being feared.

53. 'He will be in the shape of every beast,
Both on the azure sea and on land,
He will be a dragon before hosts at the onset,
He will be a wolf of every great forest.

54. 'He will be a stag with horns of silver
In the land where chariots are driven,
He will be a speckled salmon in a full pool,
He will be a seal, he will be a fair-white swan.

55. 'He will be throughout long ages
An hundred years in fair kingship,

He will cut down battalions, a lasting grave—
He will redden fields, a wheel around the track.

56. 'It will be about kings with a champion
That he will be known as a valiant hero,
Into the strongholds of a land on a height
I shall send an appointed end from Islay.

57. 'High shall I place him with princes,
He will be overcome by a son of error;
Moninnan, the son of Ler,
Will be his father, his tutor.

58. 'He will be—his time will be short—
Fifty years in this world:
A dragonstone from the sea will kill him
In the fight at Senlabor.

59. 'He will ask a drink from Loch Ló,
While he looks at the stream of blood,
The white host will take him under a wheel of clouds
To the gathering where there is no sorrow.

60. 'Steadily then let Bran row,
Not far to the Land of Women,
Emne with many hues of hospitality
Thou wilt reach before the setting of the sun.'

61. Thereupon Bran went from him. And he saw an island. He rows round about it, and a large host was gaping and laughing. They were all looking at Bran and his people, but would not stay to converse with them. They continued to give forth gusts of laughter at them. Bran sent one of his people on the island. He ranged himself with the others, and was gaping at them like the other men of the island. He kept rowing round about the island. Whenever his man came past Bran, his comrades would address him. But he would not converse with them, but would only look at them and gape at them. The name of this island is the Island of Joy. Thereupon they left him there.

62. It was not long thereafter when they reached the Land of Women. They saw the leader of the women at the port. Said the chief of the women: 'Come hither on land, O Bran son of Febal! Welcome is thy advent!' Bran did not venture to go on shore. The woman throws a ball of thread to Bran straight over his face. Bran put his hand on the ball, which clave to his palm. The thread of the ball was in the woman's hand, and she pulled the coracle towards the port. Thereupon they went into a large house, in which was a bed for every couple, even thrice nine beds. The food that was put on every dish vanished not from them. It seemed a year to them that they were there,—it chanced to be many years. No savour was wanting to them.

63. Home-sickness seized one of them, even Nechtan the son of Collbran. His kindred kept praying Bran that he should go to Ireland with him. The woman said to them their going would make them rue. However, they went, and the woman said that none of them should touch the land, and that they should visit and take with them the man whom they had left in the Island of Joy.

64. Then they went until they arrived at a gathering at Srub Brain. The men asked of them who it was came over the sea. Said Bran: 'I am Bran the son of Febal,' saith he. However, the other saith: 'We do not know such a one, though the Voyage of Bran is in our ancient stories.'

65. The man leaps from them out of the coracle. As soon as he touched the earth of Ireland, forthwith he was a heap of ashes, as though he had been in the earth for many hundred years. 'Twas then that Bran sang this quatrain:

'For Collbran's son great was the folly
To lift his hand against age,
Without any one casting a wave of pure water
Over Nechtan, Collbran's son.'

66. Thereupon, to the people of the gathering Bran told all his wanderings from the beginning until that time. And he wrote these quatrains in Ogam, and then bade them farewell. And from that hour his wanderings are not known.

Guillaume de Lorris and Jean de Meun

(Thirteenth Century)

The first 4058 lines of the medieval allegory The Romance of the Rose *were composed c. 1230 by Guillaume de Lorris; the remainder, comprising the vast bulk of the poem, were written about fifty years later by Jean de Meun. This section, lines 495–1344, describes the earthly paradise of the Garden of Pleasure.*

When I heard the birds singing, I strove with great distress to discover by what device or trick I might enter the garden. But I could find no place to get in, for I assure you that I did not know if there were any opening or pathway or place by which one might enter, nor was there a living soul there to show me, for I was alone. I was tormented by anguish, until at last I remembered that it was completely unheard of for so beautiful a garden to have no door or ladder or opening of any sort. Then I set off in great haste, skirting the enclosure and the wall that surrounded it on all sides until I found a very cramped, small, and narrow little door. No one could enter any other way. I began to knock at the door, for I did not know where to look for any other entrance. I knocked and pushed hard, listening frequently to see if I could hear anyone coming. Then the gate, which was made of hornbeam, was opened by a most lovely and beautiful maiden: her hair shone fair as a burnished bowl, her flesh was more tender than a young chick, her forehead radiant and her brows arched, her eyes not set too close together but widely and properly spaced, her nose straight and well formed, and her eyes as bright as a falcon's.

To excite the desire of the featherbrained she had sweetly scented breath, a pink and white face, a little, full-lipped mouth, and a dimpled chin. Her neck was well proportioned, her flesh softer than fleece and free from spots or sores: no woman from here to Jerusalem had a finer neck; it was smooth and soft to touch. Her throat was white as snow freshly fallen on the branch, her body well formed and slender. There was no need to search in any land for a more beautiful female form. She had a charming gold-embroidered chaplet; no maiden ever had one more elegant or unusual. I could not describe it properly if I took all day. On her gold-embroidered chaplet she had a garland of fresh roses, in her hand she held a mirror, and she had arranged her hair very richly with rich braid. For the sake of greater elegance she had sewn up her two sleeves, and in order to prevent her white hands from becoming brown, she wore white gloves. She had a tunic of rich Ghent green, edged all round with braid. You could tell from her finery that she had very little to do. When she had combed her hair carefully and decked herself out in her fine clothes, her day's work was done. She spent her time in a happy and carefree manner, being troubled or anxious over nothing except attiring herself nobly. When this well-dressed maiden had opened the gate for me, I thanked her heartily and asked her name and who she was. She was not too proud or too haughty to reply. 'Those who know me call me Idleness,' she said. 'I am a rich and powerful lady, happy especially in one thing, that I have no care but to enjoy and amuse myself, and to comb and braid my hair. I am the most intimate friend of Pleasure, the charming and elegant owner of this garden, who had the trees brought here from Alexander's lands and planted in the garden.

'When the trees had grown, Pleasure commanded that the wall you have seen be built all around, and that the images painted on the outside be set there; as you saw just now, they are neither elegant nor charming, but sad and mournful.

'Pleasure and his followers, who live in joy and happiness, often come to amuse themselves and enjoy the shade of this place. Indeed, Pleasure is doubtless already there, listening to the song of the nightingales, thrushes, and other birds. He enjoys himself there and relaxes with his followers, for he could never find a finer spot or a fairer place in which to enjoy himself. And I assure you that Pleasure's companions, whom he takes with him in his train, are the fairest people to be found anywhere.'

When Idleness had recounted this, and I had listened carefully to everything, I said to her: 'Lady Idleness, you may be quite sure that since handsome and charming Pleasure is already in the garden with his followers, I will not, if I can help it, be robbed of the chance of seeing that assembly this very day. I must see it, for I believe that the company is fair and courteous and well instructed.'

Then, without another word, I entered the garden by the door that

Idleness had opened for me, and, once inside, I grew happy, gay, and joyful; indeed I assure you that I truly believed myself to be in the earthly paradise, for the place was so delightful that it seemed quite ethereal. In fact, as I thought then, there is no paradise so good to be in as that garden, which gave me such pleasure. Many songbirds were gathered throughout the garden: in one place were nightingales, in another jays and starlings, and elsewhere were great flocks of wrens and turtledoves, goldfinches and swallows, larks and titmice. In another place were assembled calandra larks, tired from the effort of outdoing one another in song; there were blackbirds and thrushes, trying to sing more loudly than all the other birds, and elsewhere parrots and many birds throughout the groves and woods where they lived, taking pleasure in their lovely singing.

These birds that I am describing to you did most excellent service. They sang as though they were heavenly angels, and you may be sure that when I heard the sound I rejoiced greatly, for never was so sweet a melody heard by mortal man. So sweet and lovely was that song that it seemed not to be birdsong, but rather comparable with the song of the sea-sirens, who are called sirens because of their pure, sweet voices. The birds were intent on their singing, nor were they inexpert or ignorant, and I assure you that when I heard their song and saw how green everything was I grew very joyful, and had never been so happy as I then became.

The place was so very charming that I was filled with great joy, and then I knew and understood clearly that Idleness had served me well by admitting me to this delight. It was right for me to be her friend, for she had opened for me the gate of the leafy garden. From now on, I will tell you the whole story as best I can. First of all, I wish, without making a long story of it, to recount what Pleasure's office was and the company he had, and then I will tell you everything about the garden. I cannot tell you everything at once, but I will recount it all in order, so that no one will have any reproach to make.

Sweetly, pleasantly, and diligently the birds performed their service; the songs they sang, some high, some low, were amorous lays and courtly airs. I am not jesting when I say that the sweetness and melody of their song filled my heart with a new rapture. But when I had listened to the birds for a little, I could not restrain myself from going at once to see Pleasure, for I longed to see how he behaved and what kind of person he was. I set off, straight down a little path on the right, which was full of fennel and mint; but I found Pleasure quite close by, for I came at once to where he was, in a secluded place. Pleasure was disporting himself there, and he had such handsome people with him that when I saw them I could not tell where they might have come from, for in truth they seemed to be winged angels: no man living ever saw such fair folk. These people of whom I speak had begun to dance, and a lady was singing to them, whose name was Joy. She could sing well and pleasantly, and no one could have made the refrains sound better or more agreeable. Singing suited her wonderfully, for her voice was clear and pure, and she was by no means clumsy, but knew well how to move her body when dancing, to stamp her feet and have fun. It was her habit always and everywhere to be the first to sing, for singing was her favourite occupation.

Then you might have seen the dancers move and the people tread daintily, executing many fine steps and turns on the fresh grass. There you might have seen flute-players, minstrels, and *jongleurs*, one singing a *rotruenge*, another an air from Lorraine, for the airs composed in Lorraine are finer than those of any other kingdom. Around and about were many ladies performing admirably with castanets and tambourines, for they kept on throwing the tambourine up in the air and then catching it again on one finger, without ever missing. Two very charming maidens with their hair in a single braid and dressed only in their tunics were led into the dance by Pleasure, who bore himself most nobly; but I need not say how beautifully they danced: one would approach the other very elegantly, and when they were close together, their lips would touch in such a way that you might have thought they were kissing one another's faces. They knew well how to sway in the dance. I cannot describe it to you, but as long as I could have seen those people thus exerting themselves in the rounds and dances, I would never have wanted to move.

I stood watching the dance until a very mirthful lady noticed me: it was Courtesy, a worthy and gracious lady whom God preserve from harm! Courtesy then called out to me and said 'Fair friend, what are you doing there? Come here if you please and join in the dance with us.' Without delay or hesitation I joined in the dance; I was not too embarrassed, for I can tell you that I was very pleased when Courtesy asked and commanded me to dance, being very eager and anxious to dance, if only I had dared.

I then began to examine the bodies and figures and faces of those who were dancing there, and their outward forms and manners, and I shall tell you about them. Pleasure was handsome, straight, and tall: never in any company would you find a better-looking man. His face was pale, with cheeks as rosy as an apple, and he was elegant and well dressed; his eyes were bright, his mouth charming, and his nose very finely formed; his hair was blond and curly, his shoulders rather broad, and his waist slender. He was so handsome and elegant and had such shapely limbs that he looked like a painting. He was lively, spirited, and agile, the nimblest man you have ever seen, and he wore no beard or moustache except for a slight downy growth, for he was a very young man. He was richly dressed in samite embroidered with birds and decorated with beaten gold. His coat was very ornately styled, elegantly slashed and cut in various places, and he was most skilfully shod in shoes that were laced and slashed. For love and for pleasure, his sweetheart had made him a chaplet of roses, which suited him very well. And do you know the name of his sweetheart? It was Joy, with her gaiety and sweet voice, who did not hate him in the least, but had given him her love when she was no more than seven years old. Pleasure held her by the finger in the dance, and she him. They suited each other well, for he was handsome and she beautiful. The color of her tender flesh was like a rose newly sprung, for one might have torn it with a tiny thorn. Her brow was fair and smooth and unwrinkled, her eyebrows brown and arched, her eyes gay and so full of joy that they always laughed before her mouth did, as was fitting. I do not know how to describe her nose: you could not have made a better one out of wax. Her mouth was tiny, and ready to kiss her lover, and her hair was blond and shining. What more should I say? She was fair and beautifully adorned, her hair was braided with gold thread, and she wore a new gold-embroidered chaplet. I, who have seen twenty-nine, had never seen a chaplet so beautifully worked in silk. She was clothed and adorned in the same samite decorated with gold that her lover wore, and for that reason she was all the more proud of it.

On her other side stood the God of Love, who distributes the joys of love as he chooses. He it is who rules over lovers and humbles men's pride, making lords into servants, and ladies—when he finds them too haughty—into maidservants. In appearance, the God of Love was no lackey, and he was of rare beauty. I am very much afraid that I shall find it difficult to describe his robe, for it was made not of silk but rather of tiny flowers, and fashioned by courtly loves. It was decorated all over with diamond and shield shapes, birds, lions, leopards, and other animals, and was made of flowers of various colours. There were flowers of many different kinds, most skilfully arranged. No summer flower was absent, not broom nor violet nor periwinkle, not yellow nor indigo nor white, while intertwined in places were great, broad rose-leaves. On his head was a chaplet of roses, but the nightingales fluttering around his head knocked down the leaves, for he was entirely covered with birds, with parrots and nightingales, larks and titmice. He seemed to be an angel come straight from heaven. By his side stood a young man whom he kept by him and whose name was Pleasant Looks.

This young bachelor watched the dance and kept two Turkish bows belonging to the God of Love. One of these bows was made of a wood that bears an evil-tasting fruit; it was covered above and below with knots and lumps, and it was blacker than mulberry. The other bow was rather long and elegantly fashioned from the trunk of a shrub; it was well made and polished smooth, and beautifully decorated on all sides with pictures of ladies and handsome, joyful young men. Pleasant Looks, who did not look like a minion, kept these two bows, together with ten of his master's arrows. Five he held in his right hand: the nocks and flights of these were very well made, and they were painted all in gold. The points were strong and razor-sharp and would pierce deeply, though there was no iron or steel in them, indeed everything was made of gold except for the flights and the shaft, for they were tipped with barbed golden heads.

The best and swiftest of these arrows, the fairest and best-flighted, was called Beauty, while the name of the one that wounded most deeply was, I think, Simplicity. Another, named Generosity of Spirit, was feathered with valour and courtesy, and the fourth, whose name was Company, bore a very heavy point; it would not travel far, but fired at close range it could cause serious injury. The fifth was named Fair Seeming, and was the least harmful of all, although it could inflict a serious wound. Anyone struck by this arrow could expect protection and to regain his health before too long, so that his pain was less.

There were five arrows of a different kind, as ugly as you like, whose points and shafts were blacker than demons from hell. The name of the first was Pride, and the next, which was no better, was called Baseness, and was steeped in the venom of wickedness. The third was named Shame and the fourth Despair, while the name of the last was most certainly Inconstancy. The five arrows were of the same kind, all alike, and one of the bows (the hideous one, all knotted and gnarled) matched them well, being made to fire such arrows. The force of these five arrows was undoubtedly opposed to that of the others, but I shall not now tell you all about their force and their power. Their true significance will be told, for I shall not forget to do so, but will tell you what they all mean before my story is ended.

Now I shall return to my tale, for I have to tell you about the bearing, form, and appearance of the noble dancers. The God of Love had done the right thing, for he had attached himself very closely to a most worthy lady, whose name, like one of the five arrows, was Beauty. She had every good quality, for she was not dark or brunette, but resplendent as the moon, which makes the other stars look like tiny candles. Her flesh was dewy soft and she was as simple as a bride, lily-white, with a smooth, delicate face. She stood straight and slender, wearing no paint or make-up, for she had no need of adornment or embellishment. She had long blond hair falling to her heels, and her nose, eyes, and mouth were well formed. So help me God, my heart is filled with great sweetness when I remember the shapeliness of each limb, for there was no woman so beautiful in all the world. In short, she was young and blond, pleasant and agreeable, courteous and elegant, with rounded, slender form and charming and lively manners.

Next to Beauty stood Wealth, a lady of great dignity, worth, and rank. It would be a bold, arrogant man who dared say or do anything to injure her or her followers, for she had great power to harm or to help. The great power of the rich to help or to injure does not date from today or yesterday; all the greatest and the humblest honoured Wealth and sought to serve her, the better to earn her favour; each man called her his lady, for everyone feared her, and the whole world was in her power. There were many flatterers at her court, and many treacherous and envious men, such as take pains to blame and disparage all those who are better loved than they. In the beginning, these flatterers praise men in order to delude them, and ingratiate themselves with everyone, but their flatteries stab men in the back and touch the bone, so that through their deceitful compliments they cause many who should be intimate there to be ostracized and banished from court. May such envious flatterers come to a bad end, for no good man loves them.

Wealth wore a purple gown, and do not imagine that I am deceiving you when I say and affirm that there was none so beautiful, costly, or gay in all the world. The purple was all braided, and embroidered in gold with stories of dukes and kings. The neck of the gown was most richly edged with a band of gold inlaid with niello, and there were, make no mistake about it, a great many precious stones, which shone very brightly. Wealth had a most elegant belt: no woman ever wore one more costly. The buckle was made from a stone that had great power and virtue, for he who wore it need fear no poison, and no venom could harm him. Such a stone deserved to be prized; it would have been worth more to a rich man than all the gold in Rome. The clasp was made of another stone, which could cure the toothache and also had such virtue that the eyesight of the one who saw it before breakfast would be safe for the whole day.

The studs on the gold-embroidered cloth were of pure gold, and so large and heavy that each was worth fully a bezant. On her blond hair, Wealth wore a golden circlet: I do not think that such a fine one was ever seen. The circlet was of fine, toughened gold, and only an expert in the art of description could recount and describe all the stones that were in it, for it would be impossible to estimate the worth of the stones that were set in the gold. There were rubies, sapphires, zircons, emeralds of more than two ounces, and, skilfully set at the front of the circlet, a carbuncle so clear that when night fell one could, if need be, see one's way for a league ahead. Such light came from the stones that the face and countenance of Wealth shone radiantly, as did the area round about her. Wealth held by the hand a very handsome young man who was her true lover, a man who very much liked living in rich mansions. He was well shod and well dressed, and owned valuable horses, for he would have thought the presence of a hack in his stables to be as great a reproach as murder or robbery. The reason why he so much appreciated the friendship and favour of Wealth was that he was always intent upon lavish expenditure, and she was able to achieve this and to support his spending, for she gave him coins as though she had granaries full of them.

Next came Largesse, who was well trained and instructed in the art of doing honour and spending money. She was of Alexander's line, and was never happier than when she could say 'Take this.' Even wretched Avarice was not so anxious to take as Largesse was to give, and God caused her wealth to multiply, so that however much she gave away, she always had more. Largesse was greatly praised and esteemed; she had achieved so much by her generous gifts that wise and foolish alike were entirely at her mercy. If anyone happened to hate her, I believe she would make him her friend by the great service she did him, and therefore she was dearly loved by rich and poor alike. It is very foolish for a great man to be miserly; no vice is so harmful to a great man as avarice, for a miser cannot win lordship or great territory, because he does not have a large number of friends with whom he has influence. The man who wants friends should not be too attached to his possessions, but should acquire friends by giving them fine gifts, for just as the magnet subtly draws iron to itself, so the gold and silver that we give attract the hearts of men.

Largesse wore a new robe of purple from the Orient; her face was fair and well shaped, but her collar was unfastened, for a short time ago she had, there and then, given the clasp to a lady. But it rather suited her for the neck to be open and her throat disclosed, so that the soft whiteness of her skin showed through her chemise. The wise and valiant Largesse held by the hand a knight of the lineage of good King Arthur of Britain; that same Arthur bore the banner and standard of valour, and his fame is still so great that stories of him are told before kings and counts. This knight had recently come from a tournament where he had achieved many jousts and combats for the sake of his mistress; many a green helm had been uncircled, many a bossed shield pierced, many a knight unhorsed and captured through his strength and courage.

After all these came Generosity of Spirit, who was neither dark nor swarthy, but whiter than snow. She did not have an Orleans nose, for hers was long and well shaped; she had bright, laughing eyes, arched brows, and long blond hair, and she was more innocent than a dove. Her heart was gentle and gracious, and she would not have dared to speak or act towards anyone otherwise than as she ought. If she knew a man to be tormented by his love for her, I believe she would soon take pity on him, for her heart was so compassionate, so gentle and loving, that if anyone suffered harm for her sake and she failed to help him, she would be afraid of committing a great wickedness. She wore a sorquenie that was not made of sackcloth; there was none richer between here and Arras, and it fitted so well and closely that there was not a stitch that was not in the right place. Generosity of Spirit was very nicely dressed, for no dress suits a maiden so well as a sorquenie; a woman looks daintier and more elegant in a sorquenie than in a tunic. The sorquenie, which was white, signified that she who wore it was gentle and noble. A young man beside her had attached himself to Generosity of Spirit and they were side by side; I do not know his name, but he was as handsome as if he had been a son of the Lord of Windsor.

Next came Courtesy, who was greatly esteemed by everyone, for she was neither haughty nor foolish. It was she who was gracious enough to call me into the dance as soon as I arrived there. She was neither stupid nor irritable, but sensible and prudent, not given to excess, but speaking and answering fairly; she never contradicted anyone, nor did she bear anyone a grudge. She was charming, fair, and comely, with shining dark hair. I know of no more pleasing woman. She was worthy to be queen or empress in any court. By her stood a knight, agreeable in manner and conversation and one who honoured others. He was fair and handsome, very skilled in arms and beloved of his sweetheart.

Fair Idleness came next, and stayed close by me. I have certainly described to you her appearance and figure and will say no more of her, for she was the first to show me kindness, by graciously opening the door of the garden for me.

Next, as far as I remember, came Youth, with her bright, laughing face, who was not, I believe, much more than twelve years old. She was innocent, never suspecting the existence of any evil or trickery, and very joyful and gay, for, as you know, young people's only care is to amuse themselves. Her lover was so intimate with her that he kissed her as often as he liked, in full view of all the dancers. They would not have been ashamed if people had talked about the two of them; on the contrary, you could have seen them kissing each other like two doves. The boy was young and handsome, of the same age and disposition as his sweetheart.

Thus they danced there, those people and others of their household with them. They were all noble, cultivated, and well-brought-up people. When I had observed the appearance of the dancers, I wanted to go and see the garden, to walk around it and gaze on the handsome laurels, the pines, hazels, and nut-trees. The dances now came to an end, for most of the dancers went off with their sweethearts to make love in the shade of the trees. God knows they led a pleasant life, and one which it is foolish not to desire for oneself. A man who could have such a life would be prepared to do without a greater good, for there is no better paradise than having the sweetheart of one's choice. I then left that spot and set off alone, wandering happily from place to place in the garden, whereupon the God of Love instantly summoned Pleasant Looks. No longer did he want him to keep his golden bow, but ordered him without further ado to string it. Immediately and without hesitation Pleasant Looks strung the bow and gave it to him, together with five strong, shining arrows, ready to be shot. Bow in hand, the God of Love then began to follow me at a distance. Now may God keep me from mortal wound if he should happen to shoot at me. I, unheeding, continued to wander happily and freely through the garden while he made haste to follow me, but I did not stop in any place until I had been everywhere. The garden had been laid out in a perfect square, being as long as it was wide. Except for a few hideous ones, there was no fruitbearing tree of which there were not two or three or perhaps more in the garden. I well remember that there were trees bearing pomegranates, excellent fruit for the sick, and abundant nut-trees, which, at the proper season, bore fruit such as nutmeg, which is neither bitter nor bland. Many almond-trees had been planted in the garden, and he who had need of them could find many fig-trees and good date-palms. There were many spices in the garden, cloves and liquorice, fresh cardamum, zedoary, anise, and cinnamon, and many delicious spices good to eat after a meal.

John Milton

(1608–1674)

In this excerpt from book four of Paradise Lost, *Satan leaps over the walls of Eden, perches on the Tree of Life in the likeness of a cormorant, surveys the happy state of Adam and Eve, and plots their fall.*

Now to the ascent of that steep savage hill
Satan had journeyed on, pensive and slow;
But further way found none; so thick entwined,
As one continued brake, the undergrowth
Of shrubs and tangling bushes had perplexed
All path of man or beast that passed that way.
One gate there only was, and that looked east
On the other side. Which when the Arch-Felon saw,
Due entrance he disdained, and, in contempt,
At one slight bound high overleaped all bound
Of hill or highest wall, and sheer within
Lights on his feet. As when a prowling wolf,
Whom hunger drives to seek new haunt for prey,
Watching where shepherds pen their flocks at eve,
In hurdled cotes amid the field secure,
Leaps o'er the fence with ease into the fold;
Or as a thief, bent to unhoard the cash
Of some rich burgher, whose substantial doors,
Cross-barred and bolted fast, fear no assault,
In at the window climbs, or o'er the tiles;
So clomb this first grand Thief into God's fold:
So since into his Church lewd hirelings climb.
Thence up he flew, and on the Tree of Life,
The middle tree and highest there that grew,
Sat like a cormorant; yet not true life

Thereby regained, but sat devising death
To them who lived; nor on the virtue thought
Of that life-giving plant, but only used
For prospect what, well used, had been the pledge
Of immortality. So little knows
Any, but God alone, to value right
The good before him, but perverts best things
To worst abuse, or to their meanest use.
Beneath him, with new wonder, now he views,
To all delight of human sense exposed,
In narrow room Nature's whole wealth; yea, more!—
A Heaven on Earth for blissful Paradise
Of God the garden was, by him in the east
Of Eden planted. Eden stretched her line
From Auran eastward to the royal towers
Of great Seleucia, built by Grecian kings,
Or where the sons of Eden long before
Dwelt in Telassar. In this pleasant soil
His far more pleasant garden God ordained.
Out of the fertile ground he caused to grow
All trees of noblest kind for sight, smell, taste;
And all amid them stood the Tree of Life,
High eminent, blooming ambrosial fruit
Of vegetable gold; and next to life,
Our death, the Tree of Knowledge, grew fast by—
Knowledge of good, bought dear by knowing ill.
Southward through Eden went a river large,
Nor changed his course, but through the shaggy hill
Passed underneath ingulfed; for God had thrown
That mountain, as his garden-mould, high raised
Upon the rapid current, which, through veins
Of porous earth with kindly thirst up-drawn,
Rose a fresh fountain, and with many a rill
Watered the garden; thence united fell
Down the steep glade, and met the nether flood,
Which from his darksome passage now appears,
And now, divided into four main streams,
Runs diverse, wandering many a famous realm

And country whereof here needs no account;
But rather to tell how, if Art could tell
How, from that sapphire fount the crispèd brooks,
Rolling on orient pearl and sands of gold,
With mazy error under pendent shades
Ran nectar, visiting each plant, and fed
Flowers worthy of Paradise, which not nice Art
In beds and curious knots, but Nature boon
Poured forth profuse on hill, and dale, and plain,
Both where the morning sun first warmly smote
The open field, and where the unpierced shade
Imbrowned the noontide bowers. Thus was this place,
A happy rural seat of various view:
Groves whose rich trees wept odorous gums and balm;
Others whose fruit, burnished with golden rind,
Hung amiable—Hesperian fables true,
If true, here only—and of delicious taste.
Betwixt them lawns, or level downs, and flocks
Grazing the tender herb, were interposed,
Or palmy hillock; or the flowery lap
Of some irriguous valley spread her store,
Flowers of all hue, and without thorn the rose.
Another side, umbrageous grots and caves
Of cool recess, o'er which the mantling vine
Lays forth her purple grape, and gently creeps
Luxuriant; meanwhile murmuring waters fall
Down the slope hills dispersed, or in a lake,
That to the fringèd bank with myrtle crowned
Her crystal mirror holds, unite their streams.
The birds their quire apply, airs, vernal airs,
Breathing the smell of field and grove, attune
The trembling leaves, while universal Pan,
Knit with the Graces and the Hours in dance,
Led on the eternal Spring. Not that fair field
Of Enna, where Proserpin gathering flowers,
Herself a fairer flower, by gloomy Dis
Was gathered—which cost Ceres all that pain
To seek her through the world—nor that sweet grove

Of Daphne, by Orontes and the inspired
Castalian spring, might with this Paradise
Of Eden strive; nor that Nyseian isle,
Girt with the river Triton, where old Cham,
Whom Gentiles Ammon call and Libyan Jove,
Hid Amalthea, and her florid son,
Young Bacchus, from his stepdame Rhea's eye;
Nor, where Abassin kings their issue guard,
Mount Amara (though this by some supposed
True Paradise) under the Ethiop line
By Nilus' head, enclosed with shining rock,
A whole day's journey high, but wide remote
From this Assyrian garden, where the Fiend
Saw undelighted all delight, all kind
Of living creatures, new to sight and strange.
Two of far nobler shape, erect and tall,
God-like erect, with native honor clad
In naked majesty, seemed lords of all,
And worthy seemed; for in their looks divine
The image of their glorious Maker shone,
Truth, wisdom, sanctitude severe and pure—
Severe, but in true filial freedom placed,
Whence true authority in men: though both
Not equal, as their sex not equal seemed;
For contemplation he and valor formed,
For softness she and sweet attractive grace;
He for God only; she for God in him.
His fair large front and eye sublime declared
Absolute rule; and hyacinthine locks
Round from his parted forelock manly hung
Clustering, but not beneath his shoulders broad:
She, as a veil down to the slender waist,
Her unadornèd golden tresses wore
Dishevelled, but in wanton ringlets waved
As the vine curls her tendrils—which implied
Subjection, but required with gentle sway,
And by her yielded, by him best received
Yielded, with coy submission, modest pride,

And sweet, reluctant, amorous delay.
Nor those mysterious parts were then concealed;
Then was not guilty shame. Dishonest shame
Of Nature's works, honor dishonorable,
Sin-bred, how have ye troubled all mankind
With shows instead, mere shows of seeming pure,
And banished from man's life his happiest life,
Simplicity and spotless innocence!
So passed they naked on, nor shunned the sight
Of God or Angel; for they thought no ill:
So hand in hand they passed, the loveliest pair
That ever since in love's embraces met—
Adam the goodliest man of men since born
His sons; the fairest of her daughters Eve.
Under a tuft of shade that on a green
Stood whispering soft, by a fresh fountain-side,
They sat them down; and, after no more toil
Of their sweet gardening labor than sufficed
To recommend cool Zephyr, and make ease
More easy, wholesome thirst and appetite
More grateful, to their supper-fruits they fell—
Nectarine fruits, which the compliant boughs
Yielded them, sidelong as they sat recline
On the soft downy bank damasked with flowers.
The savory pulp they chew, and in the rind,
Still as they thirsted, scoop the brimming stream;
Nor gentle purpose, nor endearing smiles
Wanted, nor youthful dalliance, as beseems
Fair couple linked in happy nuptial league,
Alone as they. About them frisking played
All beasts of the earth, since wild, and of all chase
In wood or wilderness, forest or den.
Sporting the lion ramped, and in his paw
Dandled the kid; bears, tigers, ounces, pards,
Gambolled before them; the unwieldy elephant,
To make them mirth, used all his might, and wreathed
His lithe proboscis; close the serpent sly,
Insinuating, wove with Gordian twine

His braided train, and of his fatal guile
Gave proof unheeded. Others on the grass
Couched, and, now filled with pasture, gazing sat,
Or bedward ruminating; for the sun,
Declined, was hastening now with prone career
To the Ocean Isles, and in the ascending scale
Of Heaven the stars that usher evening rose:
When Satan, still in gaze as first he stood,
Scarce thus at length failed speech recovered said:—
"O Hell! what do mine eyes with grief behold?
Into our room of bliss thus high advanced
Creatures of other mould—Earth-born perhaps,
Not Spirits, yet to Heavenly Spirits bright
Little inferior—whom my thoughts pursue
With wonder, and could love; so lively shines
In them divine resemblance, and such grace
The hand that formed them on their shape hath poured.
Ah! gentle pair, ye little think how nigh
Your change approaches, when all these delights
Will vanish, and deliver ye to woe— . . ."

Bhagavata Purana

The divine Krishna sports with the cowherd wives on the banks of the Yamuna river, making an earthly paradise of the sacred city of Vrindavana.

Book X

Chapter XXXIII

The Rāsa Revels

Śrī Śuka said: When they heard those charming words of the Lord and had their longings fulfilled by the touch of His body, the Gopis shed the pangs of separation. Then Govinda began there the Rāsa dance, in which those devoted women, ornaments of their sex, joined with delight, linking their arms. The Rāsa revels, brilliant with the band of Gopis ranged in a circle, commenced with Krishna, Lord of the master-yogis, taking His place between every two of them and throwing His arms round their necks, while every Gopi imagined that He was with her alone. Instantly, the sky was crowded with hundreds of aerial cars carrying the celestials and their spouses, all eager spectators. Thereupon the kettle-drums sounded, and showers of flowers fell, and the great Gandharvas sang with their women His spotless glory. From the Rāsa circle rose the merry din of bracelet, anklet and bell, when the women found themselves with their Beloved. In their company, the exalted Lord, the Son of Devakī, shone all the more, like a great emerald between drops of gold. Footing it featly in the dance, with graceful movements of the hands, and the smiling vivacious play of eye-brows, their waists looking as if they would snap any moment, their breasts and bodices quivering, and their ear-pendants dangling against their cheeks, Krishna's loves shone like streaks of lightning from a mass of clouds, as they sang His glory, their faces covered with perspiration, their braids and zones coming undone. And as they danced, the women broke into high-pitched song, their voices graced by many a tuneful mode, their hearts thrilling to Krishna's love and the touch of His hands; that song enveloped the universe. One of them, elaborated at a high pitch melodic patterns in concert with Mukunda without the two getting mixed up; and He, greatly pleased, applauded her warmly on its excellence. And she then sang the same to the Dhruva time-measure, and He made her proud with His praise.

Thoroughly fatigued by the Rāsa dance, a Gopi, with her bracelets slipping down and the jasmine falling from her hair, flung her arm round the shoulder of the Lord Who wields the Mace, as He stood by her side. Another, inhaled the fragrance of the arm, smelling of lilies and smeared with sandal, that He had placed on her shoulder, and kissed it, the down on her body standing on end. To one, who laid against His cheek her own lit up by the flash of her ear-pendant, as it tossed about in the dance, He gave the *pan* He had chewed. A Gopi, dancing and singing to the tinkling of anklet and girdle, and feeling tired, laid on her breasts the healing lotus hand of Achyuta, Who was by her side.

Thus the Gopis, having won the love of Achyuta, the Beloved of the Goddess Śrī, to Whom She is wholly devoted, sang His glories with His arms round their necks, and were in the seventh heaven of bliss. With radiant looks, and lilies tucked behind the ears, the curls adorning their cheeks, and beads of perspiration on their faces, the Gopis danced with the Lord, as their chaplets slipped down from their tresses, in that Rāsa festival where the bees were the singers and the music came from bracelets, anklets and bells. With touch of hand and embrace, with affectionate glance and badinage, the Lord of Ramā gave Himself up to gay flirtation, sporting with the beauties of Vraja, like a child playing with his own reflection. The women of Vraja, their senses in a whirl from the ecstasy of contact with His body, their garlands and ornaments tumbling down, were unable to collect themselves sufficiently to re-fasten their hair, their upper garments or their breast-bands, O best of the Kurus. Seeing Krishna sporting thus, the celestial damsels swooned under the torment of love. The moon with the company of stars stood lost in wonder. Multiplying Himself into as many as there were Gopis, the Lord feigned enjoyment as He sported with them, though it is in the Self that He finds all delight.

Rinpung Ngawang Jigdag

(Sixteenth Century)

The learned Tibetan prince Rinpungpa wrote "The Knowledge-bearing Messenger" in 1557 as a letter to his dead father, whom he believed had been reborn in the earthly paradise of Shambhala. Using meditative visualization, Rinpungpa summoned a yogi to serve as his messenger. In this excerpt from the poem, he gives the yogi directions for reaching Shambhala.

Take this message and go to my father in Shambhala. May my words of truth, conquering the mountains of dualism, guide you along the way and help you to overcome the obstacles that lie before you.

Go first to the shrine of my father in the palace of Rinpung and pray for his blessings. Then go toward Shigatse, to the place of my tutelary deities, and ask them for help in the journey to Shambhala. After that you must travel across central Tibet, visiting shrines and monasteries along the way and seeking the audience of lamas who can bless you in your undertaking. Pay homage at the Monastery of Zalung Trubu to the great image of Maitreya, the Buddha to come. Stop also in the mountains of Nepal, at the holy shrine of Muktinath, and bathe there in the hot springs filled with scented flowers.

Then turn to the north and west and take the high plateau to the sacred mountain of Kailas, where the knowledge holders dwell. To those who see them with uncommon sight, these sages appear as tutelary deities with their diamond consorts. There, in the place of golden caves, lives the Elder Angaja, one of the sixteen disciples of the Buddha, surrounded by a thousand saints. If you listen carefully, you will hear, to the sound of bells and cymbals, the music of their enlightened teachings.

From Kailas continue northwest to Ladakh and go down through mountains and forest to the vale of Kashmir. There, scattered among green meadows, beautiful groves of saffron and sandalwood provide cool shade and fill the air with sweet scent. In that delightful place are over three million towns, all filled with houses made of jewels, surrounded by walls of crystal. Beside and between them you will find busy shops selling emeralds and rubies, coral and pearl, gold and silver. Crowds of happy people, dressed in white and singing songs, fill the streets like drifts of snow. Beautiful women with dark blue eyes and lovely breasts will send you seductive glances. Although they give nectar to the eye, they will burn the mind with the fires of passion: They are the flower arrows of the god of desire. Be careful and avoid attachments; remember your aim and go on.

Now the journey becomes more difficult. You will have to follow narrow paths that wind north through a maze of treacherous mountains. Many of these paths lead off into valleys from which the traveler can never return. If you take the wrong one, you will become hopelessly lost. But if you take heart and dedicate your efforts to the benefit of others, you will pass safely through and come out in the land of the Paksik, horsemen who wear white turbans and quilted robes filled with cotton. Although they have broad chests and look very fierce, they are quite friendly and will do you no harm. You will see much wealth in their possession, many jewels and other treasures.

Leave them behind and go north across the plains. After many days of travel, you will enter a deep forest with trees so tall that they touch the clouds. Because of that, everything below lies in utter darkness. Although you will have no light to see by, you must pass through the forest. On the far side of this dark and gloomy passage, you will come to a wild foaming river called the Sita. Its splashing water makes such a great noise that it sounds like the wind that roars when the world comes to an end. Whatever its spray touches turns to stone. Beware. Taking hold of a tree branch, carefully pull it back, and let it fling you through the air so that you fly like a bird across the river.

On the far bank you will find yourself in a tranquil park where elephants play beneath a mountain lush with grass the bluish-green tint of a peacock's neck. Branches of sandalwood, moist with drops of dew, arch overhead like cobras to form canopies of cool shade. A delicious fruit of golden color, which smells of saffron, hangs from the trees, waiting to be plucked and eaten. Does have left milk for their fawns in leaves shaped like saucers, as if the gods themselves had set it out for you to drink. Stay there and rest a while.

Rest well, for many days of trying journey through a dark and terrible forest lie ahead. Packs of killer animals with eyes like sparks of fire and shaggy manes of bloody, matted fur roam the woods, drunk on their victims' fat and blood. All around, as you go, you will hear them growling and breaking bones with a horrible noise like the sound of axes chopping wood. Pieces of flesh and bone, still warm from recent kills, lie strewn along the path. From the darkness on either side, demons' eyes, red like copper, will spy on you as you pass. During the daytime witches appear there in human form but take on the shapes of lions and tigers by night. Like messengers from the Lord of Death, hordes of ghostly night travelers who feed on flesh will try to feed on yours. By directing a deep and inexhaustible compassion toward all these threatening monsters, you can subdue their rage to kill and pass safely through the forest.

After that you will come to a great body of water that looks as vast and boundless as the open sky. By luck born from your store of merit, a boat will be waiting to carry you across the water. The virtue of your past deeds will also cause a fair wind to spring up, and if you handle the boat with skill, it will blow you to the far shore, where you wish to go.

From there to the north, a barren desert devoid of water will stretch away before you like the desolate paths of suffering that run through this world of illusion. Glaring off sand, the relentless heat of the sun will roast you as if it were the fire of a furnace melting silver into drops of molten liquid. If you try to cool off by fanning yourself with branches of dried-out leaves, you will only succeed in searing your flesh with burning air. The mournful whistle of wind blowing through parched grass will make you sigh with sadness and despair. Remember your mystical knowledge and use it to rub your tonsils so that cool nectar drips out from the secret moon within you. If you know how to drink this stream of soothing liquid, your thirst and hunger will vanish, along with old age and death.

After the desert, which takes many days and nights to cross, you will have to pass over a range of lofty mountains. As you climb, a tremendous wind will hurl rough sand and bits of leaves and twigs against your face, cracking the skin and causing great pain. Again, use your knowledge to prepare the secret ointment that shields your flesh from the wind. This medicine is very powerful and will also clear your vision and brighten your eyes.

Beyond the mountains the path leads down into the fearful Copper Forest, the lair of great serpents with jaws the size of a house. They have copper eyes and awesome black bodies that loom like mountains. Six months of the year they sleep and then they wake to kill and eat. When they breathe, poisonous steam spews out a mile and more, and whatever it touches turns to dust. But if you prepare the right antidote, it will restore your body and allow you to pass through their deadly breath unharmed.

Then you will come to a high mountain with three pointed peaks. Sharp thorns and stones cover its slopes, making it impossible for anyone with ordinary footgear to cross it. Using your secret knowledge once again, you can make the soles of your feet as hard as copper plates and walk easily over this painful obstacle.

A few miles to the north rises another peak, called Incense Mountain. From a distance its green meadows and lush foliage make it look like a heap of luminous emeralds. Medicinal herbs and incense trees grow all over its gentle slopes, filling the air with a delightful scent. Numerous sages, powerful yogis, live on the mountain in jewel-like caves. They sit erect in constant meditation, gazing straight ahead with never a flicker of their deep blue eyes. Their skin is gold and a slight smile graces their lips. As soon as you see them, prostrate yourself in homage and give them offerings of beautiful flowers. Then ask for their aid and advice in reaching Shambhala. Since they are able to accomplish whatever they wish, they can protect you from the dangers of the path and help you to overcome the obstacles that lie ahead.

Before you lies a long journey through a dangerous region of red dust storms that shoot up like fire offerings into the sky. Thunder and lightning will strike all around you, bombarding the ground with deadly showers of diamond hail. At any moment flocks of shrieking eagles can drop out of the sky with claws extended to rip you to shreds. Demons with red eyes and beings who embody nameless fears lurk in ambush, waiting to feast on your flesh. But the power and teachings of the sages will ward off these threats to your life and permit you to follow the path that leads to the north, toward Shambhala.

After many days of harrowing travel, you will come out in a beautiful land of gold and jewels—the country of fabulous beings who are neither men nor gods. Everywhere in that land there is fresh, clear water sparkling in lovely pools made of gems. You will also see houses built of precious stones, surrounded by walls of shining crystal; and in their gardens you will find wish-fulfilling trees that can grant whatever you desire. The fabulous maidens who dwell there, always happy and singing songs, have lovely moon faces, beautiful as lotus blossoms, with eyes like blue flowers. Sashes of fine cloth decorated with pearls adorn their golden bodies. Their graceful, jeweled limbs move like tree branches swaying in a gentle breeze.

As soon as the maidens see you, they will go wild with passion and swarm around you like excited bees craving honey. Smiling and looking at you out of the corners of their eyes so that it feels as if your minds merge in one, they will embrace you and wrap their seductive limbs around your body like vines around a tree. Why not take pleasure with these maidens who have attained the purity and spiritual power of enlightened dakinis? Taste the honey of their breasts, extended toward you like flowers offering you their nectar.

As you do, a great surge of joy and bliss will carry you soaring beyond all bodily sensation. The heat of an inner fire, like the fire that blazes on the southern edge of the universe, will rise through your body, burning away the thickets of mental obscurations. When it reaches the crown of your head, it will melt the mystic syllable *hum* into drops of liquid the color of a molten moon. A stream of silver nectar will cascade down into your psychic centers, causing their knots to loosen and open. As it spreads out through the thousands of nerves and channels that radiate from the centers, it will purify your body and transform it into the indestructible diamond body of bliss. In what other way can you so quickly attain it? Now that you have this marvelous body, you are certain to reach the Pure Land of Shambhala.

Now go on across the beautiful countries that lie ahead. Your path runs through idyllic towns that look like pieces of heaven dropped to earth. You will pass by mountains gleaming with the light of precious jewels and cross over rivers shining with masses of pearl-like bubbles. Go through all these lands with ease and joy in your heart.

Then you will come to the last great obstacle of the journey—a wall of mountains piled so high and deep with snow that not even the eagles can fly over it. Piercing the sky with their summits, the mountains rise like enormous demons threatening to block the way and destroy your hopes. Do not be dismayed but remember the compassionate omnipotence of the Buddha's mind and cast aside all doubts. Bring the clear light of awareness to bear on your fears and illusions so that they vanish like the mirages of darkness in the glow of a dust-free dawn. Then, to the music of golden ankle bells, the noble ones will lift you on their shoulders in a sedan chair of the gods and carry you like a load of cotton over the wall of snow mountains. Through their miraculous power you will float like an umbrella in the sky, putting even the eagles to shame.

After crossing the mountains, you will have to go through one last forest filled with snakes and wild animals, but if you show friendliness and compassion to whatever creatures you meet, you will have no trouble. Although you feel exhausted and sick from the rigors of the journey, hold onto your aim and continue to dedicate your efforts to the benefit of all beings.

Then you will see, at last, the cities of Shambhala, gleaming among ranges of snow mountains like stars on the waves of the Ocean of Milk. Flowers of light, the sight of them will remove all ignorance from your mind and leave you happy and refreshed, completely recovered from the hardships of your journey. Now you can drink and rest and enjoy the fruits of all your efforts. . . .

Thomas Traherne

(1637–1674)

Anglican priest Thomas Traherne was regarded as a minor metaphysical poet until the discovery in 1896 in a London bookstall of the manuscript of Centuries, *published in 1908. At the beginning of the third century, Traherne exults in the heavenly aspect of his early childhood.*

The Third Century

1

Will you see the Infancy of this sublime and celestial Greatness? Those Pure and Virgin Apprehensions I had from the Womb, and that Divine Light wherewith I was born, are the Best unto this Day, wherein I can see the Universe. By the Gift of GOD they attended me into the World, and by his Special favor I remember them till now. Verily they seem the Greatest Gifts His Wisdom could bestow. For without them all other Gifts had been Dead and Vain. They are unattainable by Book, and therefore I will teach them by Experience. Pray for them earnestly: for they will make you Angelical, and wholy Celestial. Certainly Adam in Paradice had not more sweet and Curious Apprehensions of the World, then I when I was a child.

2

All appeared New, and Strange at the first, inexpressibly rare, and Delightfull, and Beautifull. I was a little Stranger which at my Enterance into the World was Saluted and Surrounded with innumerable Joys. My Knowledg was Divine. I knew by Intuition those things which since my Apostasie, I Collected again, by the Highest Reason. My very Ignorance was Advantageous. I seemed as one Brought into the Estate of Innocence. All Things were Spotles and Pure and Glorious: yea, and infinitly mine, and Joyfull and Precious. I Knew not that there were any Sins, or

Complaints, or Laws. I Dreamed not of Poverties Contentions or Vices. All Tears and Quarrels, were hidden from mine Eys. Evry Thing was at Rest, Free, and Immortal. I Knew Nothing of Sickness or Death, or Exaction, in the Absence of these I was Entertained like an Angel with the Works of GOD in their Splendor and Glory; I saw all in the Peace of Eden; Heaven and Earth did sing my Creators Praises and could not make more Melody to Adam, then to me. All Time was Eternity, and a Perpetual Sabbath. Is it not Strange, that an Infant should be Heir of the World, and see those Mysteries which the Books of the Learned never unfold?

3

The Corn was Orient and Immortal Wheat, which never should be reaped, nor was ever sown. I thought it had stood from everlasting. The Dust and Stones of the Street were as Precious as GOLD. The Gates were at first the End of the World, The Green Trees when I saw them first through one of the Gates Transported and Ravished me; their Sweetnes and unusual Beauty made my Heart to leap, and almost mad with Extasie, they were such strange and Wonderfull Thing: The Men! O what Venerable and Reverend Creatures did the Aged seem! Immortal Cherubims! And yong Men Glittering and Sparkling Angels and Maids strange Seraphick Pieces of Life and Beauty! Boys and Girles Tumbling in the Street, and Playing, were moving Jewels. I knew not that they were Born or should Die. But all things abided Eternaly as they were in their Proper Places. Eternity was Manifest in the Light of the Day, and som thing infinit Behind evry thing appeared: which talked with my Expectation and moved my Desire. The Citie seemed to stand in Eden, or to be Built in Heaven. The Streets were mine, the Temple was mine, The People were mine, their Clothes and Gold and Silver was mine, as much as their Sparkling Eys Fair Skins and ruddy faces. The Skies were mine, and so were the Sun and Moon and Stars, and all the World was mine, and I the only Spectator and Enjoyer of it. I knew no Churlish Proprieties, nor Bounds nor Divisions: but all Proprieties and Divisions were mine: all Treasures and the Possessors of them. So that with much adoe I was corrupted; and made to learn the Dirty Devices of this World. Which now I unlearn, and becom as it were a little Child again, that I may enter into the Kingdom of GOD.

Hans Christian Andersen

(1805–1875)

"A Leaf from Heaven" (1855) comes from the Danish master of the fairy tale.

A Leaf from Heaven

High up in the clear, pure air flew an angel, with a flower plucked from the garden of heaven. As he was kissing the flower a very little leaf fell from it and sunk down into the soft earth in the middle of a wood. It immediately took root, sprouted, and sent out shoots among the other plants.

"What a ridiculous little shoot!" said one. "No one will recognize it; not even the thistle nor the stinging-nettle."

"It must be a kind of garden plant," said another; and so they sneered and despised the plant as a thing from a garden.

"Where are you coming?" said the tall thistles whose leaves were all armed with thorns. "It is stupid nonsense to allow yourself to shoot out in this way; we are not here to support you."

Winter came, and the plant was covered with snow, but the snow glittered over it as if it had sunshine beneath as well as above.

When spring came, the plant appeared in full bloom: a more beautiful object than any other plant in the forest. And now the professor of botany presented himself, one who could explain his knowledge in black and white. He examined and tested the plant, but it did not belong to his system of botany, nor could he possibly find out to what class it did belong. "It must be some degenerate species," said he; "I do not know it, and it is not mentioned in any system."

"Not known in any system!" repeated the thistles and the nettles.

The large trees which grew round it saw the plant and heard the remarks, but they said not a word either good or bad, which is the wisest plan for those who are ignorant.

There passed through the forest a poor innocent girl; her heart was pure, and her understanding increased by her faith. Her chief inheritance had been an old Bible, which she read and valued. From its pages she heard the voice of God speaking to her, and telling her to remember what was said of Joseph's brethren when persons wished to injure her. "They imagined evil in their hearts, but God turned it to good." If we suffer wrongfully, if we are misunderstood or despised, we must think of Him who was pure and holy, and who prayed for those who nailed Him to the cross, "Father, forgive them, for they know not what they do."

The girl stood still before the wonderful plant, for the green leaves exhaled a sweet and refreshing fragrance, and the flowers glittered and sparkled in the sunshine like colored flames, and the harmony of sweet sounds lingered round them as if each concealed within itself a deep fount of melody, which thousands of years could not exhaust. With pious gratitude the girl looked upon this glorious work of God, and bent down over one of the branches, that she might examine the flower and inhale the sweet perfume. Then a light broke in on her mind, and her heart expanded. Gladly would she have plucked a flower, but she could not overcome her reluctance to break one off. She knew it would so soon fade, so she took only a single green leaf, carried it home, and laid it in her Bible, where it remained ever green, fresh, and unfading. Between the pages of the Bible it still lay when, a few weeks afterwards, that Bible was laid under the young girl's head in her coffin. A holy calm rested on her face, as if the earthly remains bore the impress of the truth that she now stood in the presence of God.

In the forest the wonderful plant still continued to bloom till it grew and became almost a tree, and all the birds of passage bowed themselves before it.

"That plant is a foreigner, no doubt," said the thistles and the burdocks. "We can never conduct ourselves like that in this country." And the black forest snails actually spat at the flower.

Then came the swineherd; he was collecting thistles and shrubs to burn them for the ashes. He pulled up the wonderful plant, roots and all, and placed it in his bundle. "This will be as useful as any," he said, so the plant was carried away.

Not long after, the king of the country suffered from the deepest melancholy. He was diligent and industrious, but employment did him no good. They read deep and learned books to him, and then the lightest and most trifling that could be found, but all to no purpose. Then they applied for advice to one of the wise men of the world, and he sent them a message to say that there was one remedy which would relieve and cure him, and that it was a plant of heavenly origin which grew in the forest in the king's own dominions. The messenger described the flower so that its appearance could not be mistaken.

Then said the swineherd, "I am afraid I carried this plant away from the forest in my bundle, and it has been burnt to ashes long ago. But I did not know any better."

"You did not know any better! Ignorance upon ignorance indeed."

The poor swineherd took these words to heart, for they were addressed to him; he knew not that there were others who were equally ignorant. Not even a leaf of the plant could be found. There was one, but it lay in the coffin of the dead; no one knew anything about it.

Then the king, in his melancholy, wandered out to the spot in the wood. "Here is where the plant stood," he said; "it is a sacred place." Then he ordered that the place should be surrounded with a golden railing, and a sentry stationed near it.

The botanical professor wrote a long treatise about the heavenly plant, and for this he was loaded with gold, which improved the position of himself and his family.

And this part is really the most pleasant part of the story. For the plant had disappeared, and the king remained as melancholy and sad as ever, but the sentry said he had always been so.

Charles Fourier

(1772–1837)

The original French socialist, Fourier envisioned the world renewed by the creation of small cooperative communities (phalanxes) governed by love and harmony.

At last fortune has begun to smile on us; the fates are appeased, and the invention of the societary theory has opened the doors of the social prison known as civilization. . . .

If this age decides wisely to put the theory to the test, the whole globe will be transformed; humanity will rise from the depths of suffering to the heights of happiness. Everything will transpire in an instant, like a theatrical change of scenes in which Hell is replaced by Olympus. We are going to witness a spectacle which can be seen only once on each globe: the sudden transformation from industrial incoherence to societary unity. This is the most spectacular historical change which can take place in all the universes. Its expectation should console the present generation for all its misfortunes. During this metamorphosis each year will be worth centuries of existence. But the events which are going to transpire will be so remarkable that it would be wrong to disclose them without proper preparation.

Beset by long-standing misfortunes and bound by the chains of habit, the people of civilization have imagined that God destined them to a life of privations or at most to a very limited degree of happiness. It will take some time for them to become accustomed to the idea of the happiness that awaits them. They would react skeptically to an unvarnished account of the delights which they are going to enjoy in the very near future. Yet the new order is near at hand, for it will take barely two years to organize each of the societary communities and no more than six years at the longest to complete the organization of the globe.

The long delay in the establishment of the societary order will only serve to increase its magnificence. Already in the time of Solon and

Pericles the Greeks had sufficient means at their disposal to found a trial community. They had satisfied the principal requirement which is the development of large-scale industry. During the earliest times, when industrial development was limited, the societary order could not have been established and God was thus obliged to leave man in ignorance of his magnificent destiny.

Today our resources in art, industry, material elegance and refinement are at least twice those possessed by the Athenians. Thus the beginnings of the societary order will be twice as splendid. Now at last we are going to benefit from the progress of our physical sciences. Until the present time these sciences have only served to multiply the luxuries of the few and hence to increase the relative deprivation of the impoverished multitude. Until now scientific progress has benefited the idle, but it has tormented the working people. In this odious situation men had but two alternatives: to blame God or to blame civilization. Reasonable men would have opted for the latter alternative. . . . For if it is absurd not to believe in God, it is equally absurd to believe in him half-heartedly—to think that his providence is incomplete and that he has neglected to provide for our most urgent need, the need of a social order which will assure our happiness. When one beholds the marvels of our industry, such as great clipper ships and other wondrous inventions which are premature in view of our political immaturity, can one reasonably suppose that the God who has lavished such blessings upon us would want to deny us knowledge of the social art which will enable us to put our inventions to the best use. Would not God have been malicious and inconsistent in providing us with so many admirable sciences if those sciences were meant to produce nothing more than barbarism and civilization? At last humanity is going to be delivered from these disgusting and criminal societies, and their imminent downfall will be greeted by universal joy!

William James

(1842–1910)

In a talk on "What Makes a Life Significant," America's greatest and most amiable philosopher-psychologist reflects on the problem of being bored in utopia.

A few summers ago I spent a happy week at the famous Assembly Grounds on the borders of Chautauqua Lake. The moment one treads that sacred enclosure, one feels one's self in an atmosphere of success. Sobriety and industry, intelligence and goodness, orderliness and ideality, prosperity and cheerfulness, pervade the air. It is a serious and studious picnic on a gigantic scale. Here you have a town of many thousands of inhabitants, beautifully laid out in the forest and drained, and equipped with means for satisfying all the necessary lower and most of the superfluous higher wants of man. You have a first-class college in full blast. You have magnificent music—a chorus of seven hundred voices, with possibly the most perfect open-air auditorium in the world. You have every sort of athletic exercise from sailing, rowing, swimming, bicycling, to the ball-field and the more artificial doings which the gymnasium affords. You have kindergartens and model secondary schools. You have general religious services and special club-houses for the several sects. You have perpetually running soda-water fountains, and daily popular lectures by distinguished men. You have the best of company, and yet no effort. You have no zymotic diseases, no poverty, no drunkenness, no crime, no police. You have culture, you have kindness, you have cheapness, you have equality, you have the best fruits of what mankind has fought and bled and striven for under the name of civilization for centuries. You have, in short, a foretaste of what human society might be, were it all in the light, with no suffering and no dark corners.

I went in curiosity for a day. I stayed for a week, held spell-bound by the charm and ease of everything, by the middle-class paradise, without a sin, without a victim, without a blot, without a tear.

And yet what was my own astonishment, on emerging into the dark and wicked world again, to catch myself quite unexpectedly and involuntarily saying: "Ouf! what a relief! Now for something primordial and savage, even though it were as bad as an Armenian massacre, to set the balance straight again. This order is too tame, this culture too second-rate, this goodness too uninspiring. This human drama without a villain or a pang; this community so refined that ice-cream soda-water is the utmost offering it can make to the brute animal in man; this city simmering in the tepid lakeside sun; this atrocious harmlessness of all things,—I cannot abide with them. Let me take my chances again in the big outside worldly wilderness with all its sins and sufferings. There are the heights and depths, the precipices and the steep ideals, the gleams of the awful and the infinite; and there is more hope and help a thousand times than in this dead level and quintessence of every mediocrity."

Such was the sudden right-about-face performed for me by my lawless fancy! There had been spread before me the realization—on a small, sample scale of course—of all the ideals for which our civilization has been striving: security, intelligence, humanity, and order; and here was the instinctive hostile reaction, not of the natural man, but of a so-called cultivated man upon such a Utopia. There seemed thus to be a self-contradiction and paradox somewhere, which I, as a professor drawing a full salary, was in duty bound to unravel and explain, if I could.

So I meditated. And, first of all, I asked myself what the thing was that was so lacking in this Sabbatical city, and the lack of which kept one forever falling short of the higher sort of contentment. And I soon recognized that it was the element that gives to the wicked outer world all its moral style, expressiveness and picturesqueness,—the element of precipitousness, so to call it, of strength and strenuousness, intensity and danger. What excites and interests the looker-on at life, what the romances and the statues celebrate and the grim civic monuments remind us of, is the everlasting battle of the powers of light with those of darkness; with heroism, reduced to its bare chance, yet ever and anon snatching victory from the jaws of death. But in this unspeakable Chautauqua there was no potentiality of death in sight anywhere, and no point of the compass visible from which danger might possibly appear. The ideal was so completely victorious already that no sign of any previous battle remained, the place just resting on its oars. But what our human emotions seem to require is the sight of the struggle going on. The moment the fruits are being merely eaten, things become ignoble. Sweat and effort, human nature strained to its uttermost and on the rack, yet getting through alive, and then turning its back on its success to pursue another more rare and arduous still—this is the sort of thing the presence of which inspires us, and the reality of which it seems to be the function of all the higher forms of literature and fine art to bring home to us and suggest. At Chautauqua there were no racks, even in the place's historical museum; and no sweat, except possibly the gentle moisture on the brow of some lecturer, or on the sides of some player in the ball-field.

Such absence of human nature *in extremis* anywhere seemed, then, a sufficient explanation for Chautauqua's flatness and lack of zest. . . .

With these thoughts in my mind, I was speeding with the train toward Buffalo, when, near that city, the sight of a workman doing something on the dizzy edge of a sky-scaling iron construction brought me to my senses very suddenly. And now I perceived, by a flash of insight, that I had been steeping myself in pure ancestral blindness, and looking at life with the eyes of a remote spectator. Wishing for heroism and the spectacle of human nature on the rack, I had never noticed the great fields of heroism lying round about me, I had failed to see it present and alive. I could only think of it as dead and embalmed, labelled and costumed, as it is in the pages of romance. And yet there it was before me in the daily lives of the laboring classes. Not in clanging fights and desperate marches only is heroism to be looked for, but on every railway bridge and fire-proof building that is going up to-day. On freight-trains, on the decks of vessels, in cattle-yards and mines, on lumber-rafts, among the firemen and the policemen, the demand for courage is incessant; and the supply never fails. There, every day of the year somewhere, is human nature *in extremis* for you. And wherever a scythe, an axe, a pick, or a shovel is wielded, you have it sweating and aching and with its powers of patient endurance racked to the utmost under the length of hours of the strain.

As I awoke to all this unidealized heroic life around me, the scales seemed to fall from my eyes; and a wave of sympathy greater than anything I had ever before felt with the common life of common men began to fill my soul. It began to seem as if virtue with horny hands and dirty skin were the only virtue genuine and vital enough to take account of. Every other virtue poses; none is absolutely unconscious and simple, and unexpectant of decoration or recognition, like this. These are our soldiers, thought I, These our sustainers, these the very parents of our life.

Songs and Poems

"An Invitation to Lubberland"

In this seventeenth-century anonymous English ditty, Lubberland is a version of "Cockaigne," a poor-man's paradise of pastry-paved streets, rivers of wine, and dessert-bushes that has been celebrated in poetry and song since medieval times.

There is a ship, we understand,
   Now riding in the river;
'Tis newly come from Lubberland,
   The like I think was never;
You that a lazy life do love;
   I'd have you now go over,
They say the land is not above
   Two thousand leagues from Dover.

The captain and his master too,
   Do's give us this relation,
And so do's all the whole ship's crew,
   Concerning this strange nation:
"The streets are pav'd with pudding-pies,
   Nay, powder'd-beef and bacon,
They say they scorn to tell you lies";
   Who thinks it is mistaken?

The King of Knaves, and Queen of Sluts
   Reign there in peace and quiet;
You need not fear to starve your guts,
   There is such store of dyet:
There may you live free from all care,

like hogs set up a fat'ning;
The garments which the people wear
Is silver, silk and satin.

The lofty buildings of this place
For many years have lasted;
With nutmegs, pepper, cloves, and mace,
The walls are there rough-casted,
In curious hasty-pudding boil'd,
and most ingenious carving;
Likewise they are with pancakes ty'd,
Sure, here's no fear of starving.

The captain says, "In every town,
Hot roasted pigs will meet ye,
They in the streets run up and down,
Still crying out, Come eat me."
Likewise, he says, "At every feast,
The very fowls and fishes,
Nay from the biggest to the least,
Comes tumbling to the dishes.

"The rivers run with claret fine,
The brooks with rich canary,
The ponds with other sorts of wine,
To make your hearts full merry;

Nay, more than this, you may behold,
The fountains flow with brandy,
The rocks are like refined gold,
The hills are sugar-candy.

"Rose-water is the rain they have,
Which comes in pleasant showers,
All places are adorned brave,
With sweet and fragrant flowers.
Hot custards grows on ev'ry tree,

Each ditch affords rich jellies:
Now if you will be ruled by me,
Go there and fill your bellies.

"There's nothing there but holy-days
With music out of measure;
Who can forbear to speak the praise
Of such a land of pleasure?
There may you lead a lazy life,
Free from all kind of labour:
And he that is without a wife,
May borrow of his neighbor.

"There is no law nor lawyer's fees,
All man are free from fury,
For ev'ry one do's what he please,
Without a judge or jury:
The summer-time is warm they say,
The winter's ne'er the colder,
They have no landlord's rent to pay,
Each man is a free-holder."

You that are free to cross the seas
Make no more disputation;
In Lubber-land you'll live
With pleasant recreation:
The captain waits but for a gale
Of prosperous wind and weather,
And then they soon will hoist up sail,
Make haste away together.

George Herbert
(1593–1633)

After a brief academic career as public orator of Cambridge University, Herbert was ordained a priest in the Church of England and befriended Nicholas Ferrer, founder of the famed religious community at Little Gidding. On his deathbed, Herbert sent Ferrer his unpublished poems, asking his friend to destroy them or publish them. Ferrer chose the latter course, and The Temple: Sacred Poems and Private Ejaculations *(1633) ensured Herbert's fame.*

Prayer

Prayer the Churches banquet, Angels age,
  Gods breath in man returning to his birth,
  The soul in paraphrase, heart in pilgrimage,
The Christian plummet sounding heav'n and earth;
Engine against th' Almightie, sinners towre,
  Reversed thunder, Christ-side-piercing spear,
  The six-daies world transposing in an houre,
A kinde of tune, which all things heare and fear;
Softnesse, and peace, and joy, and love, and blisse,
  Exalted Manna, gladnesse of the best,
  Heaven in ordinarie, man well drest,
The milkie way, the bird of Paradise,
  Church-bels beyond the starres heard, the souls bloud,
  The land of spices; something understood.

Mikhail Lermontov
(1814–1841)

The Russian Romantic poet and novelist, soldier, and proto-revolutionary, whose life was cut short by a duel at age twenty-six, here expresses his nostalgia for paradise.

The Angel

An angel was flying through midnight's deep blue,
And softly he sang as he flew;
The moon, and the clouds, and the stars in a throng
All listened: in heavenly song

He sang of the blessings of souls without sin
In the gardens of Paradise; hymns
To God the almighty he sang, and his praise
Was pure and completely unfeigned.

He carried toward earth, with its tears and its grief,
A soul just beginning its life;
And long, long thereafter the soul could still hear
The song he sang—wordless, but clear.

The soul languished long in its worldly attire,
Still knowing a wondrous desire;
And that heavenly music was never usurped
By the wearisome songs of the earth.

Shaker Songs

These hymns were "given by inspiration" during the 1830s and 1840s to American members of the United Society of Believers in Christ's Second Appearing, the celibate millenarian sect founded by the visionary Mother Ann Lee.

Simple Gifts

Tis the gift to be simple 'tis the gift to be free,
'Tis the gift to come down where we ought to be,
And when we find ourselves in the place just right,
'Twill be in the valley of love and delight.
When true simplicity is gain'd,
To bow and to bend we shan't be asham'd,
To turn, turn will be our delight
'Till by turning, turning we come round right.

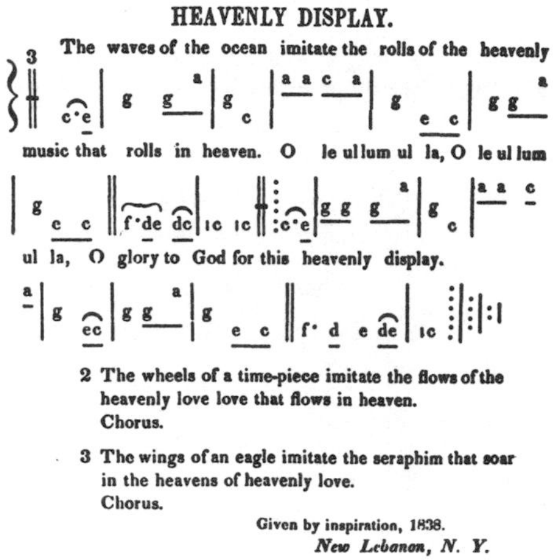
HEAVENLY DISPLAY.
The waves of the ocean imitate the rolls of the heavenly
music that rolls in heaven. O le ul lum ul la, O le ul lum
ul la, O glory to God for this heavenly display.
2 The wheels of a time-piece imitate the flows of the heavenly love love that flows in heaven.
Chorus.
3 The wings of an eagle imitate the seraphim that soar in the heavens of heavenly love.
Chorus.
Given by inspiration, 1838.
New Lebanon, N. Y.

Heavenly Display

The waves of the ocean imitate the rolls of the
heavenly music that rolls in heaven.
O le ul lum ul la, O le ul lum ul la,
O glory to God for this heavenly display.

The wheels of a time-piece imitate the flows of the
heavenly love love that flows in heaven.
Chorus.

The wings of an eagle imitate the seraphim that soar
in the heavens of heavenly love.
Chorus.

VII

New Heaven, New Earth

Introduction

The clock is running down, the earth is growing old, even the canopy of heaven is beginning to fade and curl up around the edges—so it has always seemed. If we cannot return to the paradise of beginning times, if the angel with his flaming sword still blocks the gates of Eden, then we may turn toward the paradise of end times and replace nostalgia with hope.

Expectation of the renewal of heaven and earth has inspired political revolutions; voyages of exploration, mission, and conquest; and their opposites as well: mysticism, pacifism, and quietism. Yet while attempts to calculate the date when the world will end have done incalculable mischief, end-time expectations need not always take convulsive form. There are gentler varieties of eschatological hope, in which the "still small voice" can be heard in an atmosphere of hushed expectancy.

Such is the case for the Hasidic pilgrims of S. Y. Agnon's tale, *In the Heart of the Seas*. When they leave their native Poland to go up to the land of Israel, they can expect to find little besides danger along the way and ruin upon arrival. Nonetheless, their journey feels like a return from exile; they come to the land of Israel in order "to stand at the king's gate" awaiting the promised redemption, or at least to be buried there, so that when the Last Judgment comes, they will be spared the need to roll through caves and tunnels from distant graves.

The gathering of the exiles, the restoration of Jerusalem, and the rebuilding of the Temple—with the return of the divine presence to its midst—all enter into the promise made to Isaiah: "For, behold, I create new heavens and a new earth: and the former shall not be remembered, nor come into mind. . . . And I will rejoice in Jerusalem, and joy in my people: and the voice of weeping shall be no more heard in her, nor the voice of crying." How this promise applies to the dead of Israel was only gradually spelled out, however. In the Hebrew Bible, Daniel alone states explicitly what would become the common belief of Jews: "many of them that sleep in the dust of the earth shall awake."

For St. Paul, this Jewish hope is an essential foundation for Christian faith: "If there be no resurrection of the dead, then is Christ not risen: And if Christ be not risen, then *is* our preaching vain, and your faith *is* also vain" (1 Corinthians 15:13–14). What will the resurrection be like? Indescribable, like heaven itself, but one can draw analogies: If death is like being stripped naked, the resurrection will be like being clothed in glory. If death is like returning to the soil, the resurrection will be like the quickening of the seed. If death mars creation, the resurrection will perfect it, restoring the image of God in man so that we may gaze "with open face" on the divine glory and be changed into its likeness (2 Corinthians 3:18). Immortality of the soul is not enough; soul and body together must be "swallowed up of life" (2 Corinthians 5:4). Along similar lines, in his dialogue with his sister Macrina *On the Soul and the Resurrection* (c. 380), Gregory of Nyssa speculates that on the day of the resurrection, the scattered atoms of the body will remember one another and, like the dispersed children of Israel, reassemble at God's command. This is how John Donne foresees it as well: "Arise, arise / From death, you numberlesse infinities / Of soules, and to your scattred bodies goe."

When the Prophet Muhammad taught that there would be a final resurrection and judgment of the dead, people scoffed. The verses we include from the Qur'an interpret this response as ingratitude, a sin far worse than skepticism; hence the rebuke, "which of your Lord's bounties will you and you deny?" The Zoroastrian tradition, first to articulate belief in the resurrection of the dead, had to counter similar doubts. In our selection from the Bundahishn, a ninth-century Persian scripture, Ohrmazd (Ahura Mazda, the good Creator) reasons with the skeptics: "If I created what had not been, why should it be impossible for me to recreate what once was?" Whether Zoroastrian, Islamic, Jewish, or Christian, resurrection entails the recreation of a world, not the reanimation of a corpse.

But what will this new world be like? The accounts agree on many points, including topography. In the words of the Bundahishn, "There will be neither mountains nor ridges nor pits, neither high ground nor low." Not, perhaps, a vision likely to attract Alpinists, but one designed to convey, however imperfectly, a sense of the perfection that awaits.

The nineteenth-century Ghost Dance, the subject of our excerpt from George Sword's report, provides a lesson in what can go wrong when such visions of perfection are misunderstood. A Paiute prophet and messiah-figure named Wovoka (Jack Wilson), having received divine instruction in a trance, proclaimed the imminent resurrection of the Indian dead and the advent of a new world full of buffalo and empty of white people. To accelerate this transformation, Wovoka and his followers performed a dance he had learned in the other world. Shamanic and messianic elements combined to produce a heady mixture; many participants swooned and saw visions of their dead kin. Their code was pacifist, yet rumors that this movement was taking a militant turn among the Sioux so alarmed white settlers that federal troops intervened, leaving two hundred Sioux men, women, and children dead in the snow at Wounded Knee.

St. Augustine, whose account of end times completes his masterpiece *The City of God*, was among the first Christian thinkers to suspect the dangers inherent in eschatological thinking: It is all too easy to confound the earthly city with the City of God, or to think that we might hasten the second advent by our own efforts. A healthy skepticism about latter-day prophets is perfectly compatible, Augustine believes, with the confident hope that the new heaven and earth will come in God's own good time. When it does arrive, Augustine suggests, there will be a cosmic Sabbath, leading to an endless Sunday in which "we shall rest and see, see and love, love and praise."

The difference between the new world and the old is the difference between the real world and its shadow or copy. "It's all in Plato, all in Plato: bless me, what *do* they teach them at these schools!" cries Digory in our excerpt from C. S. Lewis's children's apocalypse, *The Last Battle*. But we give the final word of this anthology to the Jubilee Singers, a choir of emancipated slaves, who know better than most what it means to look forward to the joyous freedom of "that great getting-up morning."

Belief

This brief American Hasidic tale appears in Legends of the Hasidim, *collected by Jerome R. Mintz.*

Two Jews meet and they're both a little drunk. They like to drink.

One says, "When the Meshiah comes, everything will be wonderful. The Red Sea will be brandy."

The other says, "Why not the Mediterranean? If you're going to believe in something, why believe in so little?"

Shmuel Yosef Agnon

(1888–1970)

An Israeli author of Polish Jewish descent, co-recipient of the Nobel Prize for Literature in 1966, Agnon wrote modern Hebrew prose with undertones of the archaic and magical. In the Heart of the Seas, *echoing Judah Halevi's "Songs of Zion," tells the story of a small band of Hasidic pilgrims who set forth for the Land of Israel.*

On the Sea

The ship reached the point at sea where the waters move, and sailed along calmly. Our comrades stood reciting the Prayer of the Sea and the eight verses which Jonah had recited in the belly of the fish. Then, weeping, they sang Psalm One hundred and seven, which considers the kindness of the Lord and his wonders by land and sea, how he shall redeem his redeemed ones, and gather them together from all the lands, and lead them on the straight way, and satisfy the souls of those who hunger and thirst, and fill them with all good things; even if they reach the very gates of death, God forbid, He saves them by his mercies, and delivers them from their distress, and brings them to their desired haven; so that at the last they relate his deeds in song. Even if he raises the sea against them and brings up a stormy wind, he quiets the sea at once and silences the waves; and then they rejoice and give thanks to the Holy One, blessed be he, and rise from their affliction, having seen that all that comes from the Lord is loving-kindness, but that it is necessary to consider wisely in order to see and rejoice in the mercies of the Lord.

After they finished reciting the entire Psalm, they sat down on their belongings, and took their books in hand, and read verses from the Pentateuch, the Prophets, and the Writings. When a man forsakes his home and reaches another place and finds a vessel which he had used at home, how he rejoices! How much pleasure he derives from the vessel!

This is far truer of books, which are read and studied and engaged in every day. Thus Rabbi Moshe sits reading: 'The Land must be exceedingly good if the Lord desires us and brings us unto it and gives it unto us, a land which is flowing with milk and honey.' And Rabbi Yosef Meir sits reading, 'I have forsaken my house, I have cast off my heritage'; and both of them finished by reading together: 'Afterwards the Children of Israel will return and entreat the Lord their God and David their king, and they will fear the Lord and hope for His goodness.' Finally, they put the books down and rose, and each one placed his hand on the other's shoulder, and they sang:

> 'Oh that the salvation of Israel were come out of Zion!
> When the Lord turneth the captivity of his people,
> Let Jacob rejoice, let Israel be glad.'

The ship made her way quietly and a pleasant smell came up out of the sea. The waters moved after their fashion and the waves dwelt together in peace; while birds of some kind flew above the ship and beat their wings and shrieked. The sun sank below the horizon, the face of the sea turned black, and the Holy One, blessed be he, brought forth the moon and stars and set them to give light in the heavens.

One of the company looked out and saw a kind of light shining on the sea. Brother, said he to one of the comrades, perhaps you know what that is? But he did not know, and so he asked another of the company and that one asked still another.

Then they all turned their eyes and gazed at the sea and said, If that be the lower fire which comes from hell, then where is the smoke? And if it be the eye socket of Leviathan, then no eye has ever seen it.

Suppose, said Rabbi Alter the teacher, that it is one of the evil husks of the sea.

But Rabbi Shelomo said, It is time to say the Evening Prayer. Then they promptly rose and prepared to pray, since there is no evil husk or demon that has any power or authority over a full prayer quorum.

When they stood up to pray they saw that they were lacking one for a quorum. Hananiah, who had made the journey with them, had vanished. In the morning he had gone down to the market to buy his food, but he had never come back.

Then they began to beat their heads and to wail: Woe and alas, is that the way to treat a companion! It would have been better if we had gone back and been lost. We should have held one another's hands and come up into the ship all together, but we did not. When we came aboard, each one carried his own baggage and said, 'All is well, my soul!'

How hard Hananiah had toiled until he reached them! He had gone halfway round the world, and had been stripped naked, and had fallen among thieves, and had forgotten when Sabbaths and festivals occurred, and had profaned the Day of Atonement, and had made his way barefoot, without boots. And then when he had reached them he had gone to all kinds of trouble for their sakes. He had rebound the books, and made cups for the oil lamps and boxes for their goods, and had not asked for any payment. All the trouble with the horses had been left to him on the way; they had been happy to have him because he would complete the prayer quorum. But now that they had embarked on the ship and were on the way to the Land of Israel, he had been left behind. So they stood miserable and unhappy, lamenting at heart because an unobtrusive vessel had been in their midst and had been taken away from them for their sins.

So everyone prayed separately, and while praying they beat their heads against the sides of the ship in order to divert their thoughts. Finally, everyone returned to his own place and sat down as though he were in mourning. Gradually the night grew darker and the ship went its accustomed way. The sailors tightened the masts and sails and sat down to eat and drink, while facing them our comrades sat, distress eating at their hearts. Who knew where Hananiah could be? Maybe he had been taken captive, God forbid, and sold as a slave.

The darkness grew thicker and thicker. Rats and mice were scurrying around in the lower parts of the ship and were gnawing at utensils and foodstuffs.

Where there is great anxiety, sleep helps to put it right. But who could enjoy sleep when one of their number had left them, and they had no way of knowing whether he was alive or dead. How much Hananiah had wandered about! How much trouble he had gone through! He had put himself in danger and disregarded his own life and had had no fear for his body, desiring only to go up to the Land of Israel; and yet now that his time had come to go up, something had gone wrong and he had not come aboard!

At the midnight hour the comrades sat on their baggage and uttered songs and prayers in honor of the great Name of Him who dwells in Zion. The stars moved in the sky, while the moon was now covered, now uncovered. The ship went on, the waters moved as usual, and a still small voice rose from the ship. It was the sound of song and praise rising from one firmament to another, till they reached the Gateway of White Sapphire where the prayers of Israel gather and join together until such time as the dawn comes to the Land of Israel. Corresponding to the prayers of Israel, praises of the Holy One, blessed be he, rise up from the waters.

Is it possible for water which has neither utterance nor speech so to praise the Holy One, blessed be he? But these sounds are the voices of the boys and girls who once flung themselves into the sea. After the wicked Titus destroyed Jerusalem, he brought three thousand ships and filled them with boys and girls. When they were out to sea, they said to one another, Was it not enough for us to have angered the Holy One, blessed be he, in his house, and now are we to be required to anger him in the land of Edom? Thereupon they all leaped into the sea together. What did the Holy One, blessed be he, do? He took them in his right hand and brought them to a great island planted with all manner of fine trees, and surrounded them with all kinds of beautifully colored waves, blue and marble and alabaster, looking like the stones of the Temple; and the plants from which the Temple incense was made grow there. And all those who saw that plant would weep and laugh. They would weep because they remembered the glory of the House, and they would laugh because the Holy One, blessed be he, is destined to bring that glory back.

And the boys and girls still remain as innocent as ever, fenced about from all iniquity, their faces like the rosebud, just as we learn in the tale about the rose garden which was once to be found in Jerusalem. And the brightness of their faces gives light like the planet Venus, whose light comes from the shining of the Beasts that are before God's throne.

And the children have no wrinkles either on their brows or their faces, apart from two wrinkles under the eyes from which their tears run down into the Great Sea and cool the Gehenna of those sinners of Israel who never lost their faith in the Land of Israel. These children are not subject to any prince or ruler, neither to the king of Edom nor to the king of Ishmael, nor to any flesh-and-blood monarch; but they stand in the shadow of the Holy One, blessed be he, and call him Father and he calls them my children. And all their lives long they speak of the glory of Jerusalem and the glory of the House, and the glory of the High Priests and the altar, and of those who offered the sacrifices and those who prepared the incense and those who made the shew-bread.

And whenever the Holy One, blessed be he, remembers his sons who have been exiled among the nations, who have neither Temple nor altar of atonement, nor High Priests nor Levites at their stations, nor kings and princes, he at once is filled with pity and takes those boys and girls in his arm and holds them to his heart and says to them, Sons and daughters mine, do you remember the glory of Jerusalem and the glory of Israel when the Temple still stood and Israel still possessed its splendor?

They at once begin telling Him what they saw in their childhood, and go on interpreting like Daniel, the beloved man, and Jonathan ben Uziel. The only difference is that Daniel and Jonathan wrote in Aramaic, while these children speak the Holy Tongue, which is the tongue the Holy One, blessed be he, uses. And at such times the Holy One, blessed be he, laughs with them; and you might say that at no other times does he laugh and smile as he does when he hears the praises of his House and the praises of those who came to his House. At such times he says, 'This is the people which I formed for Myself that they might tell of My praise.' And he also says, 'Comfort ye,' for in the future Jerusalem will be builded a thousand thousand times more great than she was, and the Temple will reach from one end of the world to the other and be as lofty as the stars of the heavens and the wheels of my divine Chariot; and the Divine Presence will rest upon each and every one of Israel; and each and every one of them will speak in the Holy Spirit.

Furthermore, all the years that those boys and girls have dwelt in the midst of the sea they have constantly awaited salvation, and there is no ship sailing to the Land of Israel which these boys and girls do not follow. For when they see a ship at sea, one says to the other, The time has come for the Gathering of the Exiles. Thereupon, each of them takes one of the great sea waves and mounts it as a rider mounts his horse and rides until he comes near the ship.

And as they ride they sing, 'I will bring them back from Bashan, I will bring them back from the depths of the sea.' And their voices are as golden bells in the skirts of a garment, and they are heard by those who go down to the sea. Indeed we have heard a tale from such as tell only the truth, of how they were sailing to the Land of Israel on the Great Sea and heard a voice so sweet they wished to leap into the sea and follow that voice; but the sailors tied them up with their belts until the ship had sailed a distance away from the voice.

The moon sank, the stars went in, and the planets went their way. The

Holy One, blessed be he, brought forth the dawn and lit up the world. As the dawn grew bright the travelers saw the likeness of a man on the sea. They stared and saw that he had a full beard, earlocks on either cheek and a book in his hand; and a kerchief was spread out under him and on it he sat as a man who sits at his ease. No wave of the sea rose to drown him, nor did any sea beast swallow him.

And what did the Gentiles say when they saw a man sitting on his kerchief and floating in the sea? Some of them said, Such things are often seen by seafarers and desert-farers. Others said, Whoever he is, he has a curse hanging over him so that nevermore can he rest. That is why he wanders from place to place, appearing yesterday on the dry land and today on the sea.

On that ship there were representatives of each of the seventy nations of the world, and each of them was overwhelmed and terrified at this apparition. So Israel stood on one side and the nations of the world on the other, fearful and staring, until their eyelashes became scorched by the sun. Then Rabbi Shmuel Yosef, the son of Rabbi Shalom Mordekhai ha-Levi, said, It is the Divine Presence, which is bringing back the people of Israel to their own place.

And Rabbi Moshe wept and said, 'The counsel of the Lord is with them that fear Him, and his covenant to make them know it.'

Biblical Texts

Daniel 12:1–3

And at that time shall Michael stand up, the great prince which standeth for the children of thy people: and there shall be a time of trouble, such as never was since there was a nation even to that same time: and at that time thy people shall be delivered, every one that shall be found written in the book.
2 And many of them that sleep in the dust of the earth shall awake, some to everlasting life, and some to shame and everlasting contempt.
3 And they that be wise shall shine as the brightness of the firmament; and they that turn many to righteousness as the stars for ever and ever.

Isaiah 65:17–25

For, behold, I create new heavens and a new earth: and the former shall not be remembered, nor come into mind.

18 But be ye glad and rejoice for ever in that which I create: for, behold, I create Jerusalem, and joy in my people: and the voice of weeping shall be no more heard in her, nor the voice of crying.

20 There shall be no more thence an infant of days, nor an old man that hath not filled his days: for the child shall die an hundred years old; but the sinner being an hundred years old shall be accursed.

21 And they shall build houses, and inhabit them; and they shall plant vineyards, and eat the fruit of them.

22 They shall not build, and another inhabit; they shall not plant, and another eat: for as the days of a tree are the days of my people, and mine elect shall long enjoy the work of their hands.

23 They shall not labour in vain, nor bring forth for trouble; for they are the seed of the blessed of the LORD, and their offspring with them.

24 And it shall come to pass, that before they call, I will answer; and while they are yet speaking, I will hear.

25 The wolf and the lamb shall feed together, and the lion shall eat straw like the bullock: and dust shall be the serpent's meat. They shall not hurt nor destroy in all my holy mountain, saith the LORD.

1 Corinthians 15:35–54

But some man will say, How are the dead raised up? and with what body do they come?

36 Thou fool, that which thou sowest is not quickened, except it die:

37 And that which thou sowest, thou sowest not that body that shall be, but bare grain, it may chance of wheat, or of some other grain:

38 But God giveth it a body as it hath pleased him, and to every seed his own body.

39 All flesh is not the same flesh: but there is one kind of flesh of men, another flesh of beasts, another of fishes, and another of birds.

40 There are also celestial bodies, and bodies terrestrial: but the glory of the terrestrial is another.

41 There is one glory of the sun, and another glory of the stars: for one star differeth from another star in glory.

42 So also is the resurrection of the dead. It is sown in corruption; it is raised in incorruption:

43 It is sown in dishonour; it is raised in glory: it is sown in weakness; it is raised in power:

44 It is sown a natural body; it is raised a spiritual body. There is a natural body, and there is a spiritual body.

45 And so it is written, The first man Adam was made a living soul; the last Adam was made a quickening spirit.

46 Howbeit that was not first which is spiritual, but that which is natural; and afterward that which is spiritual.

47 The first man is of the earth, earthy: the second man is of the Lord from heaven.

48 As is the earthy, such are they also that are earthy: and as is the heavenly, such are they also that are heavenly.

49 And as we have borne the image of the earthy, we shall also bear the image of the heavenly.

50 Now this I say, brethren, that flesh and blood cannot inherit the kingdom of God; neither doth corruption inherit incorruption.

51 Behold, I shew you a mystery; We shall not all sleep, but we shall all
be changed,
52 In a moment, in the twinkling of an eye, at the last trump: for the
trumpet shall sound, and the dead shall be raised incorruptible, and we
shall be changed.
53 For this corruptible must put on incorruption, and this mortal must
put on immortality.
54 So when this corruptible shall have put on incorruption, and this
mortal shall have put on immortality, then shall be brought to pass the
saying that is written, Death is swallowed up in victory.

Revelation 21:1–4

And I saw a new heaven and a new earth: for the first heaven and the
first earth were passed away; and there was no more sea.
2 And I John saw the holy city, new Jerusalem, coming down from God
out of heaven, prepared as a bride adorned for her husband.
3 And I heard a great voice out of heaven saying, Behold, the taberna-
cle of God is with men, and he will dwell with them, and they shall be his
people, and God himself shall be with them, and be their God.
4 And God shall wipe away all tears from their eyes; and there shall be
no more death, neither sorrow, nor crying, neither shall there be any
more pain: for the former things are passed away.

Qur'an

Sura 55:37–78

And when heaven is split asunder,
and turns crimson like red leather—
O which of your Lord's bounties will you and you deny?
on that day none shall be questioned
about his sin, neither man nor jinn.
O which of your Lord's bounties will you and you deny?
The sinners shall be known by their mark,
and they shall be seized by their forelocks and their feet.
O which of your Lord's bounties will you and you deny?
This is Gehenna, that sinners cried lies to;
they shall go round between it and between hot, boiling
water.
O which of your Lord's bounties will you and you deny?

But such as fears the Station of his Lord,
for them shall be two gardens—
O which of your Lord's bounties will you and you deny?
abounding in branches—
O which of your Lord's bounties will you and you deny?
therein two fountains of running water—
O which of your Lord's bounties will you and you deny?
therein of every fruit two kinds—
O which of your Lord's bounties will you and you deny?
reclining upon couches lined with brocade,
the fruits of the gardens nigh to gather—
O which of your Lord's bounties will you and you deny?
therein maidens restraining their glances,
untouched before them by any man or jinn—

O which of your Lord's bounties will you and you deny?
lovely as rubies, beautiful as coral—
O which of your Lord's bounties will you and you deny?
Shall the recompense of goodness be other than goodness?
O which of your Lord's bounties will you and you deny?

And besides these shall be two gardens—
O which of your Lord's bounties will you and you deny?
green, green pastures—
O which of your Lord's bounties will you and you deny?
therein two fountains of gushing water—
O which of your Lord's bounties will you and you deny?
therein fruits,
and palm-trees, and pomegranates—
O which of your Lord's bounties will you and you deny?
therein maidens good and comely—
O which of your Lord's bounties will you and you deny?
houris, cloistered in cool pavilions—
O which of your Lord's bounties will you and you deny?
untouched before them by any man or jinn—
O which of your Lord's bounties will you and you deny?
reclining upon green cushions and lovely druggets—
O which of your Lord's bounties will you and you deny?

Blessed be the Name of thy Lord, majestic, splendid.

Bundahishn

(Ninth Century)

This selection from a compilation of ancient Zoroastrian teachings represents one of the oldest traditions of belief in the resurrection.

'On the Raising of the Dead and the Final Body

It is said in the Religion that just as Mashyē and Mashyānē, after they had grown out of the earth, consumed water first, then plants, then milk, and then meat, so do men when they [are about to] die, abstain first from the eating of meat and milk and then from bread; but right up to the moment of death they drink water.

(2) So too in the millennium of Oshētarmāh the power of Āz (gluttony) is so diminished that men are satisfied by eating one meal every three days and nights. After that they abstain from eating meat, and eat (only) plants and the milk of domestic animals. After that they abstain from drinking milk also; then they abstain from eating plants too, and drink only water. Ten years before the coming of Sōshyans they reach a state in which they eat nothing, yet do not die.

(3) Then Sōshyans will raise up the dead, as (the Religion) says, "Zoroaster asked Ohrmazd, 'From whence can the body which the wind has carried off and the water swept away, be put together again; and how will the raising of the dead come to pass?' And Ohrmazd made answer (and said): 'When [I established] the sky without pillar on an invisible (*mēnōk*) support, its ends flung wide apart, bright with the substance of shining metal, and when I created the earth which supports the whole material creation though itself has no material support, and when I set the Sun, Moon, and stars,—forms of light,—on their courses in the atmosphere, and when I created grain on earth and scattered it abroad so that it grows up again and yields a greater crop, and when I created vari-

ous and variegated colours in the plants, and when I gave fire to the plants and other things and it did not burn (them), and when I created the embryo in its mother's womb and gave it nourishment, giving to it its several organs,—hair and skin and nails and blood, tendons and eyes and ears and other organs, and when I gave feet to the water so that it could run forward, and when I created the clouds on high (*mēnōkīk*) to carry away the waters from the earth and to rain them down wheresoever they would, and when I created the atmosphere (*vāy*) which blows through the power of the wind upwards and downwards as it wills, and this is visible to the eye though it cannot be seized by the hand,—when I created each one of these things, each was more difficult than the raising of the dead. For in the raising of the dead I have the assistance of the likes of these. When they were still [uncreated], I had [no such assistance].

(4) Behold! If I created what had not been, why should it be impossible for me to recreate what once was? For at that time I shall demand from the Spirit of the Earth the bones, from the water the blood, from the plants the hair, from the wind the spirit (*jān*) even as they received them at the primal creation'."

(5) First will be raised the bones of Gayōmart, then the bones of Mashyē and Mashyānē: then will the bones of (all) other men be raised up. For fifty-seven years will Sōshyans raise the dead and all men will be resurrected, both those who were saved and those who were damned. And each man will arise in the place where his spirit left him or where first he fell to the ground.

(6) And when the gods have restored to the whole of the material creation its proper form and shape, then will they give (men) their proper character (*adhvēnak*). And of the light that is with the Sun half will they give to Gaynōmart and half to the rest of men.

(7) Then will men recognize each other, that is, soul will recognize soul and body body (thinking), "This is my father," or "This is my brother," or "This is my wife," or "This is whatever close relative it may be." Then the assembly of Isat-vāstar will convene when men stand upon the earth in that assembly; and every man will see his good and evil deeds, and the saved will be as clearly distinguished from the damned as is a white sheep from a black.

(8) And in that assembly the damned man who had on earth a friend who was saved, will upbraid the man who was saved, saying, "Why didst thou not apprise me on earth of the good deeds that thou thyself wast

doing?" And if in truth the man who was saved did not so apprise him, then must he needs be put to shame in that assembly.

(9) Then will they separate the saved from the damned, and carry off the saved to Paradise (*garōdhmān*) and hurl the damned back into Hell; and for three days and nights these denizens of Hill will endure punishment in Hell, in their bodies and in their souls (*jān*) while the saved experience joy in their bodies during their three days and nights in Paradise.

(10) For it is said that on that day when damned is separated from saved, and saved from damned, tears will flow down from (the eyes of) all men, right down to their feet. When son is separated from the company of father, brother from brother, friend from friend, then will every man bewail the deeds he did, the saved weeping for the damned, and the damned weeping for themselves. It may be the father who is saved and the son who is damned, or it may be one brother who is saved and the other who is damned.

(11) Those who committed sins of their own free will(?) like Dahāk and Āfrāsyāb and Vātan(?) and others of this kind who committed mortal sin, will endure the *vamad-adhvēnak*(??) punishment, but no man will have to endure the punishment called *tishrām khshafnām* (the full three nights punishment).

(12) At that time when the final Rehabilitation is brought about, fifteen men and fifteen maidens from among those blessed men of whom it is written that they are (still) alive, will come to the assistance of Sōshyans.

(13) And Gōchihr, the serpent in the heavenly sphere, will fall from the summit of the Moon to the earth, and the earth will suffer pain like unto the pain a sheep feels when a wolf rends out its wool.

(14) Then will the Fire-god and the god Airyaman melt the metals that are in the mountains and hills, and they will flow over the earth like rivers. And they will make all men to pass through that molten metal and (thereby) make them clean. And it will seem to him who was saved as if he were walking through warm milk, but to the man who was damned it will seem exactly like walking through molten metal.

(15) Then will all men come together in the greatest joy, father and son, brothers and all friends. And one man will ask another, "How has thy soul fared in all these many years? Wast thou saved, or wast thou damned?" Next the soul will see its body, will question it and be answered by it.

(16) All men will become of one voice and give praise with a loud voice to Ohrmazd and the Amahraspands. At this time Ohrmazd will have

brought his creation to its consummation, and there will be no (further) work he need do.

(17) While the resurrection of the dead proceeds, Sōshyans and his helpers will perform the sacrifice of the raising of the dead, and in that sacrifice the bull Hadhayans will be slain, and from the fat of the bull they will prepare the white Hōm (Haoma), (the drink of) immortality, and give it to all men. And all men will become immortal for ever and ever.

(18) This too is said, that men who had reached middle age will be resurrected as (men of) forty years of age; and those who died young and before their prime will be resurrected as (lads of) fifteen years of age.

(19) To each man his wife and children will be restored, and they will have intercourse with their wives even as they do on earth to-day, but no children will be born to them.

(20) Then at the behest of the Creator Sōshyans will distribute to all men their wages and reward in accordance with their deeds. Some there are who are so blessed that he says, "Take them to the Paradise of Ohrmazd as is their due." They will take up their bodies, and for ever and ever they will walk together with them.

(21) And this too is said, that whoso (on earth) had not performed the sacrifice nor ordered a *gētōkhrīt* ("earthly redemption") nor given clothing in alms to those who deserved it, (will stand) there naked, and Ohrmazd will perform sacrifice on his behalf and the Spirit of the Gāthās will provide him with raiment.

(22) Then Ohrmazd will seize hold of the Destructive Spirit, Vahuman (the Good Mind) will seize Akōman (the Evil Mind), Artvahisht Indar, Shahrēvar Sāvul, Spandarmat Tarōmat (Arrogance) who is Nānghaith, Hurdāt and Amurdāt will seize Tairich and Zairich, True Speech False Speech, and the blessed Srōsh will seize upon Ēshm (Wrath) of the bloody banner.

(23) Then (only) two Lies will remain, Ahriman and Āz (Concupiscence). Ohrmazd will come (down) to earth, himself the "Zōt"-priest with the blessed Srōsh as his "Rāspik"-priest, and he will hold the sacred girdle in his hand. By that Gāthic ritual Ahriman and Āz, their weapons smashed, will be made powerless; and by the same passage through the sky by which they rushed in, they will hurtle into the darkness and gloom.

(24) And the serpent Gōchihr will be burnt up in the molten metal; and the molten metal will flow out into Hell. And (all) the stench and corruption that was in Hell will be burnt up by this molten metal and made

clean. And [the hole in(?)] Hell by which the Destructive Spirit rushed in, will be sealed up by that molten metal, and the earth that was in Hell will be brought up to the broad expanse of (this) material world.

(25) Then will the final Resurrection take place in the two worlds; and in accordance with its own desire the material world will become immortal for ever and ever.

(26) This too is said, that this earth will become flat, with neither hills nor dales. There will be neither mountains nor ridges nor pits, neither high ground nor low.'

George Sword

(?–?)

In the following selection, George Sword, an Oglala Sioux, writes about the 1890 expedition by Good Thunder, Cloud Horse, Yellow Knife, and Short Bull to investigate the Ghost Dance, the messianic Indian movement led by the Paiute prophet Wovoka, also known as Jack Wilson (1858?–1932). Wovoka taught that a cosmic upheaval would soon destroy the whites, resurrect the Indian dead, and return the bison to their former abundance. The ghost dance, so-called because it involved communion with dead ancestors, would hasten this event. Wovoka's teaching spread rapidly through many Indian nations; the movement died after the 1890 massacre at Wounded Knee.

In the story of ghost dancing, the Ogalala heard that the Son of God was truly on earth in the west from their country. This was in the year 1889. The first people knew about the messiah to be on earth were the Shoshoni and Arapaho. So in 1889 Good Thunder with four or five others visited the place where Son of God said to be. These people went there without permission. They said the messiah was there at the place, but he was there to help the Indians and not the whites; so this made the Indians happy to find out this. Good Thunder, Cloud Horse, Yellow Knife, and Short Bull visited the place again in 1890 and saw the messiah. Their story of visit to the messiah is as follows:

"From the country where the Arapaho and Shoshoni we start in the direction of northwest in train for five nights and arrived at the foot of the Rocky mountains. Here we saw him and also several tribes of Indians. The people said that the messiah will come at a place in the woods where the place was prepare for him. When we went to the place a smoke descended from heaven to the place where he was to come. When the smoke disappeared, there was a man of about forty, which was the Son of God. The man said:

"'My grandchildren! I am glad you have come far away to see your relatives. This are your people who have come back from your country.' When he said he want us to go with him, we looked and we saw a land created across the ocean on which all the nations of Indians were coming home, but, as the messiah looked at the land which was created and reached across the ocean, again disappeared, saying that it was not time for that to take place. The messiah then gave to Good Thunder some paints—Indian paint and a white paint—a green grass [sagebrush twigs?]; and said, 'My grandchildren, when you get home, go to farming and send all your children to school. And on way home if you kill any buffalo cut the head, the tail, and the four feet and leave them, and that buffalo will come to live again. When the soldiers of the white people chief want to arrest me, I shall stretch out my arms, which will knock them to nothingness, or, if not that, the earth will open and swallow them in. My father commanded me to visit the Indians on a purpose. I have came to the white people first, but they not good. They killed me, and you can see the marks of my wounds on my feet, my hands, and on my back. My father has given you life—your old life—and you have come to see your friends, but you will not take me home with you at this time. I want you to tell when you get home your people to follow my examples. Any one Indian does not obey me and tries to be on white's side will be covered over by a new land that is to come over this old one. You will, all the people, use the paints and grass I give you. In the spring when the green grass comes, your people who have gone before you will come back, and you shall see your friends then, for you have come to my call.'

"The people from every tipi send for us to visit them. They are people who died many years ago. Chasing Hawk, who died not long ago, was there, and we went to his tipi. He was living with his wife, who was killed in war long ago. They live in a buffalo skin tipi—a very large one—and he wanted all his friends to go there to live. A son of Good Thunder who died in war long ago was one who also took us to his tipi so his father saw him. When coming we come to a herd of buffaloes. We killed one and took everything except the four feet, head, and tail, and when we came a little ways from it there was the buffaloes come to life again and went off. This was one of the messiah's word came to truth. The messiah said, 'I will short your journey when you feel tired of the long ways, if you call upon me.' This we did when we were tired. The night came upon us, we stopped at a place, and we called upon the messiah to help us, because we were tired of long journey. We went to sleep and in the morning we found ourselves at a great distance from where we stopped.

"The people came back here and they got the people loyal to the government, and those not favor of the whites held a council. The agent's soldiers were sent after them and brought Good Thunder and two others to the agency and they were confined to the prison. They were asked by the agent and Captain Sword whether they saw the Son of God and whether they hold councils over their return from visit, but Good Thunder refused to say 'yes.' They were confined in the prison for two days, and upon their promising not to hold councils about their visit they were released. They went back to the people and told them about their trouble with the agent. Then they disperse without a council.

"In the following spring the people at Pine Ridge agency began to gather at the White Clay creek for councils. Just at this time Kicking Bear, from Cheyenne River agency, went on a visit to the Arapaho and said that the Arapaho there have ghost dancing. He said that people partaking in dance would get crazy and die, then the messiah is seen and all the ghosts. When they die they see strange things, they see their relatives who died long before. They saw these things when they died in ghost dance and came to life again. The person dancing becomes dizzy and finally drop dead, and the first thing they saw is an eagle comes to them and carried them to where the messiah is with his ghosts. The man said this:

"'The persons in the ghost dancing are all joined hands. A man stands and then a woman, so in that way forming a very large circle. They dance around in the circle in a continuous time until some of them become so tired and overtired that they became crazy and finally drop as though dead, with foams in mouth all wet by perspiration. All the men and women made holy shirts and dresses they wear in dance. The persons dropped in dance would all lie in great dust the dancing make. They paint the white muslins they made holy shirts and dresses out of with blue across the back, and alongside of this is a line of yellow paint. They also paint in the front part of the shirts and dresses. A picture of an eagle is made on the back of all the shirts and dresses. On the shoulders and on the sleeves they tied eagle feathers. They said that the bullets will not go through these shirts and dresses, so they all have these dresses for war. Their enemies weapon will not go through these dresses. The ghost dancers all have to wear eagle feather on head. With this feather any man would be made crazy if fan with this feather. In the ghost dance no person is allow to wear anything made of any metal, except the guns made of metal is carry by some of the dancers. When they come from ghosts or after recovery from craziness, they brought meat from the ghosts or from the supposed messiah. They also brought water, fire, and wind with which to kill all the whites or Indians who will help the chief of the whites. They made sweat house and made holes in the middle of the sweat house where they say the water will come out of these holes. Before they begin to dance they all raise their hands toward the northwest and cry in supplication to the messiah and then begin the dance with the song, *"Ate misunkala ceya omani-ye,"* etc.'"

St. Augustine

(354–430)

At the end of his massive City of God, *Augustine offers a vision of the resurrection of the dead and the life of the world to come.*

Of the eternal felicity of the city of God, and of the perpetual Sabbath.

How great shall be that felicity, which shall be fainted with no evil, which shall lack no good, and which shall afford leisure for the praises of God, who shall be all in all: For I know not what other employment there can be where no lassitude shall slacken activity, nor any want stimulate to labour. I am admonished also by the sacred song, in which I read or hear the words, "Blessed are they that dwell in Thy house, O Lord; they will be still praising Thee." All the members and organs of the incorruptible body, which now we see to be suited to various necessary uses, shall contribute to the praises of God; for in that life necessity shall have no place, but full, certain, secure, everlasting felicity. For all those parts of the bodily harmony, which are distributed through the whole body, within and without, and of which I have just been saying that they at present elude our observation, shall then be discerned; and, along with the other great and marvellous discoveries which shall then kindle rational minds in praise of the great Artificer, there shall be the enjoyment of a beauty which appeals to the reason. What power of movement such bodies shall possess, I have not the audacity rashly to define, as I have not the ability to conceive. Nevertheless I will say that in any case, both in motion and at rest, they shall be, as in their appearance, seemly; for into that state nothing which is unseemly shall be admitted. One thing is certain, the body shall forthwith be wherever the spirit wills, and the spirit shall will nothing which is unbecoming either to the spirit or to the body. True honour shall be there, for it shall be denied to none who is worthy, nor yielded to any unworthy; neither shall any unworthy person so much as sue for it, for none but the worthy shall be there. True peace shall be there, where no one shall suffer opposition either from himself or any other. God Himself, who is the Author of virtue, shall there be its reward; for, as there is nothing greater or better, He has promised Himself. What else was meant by His word through the prophet, "I will be your God, and ye shall be my people," than, I shall be their satisfaction, I shall be all that men honourably desire,—life, and health, and nourishment, and plenty, and glory, and honour, and peace, and all good things? This, too, is the right interpretation of the saying of the apostle, "That God may be all in all." He shall be the end of our desires who shall be seen without end, loved without cloy, praised without weariness. This outgoing of affection, this employment, shall certainly be, like eternal life itself, common to all.

But who can conceive, not to say describe, what degrees of honour and glory shall be awarded to the various degrees of merit? Yet it cannot be doubted that there shall be degrees. And in that blessed city there shall be this great blessing, that no inferior shall envy any superior, as now the archangels are not envied by the angels, because no one will wish to be what he has not received, though bound in strictest concord with him who has received; as in the body the finger does not seek to be the eye, though both members are harmoniously included in the complete structure of the body. And thus, along with his gift, greater or less, each shall receive this further gift of contentment to desire no more than he has.

Neither are we to suppose that because sin shall have no power to delight them, free will must be withdrawn. It will, on the contrary, be all the more truly free, because set free from delight in sinning to take unfailing delight in not sinning. For the first freedom of will which man received when he was created upright consisted in an ability not to sin, but also in an ability to sin; whereas this last freedom of will shall be superior, inasmuch as it shall not be able to sin. This, indeed, shall not be a natural ability, but the gift of God. For it is one thing to be God, another thing to be a partaker of God. God by nature cannot sin, but the partaker of God receives this inability from God. And in this divine gift there was to be observed this gradation, that man should first receive a free will by which he was able not to sin, and at last a free will by which he was not able to sin,—the former being adapted to the acquiring of merit, the latter to the enjoying of the reward. But the nature thus constituted, having sinned when it had the ability to do so, it is by a more abundant grace that it is delivered so as to reach that freedom in which it cannot sin. For as the first immortality which Adam lost by sinning consisted in his being able not to die, while the last shall consist in his not being able to die; so the first free will consisted in his being able not to sin, the last in his not being able to sin. And thus piety and justice shall be as indefeasible as happiness. For certainly by sinning we lost both piety and happiness; but when we lost happiness, we did not lose the love of it. Are we to say that God Himself is not free because He cannot sin? (In that city, then, there shall be free will, one in all the citizens, and indivisible in each, delivered from all ill, filled with all good, enjoying indefeasibly the delights of eternal joys, oblivious of sins, oblivious of sufferings, and yet not so oblivious of its deliverance as to be ungrateful to its Deliverer.)

The soul, then, shall have an intellectual remembrance of its past ills; but, so far as regards sensible experience, they shall be quite forgotten. For a skilful physician knows, indeed, professionally almost all diseases; but experimentally he is ignorant of a great number which he himself has never suffered from. As, therefore, there are two ways of knowing evil things,—one by mental insight, the other by sensible experience, for it is one thing to understand all vices by the wisdom of a cultivated mind, another to understand them by the foolishness of an abandoned life,—so also there are two ways of forgetting evils. For a well-instructed and learned man forgets them one way, and he who has experimentally suffered from them forgets them another,—the former by neglecting what he has learned, the latter by escaping what he has suffered. And in this latter way the saints shall forget their past ills, for they shall have so thoroughly escaped them all, that they shall be quite blotted out of their experience. But their intellectual knowledge, which shall be great, shall keep them acquainted not only with their own past woes, but with the eternal sufferings of the lost. For if they were not to know that they had been miserable, how could they, as the Psalmist says, for ever sing the mercies of God? Certainly that city shall have no greater joy than the celebration of the grace of Christ, who redeemed us by His blood. There shall be accomplished the words of the psalm, "Be still, and know that I am God." There shall be the great Sabbath which has no evening, which God celebrated among His first works, as it is written, "And God rested on the seventh day from all His works which He had made. And God blessed the seventh day, and sanctified it; because that in it He had rested from all His work which God began to make." For we shall ourselves be the seventh day, when we shall be filled and replenished with God's blessing and sanctification. There shall we be still, and know that He is God; that He is that which we ourselves aspired to be when we fell away from Him, and listened to the voice of the seducer, "Ye shall be as gods," and so abandoned God, who would have made us as gods, not by deserting Him, but by participating in Him. For without Him what have we accomplished, save to perish in His anger? But when we are restored by Him, and perfected with greater grace, we shall have eternal leisure to see that He is God, for we shall be full of Him when He shall be all in all. For even our good works, when they are understood to be rather His than ours, are imputed to us that we may enjoy this Sabbath rest. For if we attribute them to ourselves, they shall be servile; for it is said of the Sabbath, "Ye shall do no servile work in it." Wherefore also it is said by Ezekiel the prophet, "And I gave them my Sabbaths to be a sign between me and them, that they might know that I am the Lord who sanctify them." This knowledge shall be perfected when we shall be perfectly at rest, and shall perfectly know that He is God.

This Sabbath shall appear still more clearly if we count the ages as days, in accordance with the periods of time defined in Scripture, for that period will be found to be the seventh. The first age, as the first day, extends from Adam to the deluge; the second from the deluge to Abraham, equalling the first, not in length of time, but in the number of generations, there being ten in each. From Abraham to the advent of Christ there are, as the evangelist Matthew calculates, three periods, in each of which are fourteen generations,— one period from Abraham to David, a second from David to the captivity, a third from the captivity to the birth of Christ in the flesh. There are thus five ages in all. The sixth is now passing, and cannot be measured by any number of generations, as it has been said, "It is not for you to know the times, which the Father hath put in His own power." After this period God shall rest as on the seventh day, when He shall give us (who shall be the seventh day) rest in Himself. But there is not now space to treat of these ages; suffice it to say that the seventh shall be our Sabbath, which shall be brought to a close, not by an evening, but by the Lord's day, as an eighth and eternal day, consecrated by the resurrection of Christ, and prefiguring the eternal response not only of the spirit, but also of the body. There we shall rest and see, see and love, love and praise. This is what shall be in the end without end. For what other end do we propose to ourselves than to attain to the kingdom of which there is no end?

C. S. Lewis

(1898–1963)

Lewis was an English scholar, essayist, Christian apologist, and author of landmark works in science fiction and children's literature. Among his most popular books are the seven volumes of The Chronicles of Narnia. *In this excerpt from* The Last Battle *(1956), the Christ-like lion, Aslan, sets in motion the end of the world.*

They all stood beside Aslan, on his right side, and looked through the open doorway.

The bonfire had gone out. On the earth all was blackness: in fact you could not have told that you were looking into a wood if you had not seen where the dark shapes of the trees ended and the stars began. But when Aslan had roared yet again, out on their left they saw another black shape. That is, they saw another patch where there were no stars: and the patch rose up higher and higher and became the shape of a man, the hugest of all giants. They all knew Narnia well enough to work out where he must be standing. He must be on the high moorlands that stretched away to the North beyond the River Shribble. Then Jill and Eustace remembered how once long ago, in the deep caves beneath those moors, they had seen a great giant asleep and been told that his name was Father Time, and that he would wake on the day the world ended.

"Yes," said Aslan, though they had not spoken. "While he lay dreaming his name was Time. Now that he is awake he will have a new one."

Then the great giant raised a horn to his mouth. They could see this by the change of the black shape he made against the stars. After that—quite a bit later, because sound travels so slowly—they heard the sound of the horn: high and terrible, yet of a strange, deadly beauty.

Immediately the sky became full of shooting stars. Even one shooting star is a fine thing to see; but these were dozens, and then scores, and then hundreds, till it was like silver rain: and it went on and on. And when it had gone on for some while, one or two of them began to think that there was another dark shape against the sky as well as the giant's. It was in a different place, right overhead, up in the very roof of the sky as you might call it. "Perhaps it is a cloud," thought Edmund. At any rate, there were no stars there: just blackness. But all around, the downpour of stars went on. And then the starless patch began to grow, spreading further and further out from the center of the whole sky. And presently a quarter of the whole sky was black, and then a half, and at last the rain of shooting stars was going on only low down near the horizon.

With a thrill of wonder (and there was some terror in it too) they all suddenly realized what was happening. The spreading blackness was not a cloud at all: it was simply emptiness. The black part of the sky was the part in which there were no stars left. All the stars were falling: Aslan had called them home.

The last few seconds before the rain of stars had quite ended were very exciting. Stars began falling all round them. But stars in that world are not the great flaming globes they are in ours. They are people (Edmund and Lucy had once met one). So now they found showers of glittering people, all with long hair like burning silver and spears like white-hot metal, rushing down to them out of the black air, swifter than falling stones. They made a hissing noise as they landed and burnt the grass. And all these stars glided past them and stood somewhere behind, a little to the right.

This was a great advantage, because otherwise, now that there were no stars in the sky, everything would have been completely dark and you could have seen nothing. As it was, the crowd of stars behind them cast a fierce, white light over their shoulders. They could see mile upon mile of Narnian woods spread out before them, looking as if they were floodlit. Every bush and almost every blade of grass had its black shadow behind it. The edge of every leaf stood out so sharp that you'd think you could cut your finger on it.

On the grass before them lay their own shadows. But the great thing was Aslan's shadow. It streamed away to their left, enormous and very terrible. And all this was under a sky that would now be starless forever.

The light from behind them (and a little to their right) was so strong that it lit up even the slopes of the Northern Moors. Something was moving there. Enormous animals were crawling and sliding down into Narnia: great dragons and giant lizards and featherless birds with wings like bats' wings. They disappeared into the woods and for a few minutes there was silence. Then there came—at first from very far off—sounds of wailing and then, from every direction, a rustling and a pattering and a sound of wings. It came nearer and nearer. Soon one could distinguish the scamper of little feet from the padding of big paws, and the clack-clack of light little hoofs from the thunder of great ones. And then one could see thousands of pairs of eyes gleaming. And at last, out of the shadow of the trees, racing up the hill for dear life, by thousands and by millions, came all kinds of creatures—Talking Beasts, Dwarfs, Satyrs, Fauns, Giants, Calormenes, men from Archenland, Monopods, and strange unearthly things from the remote islands or the unknown Western lands. And all these ran up to the doorway where Aslan stood.

This part of the adventure was the only one which seemed rather like a dream at the time and rather hard to remember properly afterward. Especially, one couldn't say how long it had taken. Sometimes it seemed to have lasted only a few minutes, but at others it felt as if it might have gone on for years. Obviously, unless either the Door had grown very much larger or the creatures had suddenly grown as small as gnats, a crowd like that couldn't ever have tried to get through it. But no one thought about that sort of thing at the time.

The creatures came rushing on, their eyes brighter and brighter as they drew nearer and nearer to the standing Stars. But as they came right up to Aslan one or other of two things happened to each of them. They all looked straight in his face, I don't think they had any choice about that. And when some looked, the expression of their faces changed terribly—it was fear and hatred: except that, on the faces of Talking Beasts, the fear and hatred lasted only for a fraction of a second. You could see that they suddenly ceased to be *Talking* Beasts. They were just ordinary animals. And all the creatures who looked at Aslan in that way swerved to their right, his left, and disappeared into his huge black shadow, which (as you have heard) streamed away to the left of the doorway. The children never saw them again. I don't know what became of them. But the others looked in the face of Aslan and loved him, though some of them were very frightened at the same time. And all these came in at the Door, in on Aslan's right. There were some queer specimens among them. Eustace even recognized one of those very Dwarfs who had helped to shoot the Horses. But he had no time to wonder about that sort of thing (and anyway it was no business of his) for a great joy put everything else out of his head. Among the happy creatures who now came crowding round Tirian and his friends were all those whom they had thought dead. There was Roonwit the Centaur and Jewel the Unicorn and the good Boar and the good Bear, and Farsight the Eagle, and the dear Dogs and the Horses, and Poggin the Dwarf.

"Further in and higher up!" cried Roonwit and thundered away in a gallop to the West. And though they did not understand him, the words somehow set them tingling all over. The Boar grunted at them cheerfully. The Bear was just going to mutter that he still didn't understand, when he caught sight of the fruit-trees behind them. He waddled to those trees as fast as he could and there, no doubt, found something he understood very well. But the Dogs remained, wagging their tails, and Poggin remained, shaking hands with everyone and grinning all over his honest face. And Jewel leaned his snowy white head over the King's shoulder and the King whispered in Jewel's ear. Then everyone turned his attention again to what could be seen through the Doorway.

The Dragons and Giant Lizards now had Narnia to themselves. They went to and fro tearing up the trees by the roots and crunching them up as if they were sticks of rhubarb. Minute by minute the forests disappeared. The whole country became bare and you could see all sorts of things about its shape—all the little humps and hollows—which you had never noticed before. The grass died. Soon Tirian found that he was looking at a world of bare rock and earth. You could hardly believe that anything had ever lived there. The monsters themselves grew old and lay down and died. Their flesh shriveled up and the bones appeared: soon they were only huge skeletons that lay here and there on the dead rock, looking as if they had died thousands of years ago. For a long time everything was still.

At last something white—a long, level line of whiteness that gleamed in the light of the standing stars—came moving toward them from the Eastern end of the world. A widespread noise broke the silence: first a murmur then a rumble, then a roar. And now they could see what it was that was coming, and how fast it came. It was a foaming wall of water. The sea was rising. In that tree-less world you could see it very well. You could see all the rivers getting wider and the lakes getting larger, and separate lakes joining into one, and valleys turning into new lakes, and hills turning into islands, and then those islands vanishing. And the high moors to their left and the higher mountains to their right crumbled and slipped down with a roar and a splash into the mounting water; and the water came swirling up to the very threshold of the Doorway (but never passed it) so that the foam splashed about Aslan's forefeet. All now was level water from where they stood to where the waters met the sky.

And out there it began to grow light. A streak of dreary and disastrous dawn spread along the horizon, and widened and grew brighter, till in the end they hardly noticed the light of the stars who stood behind them. At last the sun came up. When it did, the Lord Digory and the Lady Polly looked at one another and gave a little nod: those two, in a different world, had once seen a dying sun, and so they knew at once that this sun also was dying. It was three times—twenty times—as big as it ought to be, and very dark red. As its rays fell upon the great Time-giant, he turned red too: and in the reflection of that sun the whole waste of shoreless waters looked like blood.

Then the Moon came up, quite in her wrong position, very close to the sun, and she also looked red. And at the sight of her the sun began shooting out great flames, like whiskers or snakes of crimson fire, toward her. It is as if he were an octopus trying to draw her to himself in his tentacles. And perhaps he did draw her. At any rate she came to him, slowly at first, but then more and more quickly, till at last his long flames licked round her and the two ran together and became one huge ball like a burning coal. Great lumps of fire came dropping out of it into the sea and clouds of steam rose up.

Then Aslan said, "Now make an end."

The giant threw his horn into the sea. Then he stretched out one arm—very black it looked, and thousands of miles long—across the sky till his hand reached the Sun. He took the Sun and squeezed it in his hand as you would squeeze an orange. And instantly there was total darkness.

Everyone except Aslan jumped back from the ice-cold air which now blew through the Doorway. Its edges were already covered with icicles.

"Peter, High King of Narnia," said Aslan. "Shut the Door."

Peter, shivering with cold, leaned out into the darkness and pulled the Door to. It scraped over ice as he pulled it. Then, rather clumsily (for even in that moment his hands had gone numb and blue) he took out a golden key and locked it.

They had seen strange things enough through that Doorway. But it was stranger than any of them to look round and find themselves in warm daylight, the blue sky above them, flowers at their feet, and laughter in Aslan's eyes.

He turned swiftly round, crouched lower, lashed himself with his tail and shot away like a golden arrow.

"Come further in! Come further up!" he shouted over his shoulder. But who could keep up with him at that pace? . . .

Then they all went forward together, always Westward, for that seemed to be in the direction Aslan had meant when he cried out, "Further up and further in." Many other creatures were slowly moving the same way, but that grassy country was very wide and there was no crowding.

It still seemed to be early, and the morning freshness was in the air. They kept on stopping to look round and to look behind them, partly because it was so beautiful but partly also because there was something about it which they could not understand.

"Peter," said Lucy, "where is this, do you suppose?"

"I don't know," said the High King. "It reminds me of somewhere but I can't give it a name. Could it be somewhere we once stayed for a holiday when we were very, very small?"

"It would have to have been a jolly good holiday," said Eustace. "I bet there isn't a country like this anywhere in *our* world. Look at the colors! You couldn't get a blue like the blue on those mountains in our world."

"Is it not Aslan's country?" said Tirian.

"Not like Aslan's country on top of that mountain beyond the Eastern end of the world," said Jill. "I've been there."

"If you ask me," said Edmund, "it's like somewhere in the Narnian world. Look at those mountains ahead—and the big ice-mountains beyond them. Surely they're rather like the mountains we used to see from Narnia, the ones up Westward beyond the Waterfall?"

"Yes, so they are," said Peter. "Only these are bigger."

"I don't think *those* ones are so very like anything in Narnia," said Lucy. "But look there." She pointed Southward to their left, and everyone stopped and turned to look. "Those hills," said Lucy, "the nice woody ones and the blue ones behind—aren't they very like the Southern border of Narnia?"

"Like!" cried Edmund after a moment's silence. "Why, they're exactly like. Look, there's Mount Pire with his forked head, and there's the pass into Archenland and everything!"

"And yet they're not like," said Lucy. "They're different. They have more colors on them and they look further away than I remembered and they're more . . . more . . . oh, I don't know . . . "

"More like the real thing," said the Lord Digory softly.

Suddenly Farsight the Eagle spread his wings, soared thirty or forty feet up into the air, circled round and then alighted on the ground.

"Kings and Queens," he cried, "we have all been blind. We are only beginning to see where we are. From up there I have seen it all—Ettinsmuir, Beaversdam, the Great River, and Cair Paravel still shining on the edge of the Eastern Sea. Narnia is not dead. This is Narnia."

"But how can it be?" said Peter. "For Aslan told us older ones that we should never return to Narnia, and here we are."

"Yes," said Eustace. "And we saw it all destroyed and the sun put out."

"And it's all so different," said Lucy.

"The Eagle is right," said the Lord Digory. "Listen, Peter. When Aslan said you could never go back to Narnia, he meant the Narnia you were thinking of. But that was not the real Narnia. That had a beginning and an end. It was only a shadow or a copy of the real Narnia which has always been here and always will be here: just as our own world, England and all, is only a shadow or copy of something in Aslan's real world. You need not mourn over Narnia, Lucy. All of the old Narnia that mattered, all the dear creatures, have been drawn into the real Narnia through the Door. And of course it is different; as different as a real thing is from a shadow or as waking life is from a dream." His voice stirred everyone like a trumpet as he spoke these words: but when he added under his breath "It's all in Plato, all in Plato: bless me, what *do* they teach them at these schools!" the older ones laughed. It was so exactly like the sort of thing they had heard him say long ago in that other world where his beard was gray instead of golden. He knew why they were laughing and joined in the laugh himself. But very quickly they all became grave again: for, as you know, there is a kind of happiness and wonder that makes you serious. It is too good to waste on jokes.

It is as hard to explain how this sunlit land was different from the old Narnia as it would be to tell you how the fruits of that country taste. Perhaps you will get some idea of it if you think like this. You may have been in a room in which there was a window that looked out on a lovely bay of the sea or a green valley that wound away among mountains. And in the wall of that room opposite to the window there may have been a looking-glass. And as you turned away from the window you suddenly caught sight of that sea or that valley, all over again, in the looking-glass. And the sea in the mirror, or the valley in the mirror, were in one sense just the same as the real ones: yet at the same time they were somehow different—deeper, more wonderful, more like places in a story: in a story you have never heard but very much want to know. The difference between the old Narnia and the new Narnia was like that. The new one was a deeper country: every rock and flower and blade of grass looked as if it meant more. I can't describe it any better than that: if you ever get there you will know what I mean.

It was the Unicorn who summed up what everyone was feeling. He stamped his right forehoof on the ground and neighed, and then cried:

"I have come home at last! This is my real country! I belong here. This is the land I have been looking for all my life, though I never knew it till now. The reason why we loved the old Narnia is that it sometimes looked a little like this. Bree-hee-hee! Come further up, come further in!" . . .

So they ran faster and faster till it was more like flying than running, and even the Eagle overhead was going no faster than they. And they went through winding valley after winding valley and up the steep sides of hills and, faster than ever, down the other side, following the river and sometimes crossing it and skimming across mountain lakes as if they were living speedboats, till at last at the far end of one long lake which looked as blue as a turquoise, they saw a smooth green hill. Its sides were as steep as the sides of a pyramid and round the very top of it ran a green wall: but above the wall rose the branches of trees whose leaves looked like silver and their fruit like gold.

"Further up and further in!" roared the Unicorn, and no one held back. They charged straight at the foot of the hill and then found themselves running up it almost as water from a broken wave runs up a rock out at the point of some bay. Though the slope was nearly as steep as the roof of a house and the grass was smooth as a bowling green, no one slipped. Only when they had reached the very top did they slow up; that was because they found themselves facing great golden gates. And for a moment none of them was bold enough to try if the gates would open. They all felt just as they had felt about the fruit—"Dare we? Is it right? Can it be meant for us?"

But while they were standing thus a great horn, wonderfully loud and sweet, blew from somewhere inside that walled garden and the gates swung open.

Tirian stood holding his breath and wondering who would come out. And what came was the last thing he had expected: a little, sleek, bright-eyed Talking Mouse with a red feather stuck in a circlet on its head and its left paw resting on a long sword. It bowed, a most beautiful bow, and said in its shrill voice:

"Welcome, in the Lion's name. Come further up and further in." . . .

About half an hour later—or it might have been half a hundred years later, for time there is not like time here—Lucy stood with her dear friend, her oldest Narnian friend, the Faun Tumnus, looking down over the wall of that garden, and seeing all Narnia spread out below. But when you looked down you found that this hill was much higher than you had thought: it sank down with shining cliffs, thousands of feet below them and trees in that lower world looked no bigger than grains of green salt. Then she turned inward again and stood with her back to the wall and looked at the garden.

"I see," she said at last, thoughtfully. "I see now. This garden is like the stable. It is far bigger inside than it was outside."

"Of course, Daughter of Eve," said the Faun. "The further up and the further in you go, the bigger everything gets. The inside is larger than the outside."

Lucy looked hard at the garden and saw that it was not really a garden but a whole world, with its own rivers and woods and sea and mountains. But they were not strange: she knew them all.

"I see," she said. "This is still Narnia, and more real and more beautiful than the Narnia down below, just as it was more real and more beautiful than the Narnia outside the stable door! I see . . . world within world, Narnia within Narnia. . . ."

"Yes," said Mr. Tumnus, "like an onion: except that as you continue to go in and in, each circle is larger than the last."

And Lucy looked this way and that and soon found that a new and beautiful thing had happened to her. Whatever she looked at, however far away it might be, once she had fixed her eyes steadily on it, became quite clear and close as if she were looking through a telescope. She could see the whole Southern desert and beyond it the great city of Tashbaan: to Eastward she could see Cair Paravel on the edge of the sea and the very window of the room that had once been her own. And far out to sea she could discover the islands, islands after islands to the end of the world, and, beyond the end, the huge mountain which they had called Aslan's country. But now she saw that it was part of a great chain of mountains which ringed round the whole world. In front of her it seemed to come quite close. Then she looked to her left and saw what she took to be a great bank of brightly colored cloud, cut off from them by a gap. But she looked harder and saw that it was not a cloud at all but a real land. And when she had fixed her eyes on one particular spot of it, she at once cried out, "Peter! Edmund! Come and look! Come quickly." And they came and looked, for their eyes also had become like hers.

"Why!" exclaimed Peter. "It's England. And that's the house itself—Professor Kirk's old home in the country where all our adventures began!"

"I thought that house had been destroyed," said Edmund.

"So it was," said the Faun. "But you are now looking at the England within England, the real England just as this is the real Narnia. And in that inner England no good thing is destroyed."

Suddenly they shifted their eyes to another spot, and then Peter and Edmund and Lucy gasped with amazement and shouted out and began waving: for there they saw their own father and mother, waving back at them across the great, deep valley. It was like when you see people waving at you from the deck of a big ship when you are waiting on the quay to meet them.

"How can we get at them?" said Lucy.

"That is easy," said Mr. Tumnus. "That country and this country—all the *real* countries—are only spurs jutting out from the great mountains of Aslan. We have only to walk along the ridge, upward and inward, till it joins on. And listen! There is King Frank's horn: we must all go up."

And soon they found themselves all walking together—and a great, bright procession it was—up toward mountains higher than you could see in this world even if they were there to be seen. But there was no snow on those mountains: there were forests and green slopes and sweet orchards and flashing waterfalls, one above the other, going up forever. And the land they were walking on grew narrower all the time, with a deep valley on each side: and across that valley the land which was the real England grew nearer and nearer.

The light ahead was growing stronger. Lucy saw that a great series of many-colored cliffs led up in front of them like a giant's staircase. And then she forgot everything else, because Aslan himself was coming, leaping down from cliff to cliff like a living cataract of power and beauty.

And the very first person whom Aslan called to him was Puzzle the Donkey. You never saw a donkey look feebler and sillier than Puzzle did as he walked up to Aslan, and he looked, beside Aslan, as small as a kitten looks beside a St. Bernard. The Lion bowed down his head and whispered something to Puzzle at which his long ears went down, but then he said something else at which the ears perked up again. The humans couldn't hear what he had said either time. Then Aslan turned to them and said:

"You do not yet look so happy as I mean you to be."

Lucy said, "We're so afraid of being sent away, Aslan. And you have sent us back into our own world so often."

"No fear of that," said Aslan. "Have you not guessed?"

Their hearts leaped and a wild hope rose within them.

"There *was* a real railway accident," said Aslan softly. "Your father and mother and all of you are—as you used to call it in the Shadowlands—dead. The term is over: the holidays have begun. The dream is ended: this is the morning."

And as He spoke He no longer looked to them like a lion; but the things that began to happen after that were so great and beautiful that I cannot write them. And for us this is the end of all the stories, and we can most truly say that they all lived happily ever after. But for them it was only the beginning of the real story. All their life in this world and all their adventures in Narnia had only been the cover and the title page: now at last they were beginning Chapter One of the Great Story which no one on earth has read: which goes on forever: in which every chapter is better than the one before.

Songs and Poems

Henry Vaughan
(1622–1695)

An Anglo-Welsh poet and doctor, Vaughan turned to religious verse after reading George Herbert. These poems from Silex Scintillans: Sacred Poems and Private Ejaculations *(the subtitle is borrowed from Herbert's posthumous poetry collection; see chapter 6, above) proclaim the glories of the resurrection.*

Easter-day

Thou, whose sad heart, and weeping head lyes low,
Whose Cloudy brest cold damps invade,
Who never feel'st the Sun, nor smooth'st thy brow,
But sitt'st oppressed in the shade,
Awake, awake,

And in his Resurrection partake,
Who on this day (that thou might'st rise as he,)
Rose up, and cancell'd two deaths due to thee.

Awake, awake; and, like the Sun, disperse
All mists that would usurp this day;
Where are thy Palmes, thy branches, and thy verse?
Hosanna! heark; why doest thou stay?
Arise, arise,
And with his healing bloud anoint thine Eys,
Thy inward Eys; his bloud will cure thy mind,
Whose spittle only could restore the blind.

Easter Hymn

Death, and darkness get you packing,
Nothing now to man is lacking,
All your triumphs now are ended,
And what *Adam* marr'd, is mended;
Graves are beds now for the weary,
Death a nap, to wake more merry;
Youth now, full of pious duty,
Seeks in thee for perfect beauty,
The weak, and aged tir'd, with length
Of daies, from thee look for new strength,
And Infants with thy pangs Contest
As pleasant, as if with the brest;
Then, unto him, who thus hath thrown
Even to Contempt thy kingdome down,
And by his blood did us advance
Unto his own Inheritance,
To him be glory, power, praise,
From this, unto the last of daies.

John Donne
(1572–1631)

Anglican divine and sublime love poet, Donne was the greatest of the metaphysical poets. His Holy Sonnets, *like all the religious writings of his later years, are an extended meditation on death's corruption and its reversal by the alchemy of redemption.*

At the round earths imagin'd corners, blow
Your trumpets, Angells, and arise, arise
From death, you numberlesse infinities
Of soules, and to your scattred bodies goe,
All whom the flood did, and fire shall o'erthrow,
All whom warre, dearth, age, agues, tyrannies,
Despaire, law, chance, hath slaine, and you whose eyes
Shall behold God, and never tast deaths woe.
But let them sleepe, Lord, and mee mourne a space,
For, if above all these, my sinnes abound,
'Tis late to aske abundance of thy grace,
When wee are there; here on this lowly ground,
Teach mee how to repent; for that's as good
As if thou'hadst seal'd my pardon, with thy blood.

Spirituals

These two spirituals were made famous by the Jubilee Singers, a student choir of emancipated slaves from Fisk University in Nashville, Tennessee, who toured the United States and Europe in the 1870s to great acclaim.

In That Great Getting-up Morning

As Sung by the "Hampton Students."

I'm a-going to tell you about the coming of the Saviour,
  Fare you well! Fare you well!

I'm a-going to tell you about the coming of the Saviour,
  Fare you well! Fare you well!

There's a better day a-coming,
  Fare you well! Fare you well!

Oh, preachers, fold your Bibles,
  Fare you well! Fare you well!

Prayer-makers, pray no more,
  Fare you well! Fare you well!

For the last soul's converted,
  Fare you well! Fare you well!

In that great getting-up morning,
  Fare you well! Fare you well!

In that great getting-up morning,
  Fare you well! Fare you well!

2.

The Lord spoke to Gabriel:
Go look behind the altar,
Take down the silver trumpet,
Blow your trumpet, Gabriel.
Lord, how loud shall I blow it?
Blow it right calm and easy,
Do not alarm My people,
Tell them to come to judgment;
Gabriel, blow your trumpet.
Lord, how loud shall I blow it?
Loud as seven peals of thunder!
Wake the sleeping nations.

3.

Then you'll see poor sinners rising;
Then you'll see the world on fire;
See the moon a-bleeding,
See the stars falling,
See the elements melting,
See the forked lightning,
Hear the rumbling thunder;
Earth shall reel and totter.
Then you'll see the Christians rising;
Then you'll see the righteous marching,
See them marching home to heaven.
Then you'll see my Jesus coming
With all His holy angels,
Take the righteous home to heaven,
There they'll live with God for ever.

In that Great Getting-up Morning.

No. 110. *As sung by the "Hampton Students."*

1. I'm a-going to tell you about the coming of the Saviour,
1st time.
2d time.
Fare you well! Fare you well! Fare you well! Fare you well!
There's a bet-ter day a-coming, Fare you well! Fare you well!
Prayer-makers, pray no more,
Oh, preachers, fold your Bibles, Fare you well! Fare you well!
For the last soul's converted,
In that great getting-up morning, Fare you well! Fare you well!
In that great getting-up morning, Fare you well! Fare you well!

I'll Hear the Trumpet Sound

You may bury me in the East,
You may bury me in the West;
But I'll hear the trumpet sound
    In that morning.

In that morning, my Lord,
How I long to go,
For to hear the trumpet sound,
    In that morning.

2. Father Gabriel in that day,
He'll take wings and fly away,
For to hear the trumpet sound
    In that morning.
You may bury him in the East,
You may bury him in the West;
But he'll hear the trumpet sound,
    In that morning.
        Cho.—In that morning, &c.

3. Good old Christians in that day,
They'll take wings and fly away, &c.
        Cho.—In that morning, &c.

4. Good old preachers in that day,
They'll take wings and fly away, &c
        Cho.—In that morning, &c.

5. In that dreadful Judgment day,
I'll take wings and fly away, &c.
        Cho.—In that morning, &c.

No. 11. I'll hear the Trumpet Sound.

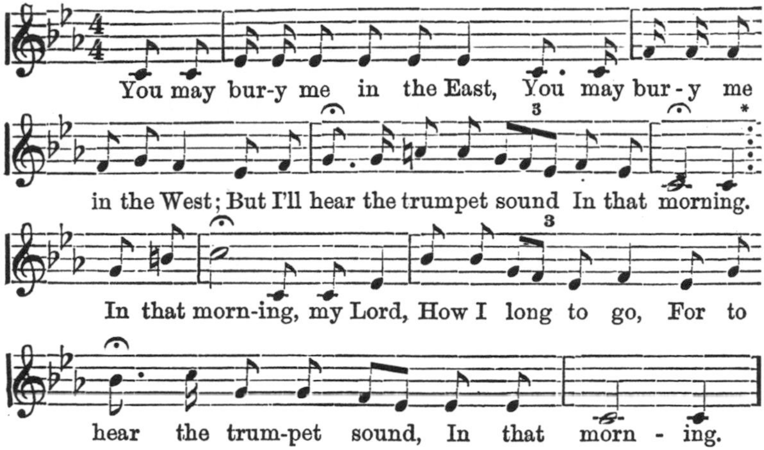
You may bur-y me in the East, You may bur - y me
in the West; But I'll hear the trumpet sound In that morning.
In that morn-ing, my Lord, How I long to go, For to
hear the trum-pet sound, In that morn - ing.

2. Father Gabriel in that day,
   He'll take wings and fly away,
   For to hear the trumpet sound
   In that morning.
   You may bury him in the East,
   You may bury him in the West;
   But he'll hear the trumpet sound,
   In that morning.

   Cho.—In that morning, &c.

3. Good old christians in that day,
   They'll take wings and fly away, &c
   Cho.—In that morning, &c.

4. Good old preachers in that day,
   They'll take wings and fly away, &c
   Cho.—In that morning, &c.

5. In that dreadful Judgement day,
   I'll take wings and fly away &c.
   Cho.—In that morning, &c.

* Repeat the music of the first strain for all the verses but the first.

Credits

Extracts from the Authorized Version of the Bible (the King James Bible), the rights in which are vested in the Crown, are reproduced by permission of the Crown's patentee, Cambridge University Press.

Chapter I

p. 15: Dante Alighieri: *The Divine Comedy. Vol. III, Paradiso*. Translated by Mark Musa. Bloomington, Indiana: Indiana University Press, 1984, Canto I, pp. 1–5. Reprinted by permission of the publisher.

p. 47: Ramanujan, A. K.: From *Folktales from India* by A.K. Ramanujan. Copyright © 1991 by A. K. Ramanujan. Reprinted by permission of Pantheon Books, a division of Random House, Inc., pp. 318–319.

p. 49: Conze, Edward, trans.: *Buddhist Scriptures*. Harmondsworth, Middlesex, England: Penguin Books, 1959, pp. 227–232. Reproduced by permission of Penguin Books, Ltd.

p. 54: Hawkes, David, trans.: *Ch'u Tz'u: The Songs of the South, an Ancient Chinese Anthology*. London: Oxford University Press, 1959, pp. 81–87. Reprinted by permission of the translator.

p. 60: Jung, C. G.: From *Memories, Dreams, Reflections* by C. G. Jung, translated by Richard and Clara Winston. Translation copyright © 1961, 1962, 1963 by Random House, Inc. Renewed 1989, 1990, 1991 by Random House, Inc. Reprinted by permission of Pantheon Books., pp. 286–296.

p. 67: Smith, Morton, trans.: From "Observations on Hekhalot Rabbati." In *Biblical and Other Studies*, edited by Alexander Altman. Cambridge, Massachusetts: Harvard University Press, 1963, pp. 158–159. Reprinted by permission of the estate of the translator and the publisher.

p. 69: Pages 67–68 from *Ancient Christian Magic* by Marvin Meyer. Copyright © 1994 by the Coptic Magical Texts Project of the Institute for Antiquity and Christianity. Reprinted by permission of HarperCollins Publishers, Inc.

Chapter II

p. 89: Ginzberg, Louis: *The Legends of the Jews, vol. I: Bible Times and Characters from the Creation to Jacob.* Translated by Henrietta Szold. Philadelphia: The Jewish Publication Society of America, 1913, pp. 8–13. Reprinted by permission of the publisher.

p. 93: Sturluson, Snorri: *The Prose Edda of Snorri Sturluson: Tales from Norse Mythology.* Translated and edited by Jean I. Young. Copyright © 1964 The Regents of the University of California. Berkeley: University of California Press, 1954, pp. 42–47, 63–66. Reprinted by permission of the publisher.

p. 102: Gomez, Luis O., trans.: *Land of Bliss: The Paradise of the Buddha of Measureless Light.* Honolulu: University of Hawai'i Press and Kyoto: Higashi Honganji Shinshu Otani-Ha, 1996, pp. 175–176, 185–186. Reprinted by permission of the publisher.

p. 106: Grant, F. C., trans.: *Ancient Roman Religion,* © 1957, pp. 147–152. Reprinted by permission of Prentice Hall, Upper Saddle River, New Jersey.

p. 111: Schwartz, Howard: "The Celestial Orchestra." In *Adam's Soul: The Complete Tales of Howard Schwartz,* pp. 99–103. Reprinted by permission of the publisher, Jason Aronson, Inc., Northvale, New Jersey © 1992.

p. 116: Shewring, W. H., trans.: *The Passion of Perpetua and Felicity; Sermons of S. Augustine upon These Saints.* London: Sheed and Ward, 1931, pp. 3–6, 11–14. Reprinted by permission of the publisher.

p. 119: Reprinted from *Black Elk Speaks,* by John G. Neihardt, by permission of the University of Nebraska Press. Copyright 1932, 1959, 1972, by John G. Neihardt. Copyright © 1961 by the John G. Neihardt Trust, pp. 15–27.

Chapter III

p. 153: St. Augustine: *The Confessions of St. Augustine.* Translated by F. J. Sheed. Indianapolis: Hackett Publishing Company, Inc., 1993, Book IX, pp. 163–165. Reprinted by permission of Hackett Publishing Company, Inc. All rights reserved.

p. 155: Jeffrey, A., trans.: *Islam: Muhammad and His Religion,* © 1958, pp. 42–46. Reprinted by permission of Prentice Hall, Upper Saddle River, New Jersey.

p. 158: Cohen, Martin Samuel: *The Shi'ur Qomah: Liturgy and Theurgy in Pre-Kabbalistic Jewish Mysticism.* Lanham, Maryland: University Press of America, 1983, pp. 187, 197–199. Reprinted by permission of the publisher.

p. 161: © Patrick Olivelle 1998. Reprinted from *Upanishads,* translated by Patrick Olivelle (Oxford World's Classics, 1998) by permission of Oxford University Press.

p. 166: Gomez, Luis O., trans.: *Land of Bliss: The Paradise of the Buddha of Measureless Light.* Honolulu: University of Hawai'i Press and Kyoto: Higashi Honganji Shinshu Otani-Ha, 1996, pp. 177–178. Reprinted by permission of the publisher.

p. 168: Dante Alighieri: *The Divine Comedy. Vol. III, Paradiso.* Translated by Mark Musa. Bloomington, Indiana: Indiana University Press, 1984, Canto XXXIII, pp. 390–394. Reprinted by permission of the publisher.

p. 182: Mbiti, John S., ed.: *African Religions and Philosophy,* 2nd edition. Oxford: Heinemann Educational Books Ltd, 1990, p. 34. Reprinted by permission of the publisher.

p. 191: Scholem, Gershom G.: *Jewish Gnosticism, Merkabah Mysticism, and Talmudic Tradition.* New York: The Jewish Theological Seminary of America, 1965, pp. 59–62. Reprinted by permission of the publisher.

Chapter IV

p. 203: Homer: *The Iliad of Homer.* Translated by Richmond Lattimore. Chicago: The University of Chicago Press, 1951, book 1, lines 493–611, pp. 72–75. Copyright 1951 by The University of Chicago. All rights reserved. Reprinted by permission of the publisher.

p. 207: Pseudo-Dionysius: *Pseudo-Dionysius: The Complete Works.* Translated by Colm Luibheid. Mahwah, New Jersey: Paulist Press, 1987, pp. 160–162. Pseudo-Dionysius translation by Colm Luibheid © 1987 by Colm Luibheid. Reprinted by permission of Paulist Press, Inc.

p. 218: Raghunathan, N., trans.: *Srimad-Bhagavatam.* Madras and Bangalore: Vighneswara Publishing House, 1976, vol. II, book VIII, pp. 49–52.

p. 239: Chesterton, G. K.: *The Man Who Was Thursday.* New York: Dodd, Mead and Company, Copyright ©1908, pp. 254–279. Reprinted by permission of A. P. Watt, Ltd., on behalf of the Royal Literary Fund.

Chapter V

p. 273: Doyle, Sir Arthur Conan: *The Land of Mist.* Garden City, New York: Doubleday, Doran & Company, 1934, pp. 140–155. Copyright © 1996 The Sir Arthur Conan Doyle Copyright Holders. Reprinted by kind permission of Jonathan Clowes Ltd., London, on behalf of Andrea Plunket, Administrator of the Sir Arthur Conan Doyle Copyrights.

p. 286: From *A History of the World in 10½ Chapters* by Julian Barnes. Copyright © 1989 by Julian Barnes. Reprinted by permission of Alfred A. Knopf, Inc. and Peters Fraser & Dunlop Group, Ltd., pp. 281–284, 297–302.

p. 295: Hildegard of Bingen: *The Book of the Rewards of Life*. Translated by Bruce W. Hozeski. New York and London: Garland Publishing, Inc., 1994, pp. 281–283. Reprinted by permission of the publisher.

p. 298: St. Thérèse of Lisieux. From *Story of a Soul*, translated by John Clarke, O.C.D. © 1975, 1976 by Washington Province of Discalced Carmelite Friars, ICS Publications, 2131 Lincoln Road N.E., Washington, D.C., 20002, pp. 190–192.

p. 304: Ginzberg, Louis: *The Legends of the Jews, vol. IV. Bible Times and Characters from Joshua to Esther*. Translated by Henrietta Szold. Philadelphia: The Jewish Publication Society of America, 1913, 1936, pp. 200–211. Reprinted by permission of the publisher.

p. 311: Nicholson, Reynold A., trans.: *Rumi: Poet and Mystic*. London: George Allen and Unwin Ltd., 1950, p. 41. Reprinted by permission of HarperCollins Publishers.

Chapter VI

p. 330: © Frances Horgan 1994. Reprinted from *The Romance of the Rose* by Guillaume de Lorris and Jean de Meun, translated and edited by Frances Horgan (World's Classics, 1994) by permission of Oxford University Press.

p. 347: Raghunathan, N., trans.: *Srimad-Bhagavatam*. Madras and Bangalore: Vighneswara Publishing House, 1976, vol. II, book X (part 1), lines 1–20, pp. 280–282.

p. 349: Bernbaum, Edwin: *The Way to Shambhala*. Garden City, New York: Doubleday, Anchor Books, 1980, pp. 197–202. Reprinted by permission of the author.

p. 360: Reprinted from *The Utopian Vision of Charles Fourier: Selected Texts on Work, Love, and Passionate Attraction*, edited by Richard Bienvenu and Jonathan Beecher, by permission of the University of Missouri Press. Copyright © 1983 by Richard Bienvenu and Jonathan Beecher, pp. 201–203.

p. 369: Daniels, Guy, trans. and ed.: *A Lermontov Reader*. New York: The Macmillan Company, 1965, pp. 74–75. Reprinted by permission of the estate of Guy Daniels.

CHAPTER VII

p. 377: Mintz, Jerome R.: *Legends of the Hasidim: An Introduction to Hasidic Culture and Oral Tradition in the New World*. Chicago and London: The University of Chicago Press, 1968, p. 409. Reprinted by permission of Betty Mintz, trustee u/w/o Jerome R. Mintz.

p. 378: From *In the Heart of the Seas* by Shmuel Yosef Agnon, translated by I. M. Lask. Copyright © 1948, 1975 by Schocken Books, Inc. Reprinted by permission of Schocken Books, distributed by Pantheon Books, a division of Random House, Inc., pp. 57–65.

p. 389: Arberry, Arthur J.: *The Koran Interpreted*, Vol. II. London: George Allen & Unwin Ltd.; New York: The Macmillan Company, 1955, pp. 251–253. Reprinted by permission of HarperCollins Publishers.

p. 391: Zaehner, R. C.: *The Teachings of the Magi: A Compendium of Zoroastrian Beliefs*. New York: Oxford University Press, 1976, pp. 145–150. First published in 1956 in Great Britain by George Allen & Unwin Ltd. Reprinted by permission of Sheldon Press.

p. 405: Lewis, C. S.: *The Last Battle. Book VII of The Chronicles of Narnia*. New York: HarperCollins, 1994, pp. 187–198, 208–213, 219–220, 224–228. Copyright © 1956 by C. S. Lewis (Pte) Limited; copyright renewed 1984 by C. S. Lewis (Pte) Limited. All rights reserved. Reprinted by permission of HarperCollins Publishers.

Although every effort has been made to trace and contact copyright holders before publication, this has not been possible in a few cases. If notified, we will be pleased to rectify any errors or omissions at the earliest opportunity.

Name Index

Numbers in boldface type refer to pages on which works appear.

Adamnan, Saint, 199, **210**
Agnon, Shmuel Yosef, 373, **378**
Andersen, Hans Christian, 315, **357**
Ar-Rumi, Jalal ad-Din. *See* Rumi
As-Suyuti, 150, **155**
Augustine, Saint, 149, **153**, 375, **400**

Barnes, Julian, 9, 251, **286**
Bede, Saint (the Venerable), 12, 13, **21**
Black Elk, Nicholas, **119**, 315
Blake, William, 221, 266
Brooke, Rupert, 6, 9, 79, **85**
Bunyan, John, 12, 13, **27**
Byron, Lord. *See* Gordon, George (Lord Byron)

Chatterton, Thomas, 13
Chesterton, G. K., 3, 6, **239**
Ch'ü Yüan, **54**
Cicero, Marcus Tullius, 80, **106**
Clemens, Samuel Langhorne. *See* Twain, Mark
Confucius, 6
Conze, Edward, **49**
Corelli, Marie, 151, **176**

Dana, Charles, 316
Dante Alighieri, 5, 11–12, 13, **15**, 82, 150, 151, **168**
De Lorris, Guillaume, **330**
De Meun, Jean, **330**
Donne, John, 3, 5, 374, **418**
Doyle, Sir Arthur Conan, 252, **273**

Edwards, Jonathan, 150, **174**

Ferrer, Nicholas, 368
Fielding, Henry, 6, 9, 12, **35**
Fourier, Charles, 315–16, **360**

Ginzberg, Louis, 81–82, **89**, **304**
Gordon, George (Lord Byron), 9, 226, **228**
Gregory of Nyssa, 374

Halevi, Judah, 378
Hare, Robert, 82, **127**
Hasanoanda, **75**
Hawking, Stephen, 9
Hawthorne, Nathaniel, 316
Herbert, George, 5, **368**, 416
Hildegard of Bingen, 252, **295**
Hilton, James, 314
Homer, **203**

James, William, 316, **362**
Jigdag, Rinpung Ngawang, **349**
Jubilee Singers, 376, **416**

Julian of Norwich, 10
Jung, C. G., 13, **60**

Kant, Immanuel, 266
Keats, John, 13, 42

Lamont, Corliss, 9
Lao Tzu, 6
Lee, Mother Ann, 370
Lermontov, Mikhail, 315, **369**
Lewis, C. S., 5, 376, **405**
Lucan, 13

Mackay, Mary. *See* Corelli, Marie
Milton, John, 316, **341, 221**
Mintz, Jerome R., **377**

Neihardt, John G., **119**
Newman, John Henry (Cardinal), **197, 233**

Parker, Ely S. *See* Hasanoanda
Paul, Saint, 4, 149, 374, **386**
Phelps, Elizabeth Stuart, **135**, 255
Pius XII, 199, **237**
Plato, 5, 313, **317**, 376
Pseudo-Dionysius, 199, **207**
Pythagoras, 80

Ralegh, Sir Walter, 13, **73**
Ramanujan, A. K., **47**
Rinpunga, Prince. *See* Jigdag, Rinpung Ngawang
Rumi, **311**

Schwartz, Howard, 80, **111**
Shelley, Percy Bysshe, 13, **42**
Sidney, Philip, 13
Socrates, 313, 317
Southey, Robert, 226, **228**
Spenser, Edmund, 5, **193**
Stevens, Wallace, 9
Sturluson, Snorri, **93**
Swedenborg, Emanuel, 6, 252, **266**
Sword, George, 375, **396**
Thérèse, Saint (of Lisieux), **298**
Thompson, A. C., 83
Traherne, Thomas, 5, 315, **355**
Twain, Mark, 6, 9, 251, **255**
Underhill, Evelyn, **301**

Vaughan, Henry, 5, **416, 417**

Wilson, Jack. *See* Wovoka
Wordsworth, William, 315
Wovoka, 375, **396**

Young, T. C., 182